The Levellers

A History of the Writings of
Three Seventeenth-Century Social Democrats:
John Lilburne, Richard Overton, William Walwyn

The Levellers

A History of the Writings of
Three Seventeenth-Century Social Democrats:
John Lilburne, Richard Overton, William Walwyn

by Joseph Frank

HARVARD UNIVERSITY PRESS
Cambridge, Massachusetts
1955

Acknowledgments

Writing a scholarly book is like climbing a mountain: it is almost impossible to do alone. Consequently it is both appropriate and pleasant to acknowledge the help I have received in crossing the Great Divide of publication, not only the help of those earlier trail-blazers who are cited in the Bibliography but the help of those friends and associates who held the upper end of the rope. First is Professor Douglas Bush of Harvard University, who always managed to be a painstaking and compassionate teacher and critic. Next is William Haller, Professor Emeritus of Barnard College, whose books and whose conversation were invariably stimulating. Three of my colleagues at the University of Rochester have also aided in pulling me over some rough spots: Bernard Schilling, who helped me to get started; Willson Coates, who read my manuscript with a careful and understanding eye; and Allan Wendt, who was invaluable in steering me into the proper paths of the English language. I am also particularly indebted to two libraries: the Huntington, which allowed me to go through its collection of Interregnum newspapers; and the Rush Rhees Library of the University of Rochester under John Russell — who, with his staff, did everything he could to make my task easy and enjoyable. Finally, I would also like to thank the Harvard Library, the Yale Library, and the British Museum for their coöperation in sending me microfilm and photostats; Professor Herschel Baker of Harvard University, who, along with Douglas Bush, first got me interested in the seventeenth century; and President Wilbur Knight Jordan of Radcliffe, whose encouragement helped a dissertation grow into a book.

June 1955   J. F.

CONTENTS

The Levellers

A History of the Writings of
Three Seventeenth-Century Social Democrats:
John Lilburne, Richard Overton, William Walwyn

The Ancestry of The Levellers

The Levellers of seventeenth-century England faced, and faced up to, many of the social problems which are today plaguing the Western world. Such current issues in the United States as the propriety of loyalty oaths or the need to limit the scope of legislative investigating committees were issues which three hundred years ago helped to determine both the aims and techniques of the Leveller party. Indeed, the words of the chief Leveller spokesmen are often echoed with startling accuracy on the more progressive editorial pages of the 1950's. Today one may yearn for the peace of the Augustans or the external stability of the Victorians but he would find himself excitingly and alarmingly at home in the political and intellectual ferment of the English Civil War.

The close resemblance between the political problems of that day and this is at once an advantage and a disadvantage to the person who wishes to study the England of the Interregnum.[1] Since the central domestic issue, in its broadest terms, was then as now how to work out and apply a pragmatic concept of the power of government, and since the opposing forces of the mid-seventeenth century employed many of the techniques and much of the phraseology still current, one can move from Capitol Hill to the Westminster of three centuries ago with little intellectual difficulty — though such ease of identification may easily lead to anachronism and distortion. Thus it is both correct and incorrect to compare Lilburne, the most vocal of the Levellers, with a demagogue like Huey Long or an extreme democrat like Norman Thomas; or, as certain modern authors have done, to compare Cromwell with Napoleon, Lincoln, Hitler, and Franklin Roosevelt.[2]

Yet it remains a truism that each age must reinterpret the past. The protean standards which are characteristic of today have accelerated that process of reinterpretation, particularly in those areas which represent significant battlegrounds of ideas. Such a battleground was the England of the Interregnum. Consequently a new study of one minor but provocative phase of that period is again justified. Moreover, since no previous work on the Levellers has dealt with all the writings of the leaders of that party or has tried to reconstruct the story of the Leveller movement by working outward from its publications — by seeing its inception, maturation, and disintegration mainly through the eyes of its chief protagonists — a supplement to previous scholarship is further warranted.[3] Hence the pages which follow constitute an attempt to bring together and to analyze all the works by or directly relevant to the men who led the Leveller party. This examination will therefore be focused on the works themselves, but at the same time it may lead to a history of the Leveller movement which, without doing violence to the words of its leaders, can be contemporary to the twentieth century.

The Leveller party had only a brief and abortive life: born in 1646, it died in 1649 without ever having crossed the threshold to actual political power. Even the appellation "Leveller" was a late and generally opprobrious term. First used in connection with this new political party late in 1647, it became the accepted name for this group only among its opponents.[4] None the less, the term "Leveller" is, in its political implications, a convenient and accurate designation for those diverse men who briefly joined together to form a militant, articulate, and radical organization: an organization which, though actually short-lived and in its time comparatively inconsequential, can be given a relatively important role in the history of modern ideas.

Even so, in the large perspective of modern history, the Leveller movement was an evanescent phenomenon. Arising from the matrix of the Reformation, it had disappeared by the time the Restoration was an accomplished fact. Yet its direct ancestry is fully as complex and ramified as its indirect present-day descendants; and in the same simplified way that these descendants can be subsumed under the head of constitutional democrats, so the ancestors of the Levellers can generally be labeled Calvinists. This term signifies that the Leveller movement was a product of the Reformation rather than of the Renaissance — a distinction which means, in turn, that both the roots and the original impelling force of the movement were predominantly religious.

The chief doctrinal offshoot of Calvinism's stress on the absolute omnipotence of God was the belief in predestination: the conviction that a few had been chosen by God, the many, incorrigibly tainted by original sin, consigned to eternal damnation. But even though this underlying sense of sin does much to distinguish seventeenth-century liberalism from the perfectibilitarian hopes of the nineteenth century, Calvinism was far more than a religion of deterministic pessimism or spiritual snobbery; and even though it could operate with great efficiency to invoke the certitude and regimentation of organized intolerance — as it did in Geneva and Massachusetts — it could also produce an individualism which was potentially revolutionary in both its religious and political manifestations.[5] For, though the Calvinist theologians and their pulpit interpreters might argue that the great majority of men were doomed to hell, they found it "practically inadvisable as well as theoretically impossible to name the many who might not be saved." [6] On the contrary, in attempting to win a large number to the "Covenant of Grace," the preachers of Calvinism more and more emphasized the possibility of every convert's becoming a "Saint." Further, in all likelihood those who heard these sermons equated the desire to be saved with the certainty of their own salvation. One inevitable result was that membership in the elect became increasingly less exclusive.

Consequently in its first century Calvinism succeeded in undercutting its own doctrine of spiritual aristocracy by fostering a potential egalitarianism of the spirit which could lead to a congregation of the elect as inclusive as Elizabeth's expedient arrangement. But, at the same time, the Calvinist emphasis on predestination helped to produce two other important manifestations: obscurantism and anticlericalism. If faith in one's own election was a personal rather than an institutional matter, then neither learning nor a professional intermediary was necessary for "Sainthood." Despite the fact that Calvinism was originally conservative in its politics and monolithic in its structure, it thus displayed its own Protestantism by nurturing the radical and disintegrative tendency toward separatism. Particularly in those places where, because it was frowned on by the government, it had little secular authority, Calvinism not only contained but fructified the seeds of religious schism: the increasingly centrifugal tendency of groups of believers to break away from their parent religious body in order to form smaller and purer congregations.[7]

Such a process of fission was, of course, inherent in a Protestantism which stressed man's personal relationship to the word of God as expressed in the Bible; but in the England of the early seventeenth century it was the Presbyterians, the organized Calvinists, who gave sectarianism its strongest push. Elizabeth's church settlement had, by its tolerance, acted to embrace all who were neither aggressively intolerant nor politically dangerous, as well as those who were spiritually indifferent. In opposition to this convenient national church the Presbyterians cited the taint of association with the ungodly, an argument which could be used, however, each time a Puritan splinter group wished to decontaminate itself by removal from those brethren who were not of the elect. And the Bible itself, read avidly and literally but capable of an infinity of semi-allegorical interpretations, managed to supply any and all such groups with infallible grounds for breaking away from either the historical church or its proliferating offshoots. Notwithstanding the Presbyterians' chronic fear of civil and religious disorder, and their elaborate theoretical edifice of church discipline to eliminate future disturbances, it was their increasingly militant opposition to the originally flexible unity of Elizabethan prelacy that did much to pave the way for the Civil War.[8]

These aggressive Calvinists of the early seventeenth century — the Puritans — whether actually separatist or still nominally within the official religion of the nation, were the Levellers' direct ancestors. In addition, the organizational covenants of a variety of splinter congregations helped to father the democratic constitutions later proposed by the Levellers; while the Leveller belief in full religious freedom stemmed in part from the mutual recrimination practiced by a growing number of competing congregations. Hence from the authoritarian watershed of Geneva flowed the currents of political as well as religious schism.[9] In England under James and Charles these largely theoretical currents were channeled and swollen by a complex of political and economic factors until they became, in 1642, an actual flood.

But Calvinism also helped to pave the way for the Levellers with what can be called philosophical or temperamental preparation. The expected behavior pattern of the person who considered himself a member of the elect was neither contemplative nor monastic, but active and gregarious. Such a pattern resulted in the concept of a "calling," of a life of disciplined and purposeful activity. Theologically this way of life might not be a guarantee of salvation, but it could and did become the psychological method whereby many of the "Saints" seemed to rid themselves of the fear of damnation and to gain a positive hope of grace.[10] Thus the life of the true Puritan was conceived of as planned, self-controlled, and, in the world of the seventeenth century, embattled. Calvin's allegiance to the doctrine of political passive obedience was further weakened, then, by the inculcation of an essentially aggressive state of mind among the more vehement of his followers.

This concept of a calling may have been either an effect or a cause of the fact that seventeenth-century Puritanism, both in its membership and in its morality, became largely a middle-class movement. In England during the century beginning about 1540 the growth of Puritan sentiment happened to parallel a rise in prices.[11] Together they produced an era of comparatively intense economic enterprise: an era in which traditional class barriers began to be weakened and the medieval idea of fixed status to be replaced by the modern concept of a fluid economy.[12] This further accelerated the disintegrative forces already long at work in the national economy of England, and thus also in the field of economics Calvinism's embattled vanguard contributed to the tendency toward social fragmentation which preceded the Civil War.

These centrifugal tendencies in militant Calvinism represent the chief branches of the Levellers' genealogy; but there is a second distinguishable strain, though one far less important, in their background. Calvinism, and particularly English Puritanism, was primarily and literally a protest-ant force, an iconoclastic movement. Iconoclasm always accompanies revolution, but so does some form of utopianism. In the case of the Levellers, this second and sub-ordinate progenitor is represented by a potentially utopian tradition which can be labeled the belief in a law of nature. In contradistinc-tion to Calvinism, the orientation of such a belief was, on the whole, political rather than religious, its initial impact synthetic rather than disintegrative, and its vitality late and dispersed rather than immediate and concentrated.

As the lesser intellectual ancestor of the Leveller movement, this belief in a law of nature is the chief theoretical link between the Levellers and the Renaissance. The idea of natural law goes back at least to the Stoics of ancient Greece and Rome.[13] From their state-ment that there was some basic, universal, and rational law to govern human behavior, through Cicero's elaboration that civil laws represented merely the application of an eternal law to man in society, to the medieval view that natural law was superior to and at least potentially independent of the state, there was little doubt expressed as to the existence of some such fundamental law. But that this "law" was amorphous is proved by the fact that the Middle Ages invoked it to restrain economic self-interest, the Levellers to justify democracy, and the conservatives of the eighteenth century to oppose institutional change.[14]

By the early seventeenth century, however, the protean and tradi-tional idea of a law of nature had begun to be a little less vague, gain-ing relative precision in proportion to its accidental breakdown into three constituent beliefs: first, the contention, cited among others by the religious separatists, that a specific social contract could solve certain actual political and doctrinal problems; second, the rise to greater importance of the theory that the decisions of the common-law judges had put on record various definite and basic rules about man's relationship to man; and third, the renewed faith that Magna Carta had at least in part defined for England the actual meaning of a law of nature.

In the first decades of the seventeenth century, coincident with the establishment of the earliest English separatist congregations, the principle of a precise and binding social contract had begun to be accepted both by the schismatics who employed it and by the many political theorists who countenanced it.[15] The Mayflower Covenant of 1620 is merely one example of a group of people deliberately organizing themselves and their society on the basis of a written contract.

By this date, too, the common law of England had undergone a change in the direction of precision. Under such men as Bacon and Coke, the accumulation of judicial precedents was given more penetrating analysis than ever before, and in a series of interpretive commentaries these precedents were made at once more functional and, collectively, more fundamental. Furthermore, as these precedents had been assembled through the centuries, so customary laws and customary rulings had tended to become inviolable, "natural." [16]

Similar to this development toward theoretical inviolability was the history of Magna Carta. For four centuries its confirmations had been progressively "enshrined in Parliament and statute roll, permanently recorded in such form as to convince later generations that here was . . . a law of laws." [17] Each succeeding confirmation of Magna Carta served to strengthen its own suggestion that it was a fundamental or natural law, the cornerstone of England's traditionally limited monarchy; and the constitutional controversies of the reigns of James and Charles acted to bring this document even further into the limelight of renewed argument and analysis.[18]

It is highly probable that some sort of correlation might be worked out which would show that the belief in a law of nature, a law, that is, superior to actual statutes, flourishes at those moments when the central government is either least strong or least popular. If so, the rapid growth of this latent theory just before and during the Civil War is not at all surprising. In fact, the Leveller Agreements of the People — which were attempts to make the contractarian principle of written consent, the traditional "natural" rights embodied in the common law, and the alleged basic constitutionalism of Magna Carta explicit and unalterable — were offshoots of a political tradition that had long believed that the implementation of the law of nature was the *raison d'être* of government. But that this belief could emphasize either conservative precedent or radical abstract rights did little in the mid-seventeenth century to discourage its use as a battle cry by most parties in the Puritan Revolution.

Leveller genealogy thus consists mainly of the iconoclasm inherent in militant Calvinism and, to a much lesser degree, of the utopianism potential in the belief in the supremacy of natural law.

However, as one moves to the immediate forbears of the Leveller party, the disintegrative tendencies manifested in seventeenth-century Puritanism can be seen to be predominant. During the first forty years of that century the Puritan party grew in numbers, wealth, and political strength. At the same time, the spread of Arminian doctrines and the increase in the number of separatist congregations tended to weaken the fundamental Calvinist concept of an aristocracy of the elect. Moreover, the opponents of the established church increasingly identified that church with the evils of popery; to which the prelates, now on the defensive, responded by generally wedding themselves ever more closely to the monarchy.

This religious and political cleavage was complicated by the fact that the nature of separatism had by 1630 begun to experience a change: the breakup of Puritanism into "pure" but still predestinarian groups was now complemented by the rise of mystical and increasingly antinomian sects. Though small in number and insignificant in terms of their political and economic strength, these sects were pregnant with further change. An official report in 1634 listed "Brownists, Anabaptists, Arians, Traskites, Familists and some other sorts" as people to be watched.[19] The government and the Presbyterians agreed, for many of these sects were not only democratic, even proletarian, in their membership, but most of them had in common — and in opposition to both the established hierarchy and to Calvinist predestinarianism — the clearly stated conviction that God's grace was available to all who sought it: that God was a God of love, and that the gates of salvation were open to the most humble. Hence these sectarian splinter groups reflected a further step in the disintegration of the monolithic society which Calvin had tried to establish, and which the Presbyterians in the Westminster Assembly continued to hypothesize.

Of greater import to these divisive pressures was the rise of a new capitalist class whose source of wealth was not primarily land. At first this group was strengthened by the growth of monopoly under the early Stuarts. But Charles's policy of bringing large-scale enterprise under the control of the Privy Council increasingly conflicted with the rich merchants and enlightened landlords at a time when their power had reached the point where, as a body, they might resist the King.[20] Though this group of men dominated Charles's first three Parliaments, the conflict between them and the throne was not a simple issue of *laissez-faire* liberalism versus authoritarian reaction. Between 1629 and 1640, the period of the King's most arbitrary rule, the Privy Council, for instance, attempted to enforce a system of complicated industrial regulation in an effort to keep up wages, to maintain high standards in the administration of poor relief, and to curb — if for the benefit of the royal exchequer — certain monopolies.[21] None the less, just as the Puritans identified the church of James and Charles with popery, so the richer *bourgeoisie*, themselves largely Puritan, viewed the government's economic policy as largely feudal, corrupt, and restrictive.

To the Puritans in the decade before the Civil War the chief spokesman for English popery and official reaction was Archbishop Laud, a man whose self-confident zeal often led him into attacks on religious nonconformity and economic individualism which seemed calculated to bring down on him the wrath of articulate Puritanism. Acting on the assumption that the opposition to him was intolerant and destructive, Laud worked with the Crown to establish an ecclesiastical system which would be harmonious, monarchical, and Arminian. But the absolutism necessary in a post-Elizabethan era to realize this ambition involved interference in many areas of national life, particularly in those areas in which the Puritans were most strongly organized. Consequently the attacks on him became increasingly threatening.

During the seven years before 1640 Charles coöperated closely with his archbishop. James had identified the cause of the Crown with that of the bishops; Charles narrowed this coalition further by equating the cause of the bishops with that of Laud and the "High Church" party. During these years, in attempting to govern without Parliament, Charles was also trying to govern without the aid of, and in opposition to, those classes upon which his revenue, in the long run, depended.[22] The sale of titles and of monopolistic licenses could keep the throne solvent only as long as it avoided expensive foreign or military adventures, and Charles's restatement of his father's dictum that he ruled by divine right raised no cash: instead it further antagonized those businessmen and Parliamentarians who were already taking a stand against Royalist absolutism.

Though neither the theory of the divine right of the king nor the developing countertheory of Parliamentary omnipotence had any real basis in English history or in the accumulation of common-law precedents, as early as 1628 the incipient cleavage between Puritan and Royalist had begun to reach the point where each was proclaiming a theory of power potentially irreconcilable with that of its opponent.[23] In that year the Parliament passed, and the King reluctantly consented to, the Petition of Right, "the first statutory restriction on the powers of the Crown since the accession of the Tudor dynasty." [24] Less than a year later Charles adjourned his intransigent third Parliament, and in 1633 Laud was appointed Archbishop of Canterbury.

Laud's administration coincided with the mounting disaffection in England, of which Hampden's refusal to pay ship-money was a dramatic symbol, with Strafford's ruthlessly efficient rule in Ireland, and with the increasing antiprelatical turbulence in Scotland. In 1638 this turbulence reached a climax when a large majority of the men of Scotland signed the National Covenant against episcopacy. Later that year the Scottish General Assembly, a body completely dominated by the Presbyterians, renounced the authority of the king and abolished his form of church government. After Charles's brief and abortive attempt to crush this rebellion, he summoned but promptly dissolved the short Parliament. A second war with Scotland also ended in the defeat of Charles; and, in November 1640, financially and militarily crippled, he called to Westminster that group of men to be known as the Long Parliament. This Parliament, instead of filling its traditional role as the symbol of unity between king and people, managed after a year of sporadic compromise to bring to a head the issues over which the Civil War was to be fought.

These issues embraced the fields of religion, politics, and economics. Though only a small segment of the people of England aligned themselves firmly with the opposing sides in these disputes or even articulated their own grievances, the cleavage between prelate and presbyter, between monarchist and Parliamentarian, between feudal landlord and capitalist entrepreneur, had by 1641 reached the point where it would affect the lives of most of the people, and possibly determine the nature of the church, the government, and the economy under which their posterity would live. In

that year the Act against Dissolving the Long Parliament was
passed; and six months and many debates later the Grand Remonstrance announced that the struggle for actual power had begun.
The start of the Civil War in the summer of 1642 merely replaced
the verbal artillery of Westminster with the only slightly more
dangerous bullets of Edgehill.

The immediate background of the Leveller party was therefore
the explosive controversies of the late 1630's and early 1640's, when
the disintegrative forces inherent in militant Puritanism collided
with a government that had become increasingly rigid in its theology,
authoritarian in its politics, and desperate in its economics. The
Leveller fight for full freedom of religion, for a constitutional
democracy, and for a laissez-faire economy was an unexpected
product of this collision. Unlike the Independents, who never broke
away from their Puritan ancestry and who reaped the benefits of
Parliament's victory in the Civil War, the Levellers became the
biological "sport" of the Interregnum. Sired by Puritanism, they
none the less so combined a diversity of ideas and talents that they
developed into a strange hybrid, and, true to form, they had no direct
descendants. Yet the incubation period of the party during the early
years of the war was orthodox in its Puritanism; and John Lilburne,
the best known and most active of the Levellers, never really divested
himself of that aggressive Calvinism which ultimately fathered him
and his party. Consequently the Leveller movement is trebly an
anomaly: conceived in Puritanism, it largely renounced its ancestry;
led by a Puritan, an antinomian, and a skeptic, it achieved a militant
unity; for a brief moment the highly organized spearhead of a
potentially mass movement, it quickly vanished into almost total
oblivion. The case history of John Lilburne, however, reflects the
story of the Leveller party at its least anomalous, at its most traditional.

John Lilburne: Puritan Apprentice

I. 1615–1637: The Apprentice

John Lilburne transformed the dramatic facts of his life into a political program, and his biography — from his family's antecedents to his death as a Quaker — provided much of the material with which he and his colleagues constructed and publicized their social theories. He was born probably in 1615.[1] As he often emphasized, he was no social upstart. Before him for at least a generation the family had had its own coat of arms, and a will probated in 1565 shows that the Lilburnes had long belonged financially to that upper middle class which supplied a large part of the leadership of the Puritan Revolution.[2]

Though his father was the last man in England to demand trial by battle in the settlement of a civil law suit,[3] the elder Lilburnes were both inconspicuous minor courtiers. Shortly after their son's birth, Mrs. Lilburne died and the family returned from Greenwich to their "hereditary habitation" near Durham. Of his early education there, Lilburne wrote that he was "brought up well neigh ten yeares together in the best Schooles in the North," and that he was by no means "one of the dronessest Schoole Boyes." [4] Despite the fact that he several times referred to himself as "noe scoller, according to that which the world counts scollership," he remained proud of his small Latin and less Greek.[5]

Since Lilburne was neither the eldest son nor on good terms with his family, his formal education ended before he was fifteen. Late in

1630 his father brought him to London and apprenticed him to Thomas Hewson, a successful wholesale trader in cloth.[6] Lilburne describes his vocational training in these words:

I served as faithfully about six yeare as ever Apprentice served a Master; and though he had no more but my self, and many thousand of Pounds went through my hands, . . . yet directly nor indirectly I cannot remember that I ever wronged him of a Groat . . . or that ever all the time I was with him, I was ever branded or taxed with one base visible action; or that I either ever gave or took a box on the eare . . . or ever quarrelled with any flesh alive all the time I was there (although I had as much mettle, life and spirit as most young men in London had).[7]

But he continues his account with an episode far more indicative of his own disputatious future: "I must confess my old Master offered me sometimes some abuse, for which I carryed him before the Chamberlain of London."[8]

Working in Hewson's warehouse left Lilburne with "spare time enough," which, he avows, he never wasted. His leisure hours were, he goes on,

continually spent . . . in reading the Bible, the Book of Martyrs, Luthers, Calvins, Bezaes, Cartwrights, Perkins, Molins [Du Moulin], Burtons, and Rogers Works, with multitude of other such like books that I bought with my own money.[9] [In a second edition of the work in which this quotation appears, Lilburne adds the phrase "with histories" after "such like books."] [10]

The Bible, particularly the historical portions of the Old Testament and the apocalyptic visions of Isaiah, Jeremiah, Daniel, and St. John, was of central importance to him as a source of inspiration, ideas, and vocabulary. From Foxe he probably imbibed much of his fervid nationalism, and he certainly identified himself with many of the martyrs dramatically portrayed by Foxe, as well as with the much tried Calvin of Beza's biography. Lilburne also seems to have been impressed by Luther's political conservatism and by Calvin's legalistic theology. In addition, the "histories" which he read at this time — the works of Speed, Holinshed, Daniel, and Raleigh — had a durable influence on him, as did his early reading in books of jurisprudence.[11]

Despite the Puritan orientation of his reading, Lilburne, at the end of his apprenticeship in 1636, was still not a formal member of any religious congregation. His close friend of this period, William Kiffin, shows, however, that this lack of affiliation was not the result of laziness or indifference:

I began to get acquainted with several young men, who diligently attended on the means of grace. . . . And, being apprentices as well as myself, they had no opportunity to converse but on the Lord's days. It was our constant practice to attend the morning lecture which began at six o'clock. . . . We also appointed to meet together an hour before service, to spend it in prayer and in communicating to each other what experience we had received from the Lord, or else to repeat some sermon which we had heard before. After a little time we also read some portion of Scripture, and spake from it what it pleased God to enable us.[12]

Two other young men who accompanied Lilburne on these theological voyages of discovery — on this disciplined sampling of Independent preaching — were Edmund Rozer, who with Kiffin soon became active in England's first Particular Baptist Church, and William Larner, a man for many years closely associated with the printing of Leveller works.[13] It was through his friendship with such men that Lilburne came in direct contact with nonconformist Calvinism in its most enthusiastic form; and the evident zeal with which he met persecution undoubtedly had its foundation both in the extreme Puritanism of his reading and in his gregarious search for religious certainty. The combination of the histrionic and the personal inherent in this search also resulted in Lilburne's increasingly well-defined picture of himself as a "spiritual warrior enlisted under the banners of Christ"[14] — a picture patterned upon the hero of the many Puritan sermons he had heard and Protestant books he had read. Moreover, it was this somewhat self-conscious hero who occupied the central position in Lilburne's youthful pamphlets, and who never disappeared from his works.

Early in 1637 Lilburne temporarily found the solution to his immediate problems, both economic and spiritual, when Edmund Rozer took him to visit Dr. John Bastwick.[15] Bastwick's career is almost an epitome of that rigorous Presbyterianism which at once helped to promote the Civil War and attempted to keep it from being more than a nonrevolutionary struggle for power. He had spent a short time at Cambridge, had received an M.D. from Padua, and, after a brief period as a doctor, had written two Latin treatises, one violently attacking Catholicism, the other justifying Presbyterianism. For these he was fined £1,000 and sentenced to the relatively easy confinement of Gatehouse Prison.[16] There his zeal for the Presbyterian cause continued to need little prodding. When a "cheerfull, merry old man," Mr. Wharton, urged him to write an attack in English on the bishops, he promptly complied with the first part of the *Letany of John Bastwick*. Wharton's glee at this tract resulted in a series of prison parties for its author, at which the chief diversion was reading the *Letany* aloud. Bastwick's guests then saw that it received a relatively wide circulation, a favor which resulted in a sudden increase in Bastwick's notoriety — until in June 1637 he, with Burton and Prynne, was publicly punished by Laud.[17] Among Bastwick's more active guests had been John Lilburne.

Bastwick's account of his early relations with Lilburne is not especially flattering. Not only was Lilburne deficient in capital, but, "though he were Honest and Religious, yet he was but a meere country courtier, and very rough hewen, so that he could neither make a legge with grace, nor put off his hat seemly." [18] Bastwick then alleges that he began to improve Lilburne's manners and to give him instruction in the techniques of religious controversy. Lilburne, in return, asked the older man to give him a copy of the *Letany* and of Bastwick's answer in Star Chamber to the Bill of Information against him, saying that "hee doubted not hee should get enough money by them, for he perceived that they were well approved by all that read . . . them." [19] Lilburne planned to take these two works to Holland, there to have them printed, and, through certain confederates, to market them in England. Bastwick agreed to this scheme. Hence, at about the same time that he and Burton and Prynne were having their ears cropped in the pillory, Lilburne was crossing the Channel to Holland.

Lilburne has little to say about his six months there. Despite his subsequent legalistic evasions when cross-questioned about his part in printing the *Letany*, it is obvious that his major occupation was this profitable, zealous, and dangerous activity.[20] In both Rotterdam and Amsterdam he established contact with men who printed books to be smuggled into England — a thriving business which had been going on since the days of Queen Mary, and one which he soon utilized for some of his own pamphlets.[21] Then, in December 1637, he followed several thousand copies of Bastwick's *Letany* back to England. There one of his accomplices denounced him to the Archbishop's agents. Lilburne was promptly arrested, and two months later indicted in Star Chamber.[22]

In March 1638 he wrote his first pamphlet, *A Christian Mans Triall*, in which he told of his recent vicissitudes. With this work Lilburne began his almost continuous self-portrait and, indirectly, his saga of the Leveller movement — from its origin in Calvinist enthusiasm to its disintegration before the hard realities of power politics.

II. *1638–1640: The Martyr*

Facing prison for the first of many times, Lilburne could find reassurance in the strength of his own Puritanism. Though as a Calvinist he could not consider himself Sir Galahad, the young Lancelot felt that he was ready to do battle against the foes of Christ. The nature of that battle, however, was likely to be legalistic. Calvin's emphasis on Old Testament institutions included an emphasis on the idea that man's original violation of a cosmic contract had eventuated in the need for many laws to curb him in his fallen state. Since the later years of Elizabeth's reign there had also been a growing disposition to think of the conflict between Crown and Parliament, between Episcopacy and Presbyterianism, in legal terms.[23] In 1638 the law was, for Lilburne, an untried but inviting weapon. Despite his reading in such authors as Coke, he had developed no theory of English law, but in that year, as throughout his life, the theory came after the practice.

A Christian Mans Triall, written in the Fleet, tells Lilburne's story from his arrest in December 1637 through his arraignment and conviction in February 1638.[24] More than half of it is a legalistic document detailing the author's refusal to answer certain questions put to him by the king's attorney and to take the ex-officio oath customary for those brought before Star Chamber.[25] The defiant attitude of the accused, as well as his mixture of faith and Coke, can be seen in his answer to the Crown's legal representative:

If you will not aske me about the thing laid to my charge, I shall answer no more. And of any other matter that you have to accuse me of, I know it is warrantable by the Law of God, and I thinke by the Law of the Land, that I may stand upon my just defence and not answer to your intergatorie.[26]

The Puritan God who enabled the young apprentice to defy the august members of Star Chamber, and apparently to enjoy doing it, also served as counsel for the defense: "God shewed his goodness to me, in keeping mee (a poore weak worme) that they could not in the least intangle mee, though I was altogether ignorant of the manner of their proceedings."[27] Despite such occasional self-deprecatory interjections, a profound optimism underlay Lilburne's actions. When first apprehended he had resisted arrest, then joked with his captors; now he could address the members of Star Chamber "without any dantedness of spirit . . . as they had been my equals. . . . For I knew God . . . would be with me . . . [and] be a mouth unto me."[28] But that this attitude was the result of religious faith and not of any incipient democratic conviction Lilburne immediately, if inadvertently, proved:

. . . the court had proceeded against some that had harbored Jesuits and Seminary-Priests (those Traitors) who refused to be examined under Oath . . . so they were the president [precedent] by which we were censured, though their cause and ours be much unlike, in regard theirs were little better than Treason.[29]

Lilburne's legal double standard did not convince the court. He was sentenced to be whipped, and in the interim was confined close prisoner. His evasiveness both invited this sentence and corroborated the inference that Lilburne in Holland and Wharton in England had been largely responsible for the dissemination of Bastwick's *Letany*, as well as of other antiprelatical works.[30] Whether Lilburne's distortion of fact in the cause of what he considered a larger justice was warranted is an issue which comes up again and again in the course of his controversial career.

The style of *A Christian Mans Triall*, like that of his later works, is hasty, emotional, undisciplined. His sentences are long, with little or no internal architecture, and his paragraphing is whimsical. What unity his tracts have is mainly unity of tone, not of content or structure. Thus in *A Triall* the cohesive force is largely the self-assurance of God's champion. Lilburne's intimate acquaintance with Reformation polemics and Puritan sermons not only contributed to this note of confidence, but helped to mold the style in which that mood was expressed. His simple and colloquial vocabulary, his neglect of formal rhetorical devices, and the instinctively close identification which he makes between writer and reader are, in fact, all aspects of a tradition which extends from the Lollards to Bunyan.

Lilburne's second tract, *A Worke of the Beast*, replaces this air of confident defiance with an air of confident martyrdom.[31] Printed shortly after his punishment in April 1638, *A Worke* tells how its author was whipped through the streets of London, pilloried, and finally returned to close imprisonment. Besides this account of events, it provides a clear insight into the spirit of the youthful Lilburne; for in the same manner that Bastwick, Burton, and Prynne had used their punishment as an instrument of publicity for themselves and their cause, so Lilburne utilized the pillory as his podium. He tells how he promptly gained the crowd's sympathetic attention: first, while being whipped at the cart's tail, how he harangued them until he was forcibly gagged; and then how he climaxed his speech by dramatically flinging copies of Bastwick's banned work to his apparently enthralled listeners.[32] Yet *A Worke of the Beast* also shows that behind this dramatic exhibitionism was Lilburne's spiritual assurance that his role as a Puritan martyr was valid and ultimately rewarding.

Exactly when Lilburne arrived at this certainty cannot be specified. His conviction that God was on his side had certainly been evident in *A Christian Mans Triall*. But at the time of his actual punishment this conviction apparently became more articulate, more intense, and more self-conscious: in *A Worke of the Beast* Lilburne both identifies his tribulations with those of Christ and views them as the ceremonials of a holy marriage. Of his experience in the pillory he says, for instance:

And this I counted my wedding day in which I was married to the Lord Jesus Christ; for now I know he loves me in that he hath bestowed soe rich apparrell this day upon me, and counted me worthye to suffer for his sake.[33]

Twice Lilburne explicitly states that he is now assured of election, of an "immortall Crowne." More than a bridegroom, he is also a soldier fighting "under the banner of the great and mightie Captaine the Lord Jesus Christ"; and, at the same time, the humble and ascetic, if somewhat plaintive, servant of the Lord:

I am a young man and likelie to have lived well and in plentie, according to the fashion of the world. Yet notwithstanding, for the cause of Christ, and to doe him service, I have and doe bid adue to Father, Friends, Riches, pleasures, ease, contented life, and bloud.[34]

Such a complex of attitudes was, in fact, typical of enthusiastic Calvinism. In his speech from the pillory, as reported in *A Worke of the Beast*, Lilburne not only expressed his admiration for Bastwick, Burton, and Prynne, and devoted much attention to advancing the standard Puritan arguments against the bishops, but he displayed the traditional pattern of self-elevation to the ranks of the Saints, a pattern made up of assurance, militancy, and self-sacrifice. Since Lilburne's service to Christ was obviously based on the assumption that it would be everlastingly rewarded, such service could be fearless, zealous, even joyous, particularly if it involved public martyrdom by the Lord's enemies. Hence it was logical for him to conclude his tract with these defiant words:

If the Bishop of Canterbury be offended at that which I spoke yesterday, tell him I will seale it with my bloud. And if he please to send for me, I will justifie it to his face, and if I be not able to make it good before any noble man in the Kingdome, let me loose my life.[35]

Lilburne almost did lose his life; for four months he was placed in solitary confinement, under prison conditions which required both certitude and fortitude for survival.

In September 1638, though his confinement was still onerous, Lilburne was able to compose his third pamphlet, *Come out of her my people*.[36] This work was addressed to an unnamed woman who had criticized Lilburne for saying he would rather listen to the devil than to certain Episcopal ministers. Though Lilburne denies this specific statement, much of his answer is devoted to proving that the prelates and their underlings are agents of Satan. In this he again follows the loose and commonplace Puritan syllogism that the

Pope's power is from the devil, the bishops get their power from the Pope, and therefore all "God's people" are bound to withdraw their spiritual obedience from the present established church. In several places, moreover, Lilburne strongly implies that the prelatical clergy has no right to preach: "the enemies of God's people" are not only wrong, they are evil — the word "Antichrist" rolls easily off Lilburne's pen.

In addition to attacking the prelates, Lilburne now explicitly defends "Totall Separation," the right of the godly to separate from the inclusive church of the ungodly.[37] The cumulative oppression of prison life had apparently strengthened his anger against his persecutors, while, at the same time, it had intensified his conviction that he was one of God's elect:

For before I was not only a Novice but a very Idiot in the right wayes of God, having muddy affections, but wanted inward principles, having fiery zeal, but it was without grounded spirituall knowledge; but now the Lord hath made knowne to me, by his spirit, the way wherein to serve and worship him; And he hath made me by his power and strength as unmoveable as an Iron Pillar or a Brazen Wall.[38]

During this progress toward certainty, Lilburne returned to the Bible for additional assurance.[39] Since at this stage of his religious development it was the Book of Revelation which dominated his thinking and writing, he could, like so many of his dispossessed contemporaries, stifle present pains in apocalyptic visions of the coming victory over the mighty of the world. Such millenarianism usually had two corollaries, both of which *Come out of her my people* exhibits. The first is self-confident obscurantism:

And though my Adversaries are learned in the Phariseicall, Philosofical, deceivable learning of the world . . . and have studied and beat their braines in their Universities and else where for many yeares together, yet in one six months in a Prison and fettered condition, I have got more true spirituall learning and knowledge in the misteries of Godliness then is amongst them all.[40]

The second is the willingness to submit physically to those whose power is soon to vanish before the wrath of God:

Yet I will submit my body to them and suffer cheerfully, . . . for I doe hold it unlawfull for any of Gods people, in their greatest opression by the Magistrate, to rebell or to take up any Temporal armes against them, . . . but only to pray and . . . wait . . . with patience for redresse and deliverance.[41]

Neither of these offshoots of Lilburne's chiliasm was, however, quite as out of keeping with his later career as first seems apparent. His anti-intellectualism is partially undercut by his challenge to Laud and his bishops to meet him in public debate on the theological issues in question; and again and again he abuses their recourse to "clubb law." Lilburne also slightly qualifies his adherence to the doctrine of submission. He affirms his loyalty to the king and his royal magistrates: to them he will submit, but should they command anything which is against the word of God, then, though he will not resist, his submission will be only physical and passive. In this respect Lilburne seems more conservative than Calvin; yet his actions since his first meeting with Bastwick, the over-all tone of his early pamphlets, and his vilification of the prelates in *Come out of her my people* are all symptoms of an obedience which was scarcely passive. This political ambivalence, along with his enthusiastic Calvinism, indicates that Lilburne at the end of 1638 was still very much in the main stream of conventional Puritanism.

His relative orthodoxy is corroborated in a letter Lilburne wrote in November 1638.[42] Deserted by most of his friends, he had received an admiring note from a woman who had been in prison with him during the first days of his confinement. For twenty-one pages — which he calls a "few lines" — he pours out his gratitude to her and to the God who has enabled him to bear sickness, loneliness, pain, contumely. He reiterates his conviction that he, one of the lowly, has been chosen, and that therefore his cell has become a place of spiritual joy and exaltation. Indeed, the idea that the elect are the world's weak and dispossessed has become ever more inviting to him as his own earthly prospects have grown more hopeless.

Lilburne describes more fully the premises of his early theology in his next pamphlet, *An Answer to Nine Arguments*, written in all likelihood at the end of 1638.[43] In the form of a letter in answer to certain propositions advanced by a proponent of the established church, this tract is verbose, arrogant, and entirely unoriginal. Lilburne's starting point is that the Bible is the only touchstone of truth: logic and philosophy are the weapons of Antichrist, for that which is not explicitly supported by Scripture is, at best, mere sophistry. Then, on this antihumanist basis, Lilburne constructs the traditional separatist argument: a true church can consist only of the elect, for a policy of inclusiveness is contrary to the word of God. Moreover, the ministers of the prelatical church are neither truly Christian nor apostolic, and the sins of their false religion are increased by their cruelty and corruption, as well as by their diabolic affiliation with the Church of Rome. Though Lilburne says that he has had little formal contact with separatism,[44] his reasons for supporting it are distinctly conventional; *An Answer to Nine Arguments* stresses the iniquities of the established church rather than the virtues of separatism. Thus his fervent reliance on Scripture had supplied him with an individual faith and a polemical weapon, but it had not yet given him a point of view which was rationalistic, tolerant, or radical.

Lilburne's subsequent prison writings, prior to his release at the end of 1640, add little to a knowledge of his religion. He continued to berate the bishops and to identify himself with the celebrated martyrs of Protestantism. But though protestations of his own election recurred, there was a shift in emphasis from the exaltation of salvation to the vicissitudes of prison life, and his ideas on his own secular role — his embryonic political and social convictions — began to assume more definite shape.

Two immediate forces were instrumental in determining that shape. The first was Lilburne's spiritual optimism, the assurance behind his opposition to the ecclesiastical *status quo* that he was one of God's saints. The second was the actual environment of his prison, an environment which helped to confirm Lilburne's proclivities for dramatic self-publicizing, popular martyrdom, and social reform. His reaction to the burdens of prison life thus moved from spiritual egocentricity and alleged submission toward angrier and more explicit attacks on the actual circumstances in which he found himself:[45] in short, his pamphlets ceased to be primarily theological.

The subtitle of *The Poore Mans Cry*, dated by Lilburne December 20, 1638, illustrates this change. It reads, "Wherein is shewed the present miserable estate of mee John Lilburne" — a sharp contrast to the superscription to his letter of the month before, "Let the quintessence of sweetnesse which is in the Lord Jesus Christ, be alwayes your delight." *The Poore Mans Cry* recounts Lilburne's bodily pains and torments, blaming them on the cruelty of the prelates and their henchmen, the wardens of the Fleet. But, after describing his persecution by the clergy, Lilburne appeals to the House of Lords for rescue, threatening, at the same time, to make the kingdom ring with his "just and murnefull complaints."

This supplication to the Lords against the bishops is the earliest extensive example of Lilburne's calculated technique of concentrating on that group of his opponents most immediately in conflict with him, in the hope of winning new if temporary allies. For this reason, as well as to show his loyalty and patriotism, *The Poore Mans Cry* vehemently reaffirms Lilburne's allegiance to the king. Further, the marginal notes which crowd its pages concentrate their scorn on the prelates, citing them as the real subverters of king and Lords, as the real traitors to England. Thus, essentially, Lilburne's political position at this period of his life was also marked by Puritan orthodoxy: the Preamble to the Root and Branch Petition at the start of the Civil War, for instance, similarly laid the blame for England's woes at the feet of the established clergy.

During the first four months of 1639 Lilburne, who now apparently had readier access to pen and paper, continued to air his grievances. Though none of his petitions of this period have survived, it is evident that they stressed the sufferings of the prisoner and the nefariousness of the bishops.[46] Then in May, Lilburne addressed a plea "To all the grave and worthy citizens of the famous city of London, but especially to the . . . Lord Maior," which he called *A Cry for Justice*.[47] Picturing himself as "a poor distressed innocent young man, and a Prentice of this Honourable City," Lilburne was obviously trying to enlist the Lord Mayor's aid in furthering his appeal to the Lords. Yet *A Cry* continues to show the nonradical and essentially expedient nature of Lilburne's early political views; for, though it toys with the vocabulary of political theory, it concentrates on his own immediate wrongs.

Three techniques in this tract, however, can be seen as foreshadowing the Lilburne of the later 1640's. The first is his explicit accusation against Laud of high treason for the Archbishop's illegal censure of Bastwick. Though Bastwick had already made this same accusation, and though Lilburne had repeated it in 1638, he here uses this charge, and the legal precedents which support it, to strengthen the inference of his own traditional patriotism. In other words, Lilburne carefully builds up his own case by debasing its opponents. The second technique is shown in his treatment of prison abuses, whereby the reader's sympathy for Lilburne's sufferings is interwoven with a larger issue, in this case the need for prison reform. Thus the wardens' maltreatment of the poor, as well as the prevalent bribery and corruption, are particularized as they affect Lilburne, and generalized — with many examples — as they affect the entire Fleet Prison. Lilburne, in short, has also developed in his writing the knack which he first displayed on the pillory of consciously dramatizing himself as the focal point of a broader issue. The third technique which *A Cry for Justice* reveals is his willingness to take his case to the people. Though he had likewise anticipated this threat, now it is more explicit, more ominous.[48]

Within a month of the publication of *A Cry for Justice*, a group of London apprentices rioted against Laud. Largely provoked by the turmoil incident to Charles's Scottish adventure, they were also probably stirred by Lilburne's appeal in *A Cry*, and by his next tract, the distribution of which coincided with the time and place of their riot. *To all the brave, courageous, and valiant Apprentizes of . . . London, but especially those that appertain to the worshipful Company of Cloth workers (of which company, if I live I hope to be a Free Man)* [49] in melodramatic language urges the apprentices to go to the Lord Mayor, "by hundred or thousands," and to importune him to save the life of their fellow-apprentice. But, even if they do not help him, Lilburne announces that

I am resolved by the might and strength of my God, for the honour of my King and Country, and the good of future generations, to fight it out so long as I have a legge to stand on, and to wage professed warre so long as I have a drop of blood in my bellie with the domestick and home bred enemies of the King and State, for I have a souldiers heart within my innocent breast.[50]

Twice he warns the apprentices not to raise any "tumult or uproare" in his behalf, but then he concludes with this exhortation:

Wherefore unto all you stout and valiant Prentizes, I cry out murther,

murther and murther, wherefore as you pitty the most miserable and deplorable condition of one who am your stout and courageous (though sore) afflicted fellow Prentize, give the Lord Maior no rest till he . . . fulfill my just and equall desire, that so my innocent blood may be preserved.[51]

Thus, if on a comparatively small scale, Lilburne was for the first time effectively calling for mass action, impelled to do so not by any conscious political theory, but by the personal exigencies of his imprisonment.

None the less, that imprisonment was to last another year and a half, until November 1640. However, the events in the outside world which progessively threatened the Royalist position made Lilburne's lot somewhat easier, and his few complaints were now written largely in the past tense. Only two items from his pen survive from this period. The first, dated October 4, 1640, is a letter addressed to the wardens of the Fleet.[52] It is vituperative and threatening, and it suggests that its author will soon be vindicated not by God's ultimate sanction but by the immediate pressure of onrushing history. The second is Lilburne's petition to the Long Parliament which assisted in securing his release.[53]

After three years in prison, Lilburne, at the age of twenty-six, would soon be free to take his part in the revolution which was coming to a head. Since both his theology and his politics were still very much in the main stream of conventional Puritanism, he was well suited to join that coalition now temporarily united in opposition to the king-supported Episcopal church — a church which had both persecuted him and helped him to create his picture of himself as a Puritan Saint and as fledgling spokesman of the people.

III. *1641–1645: The Soldier*

Immediately after the opening of the Long Parliament in November 1640, Lilburne was released from prison.[54] It is paradoxical that, within the first week of his freedom, a petition that his wrongs be righted was presented to Parliament by Oliver Cromwell, a man with whom Lilburne's future career was strangely intertwined.[55] Despite Cromwell's intercession, it was not until six months later that the House of Commons voted that Lilburne's imprisonment had been "Bloody, Wicked, Cruill, Barbarous, and Tyrannicall"; [56] and the reparations which he claimed were his due had only a long, complicated, and abortive history in various Parliamentary committees.

Shortly after his release, Lilburne, with the financial help of his uncle, set up a brew house which quickly prospered, and which enabled him to get married.[57] During these early years of the Long Parliament Lilburne remained a staunch Parliamentarian. From the beginning he followed Parliament's prosecution of Strafford with such enthusiastic interest that he was brought before the House of Lords on a charge of high treason for allegedly having uttered violence against the king — a charge which was quickly proved to be substantially false.[58] The vehemence of his antiprelatical views, however, got him into further trouble when he took part in the riot of December 1641 which prevented the bishops from taking their seats in the House of Lords. His admiration for Parliament on the eve of the Civil War can be seen in his account of this affair:

I fought with . . . divers . . . at Westminster, (who drew first) with my sword in my hand, to save the Parliament mens throats from being cut, conscienciously judging that nothing I had too good to hazard for so just an authority as I then judged them to be.[59]

Then, late in the summer of 1642, having studied all of Parliament's "most excellent declarations," and having "sufficiently smarted under the Kings irregular government," Lilburne enrolled in the Parliamentary army.[60] He was commissioned as a captain in Lord Brooke's regiment, took part in the indecisive Battle of Edgehill, and a few weeks later was taken prisoner by the Royalists and sent to Oxford, there to await trial and, probably, execution for high treason against the king.[61]

His views on politics and religion had undergone little change since his earlier imprisonment. In making up his mind to enlist, he had probably read, among other contemporary works, Brooke's *A Discourse opening the Nature of that Episcopacie*, and perhaps imbibed some of its rationalism and tolerance.[62] He had also very possibly encountered Henry Parker's *Observations upon some of his Majesties late Answers and Expresses*, where Parker, in support of the war against the king, advanced the myth of a semidemocratic social contract.[63] Even so, Lilburne continued to follow the official Parliamentary explanation for the Civil War, an explanation which had been central to the indictment of Strafford, that the king was a "prisoner" of his evil advisers. Moreover, his unquestioning zeal in the Parliamentary cause shows that he continued to believe that he was battling in the service of Christ against prelatical evils and "Romish innovations."

Lilburne's one published letter from these years, written late in 1642, is relatively high-spirited: [64] his imprisonment by the Royalists is not too onerous, he is sure that Parliamentary pressure will prevent his execution, and, though he is personally loyal to the king, his ardor for the cause of God and Parliament continues unabated. His cheerfulness was justified: within a month, under the threat of retaliation by Parliament, the Cavaliers exchanged Lilburne.[65]

He was greeted with public joy on his return to London, presented with £300 by the Earl of Essex, and told by his wife that she had secured him a well-paying government job. The first two he accepted gladly; the latter he rejected, telling his wife

I must rather fight (though it were) for 8 pence a day, till I see the liberties and peace of England settled, then set me down in a rich place for mine own advantage, in the midst of so many grand distractions.[66]

Lilburne was true to his word. For two more years he fought actively in the army of Parliament, from which he resigned almost a poor man.[67] He first served as a major under Colonel King, in which capacity he showed a fervor which many of his superiors found galling. The immediate outcome of his zeal was a dispute with King, and Lilburne's promotion to Lieutenant-Colonel under the Earl of Manchester; its delayed outcome was his later battle with the House of Lords, then with the House of Commons and Cromwell. But as early as the summer of 1644 Lilburne was again in trouble: in defiance of orders he captured a Royalist castle, whereupon Manchester threatened to hang him. Cromwell intervened, and Lilburne immediately became involved in the growing quarrel between the two generals. On one side of this quarrel were those who wished vigorously to prosecute the war; on the other, those whose chief aim was to make a quick peace in order to restore some sort of national religious unity, probably Presbyterian, and to regain political stability under an only slightly limited monarchy. The widening rift in the Parliamentary coalition had thus spread to the army on the eve of its New Modelling, and Lilburne threw his lot with the forces that opposed Manchester and the relative neutralism for which he stood. Consequently, at the end of April 1645, irritated by Manchester's treatment of him and by the frustrations incident to a divided high command, Lilburne resigned his commission and returned to London.

The principal reason for this return to civilian life, however, was Lilburne's refusal to subscribe to the Solemn League and Covenant, now a precondition to service in the New Model. Against this covenant and the compromises for which it stood, he now intended to exercise his polemical talents.[68] This intention marks Lilburne's first significant major departure from the main current of Puritan thought, and it is proof that his political apprenticeship was coming to an end, that his career as a journeyman in radical politics was about to begin. His new "master" was to be neither Hewson nor Bastwick, but William Walwyn.

Walwyn and Overton: The Early Fight for Religious Liberty

I. William Walwyn: His Life to 1645

Compared to Lilburne's stormy and self-publicized career, that of William Walwyn was relatively sedate and obscure. His role in the Leveller movement is still somewhat of an enigma, and the measure of his influence on his colleagues is often a matter of conjecture.[1] Yet whereas Lilburne was usually the dramatic spokesman for this group, it was in all probability Walwyn who did most to give it a cohesive philosophy, a radical bent, and a political organization.

Walwyn was born in 1600 near Malvern in Worcestershire. His father, Robert Walwyn, was "a man of good Life and Repute in his Country, and of between three and four hundred pounds Annual Estate. . . . His Mother . . . was Daughter to . . . [the] Bishop of Hereford."[2] A younger brother like Lilburne, Walwyn too was bound apprentice in London, where he "served out his Time with a Silk-man in Pater-noster row."[3] About 1631 he was made a member of the Merchant Adventurers' Company. He achieved quick success as a cloth merchant, for during the first twenty-one years of his marriage, from 1628 to 1649, he was able to support his wife and approximately twenty children in "a middle and moderate but contentful condition."[4] During this period, except for his involvement in the Leveller tumults, Walwyn and his family enjoyed a comfortable upper-middle-class life.

It was from a relatively respectable background, then, that Walwyn emerged as the most consistently radical thinker among the Levellers. Part of the explanation for his radicalism, for his unorthodox approach to religion and politics, can be found in the not uncommon mixture of classical and theological reading which constituted his informal education. In a pamphlet written in 1649 to defend himself against the charge of heresy, Walwyn says he has been reading "humane authors" for twenty years. He then goes on, in a passage which shows his candor, his inclination toward didacticism, and his wry humility, to comment on his own intellectual habits:

but I used them (the humane authors) alwayes in their due place; being very studious all that time in the Scriptures, and other divine authors, as some of Mr. Perkins works, Mr. Downhams divinity, I had, as it were, without book, also Doctor Halls meditations, and vowes, and his heaven upon earth, and those peeces annexed to Mr. Hookers *Ecclesiasticall policy*. Hearing, and reading continually; using Seneca, Plutarchs Lives, and Charon of humane wisdom, as things of recreation, wherein I was both pleased, and profited; and truly, I do not see I have cause to repent me of taking liberty in this kinde, having never in my life, I blesse God, made an ill use thereof; amongst which Lucian for his good ends in discovering the vanity of things in worldly esteem, I like very well, whereof I can read only such as are translated into English; such a wise Jesuite I am, that with all my skill, I cannot construe three lines of any Latin author, nor do understand any, except such common proverbs, as are more familiar in Latine then in English, which sometimes I use not to dignifie myselfe, but because of the pertinency of them in some occasions.[5]

The judicious range of Walwyn's reading is further indicated not only by other references to the standard classics, but by his allusions to such unexpected sources of wisdom as a *Life of Mahomet* and Montaigne's *Essays*.[6] In 1649 he even recommended the latter to his accusers, with the advice, "Go to this honest Papist, or to these innocent Cannibals . . . to learn civility, humanity, simplicity of heart; yea, charity and Christianity."[7] This interest in a wide variety of books Walwyn helps to explain by saying that for many years his only recreations have been "honest and discoursing" friends and good books, but especially the Bible.[8] Indeed, Walwyn's reverence for and close knowledge of the Bible pervades almost every line he ever wrote.

Though Walwyn says nothing directly about his own formal education, his few scattered observations on education in general throw some light on the development of his social thinking. Walwyn's son-in-law, Humphrey Brooke, quotes him as criticizing the inefficiency with which foreign languages are taught, and adds that Walwyn

dislikes in the education of Children, that the languages only are proposed, and not the principles of Divinity, and the precepts of Morality, in such a manner as that their understandings may be possessed therewith, whereby they may be made both religious and true Common-wealthsmen. And that also some Art, Mechanick, or Manufacture be taught according as their genius and disposition of body shall encline them; so that they may be both able to provide for themselves, and be serviceable to the Common-wealth.[9]

To this mixture of Bacon and Milton, Walwyn also contributes several anti-Scholastic remarks, of which the following can serve as a sample:

I have, indeed, bemoaned the breeding of the Youth of this Nation, as being bred so as to be artificiall and crafty, rather than truly wise and honest; to be Sophisters and Pedantick Disputers, and Wranglers about words, then of solid judgment.[10]

But the core of Walwyn's philosophy and the key to his political activities was his religion, his personal attitude toward God. Less zealous than Lilburne, Walwyn practiced to a conspicuously small degree that separation of the holy and the secular which Woodhouse finds characteristic of Interregnum radicalism.[11] The fusion in him of the divine and the profane is, in fact, the hallmark of his reading, his writing, and his life.

Throughout this long life Walwyn remained an Independent in religion, though there is some doubt as to whether he continued for a long time a formal member of any specific congregation.[12] More important than his nominal Independence was his early adherence to antinomianism. Writing in 1649, Walwyn says that he

had long before been established in that part of doctrine . . . of free justification by Christ alone; and . . . was at much more ease and freedom then others, who were entangled with those yokes of bondage unto

which Sermons and Doctrines mixt of Law and Gospel do subject distressed consciences.[13]

This belief in free justification for all men certainly came to Walwyn
some time before 1640.[14] Presumably it was the result of his reading
in both pagan and Protestant authors, including certain mystical and
sectarian writers, and of his deliberately Socratic examination of
Scripture.[15] Troubled by certain apparent contradictions between
the word and the spirit of the Bible, he had diligently applied himself to its text. Then he had proceeded to examine it and himself
until he not only resolved these contradictions, but reached a state of
deductive certainty about the promise of universal grace which he
found in the spirit of the New Testament. Moreover, like Socrates,
he continually attempted to learn about other religions, to observe
their adherents with sympathy and understanding; in this respect
he twice refers to himself as a "Seeker" — as one who searches for
useful truth.[16]

At the time when Lilburne was still suffering his initial imprisonment, when open civil war was imminent, Walwyn was thus both a
successful man of business and a wise and experienced amateur
theologian. Further, he had had some experience in local politics,[17]
and was prepared, therefore, to take up arms against the oncoming
sea of national troubles. His first plunge was into the fight for religious liberty, and until 1646 freedom of conscience was the major
theme of all his pamphlets.

In November 1641 a short pamphlet entitled *The Humble Petition
of the Brownists* appeared. It was probably the work of William
Walwyn.[18] Pretending to be a petition to Parliament, this tract was
one of the first and one of the most effective of the many Civil War
pleas for unrestricted religious liberty. Its tone is mild, rational, at
times slightly sardonic. Of the despised Adamites, for instance, the
author says:

Let . . . [them] Preach in vaults & caves as naked as their nailes, and
starve themselves with cold, they think themselves as innocent as Adam
& Eve were in their nakednesse before their fall, let them therefore alone
till some innocent Eve bee so curious as to eate forbidden fruite, and then
they will all make themselves aprons of figge leaves perceiving their
nakednesse.[19]

In a similar manner the tract goes on to plead for toleration for Brownists, Puritans, Socinians, Familists, Arminians, and Papists — a controversial sampling extending from sectarian extremes to ultramontane Catholicism. Walwyn thus goes beyond Milton when he says, for example, "If the Papists will have altars, Priests, Sacrifice and Ceremonies, and the Pope for their supreme head in Spirituall affaires . . . let them alone with their pretended prescription." [20]

Both religion and reason, the author argues, cry out for full toleration. Only by complete religious freedom can England achieve order and harmony, and individual judgment and conscience avoid violation: "for the quiet of the state . . . the comfort of the subject, and . . . the love of truth" necessitate that "every one shall freely enjoy his conscience." [21] Thus in 1641, Walwyn, if he wrote this cogent and rational pamphlet, not only entered the arena of political-religious conflict, but reached ahead to a solution that was not to come until the Toleration Act of 1689. Unfortunately, *The Humble Petition of the Brownists* attracted almost no attention amid the competition of more violent, if not more crucial, issues.

Within the following year Walwyn took the side of Parliament against the king. By November 1642 he was a Parliamentary Committeeman for one of the London wards, with the duty of helping to raise soldiers and arms for the cause.[22] In this same month a second pamphlet probably from his hand was published, *Some Considerations Tending to the undeceiving those, whose judgements are misinformed by Politique Protestations, Declarations, &c.*[23] In the main, this work was an appeal for unity among the components of the Parliamentary coalition, particularly in the face of the machinations of the prelatical clergy. As such, it is typical of many of the hortatory pamphlets and newspapers which were then flooding London. However, there are certain aspects of this appeal which are peculiarly relevant to Walwyn and to future Leveller developments.

First, Walwyn makes an unusually sharp distinction between those who are in the Royalist camp and those who oppose them, and in the latter category he stresses the common denominator of victimization. The supporters of Parliament are, by and large, those who have suffered from religious repression and from the abuses of lawyers and monoplies, and those "who are sensible either by their owne or their neighbors sufferings of the injuries of former times, or desirous to prevent and divert our oppression and slavery for the future." [24]

Second, Walwyn's implication that the Civil War is and should be revolutionary in both religious and economic terms, though by no means unique in 1642, is somewhat novel in that it emphasizes the inherent rationalism of the common man. Thus in warning his readers about the Royalist technique of "divide and conquer," of "deceit and delusion," Walwyn asserts that his friends ("for all good men are such") need only to think in order to penetrate the wily prelatical stratagems. A precondition to this ability to think is, however, mutual toleration; hence the members of the Puritan coalition must, in a spirit of love, disregard indifferent matters of ceremonial and worship for the sake of overcoming their common enemy.

Third, several pages of *Some Considerations* are concerned with a strongly partisan analysis of Caroline corruption, which, Walwyn alleges, has been largely caused by the bishops and their hirelings, abetted by monopolists, lawyers, and courtiers. Against this corruption the Puritans have stood steadfast. Consequently, Walwyn continues, let us not find fault with them, despite the fact that often the Puritan "is to blame in his not observing all he can to win by love . . . such as differ from him in opinion, [and] in not endeavoring all he can to bridle his passion." [25] For, notwithstanding, it will be only by the union of all devout men, including explicitly Brownists and Anabaptists, that slavery to prelatical oppression and a misled monarch can be avoided. Without fanaticism, Walwyn had thus taken a pragmatic, liberal stand which was not to become relatively common for another two years. Even then, full freedom of conscience remained a doctrine that to the Presbyterians and conservative Independents was sinful, to most of the Erastians anarchical.

Walwyn's probable third pamphlet, published in September 1643, relies still more heavily on his belief in man's innate rationalism, in the capacity of every man to approach the truth by means of his own comparatively unaided and unsophisticated reason. Consequently, *The Power of Love*,[26] to a greater degree than his two preceding tracts, is devoted to a direct defense of the sects; and, in order to state his case with maximum effectiveness, Walwyn in his opening sentence pretends to be a member of the small, mystical, and unpopular sect, the Family of Love. He then goes on, in the prefatory "To Every Reader," to reveal his own basic religious conviction and to show succinctly how that conviction is at once mystical and intensely secular:

looke about you and you will finde in these woefull dayes thousands of miserable, distressed, starved, imprisoned Christians: see how pale and wan they looke: how coldly, raggedly, & unwholsomely they are cloathed; live one weeke with them in their poore houses, lodge as they lodge, eate as they eate, and no oftener, and bee at the same passe to get that wretched food for a sickly wife, and hunger-starved children (if you dare doe this for feare of death or diseases); then walke abroad, and observe the generall plenty of all necessaries, observe the gallant bravery of multitudes of men and women abounding in all things that can be imagined: observe likewise the innumerable numbers of these that have more than sufficeth, . . . and the wants and distresses of the poore will testifie that the love of God they have not.[27]

Walwyn next anticipates the charge of communism that such a statement invites by saying that the apostles held all things in common, and that distinctions between men should be based only on the extent to which they love their brethren. From here he moves to warning his readers not to be diverted by name-calling:

reade the ensuing discourse impartially, and . . . finde the minde of him that hateth no man for his opinion: . . . plaine truth will prove all; . . . give her but her due and patient audience, and her perswasions are ten thousand times more powerfull to worke upon the dull, refractory minde, than all the adulterate allurements and deceivings of art.[28]

Despite Walwyn's abjuration of "art," this preface shows his flair for the quietly dramatic, his intimacy of tone, and his restrained forcefulness — qualities which make his appeal to love and reason a weapon for social reform rather than a series of pious platitudes.

The body of *The Power of Love* is less concise, less hard-hitting, than its preface, but it contains, at least in embryo, most of Walwyn's later ideas. Referring to himself as a "Minister of reconciliation," he begins with an exposition of his doctrine of free and universal grace through Christ's love: not the law of the Old Testament but the spirit of the New is man's clue to salvation. Even Calvinistic man, bowed down under his own sense of depravity — "Many of you through sense of sinne, and of wrath due for sinne, walke in a very disconsolate condition: feares and terrors . . . abound in you" — can be saved, for Christ died for all men.[29] Then, as a corollary to his fundamental doctrine of the "power of Love," Walwyn reiterates the need for full toleration: "[it is] a universall mistake, that men are sooner perswaded from their vanities, through pressures of the law, and affrighting terrors of wrath and hell, then by the cordes of love."[30] Christianity itself hates oppression; and its true enemies are those who are now trying to divide and calumniate the Puritan forces. Thus, in part, *The Power of Love* repeats the political message of *Some Considerations*, as it does, though with greater fullness, Walwyn's central and hopeful belief in the potentialities of human reason: "for men never reforme their vices till first their judgements be well informed, and then they kindly reforme themselves."[31]

Walwyn's optimistic rationalism may here suggest certain smug assumptions of early eighteenth-century conservatism; yet ultimately his rationalism has closer affinities with the romantic primitivism of the late eighteenth century. Like Goldsmith, for instance, Walwyn claims that the natural reason with which man was originally endowed has been corrupted by so many "inventions of superstitious subtilities and artificiall things," that, "now in these later times we see nothing but mens inventions in esteeme, and the newer the more precious."[32] And, with Rousseau (and Montaigne), Walwyn complains that men are no longer leading a life "according to nature," but are living instead in a manner which "heathen and meere naturall men would be ashamed of."[33]

From this reverence for natural, uncorrupted man springs Walwyn's obscurantist opposition to higher education. The prelates and their followers — those, that is, who oppose a society based on love, toleration, and innate reason — are the products of the universities, and their counsels are devious, subtle, learned, and destructive. Therefore, as part of his warning against the divisive practices of the Royalists, Walwyn equates natural man with simple man, and subversive aristocrat with the product of higher education. But this primitivistic view of man probably arose, in turn, from Walwyn's belief in free grace. Again with the New Testament as his starting point, and with the support of such "profane" authors as Seneca and

Montaigne, he emphasizes not man's fall but his salvation. As *The Power of Love* makes clear, since man is to be saved, presumably he is well worth saving. This is true primarily because of Christ's loving sacrifice, but also because all men have been endowed with the God-given quality of reason. The impediments in the way of men's salvation are not natural depravities but institutionalized corruptions. As a result, the return to a natural Eden which Walwyn advocates is not so much a return to moral naïveté as it is the dream of a sort of rural, idyllic anarchy, wherein man, like Adam, "judging rightly of all things, and desiring only what . . . [is] necessary . . . [can pass] his days with abundance of delight and content-ment." [34]

Walwyn's increasing involvement in postlapsarian politics can be seen in the next tract probably from his pen, *The Compassionate Samaritane*, which appeared in the summer of 1644.[35] Continuing to operate from the premise that a loving God has endowed all men with the capacity for goodness and reason, Walwyn again pleads for liberty of conscience. In the course of this appeal, his attack on con-temporary vested interests becomes more explicit, more polemical. Also, though he makes it clear that he holds "fellowship and com-munion with the Parochiall congregations," he strongly defends the sects and castigates those who either attack them or condescendingly apologize for them.[36]

The first brief section, one of the three major divisions of *The Compassionate Samaritane*, is addressed to the House of Commons, and it pleads with them in a hopeful vein to put an end to the "sufferings of the Separation." The second and much longer section then goes on to defend unlimited toleration, though at first glance it often appears to be digressive and undisciplined. This defense is based on three premises, each of which shows why "every man ought to have Liberty of Conscience of what Opinion soever," provided that such liberty is not directly prejudicial to the Commonwealth; why, specifically, all statutes limiting religious freedom should be repealed, and freedom of the press, again provided it not be abused to the immediate danger of the state, guaranteed. These three premises are: first, that one necessarily believes what his own reason dictates, and "where there is necessity there ought to be no punish-ment, for punishment is the recompense of voluntary actions"; second, that all mortal knowledge is uncertain; and third, that compulsion against one's conscience is as useless as it is sinful.

It is in the amplification of his second reason, the uncertainty of human knowledge, that Walwyn's ostensible digressions can be seen to have a fundamental intellectual consistency. Asserting that uniformity is not a desirable goal, Walwyn goes on to amplify Milton's dictum that "New Presbyter is but old Priest writ large." Next, as a corrective to Presbyterian intolerance, Walwyn advocates the separation of church and state, with the state being supreme and secular, but without the power to interfere in matters of conscience. From here he moves to the assertion that distinctions between clergy and laity are false and destructive, a proposition which he reinforces by his belief in human reason and his suspicions of formal education. Indeed, it has been the most learned who have long been "the troublers of the world, . . . the poore and unlearned Fishermen and Tent-makers [who] were made choyce of for Christs Disciples and Apostles." [37] But the class-conscious momentum inherent in Walwyn's sharp distinction between innate reason and formal learning does not allow him to stop here. He goes on to attack the vested interests of the clergy, both prelatical and Presbyterian. He berates their stake in higher education, their exaction of tithes, and their attempts to maintain their unwarranted power by control of the press. Against such oppression and tyranny the common people who constitute the varied sects have been the most consistent and valiant battlers. Walwyn's conviction that human knowledge is uncertain had thus brought him a long way toward active support of democratic agitation.

The third major section of *The Compassionate Samaritane* explicitly supports certain of the sects, and thereby carries on the revolutionary implications of his belief in full toleration. In answer to a variety of divisive allegations, Walwyn claims that he stands with Christ and the apostles against either prelatical or Puritan intolerance, and with considerable detail he counters the favorite conservative red herrings: the Anabaptists are not anarchists, they are merely opponents of tyrannical government; the Antinomians are truly godly, not preachers of immorality and licentiousness; the Brownists, Separatists, and Independents by and large believe in religious freedom for all, and most of them do not hold that "all other

Protestants are in a damnable condition." [38] Walwyn then concludes with a plea for unity and harmony among all those devout men who are engaged in the struggle for human rights, a plea similar in tone and intent to that of *The Humble Petition of the Brownists* of three years earlier.

Thus, while Walwyn's intellectual position and underlying philosophy had remained essentially the same, the events of the day were pushing him to the left. As those leading the opposition to king and bishop came closer to power they tended to renege on the implications of their own democratic slogans. Consequently Walwyn more and more found his allies among the political outcasts, the sectaries, who saw in the success of the Puritan Revolution the only guarantee of their own continuance. Himself no sectary, he was compelled by his liberal antinomianism to identify himself with the persecuted and dispossessed, as well as with those whose religion and politics were, in the context of the seventeenth century, most truly revolutionary. However, it was only during the brief period when the Levellers became an organized movement that his political activities were to be directly secular and, so to speak, physical, rather than sectarian and spiritual. Therefore, for the Leveller movement to be more than a series of hopeful visions and sporadic efforts, just as Lilburne was complemented by Walwyn, so Walwyn needed both Lilburne and Overton in order for his ideals to achieve a greater degree of historical reality.

II. Richard Overton: His Life to 1645

Less is known about the third of the leading Levellers, Richard Overton, than about Walwyn. A man with a strong sense of humor and adventure, he often deliberately surrounded himself with a cloak of mystery, and to his contemporaries he was the most elusive of the prominent radicals.[39] Born at the close of the sixteenth century, by 1615 he was in Holland, where he joined a congregation of non-Calvinist Baptists. In his confession of faith at that time Overton is reported to have said:

Lately of the English church, but convinced by the Word and Holy Spirit of God, I give up all its errors, and renounce its maternity, and with the whole soul and mind desire to enter by baptism into the true church.[40]

At least until 1649, when his ideas on religion are lost sight of, Overton ostensibly remained an adherent to the major articles of faith of the General Baptists. As a result, his emphasis on individual revelation was typically Calvinist, though his attitude of expectant waiting brought him close to the antinomianism of Walwyn. Yet this attitude did not mean an absence of worldly activity, for despite the fact that the General Baptists may have felt themselves set apart from others because of their state of inner religious grace, Overton and his coreligionists were aggressive in their demands for toleration and for the separation of church and state. Indeed, the General Baptists, partly because they came under the direct influence of Continental Anabaptism, became in the mid-seventeenth century the source for many of the members of the extreme sects and the more radical political groups.[41]

Sometime before 1641 Overton returned to England. There he became an unlicensed printer.[42] Possibly by 1642, certainly by 1645, he was helping to print his own and some of Lilburne's tracts, having probably got his start in this trade through a relative who had printed and sold books in London since 1629.[43] Little else is now known about this man's early life. By 1645, however, under the pseudonym of Martin Mar-Priest, Overton achieved, if only briefly, wide notoriety.

Before this, in January 1642, Overton published his first signed work, most of it a rough poem, called *Articles of High Treason Exhibited against Cheap-side Crosse*. Two months later his second work, also signed by him and this time completely in verse, appeared, under the title of *New Lambeth Fayre*. Both are uneven, rollicking profusions of anti-Catholic and antiprelatical clichés, and their only significance for his later work lies in their revelation of his zeal in behalf of Puritanism and his propensity for graphic allegory. But as a poet he was at best a writer of facile doggerel.

Early in 1644, however, Overton published *Mans Mortallitie*, a lengthy pamphlet which separates him not only from the Puritan scribblers but also from most of his contemporaries. (For the near certainty with which this tract can be attributed to him, see the Appendix.) This work reaches back to a long tradition of skepticism, and forward, through Hobbes, to the materialism of Marx. Its title page, in fact, sets forth both its implicit skepticism and its quasi-materialistic purpose, when, in addition to citing Ecclesiastes, it describes *Mans Mortallitie* as a "Treatise,"

Wherein 'tis proved, both Theologically and Philosophically, that whole Man (as a Rationall Creature) is a Compound wholly mortall, contrary to that common distinction of Soul and Body: And that the present going of the Soule into Heaven or Hell is a meer Fiction: And that at the Resurrection is the beginning of our immortality, And then Condemnation, and Salvation, and not before.

But like Milton in *Paradist Lost*, the author postpones this Resurrection to a distant and indefinite future: the emphasis of Overton's treatise is on man's mortality, and the final mystical union with Christ is asserted only in an undefined and brief manner, in occasional tangents to the main argument.[44] Perhaps, as in Hobbes, such references had the ulterior purpose of forestalling a charge of atheism; for though Overton treats the Fall in almost a traditional manner, and though this work is full of Scriptural citations, its tone often suggests an antireligious attitude.

Overton's opening premise is that Adam, though created immortal, through his fall bequeathed mortality to his posterity. This "mortalization" is of the whole man, both his body and soul, as the author attempts to show by many passages from the Bible and by means of "Naturall Reason." In fact, he continues, the soul is "elementall, and . . . finite"; for, says Overton, paraphrasing Aristotle,

Man is but a creature whose severall parts and members are endowed with proper natures of Faculties, each subservient to other, to make him a living Rationall Creature, whose degrees or excellencies of naturall Faculties make him in his kind more excellent then the Beasts.[45]

Thus what men call the soul is merely an agglomeration of man's nonphysical "Faculties," faculties which animals also possess though to a lesser degree. Then, arguing from biological and rudimentary psychological grounds, Overton goes on to show that man by and large is merely a higher animal, and that the "fictions" concerning the soul would be ridiculous if carried to their logical conclusions in relation to a lower species.

From here, in a chapter consisting mainly of Scriptural exegesis, Overton proceeds to show that "whole man" suffers death. Human procreation, birth, growth, decline, and death are all natural processes, since "by this mortall flesh cannot be generated an immortall spirit or soule that can subsist by it selfe dissolved from the flesh." [46] Then, in answering objections to this theory, Overton resorts to the weapon of ridicule, calling attention, for instance, to the absurdity of sexual activity between "He soules and She soules." Several times he reaffirms the core of the mortalist doctrine that, until the final Resurrection, the soul cannot exist apart from the body, and that a disembodied soul has no function within the universal cycle of birth, maturation, and death.

Moreover, if the body is only the instrument of the soul, and if the soul comes directly from God, then is God

Author of all sinne, and . . . only prone to all sinne, and not the flesh, no more than a conduite though a meet instrument to convey water is the author or fount of water, . . . so [if] Gods immediate hand is the cause of all sin . . . man had better been born without this soul.[47]

The traditional concept of God, in fact, makes Him "like the tyrant Mezentius, that bound living men to dead bodyes, till the putrefaction and corruption of the stinking corps had killed them." [48] This, says Overton, is impossible, and the only conceivable alternative is that "corruptible man begets nothing but what is corruptible . . . totally mortal." [49] But Overton proceeds to qualify this ostensible message of despair:

If it be scrupled that this destroyeth the hope of our faith, I answer, It doth but remove it from a false principle to a true, from a deceitful fancie to an infallible object, the Resurrection.[50]

And the concluding sentence of *Mans Mortallitie* reminds its readers that, though "man hath not wherewith at all to boast no more then of dirt under his feet," yet if he casts himself "wholy on Jesus Christ," then at the final Resurrection his dust shall be made immortal.[51]

There are, of course, many strongly traditional elements in this treatise. The Fall and its ramifications are treated in a by no means unusual manner; Overton's emphasis on man's corruption, on his vast distance from God, seems on the surface to be in the Pauline-Augustinian-Calvinist tradition; and the anti-Catholicism of the typical Puritan is very much in evidence. Also, the whole apparatus of Scriptural citation to support a point, as well as the use of complicated allegory to dilute or dispose of conflicting passages, is in keeping with the elaborate scaffolding of most seventeenth-century theological writing. Finally, Overton's treatment of the Resurrection as the ultimate hope of those who by faith embrace Christ could be devout; certainly the pessimism inherent in the postponement of this looked-for event was not uncommon in an era when the idea of universal decline was at least as widely accepted as the idea of progress.[52]

None the less, the underlying configuration and attitude of *Mans Mortallitie* seem to be not only untraditional but, by implication, startling. Most striking in this respect is the tone of skepticism, even on occasion of mockery, which pervades much of Overton's text. Such overt skepticism is rare in England in the mid-seventeenth century, and it is almost unique in a work which purports to be a serious treatment of Christian theology. At the same time, this skepticism can contribute to a fuller understanding of Overton's vigorous fight for complete toleration. Despite the fervor with which he later battled for religious liberty, Overton's views on this subject have more in common with the philosophic indifference of many eighteenth-century tolerationists than with the majority of his own nonpersecuting contemporaries — who tended to advocate freedom of conscience either because of their desire to survive as a minority or because their religion hallowed the concept of a personalized and inviolable inner light, and to whom persecution was sinful rather than foolish.

Of almost equal importance in regard to the untraditional quality of *Mans Mortallitie* is its author's extension of teleological arguments in order to arrive at an unusual conclusion. On the basis of analogies in the fields of biology and psychology, with even an occasional nod in the direction of present-day pathology, Overton approaches a form of materialism which, if unconsciously and incompletely, at once goes back to Pliny and foreshadows Pavlov; for, rather than stressing man's middle position in a cosmic chain of being, *Mans Mortallitie* implies that the human being, though capable of reason, is merely and solely a higher animal, extremely remote from a semideistic God. This incipient materialism probably also helped to direct Overton's political efforts, since his reformist proclivities as a General Baptist may well have been strengthened by the self-reliance implicit in his "mortalism." [53]

Finally, *Mans Mortallitie* can serve as a partial explanation for the skillfully sardonic quality of much of Overton's later writing, and the effectiveness of his mockery can very possibly be related to the underlying secularism of his philosophy. Of all the Levellers, Overton became the most adept at combining rapier with bludgeon in his attacks on the ideas and powers that be, whether such powers were people, institutions, or traditional beliefs. Thus by 1644 Overton had not only entered the political-theological arena, but he was armed with a pen and a point of view which were well suited to the battle within the Puritan ranks that was about to break into the open.

The Coming Together of The Levellers

I. January to July 1645: The Battle for Religious Freedom

The pamphlets examined above were only drops in the published torrent which dealt with theology and politics, especially with the issue of toleration, between 1641 and the end of 1644.[1] Concurrently with this debate in print, the conservatives — those, that is, who wished to curb the impact of the Civil War — were increasing their efforts to attain their goals by legislation. (The Solemn League and Covenant, which Lilburne had refused to sign, was, in this sense, an example of military and legislative expediency engineered by a combination of English and Scotch Presbyterians.) Yet despite its apparent gains, the Puritan right wing, aware of the advances the Independents were making in the New Model Army and in London, also stepped up its efforts in the battle of press and pulpit over the course the war was to take.

The major issue of that battle was the question of religious freedom. Along with the Presbyterians, the most ardent opponents of toleration were certain of the Erastians, and the most virulent spokesman for both groups was William Prynne, once with Burton and Bastwick the object of Lilburne's admiration.[2] In the autumn of 1644 Prynne shifted his attack from priests and bishops to Independents and sectaries, from Laud to Goodwin, from support of the Parliamentary coalition to castigation of toleration and its supporters. On January 2, 1645, he published a violent assault on the leading Independents. Its title, as with so many of Prynne's diarrhetic pamphlets, serves as an adequate table of contents, *Truth Triumphing over*

Falsehood, Antiquity over Novelty: Or, *A Seasonable Vindication of*
the Undoubted Ecclesiastical Jurisdiction, Right, Legislative and
Coercive Power of Christian Emperors, etc. in Matters of Religion.
Along with John Goodwin and Henry Robinson, Lilburne wrote an
immediate answer to Prynne, *A Copie of a Letter . . . To Mr. William Prinne Esq.,* dated January 7, 1645.[3]

Having lost his brewery and being unable to get into the cloth
trade because of the monopoly of the Merchant Adventurers, Lilburne challenged the man who for many years was to be one of his
chief antagonists, and who now served as his symbol for the repressive turn which events in Parliament and the Westminster Assembly seemed to be taking. It was a dramatic challenge: "I am,"
wrote Lilburne to Prynne,

> desirous to try a fall with you, though one of your friends not long since
> told me there was as great disproportion betwixt you and me . . . as
> there is betwixt a tall Cedar and a little shrub. . . . I replyed, goe you,
> and tell this tall Cedar the little shrub will have a bout with him.[4]

The bout which Lilburne then proposed was a public debate on the
question of toleration.

In unsavoury language Lilburne's letter takes Prynne to task for
using "unsavoury Language against the poore Saints of God," for
allying himself with the persecuting Presbyterians, and for playing
the part of a Jesuit — an abusive term, paralleled today in the multi-
plicity, ubiquity, and vagueness of its uses by the word "Communist."
Lilburne also complains of the curtailment of freedom of the press
to those who have been most active in the fight against tyranny,
and he concludes his letter with a blast against tithes. The intellectual
heart of this epistle, however, is its central proposition that "to
persecute for conscience is not from God, but of and from the Divell
and Antichrist." In behalf of the holy cause of toleration, Lilburne is
careful to point out, those martyrs whom Foxe celebrated, as well as
those in King Charles's reign — "my selfe and many others" — have
all been persecuted. But Lilburne's attitude toward religious freedom
had not yet developed to the inclusive and rationalistic level already
reached by Walwyn. Rather, toleration is the due of the Saints, the
Independent elect, and the implication persists that Papists and Prelatists, as well as non-Christians, are to be excluded.

Prynne did not accept Lilburne's challenge; instead he undertook to have Parliament silence him.[5] Meanwhile, less than a month later, Walwyn, though still personally unacquainted with Lilburne, joined in the fray. Largely in answer to an earlier tract by Prynne which had attacked the leading Independents (*Independency Examined, Unmasked, Refuted*, September 1644), Walwyn both skillfully flayed Prynne and expounded his own broad and increasingly pragmatic view of toleration. Using the same general format that Prynne had used, Walwyn's *A Helpe to the right understanding of a Discourse concerning Independency* at first glance suggests that it is another tract by William Prynne.[6]

This impression is at once dispelled, for *A Helpe* begins by conjecturing what has made Prynne, once a good man, fall. Walwyn suggests self-interest, then that Prynne is "defective . . . in his understanding and easily outwitted"; and as an example of the latter he inserts an account of the sympathy for Laud which Prynne's vitriolic attacks on the Archbishop have occasioned. The "spleene" is another possible cause for Prynne's decline into malevolence. But the most likely explanation for his fall is that Prynne is a lawyer — a man who charges excessive fees, who does not labor with his hands, and who takes unfair advantage of the fact that England's laws are written in an unknown language and are the reverse of plain and simple.[7]

After this semi-ironic beginning, Walwyn shifts to a positive defense of full religious freedom. No man, he says, can go against his own reason and conscience, and "no man can refer matters of religion to any others regulation." Thus no governing body, either civil or religious, can have any repressive jurisdiction in matters of conscience. The state can, if it so desires, set up an official church, but only provided that this church grants full toleration to dissenters. Further,

as for disturbance to the State: admit any mans judgement to be so misinformed as to beleeve there is no sinne: if this man . . . should take away another mans goods, or commit murder or adultery, the Law is open, and he is to be punished as a malefactor.[8]

Moreover, toleration has its practical side. It is both essential to the unity of the "wel-affected party" and the cornerstone of true patriotism:

> for where the government equally respecteth the good and peace of all sorts of virtuous men, without respect to their different judgement in matters of Religion: there all sorts of judgement cannot but love the government, and esteem nothing too pretious to spend in defence thereof.[9]

In fact, as Walwyn goes on to point out, the disturbances created by intolerance can disrupt the economy of a country and send its workers and traders to other, freer lands.

Walwyn's contributions to the fight for liberty of conscience were not original. The assertion that the people cannot entrust a government with the power to control religion goes back at least to the early seventeenth century when Thomas Helwys and Leonard Busher spoke out against persecution and denied the magistrate any jurisdiction in matters of individual conscience. The utilitarian argument in behalf of full toleration also predates Walwyn. A year before, for instance, Henry Robinson's *Liberty of Conscience* logically demonstrated the threat to an expanding capitalism inherent in religious persecution; and during the summer of 1644 Roger Williams' *The Bloudy Tenent* set forth in full and stirring terms the case for complete liberty of conscience. Nor does *A Helpe* add very much to what Walwyn had already said on this subject in his earlier pamphlets, though it does indicate his growing effectiveness as a propagandist.

Two months later, in April 1645, a more aggressive ally than Walwyn began to launch his own diversionary attacks on Prynne and the Presbyterians: Richard Overton, under the pseudonym of Martin Mar-Priest, published the first of his bitingly humorous indictments of intolerance, *The Araignement of Mr. Persecution*.[10] Though not the first to revive the famous Elizabethan pen name Martin Marprelate, Overton alone succeeded in making Martin's seventeenth-century descendant notorious.[11] The title page of this pamphlet helps to explain why. The author is given as "Yongue Martin Mar-Priest, Son to Old Martin the Metropolitiane." His work is "Licensed and Printed according to Holy Order, but not entered into the Stationers Monopole." The place of printing is given

as Europe, to which is added: "Printed by Martin Claw Clergie,
Printer to the Reverend Assembly of Divines, and are to be should
[sold] at his Shop in Toleration Street, at the Signe of the Subjects
Liberty, right opposite to Persecuting Court."

In the same spirit, the Dedicatory Epistle is addressed to the
Scottish clergy and the Westminster Assembly. In it Martin says
that he lacks nothing but preferment, and that he is well qualified
to be the spokesman for these two groups:

Reverend Yongue Martin can thunder-thump the Pulpit. O, he can staer
most devoutly, raile and bawle most fervently, storme most tempestuously
even till he foame at mouth most precisely; oh how he can spetter't out!
O these cursed Anabaptists, these wicked Brownists, these Heretickes,
these Schismatickes, these Sectaries; O Martin hath it at his fingers end,
he's an University Man, skild in the Tongues and Sciences, and can
sophisticate any Text, O he is excellent at false Glosses, and Scholastike
Interpretations . . . an excellent man to make a Presbyter.[12]

This is followed by a mock notice from the Westminster Assembly
thanking Martin for his efforts!

Overton's satire may be obvious, but his invective, like that of his
Elizabethan prototype, is zestful and kinetic. At the same time, *The
Araignement* contains almost all of Overton's ideas on toleration and
on the potential power of reason to regulate human affairs. It likewise has several touches of his own strong skepticism and of Walwyn's obscurantism. Further, despite its slapdash style, its involved
allegory, and its attempt to achieve some dramatic suspense, *The
Araignement* fully articulates those charges which had become
standard to the case against persecution.

The Araignement's cast of characters itself points out this traditional element, as it does the elaborate but distinct allegory.[13] The
judge is Lord Parliament. Two of the justices of the peace are
Reason and Humanity. Among the members of the grand jury
which has indicted the defendants — Sir Symon Synod, Sir John
Presbyter, and Mr. Persecution — are such personifications as Sov-
eraignty-of-Christ, Nationall-Strength, and Publike-Good; while on
the trial jury serve Gospel, Liberty-of-Subject, Light-of-Nature, and
Good Samaritane — perhaps a reference to Walwyn. Gods-Vengeance is the prosecutor, and among the witnesses he calls are

Christian-Martyrs and Liberty-of-Conscience. Finally, in sharp contrast, is the jury which Sir Symon Synod asks for: it includes Satan, Spanish-Inquisition, Scotch-Government, and Pontificall-Revenue.

The arraignment gets under way with the pragmatic testimony of the grand jurors, among whom Mr. United-Provinces cites his own prosperity to show the utility of tolerance, and Mr. Desolate-Germanie illustrates the ruinous effects of persecution by his own sad condition. The indictment, in fact, accuses Mr. Persecution of being responsible for most of the blood which has been shed between Abel's murder and April 1645. Even so, the bill of particulars against Mr. Persecution consists of only a few points, though they are restated in many ways and with a rising degree of anger. The majority of them are brought out in the opening speech of the prosecutor, Gods-Vengeance. Primarily, persecution is destructive: it disrupts temporal life and kills spiritual life, it breaks the "bonds of Peace and Friendship Nationall and Domestike," it throws men in jail merely for following their own consciences, and it curtails the free interchange of knowledge. Furthermore, persecution is a vicious circle: the Protestants "hate & persecute the Papists because the Papists hate and persecute them."

The only escape from this vicious circle is complete religious liberty, which Overton extends explicitly to Catholic, Jew, Mohammedan, and pagan, as well as to all the sects. This liberty, in turn, is based on two premises, one primarily secular, the other primarily religious. The first, Overton sums up with this somewhat Hobbesian assertion:

Where two stand at enmity, there must needs be Mastery, or else no safety: When one knoweth the other is his mortall enemy, he will use all the Means, Strength and Pollicy that he can to subdue him. This enrageth to all manner of Tyranny and Bloodshed . . . built upon this rotten & devouring principle of forcing the consciences.[14]

The second premise, having to do with spiritual love rather than political accommodation, Overton suggests by a rhetorical question which might have been asked by Walwyn or any other believer in free justification: "Why should we hate and destroy one another? are we not all the Creatures of One God? redeemed by our Lord Jesus Christ?"[15]

But Overton is his most effective when he tries to hoist Presbyterianism by its own petard. Thus, for instance, Sir Symon Synod, who as one of the proponents of "Present Reformation" is the active agent of Mr. Persecution, exhorts the court:

This fellow Liberty-of-Conscience is a Free-Willer, a loose libertine, one that opens the gate to all manner of prophanes, . . . a man of all Religions and of no Religion, a compound of all heresies, scisme, and faction; a pestelent enemie to Nationall Conformity, our Late Solemn League and Covenant, a Traytour to your [Parliament's] late sacred and blessed Ordinance for Tythes, a worke of Superarrogation! a confuter of our mighty champions Mr. Prinne, Edwards, &c. . . . This is he would [permit] every mecannicke illiterate fellow to turne preacher, and be as good as their Minister, no distinction made betwixt the Clergie and the Laity, our Canonicall Coates, Girdles . . . and Black Gownes made a derision, a taunt, and a curse. . . . Our holy Tythes . . . be turned into voluntary Contribution, oh insufferable sacraledge! from the good will of the people good Lord preserve us.[16]

Much of *The Araignement* is a similar free-swinging attack on Presbyterian policies. The "Black Coates" are accused of being greedy and mercenary: their chief interest is in tithes and benefices, "so that now the Trade of a Presbyter is the best Trade in England" — in contrast to those true patriots, the Independents and sectaries, who have sacrificed much for the cause of liberty. The Presbyterians are also hypocrites: they, who complained most loudly about prelatical oppression, now "breathe out threatnings, menaces, and persecutions openly," and they have substituted the Assembly of Divines for Charles's High Commission. Moreover, their Solemn League and Covenant is only a system of "Persecution by Covenant" which has to be enforced by a misled Scottish army. Finally, the Presbyterian religion "is moved upon the Wheele of the State," for its supporters will plot and scheme to augment their wealth and to attain that cruel "Monopole of the Spirit" which is their "Jesuiticall" goal. For all these reasons the court sentences Mr. Persecution, along with Sir Symon and Sir John, to eternal punishment in the "Lake of fire and brimstone."

Running through *The Araignement*, however, is the hint of a developing political program on Overton's part. Its basic postulate, as in Walwyn's social theory, is that man is rational, educable:

What we know, we receive it by degrees, now a little and then a little; he that knowes the most was once as ignorant as he that knows the least; nay, is it not frequent amongst us that the thing that we judged heresie we now believe is orthodox? [17]

Overton then supplements this postulate with a second assumption, one that was employed at least verbally by all the major political factions in the Civil War, *salus populi suprema lex*. But Overton gives this slogan a modified direction and a potentially more revolutionary impact when he applies it specifically to the limitations on, and duties of, Parliament. In the words of one of the justices of the peace, Reason, addressing the judge, Lord Parliament:

The people . . . did not in chusing your Lordship to this place . . . intend the makeing of themselves slaves in any the least kind . . . or to put themselves at so vast a distance, as to make their addresses to you as to some Dietie, but . . . authorized and entrusted you to vindicate and preserve their native and just Liberties. . . . Therefore you cannot, without betraing this Trust, by any coercive power subject any of their consciences, persons, or estates to any Ecclesiaticall Jurisdiction whatsoever.[18]

Here, in embryo, is the later Leveller doctrine of a popularly elected Parliament, directly responsible to its electors, with its powers curbed by some form of historically valid and unchangeable bill of rights.

None the less, Overton was not yet a democrat, not even a confirmed republican. He says, for instance, that a king, provided he gives his people protection from persecution, is to be supported. He also acknowledges the power of the magistrate over all civil offenses, without bothering to set up any system of safeguards to limit that power. On the other hand, Overton is strangely ahead of his time in his internationalism, for, citing Ireland as a dramatic case in point, he shows how persecution has been the principal barrier to world peace. Yet, in general terms, the author of *Man's Mortallitie*, by opposing the restrictive — and hence antirational and antidemocratic — "Machiavellisme" of the Presbyterians and Erastians with his own rationalism, pragmatism, and incipient democracy, was now showing himself more fully qualified to help form a radical and secular political organization.

But the actual birth of the Leveller party was still almost two years away, and at the end of May Overton, continuing his role as Young

Martin Mar-Priest, issued his second provocative attack on the Presbyterians, *A Sacred Decretall, Or Hue and Cry, From his superlative
Holinesse, Sir Symon Synod, for the Apprehension of Reverend
Young Martin Mar-Priest*. Though intellectually this tract adds little
to *The Araignement*, Overton's satiric technique is here somewhat
more disciplined, sharper. It is at its best in its ironically extravagant
denunciation of Martin for his opposition to tithes and for his faith
in the common people. Again the Presbyterians are equated with the
bishops, and both are again contrasted to the self-sacrificing, patriotic
Independents and sectaries. *A Sacred Decretall* opens, therefore,
with a complaint from the Assembly of Divines that its enemies are
attempting to curtail clerical revenues and "trayterously and
blasphemously" to subvert some of its members into working for the
good of the people, and it concludes with an account of the Assembly's unsuccessful efforts to bribe Young Martin.

A third Mar-Priest tract, *Martins Eccho*, of June 1645, carries on
Overton's effective goading of his opponents. His central theme remains the "unreason of persecution"; but stylistically this work, with
its short phrases strung like beads into long and breath-straining
sentences, seems closest to its Elizabethan model.[19] Also present is a
stronger note of threat and braggadocio, particularly when, after
again scorning the bribes of the Presbyterians, Overton offers them a
variety of facetious ways to deal with Martin.

Martins Eccho, however, brings up two new aspects of Overton's
political thought. In addition to attacking persecution and tithes, he
now includes the nonpayment of the army's arrears among the sins
of those who are not properly prosecuting the Civil War. This issue
was to be one of the cornerstones of Leveller popularity in the New
Model, and Overton was the first of the Levellers, though probably
not the first pamphleteer, to tie it in with the larger questions of
toleration and political reform. Also in *Martins Eccho* he, like
Walwyn, closely links the Presbyterians with wealth and social
position, the separatists, especially the members of the sects, with
the lower classes — and it is this class-consciousness which now adds
a sharper note to Overton's invective. Martin, pretending he is the
Synod's servant, berates his presumed master in increasingly rough
and menacing terms. Tithes are a symbol of Presbyterian greed; the
Directory is a Satanic device for persecution; the name-calling,

slander, and oppression indulged in by the Westminster Divines are subversive; and the recent military defeats suffered by the Parliamentary forces are "tokens of Gods wrath" against such men as Prynne, Edwards, Pagitt, and their fellow "superlative Holinesses." But as the intensity of Martin's railing increases, the positive content of his argument decreases, and much of *Martins Eccho* is a diatribe in which Overton devotes his energies to the ever popular sport of mud-slinging.

In his vituperative attacks Overton did not rely exclusively on Martin. A week after his *Eccho* the Presbyterians were assailed with *The Nativity of Sir John Presbyter*, "Calculated by Christopher Scale-Sky, Mathematitian in chief to the Ass-embly of Divines," and "Licensed by Rowland Rattle-Priest, a terrible Imprimatur." This horoscope, drawn up for the Westminster Assembly, sets forth a gloomy series of predictions for Presbyterianism. Every planet in every position indicates nothing that is not wicked in Sir John's character, and forebodes nothing but evil in his future. Ostensibly straight-faced, with all the paraphernalia and technical terminology of astrology, *The Nativity* links Overton to Ben Jonson as well as to Martin Marprelate, for it is reminiscent of *The Alchemist* in both its humor and its scathing portraiture. But, again, this pamphlet shows Overton's literary versatility rather than any further development in his social thinking.

By this time, the summer of 1645, Overton's attacks were beginning to take effect. The Stationers' Company had stepped up its efforts to locate the secret press which printed the Martin tracts,[20] while ever more strident outcries against Martin came, as might be expected, from William Prynne, the favorite butt of Overton's jibes. At the end of July, Prynne's *A Fresh Discovery of some Prodigious New Wandring-Blasing Stars, & Firebrands, Stiling Themselves New-Lights, firing our Church and State into New Combustions* objected strenuously to the laxity in licensing and enforcement which allowed the nefarious Martin tracts to be printed. Martin, whoever he is, says Prynne, is seditious and impious, and should be punished as well as muzzled. Thus the heat was on; presumably the secret press used by Overton was dismantled and moved, for his next Mar-Priest pamphlet, *The Ordinance for Tythes Dismounted*, did not appear until the very end of the year.

Prynne's splenetic outburst was, in part, occasioned by Lilburne. In January Prynne had ignored his challenge to debate the subject of toleration, and had referred Lilburne's *Letter to Prinne* to a Parliamentary Committee.[21] Then, early in June, Lilburne attended a meeting at the Windmill Tavern to discuss the repercussions of the recent Parliamentary defeat at Leicester — one of the "tokens of Gods wrath" against the Presbyterians referred to in *Martins Eccho*. Prynne and Lilburne differed in their accounts of this meeting. The former accused Lilburne of acting as its chairman and of convening the meeting for subversive purposes.[22] Lilburne denied both allegations. He stated, instead, that the meeting had been called for a patriotic purpose; that, after a long debate, it was proposed that Parliament be prorogued for a month and that its members, as well as the Assembly of Divines, disperse to their homes to rally the people again to the antiprelatical cause; and that he himself was chosen as one of a large committee to present the sense of this meeting to Parliament.[23]

Even if Lilburne's account is correct, Prynne's anger at the Windmill Tavern gathering can be explained by the fact that he viewed it both as an attempt to break up the Westminster Assembly and as a manifestation of radical intransigence against the leadership of the conservative majority in Parliament. His fears might have been better grounded had he realized that this meeting was indirectly to result in the active alliance of Lilburne and Walwyn. During the winter of 1644–1645, Walwyn had begun to take part in the discussions of a group of citizens at Salter's Hall. From these discussions, Walwyn says, "much good issued to the whole City and Kingdom." [24] One such "good" was the fact that Walwyn was also present at the Windmill Tavern in June.[25] Then, on July 19, when Lilburne was at Westminster to testify against one of the leading conservative members of Parliament, Walwyn, with a committee from Salter's Hall, was also waiting outside the House of Commons to present charges against its speaker. In all likelihood, Lilburne and Walwyn there met face to face for the first time.[26]

Prynne's preliminary anger was further augmented because, at about the same time as the Windmill Tavern meeting, Lilburne published a short tract entitled *The Reasons of Lieu. Col. Lilbournes sending his Letter to Mr. Prin.* Here he unbashfully contrasts his own patriotic activities to the destructive tactics of the Presbyterians and reactionary Erastians. Moreover, he goes on, since Prynne's venomous harangues have contributed much to the present disunity among the proponents of the good cause, since Prynne has also continued to oppose that liberty of conscience which is essential to victory against king and prelates, and since he has persisted in his personal animus against Lilburne, Lilburne has felt compelled to vindicate his original challenge from the "little shrub" to the "tall Cedar."

A final specific factor in the tension between radical and conservative, as epitomized in the Prynne-Lilburne quarrel, was an official report Lilburne made to the House of Commons on July 10 telling of a recent victory of the army under Fairfax.[27] Lilburne, who had been in Somerset gathering material for his charges against Colonel King, was given the minor honor of reporting this triumph of the increasingly pro-Independent New Model. His account was straightforward, probably eyewitness, and appended to it was a request from the army for added supplies and encouragement from Parliament. In historical context, this request was a further small symptom of the growing breach between Westminster and the New Model and the ideals for which each was beginning to stand. On July 19, 1645, these conflicting ideals came into sharp if trivial conflict at the door of the House of Commons.

II. July to October 1645: "England's Birth-Right"

On that summer day in 1645 Lilburne's former mentor John Bastwick was also hovering about Westminster. Probably overhearing some of the remarks exchanged between the Salter's Hall and Windmill Tavern contingents, and incensed at Lilburne for reasons similar to Prynne's, Bastwick reported to the House that Lilburne has accused Speaker Lenthall of sending £60,000 to the enemy at Oxford.[28] Despite the fact that Bastwick's charge was probably a fabrication, Lilburne was promptly arrested.[29]

On July 24 he was summoned before the Parliamentary Committee on Examinations. Asked to affirm or deny Bastwick's charge, Lilburne, as he had done six years earlier, refused to answer without first being properly informed as to the cause of his commitment.

The committee chairman, now angered, repeated the question; and Lilburne, with his lifelong propensity for martyrdom and his dramatic skill in making his own predicament the testing ground for a broader issue, answered:

I am a free man, yea, a free borne Denizen of England, and I have been in the field with my Sword in my hand, to adventure my life and my blood (against Tyrants) for the preservation of my just freedome, and I doe not know that I ever did an Act in all my life that disenfranchised me of my freedome, and by vertue of my being a free man (I conceive) I have as true a right to all the priviledges that do belong to a free man as the greatest man in England whatsoever he be, whether Lord or Commoner, and the foundation of my freedome I build upon the grand Charter of England. . . . Sir, the priviledges contained herein are my Birthright and inheritance.[30]

Lilburne, though again warned to take heed of what he was saying, reaffirmed that he would live and die by what he had just spoken. Forthwith he was returned to jail. The loose organization that grew into the Leveller party arose largely in response to Lilburne's present "martyrdom" in the cause of political liberty.

The first step, however, was to publicize that martyrdom. This Lilburne promptly did: the day after his examination, *The Copy of a Letter From . . . Lilburne to a Friend* was already in circulation. Here Lilburne recapitulates the story of his arrest and of his vindication of English rights, and then depicts the ingratitude of Parliament toward a man whom they once esteemed, interlarding his account with many well-placed references to his sufferings at the hands of the bishops, to his courageous military career, and to his unjust persecution by Prynne and the Presbyterians. Next, having cited Magna Carta, the Petition of Right, and the *Book of Declarations* in support of his position, Lilburne comes to the intellectual heart of his case:

For my part, I look upon the House of Commons as the supream Power of England, who have residing in them that power that is inherent in the people, who yet are not to act according to their own wills and pleasure, but according to the fundamentall Constitutions and Customes of the Land, which I conceive provides for the safety and preservation of the People.[31]

At no future date does Lilburne state the basic political principles of the Levellers more succinctly. Indeed, in one sense the later Agreements of the People can be considered a clarification and amplification of this statement, just as the major political contribution of Walwyn and Overton in the years immediately following 1645 can be considered an attempt to provide a theoretical scaffolding for Lilburne's relatively untutored political utterances, as well as a practical method of applying them to the reform of existing institutions.

After thus postulating his fundamental concept on the role of Parliament, Lilburne proceeds to take a stand on the proper functioning of a legislative investigating committee — a stand which is still painfully pertinent:

> For either it is a Court of Justice, or no Court of Justice, and either it is tyed unto Rules, or not tyed; but if it be a Court of Justice, and tyed unto Rules, when it sits upon criminall causes betwixt man and man, concerning life, liberty, or Estate . . . me thinks they should observe the method of other Courts of Justice.[32]

None the less, in the *Letter . . . to a Friend* Lilburne the theorist is, as usual, subordinate to Lilburne the self-propagandist: after a single page of concentrated political analysis, he returns to the saga of his own sufferings.

Two weeks later Lilburne was again called before the Committee on Examinations, this time to determine if he was the author of the *Letter . . . to a Friend*; if he was, the committee was to have "power to commit him to what prison they please." They chose Newgate, for Lilburne's answer was essentially unchanged.[33] Two days later, on August 11, the full House of Commons approved the committee's sentence on Lilburne for his "affront and contempt," and ordered him tried at the next London Quarter Sessions.[34] For the third but by no means the last time Lilburne faced the prospect of a long period behind bars.

It is obvious from Lilburne's relatively able statements of political and judicial principles in his two examinations that his reading since 1642 had branched out. Most important among his recent intellectual acquisitions was the second part of Coke's *Institutes*, published in 1642. Though he may well have been acquainted as early as 1638 with Coke's *First Institute*, published in 1628, his major source of legal ideas and quotations, from 1645 to the end of his life, was the section in Coke's *Second Institutes* dealing with Magna Carta, and to a lesser degree that dealing with the aggregations of significant Edwardian statutes. After 1645 his writings show the impact of Coke's emphasis on historical continuity, on Parliament's function as a high court, on Magna Carta as a fundamental law, on the major historical function of judicial decisions, and on the underlying role of reason as the principal criterion by which to judge a law. Any similarities between Lilburne and Burke can therefore probably be attributed to their sharing Coke's belief in the organic growth of English constitutional law — a belief which could be either radical or conservative in its ramifications.

Lilburne's second new major source of both principles and references was the so-called *Book of Declarations*, published in 1643. Its formal title explains its contents, *An exact Collection of all Remonstrances, Declarations, Ordinances, and other passages betweene the Kings Majesty and his Parliament . . . from Dec. 1641 . . . until March, 1643*. Along with the historical and apocalyptic books of the Old Testament, Coke and the *Book of Declarations* provided Lilburne's text and marginalia with a profusion of quotations and allusions; but, as might be expected, the Bible remained predominant. Presumably, too, Lilburne continued to read in the English chroniclers, and possibly in a few well-known works on political theory.[35] He certainly kept himself informed concerning the more important contemporary pamphlets which bobbed on the flood daily pouring from the London presses.

The explanation for Lilburne's growing skill as a propagandist can, in fact, be partly attributed to this familiarity with current pamphlet subliterature. His frequent juxtaposition of indignation and pathos was a common device. So, too, was the apparatus of erudition, of which the conspicuous overloading of margins, the insertion of Latin phrases, and the plethora of Scriptural allusions were all parts. In addition, Biblical echoes pervaded the works of the day, often even the most scurrilous or facetious. Lilburne's technique of personalizing an issue, of making himself the focal point of a principle, was also common to an era in which a religion stressing individual salvation set the spiritual tone. Finally, most of the

pamphleteers, despite their tendency to use labyrinthine sentences
(ranch-house is a more descriptive adjective in this connection than
baroque), had the knack of pungent and colloquial utterance when
the occasion demanded. This skill was confined to no religious or
political group, and stylistically it raises many of these ephemeral
tracts above the level of verbose mediocrity.

Lilburne's well-advertised vicissitudes often seemed to act as a
spur to the publication of strongly worded tracts, both for and
against him. The first effective answer to his own account of his
arrest and imprisonment was *A Just Defence of John Bastwick*.[36] In
often racy prose, Bastwick denies that he has informed against Lilburne, abuses his former disciple, and justifies Parliament's sentence
against him. Bastwick accuses him of being the spokesman for the
Independents, and, with a mixture of Presbyterian zeal and political acumen, proceeds to correlate Independency with radicalism. The
belief that power resides in the people, Bastwick predicts, will lead
to the destruction of religious discipline and to the eventual elimination of social distinctions. Lilburne speaks for that faction which
is not only revolutionary but greedy for power and wealth — unlike
such stalwart defenders of stability and truth as Prynne and John
Bastwick.[37]

Concurrently with the appearance of Bastwick's *Just Defence*
was a petition in Lilburne's behalf presented to the House of Commons on August 26, and signed by between two and three thousand
people, some of whose names were presumably secured by William
Walwyn.[38] In addition to this mass petition, a glimpse of the partisan excitement of the summer of 1645 can be seen in the minor
plotting and counterplotting which went on in the struggle for publicity, now that for the first time in English history the combination of cheap printing and democratic ferment made the public ear
both available and important. For instance, at the instigation of
Colonel King, Bastwick, and Prynne, so Lilburne alleges, rumors
and papers were deliberately circulated, purportedly from Lilburne's
adherents, threatening civil bloodshed if the prisoner were not released. The prisoner's prompt response was a nonsecret letter to the
Lord Mayor avowing that "he would rather chuse to die in prison,
then to take any such unjust way for . . . deliverance." [39]

But in mid-September an intellectualized defense of Lilburne succinctly restated the issues involved. The anonymous *Englands Miserie and Remedie* is a closely reasoned exposition of the claim that Lilburne is justly attempting to vindicate the rights of all freeborn Englishmen.[40] The House of Commons, it asserts, is the "representative body of the people"; as such, it is the servant of the people who elect it, and it must not abuse the power which they delegate to it. Lilburne's plight is therefore a dramatic example of the wicked, arbitrary, and dangerous abuse of power by the House of Commons, an abuse which, the author continues, is symptomatic of Parliament's increasing tendency to violate Magna Carta and to encroach on the people's liberties.

And let no man deceive himselfe, to thinke with senceless and frivolous distinctions to award the dishonor and danger, which may arise to the Parliament hence, as to say that the Great Charter is but suspended as to Lilburne, but not abrogated; and that the duty of the Parliament is to provide for generalities, but is not at leysure to attend particular grievances; these answers satisfie none but Ideots, or those that suck profit under their command.[41]

Then, early in October, Lilburne again appealed to the public against Parliament's handling of both generalities and particular grievances. *Englands Birth-Right Justified* is a mélange of Biblical citation and legal precedent, of personal pique and large principle, of invective and positive political analysis.[42] Throughout, however, it is informed with the burning conviction that the case of Lilburne is that of all Englishmen, and that all Englishmen — the public, that is, to whom Lilburne now appeals in his pamphlets — are capable of concerted democratic action. Thus despite its stylistic and intellectual ups and downs, *Englands Birth-Right* is also a rudimentary party platform in terms of both its planks and its intended rhetorical effects.

In a series of queries, largely buried amid lengthy digressions, Lilburne sets forth his own grievances and the applicable principles which they invoke. His first and here most basic principle is that there is a fundamental distinction between the equity and the letter of the law. As a corollary, he asserts that the law, like the Bible, should be written in simple English, "so every Free-man may read it." This leads him to a violent attack on lawyers, who, says Lil-

burne, have long been a curse on the land. Thence he proceeds to
assail other vested interests, each of which was becoming increasingly popular as an object of public contumely: the monopoly of
preaching in the hands of prelate and presbyter; the cloth monopoly
of the Merchant Adventurers; the monopoly of the press under a
combination of Parliamentary conservatives and the members of the
Stationers' Company, a monopoly which, as Lilburne is careful to
point out, does not interfere with Royalist publications in Oxford;
and, as an alarming culmination, the threatened monopoly on bread
and beer.[43] "Oh Englishmen!" he asks, "Where is your freedom?
And what is become of your Liberties and Priviledges that you have
been fighting for all this while?"[44]

From this attack on monopoly Lilburne moves to an attack on the
Solemn League and Covenant, with the now almost inevitable correlation on the part of the radicals of Presbyterian discipline with
prelatical oppression. Both, says Lilburne, are antichristian, and both
utilize the "Papist device" of tithes to maintain their "intollerable
oppressing . . . burthen" on the backs of the common people. A
similar burden is that imposed on the commons of London by certain aldermen who are treading in "Strafford's pathes of Arbitrary
Government." In addition to such encroachments on the people's
rights and liberties are the neutralism in high places and the widespread graft which, between them, are making a mockery of the
Puritan Revolution.

Then, toward the end of his pamphlet, Lilburne suggests certain
specific courses of action to alleviate his own and England's suffering. Justice is to be administered impartially and equitably. The
people of London should be restored to their true rights. The war,
under the leadership of Cromwell, must be prosecuted to a successful conclusion.[45] All of those who have cheated the Commonwealth
or grown rich through its establishment are to be punished, and
all monopolies ended. These are only the more important of the
war aims which Lilburne outlines, but they were enough to provide a basis for future popular action. That he had some sort of
democratic action in mind is indicated by Lilburne's final plea, his
class-conscious advocacy of proportional taxation.

Despite the heavy weight of vanity and demagoguery in this
pamphlet, Lilburne was by no means a mere rabble-rouser, nor was

his political-economic program entirely haphazard. Though his thinking was still chaotic and undisciplined, it was not illogical. Thus again and again in *Englands Birth-Right* he refers to his basic belief in government by law, provided only that that law be founded on principles of equity. His typically radical proposition that the laws of England be reduced to simple English is itself sufficient answer to the charge of anarchy. Moreover, since Parliament theoretically represents the people, it has the function, both legislative and judicial, of preserving the people's traditional liberties. These liberties, in turn, are traditional because they stem from Magna Carta, from its confirmations, and, more recently, from the Petition of Right. Thus both logically and historically Parliament should be sensitive to the will of the people and to their grievances. The implied syllogism on which *Englands Birth-Right* is based does, in fact, arrive at a democratic conclusion: Parliament must be subject to frequent elections, and in these elections all the people should be allowed to vote. Specifically Lilburne advocates annual elections, and he suggests, though somewhat in passing, that he believes in universal manhood suffrage.[46]

Because this later demand was to be central to the Leveller political program, it is worth recapitulating the partially buried logic of *Englands Birth-Right*. Law, if it conforms to reason (or equity), is paramount; and since the House of Commons is the only institution which can properly represent the collective reason of the people, it must be truly and continuously representative. Such, says Lilburne in essence, is the message of English constitutional history. *Englands Birth-Right* was therefore of special importance because it helped to set forth a potentially radical philosophy of history as well as a potentially wide-ranging program of democratic action. But, as this pamphlet also shows, Lilburne still lacked two essentials: the ability to articulate a cohesive and practicable political theory, and a functioning organization to guide and implement such a theory. In short, Lilburne needed Walwyn.

III. *October 1645 to June 1646: Walwyn Versus Edwards*

Walwyn was not remiss. On October 11, 1645, the day after *Englands Birth-Right* was published, *Englands Lamentable Slaverie,* in all probability the work of Walwyn, appeared.[47] Though its main purpose was to support Lilburne and to warn him against placing too much reliance on Magna Carta, it also provided Walwyn's contemporaries with a sharp portrait of his own character. Thus the opening sentence establishes Walwyn's intellectual relationship to Lilburne:

> Although there is some difference between you and mee in matters of Religion, yet that hath no white abated in me that great love and respect justly due unto you for your constant zealous affection to the Common Wealth, and for your undaunted resolution in defence of the common freedome of the People.

This "love and respect," Walwyn continues, is based neither on prejudice nor rumor, for it has long been his habit to be "rightly informed" about what is going on in England. Now, having become so informed, he is indignant at the fact that Lilburne was asked to testify against himself and that he was imprisoned "without cause declared."

But despite the over-all righteousness of Lilburne's defense of himself, Walwyn goes on to advise the younger man not to pin too many of his hopes on Magna Carta. This document is "but a part of the peoples rights and liberties, being no more but what with much striving and fighting was . . . wrestled out of the pawes of those Kings, who had by force conquered the Nation." [48] Nor has the history of England in the past four centuries been potentially onward and upward as Lilburne had assumed. On the contrary, even Magna Carta, "the best we have," has been constantly abridged, while the history of Parliament has largely been a story of "vexation of the people":

> See how busie they have been about the regulating of petty inferior trades and exercises, about the ordering of hunting, who should keep Deere and who should not, who should keep a Greyhound, and who a Pigeon-house . . . who should weare cloth of such a price, who Velvet, Gold, and Silver, what wages poore Labourers should have, and the like precious and rare business, being most of them put on purpose to divert them from the very thoughts of freedome suitable to the representative body of so great a people.
> And when by accident or intollerable oppression they were roused out of those waking dreams, then whats the greatest thing they ayme at?

Hough wth [how with] one consent cry out for Magna Carta . . .
calling that messe of pottage their birthright, the great inheritance of
the people, the great Charter of England.[49]

Such was Walwyn's incisive and sardonic reading of history. Yet
he was able to end *Englands Lamentable Slaverie* with the assurance to Lilburne that "the honest and plaine men of England . . .
shall be your judges," and that consequently Lilburne should live
to be an honor to his country.

Meanwhile the London Quarter Sessions had started. Lilburne
appeared in court but was told that no formal charges had been
brought against him. He therefore wrote the Lord Mayor petitioning for release, and on October 14 he was discharged from prison.[50]
Concurrently with Lilburne's release, Prynne, still the most powerful of his "persecutors," published *The Lyar Confounded, or a
Briefe Refutation of John Lilburnes miserably, mistated Case against
the Parliament*. Largely directed against Lilburne's *Letter . . . to a
Friend* of the previous July, Prynne's pamphlet also indulges in a
good deal of generalized and vindictive pummeling of "poor upstart John." Yet the author's "inveterate malice" does provide a key
to an understanding of the conservative reaction against the growing revolutionary ardor of the radicals. Thus with some justice
Prynne says that Lilburne

is lately swelled to such an altitude of worth and merit in his own
conceite . . . that he thinks the whole Parliament guilty of a breach of
Magna Charta for not setting all public business aside to hear his private
petitions and give him reparations.[51]

Indeed, Prynne's alarm at the social upheaval implicit in Lilburne's
actions and his horror at Lilburne's amateur legal activities were so
intense that he characterizes Lilburne as a defamer, felon, liar, demagogue, ingrate, illiterate, malefactor, and traitor, against whom Parliament, in conformity with Magna Carta, must proceed, and against
whom all good men must continue to be alert. In short, Prynne and
Walwyn did not agree in their evaluations of Lilburne.

Lilburne's view of himself was closer to Walwyn's. This is made
extremely clear in *Innocency and Truth Justified*, which Lilburne
published in answer to Prynne early in January 1646. It is a digressive
and angry torrent that supplies a great deal of information about

Lilburne as an embattled and patriotic saint but little that is new
to the development of his ideas. Yet it is possible to see in this
pamphlet traces of the stylistic influence of Overton, with whom
Lilburne in all likelihood had begun an alliance shortly after his
release from Newgate in October. Here, too, Prynne played an important part. His efforts had caused a hiatus in the publication of the
Mar-Priest tracts, and had forced Larner, Overton's printer and the
early friend of Lilburne, to move his secret press twice between
July 1645 and March 1646.[52] By the end of 1645 Larner had also
become the printer for some of Lilburne's more incendiary tracts.[53]
Consequently, either through Larner or because they shared many
of the same ideas, Lilburne and Overton began their active connection sometime before Lilburne issued his ponderous and egocentric
though often hard-hitting answer to Prynne.

It is even possible that the relative seriousness of Young Martin
Mar-Priest's renewed attacks on intolerance was a result of Overton's acquaintance with Lilburne, and, through him, with Walwyn.
In any case, at the very end of 1645 Martin reëntered the fray with
The Ordinance for Tythes Dismounted. The object of Overton's
contumely is still Presbyterian persecution, but his central focus is
now on their greed, on their unjust economic encroachments. The
fourth of the Mar-Priest tracts is thus somewhat graver than its
predecessors: it is longer and, despite much that is still boisterous,
there is far more Scriptural underpinning. One can sense that the
issues Overton probes have reached a more explosive stage, that the
personal and ideological stakes seem higher.

The pamphlet itself, after a derisive dedication to the Assembly
of Divines, is divided into three parts, each dealing with one aspect
of the clergy's false claim to the exaction of tithes. In the first section the Presbyterian yoke is again found heavier than that of the
bishops. This is proved by the spate of recent pro-Presbyterian ordinances passed by Parliament: "whole Cart-loades," that is, of oppressive statutes.[54] Nor do the Presbyterians realize, says Overton in
agreement with Walwyn, that the New Testament has superseded
the "laws of the Levites," and that therefore the "Reverend Brethren"
should not continue to demand Moses' wages for doing Christ's
work. From here Overton moves to an attack on all ecclesiastical
courts, and thence to an indictment of the pyramidal system of

church government. He concludes this section of *The Ordinance for Tythes Dismounted* with the assertion that the greed of the Presbyterians exceeds even that of the priests of Moses: the Levites exacted tithes only from those well able to pay them! The amount of Scriptural exegesis and scaffolding, the emphasis on precedent — here Biblical rather than historical — and the serious awareness of the growing split between rich and poor, all contribute to making these pages seem closer to Lilburne's zealous works than to Overton's more gamesome Martin tracts. This relative gravity continues in the second section, where contemporary Presbyterian avarice is contrasted to the welfare point of view of the primitive church, and the author of *Mans Mortallitie* is evident both in the undercurrent of anticlericalism and in the scholastic skill with which he disposes of certain Biblical passages that seem to support tithes. But the brief concluding section of *The Ordinance for Tythes Dismounted* is more in keeping with the Martin of the year before, particularly in its sprightly attack on the alleged divinity of Parliamentary ordinances. Yet Overton closes on a note of menace: any law in behalf of forced maintenance is "Transgressant: . . . [it] is not truly Magesteriall, and cannot in equity engage either in Divine or Humane obligement"; for such a law is necessarily an encroachment on Christ's prerogative and an unwarranted interference with individual freedom.

At the same time that Overton's pamphlet appeared, the heavy artillery of the Presbyterians sent forth *A Letter of the Ministers . . . of London . . . against Toleration*. Within a few weeks Overton, in his final Mar-Priest effusion, answered this weighty appeal for conformity and stability. *Divine Observations Upon the London Ministers Letter* marks a return to his earlier style. It is signed by "his Synodicall, Priest-byter-all, Nationall, Provinciall, Congregationall, Superlative, Un-erring, Clericall, Academicall Holynesse, Reverend Yongue Martin Mar-Priest," and it uses the arguments of the London ministers, though with several new twists and turns, to justify the toleration of his own "Sacred Person . . . [and] the whole Independent Fraternity."

Overton's vigorous reaffirmation of full religious liberty invokes no new ideas, but it does give effective expression to the position which Walwyn had achieved five years earlier and which Lilburne was only now approaching. Moreover, Overton, in his prophetic analysis of the lengths to which the Presbyterians would go in order to curb the impact of the Civil War, penetrates to both the essential strength and weakness of the conservative position. Of Presbyterian political pliability and eventual strong survival, Overton says: "And this I dare be bold to affirme, That if the King should conquer and confound the Parliament, the now Parliamentized-Presbyters . . . would therewith be Royalized." [55] But their religious inflexibility and oppression — the cause of their imminent decline in power — he characterizes as the "very spirit, marrow, root, and quintecense of Popery." It is this "Popery" which forces Overton to conclude his pamphlet with these words — a sentence which could have just as easily been written by Lilburne or Walwyn:

And this my contestation and defyance of Presbytery is no otherwise against it, but onely as it is Exorbitant, Tyranically Prelaticall, Cruell and Ambitious; as for honest, meek, Evangellicall Presbytery, I am ready . . . to seal it with my blood, even out of an unfained love thereunto; So that in brief, my enmity is only against Tyranny, where ever I find it, whether in Emperour, King, Prince, Parliament, Presbyters, or People.[56]

This list of Overton's potential opponents can serve as a fitting epitaph for Young Martin Mar-Priest. Overton was now about to move from the battle for religious freedom to the battle for secular freedom. Though the two cannot really be separated, it was in the more secular arena that the Levellers mainly attempted to make the defeat of king and bishops a positive accomplishment. Freedom of conscience remained a major stumbling block to any permanent settlement during the years remaining before the Restoration, but the Levellers, in their progress toward the formation of a political organization, became increasingly worldly in both their techniques and their purposes. Within half a year, in fact, Overton side by side with Lilburne was engaged in open conflict with the House of Lords on the question of due process of law.

Similarly, Walwyn's progressive disillusion with the course of events led him, in the summer of 1646, to supplement his defense of religious freedom with a defense of Lilburne against the House of Lords, and shortly thereafter to transfer his hopes and his talents from support of Parliament to support of the fledgling Leveller party. Part of the background for Walwyn's disillusion and for his shift from the religious to the secular can be seen, if somewhat indirectly, in the seven tracts which he wrote between January and October 1646 on the question of liberty of conscience.

The first of these, like Overton's *Divine Observations,* was written in reply to the *Letter . . . against Toleration* of the London ministers. But unlike Overton, Walwyn in *Tolleration Justified, and Persecution Condemnd* "mildly examines" the barrage of the London ministers.[57] Though he tries to answer its various specific allegations, Walwyn's responses all fall back on his belief in the supremacy of human reason and in God as a God of love. Persecution is the greatest threat to brotherly love and to social harmony, and it springs mainly from a lack of self-confidence in the persecutor. This lack of self-confidence, in turn, prevents him from realizing that reason, not force, is the best antidote to heresy. Only if there is total toleration will each man be free to examine the word of God and thus to seek the truth. Walwyn then concludes his rationalistic defense of the Independents and sectaries against the Presbyterians with the confident assertion that "Parliament will judge justly between the two parties."

A month later the first part of Thomas Edwards' *Gangraena* plumped into the middle of the pamphlet war. Professor Haller's description of its author cannot be surpassed:

But the man who outdid all others in what Vicars called the practical rather than the dogmatical way of writing was Thomas Edwards. Edwards did not sit in his study dredging for texts with which to smite the heretics. He made it his business to read, if with starting eyes, the flood of heretical and seditious literature as it poured from the press. From this, from his own observation, from acquaintances and correspondents, he collected nearly three hundred dangerous opinions of the time, and heaped about them a prodigious assortment of distorted and libelous information concerning those who espoused them. All this he issued in the three amorphous parts, over six hundred pages in all, of his *Gangraena: Or a Catalogue and Discovery of many of the Errours, Heresies, Blasphemies, and Pernicious Practices of the Sectaries of this time.* He sacrificed every canon of logic, of good taste, and, as John Goodwin pointed out, even of syntax, in the effort to make his readers realize what was happening about them. He mentioned names, dates, and places. . . . The effect of this method may perhaps be measured by the fact that its author was visited with the full weight of Goodwin in refutation, that he achieved the immortality of mention in a sonnet of Milton's. . . . A host of lesser pens helped to make his name a byword for bigotry run mad.[58]

It was in answer to Part I of this torrent of abuse, particularly to some of the drops which were labeled with his own name, that Walwyn wrote his first signed tract, *A Whisper in the Eare of Mr. Thomas Edwards Minister*.[59] Here, in opposition to Presbyterian fears and restraints, he continues to plead for complete liberty of conscience. But in so doing he now displays his matured skill as an ironist, particularly in his predictions about the decline of Presbyterianism if such of its proponents as Edwards persist in their "inconsiderate rashnes, violent railing, and adventuring on unheard of waies to compasse . . . [their] ends." These predictions reach their culmination when Walwyn suggests that Edwards repent, in which case Edwards could petition Parliament in behalf of religious freedom in order to "make some amends for the evill" accomplished by his *Gangraena*. Walwyn then appends the meek and mild petition which Edwards allegedly might compose.

Throughout *A Whisper* runs the contrast between the two men. In contradistinction to the mercenary and splenetic Edwards, Walwyn characterizes himself as a type of Puritan Socrates — a man whose chief desire is to win friends, by rational persuasion, to the cause he loves. This "cause," in its widest meaning, has been that "all men might come to the knowledge of truth." In pursuit of this large aim, Walwyn has made it his lifelong habit to inform himself on "all the severall doctrines and waies of worship that are extant." [60] As a result, unlike Edwards' antipodal reaction to a similar process of investigation, Walwyn has become tolerant and sympathetic. Even when answering Edwards' charge that he is "a seeker, and a dangerous man, a strong head," Walwyn merely reasserts the pragmatic antinomianism which was the ethical foundation for his conduct:

I a seeker, good now: whose your author [authority]? Am I one because I know many, and have been amongst them often, that I might know them fully; so have I been with all other judgments, but I carry with mee in all places a Touch-stone that tryeth all things, and labours to hold nothing but what upon plain grounds appeareth good and usefull.

. . . My manner is in all disputes . . . to enquire what is the use, and if I find it not very materiall, I abandon it; there are plain useful doctrines sufficient to give peace to my mind, direction and comfort to my life; and to draw all men to a consideration of things evidently usefull hath been a speciall cause that I have applyed my selfe in a friendly manner unto all. . . . Had I all the power or strength in the World at my disposal, in cases of religion I conceive I should sinne if I should do more then in a loving way offer my argument, and gently perswade to what I conceive is both evidently true and really usefull.[61]

It is this method of behavior which has given Walwyn the reputation of being "a dangerous man, a strong head" among the bigots who are afraid of the free interchange of ideas, who, if granted the power, would silence any and all opposition, and who fail completely to understand the redemptive power of Christ's love — the bigots, in short, whose efforts produce neither truth nor utility.

A Word More to Mr. Thomas Edwards of a week later is largely a postscript to *A Whisper*; but Walwyn also uses it to explain how a man with his convictions was able to sign the Solemn League and Covenant, for according to his own broad interpretation of its first two articles, he found nothing necessarily inconsistent with a belief in full liberty of conscience. His continued ostensible confidence that Edwards will soon repent is again effectively ironic. Yet despite such irony, Walwyn's method in this tract, as in all of his signed tracts of the first half of 1646, is to emphasize rational "perswasion" and to play down direct abuse. Lilburne's far more violent reactions to the Covenant thus point up Walwyn's comparative isolation from his contemporaries in the restrained style of his polemics.

But this isolation was only literary. Walwyn's efforts in behalf of liberty of conscience soon got him involved in the organizational side of radical national politics. This can be seen in the circumstances surrounding the distribution of his next tract, *A word in season*, in May 1646.[62] At this time, when Charles was bending every effort to widen the breach between the parties making up the Puritan coalition, the acrimony of the pamphlet war was further heightened by an angry debate within the conservative-dominated London Common Council. This debate concerned a Presbyterian resolution which requested Parliament to suppress heresy, establish the Presbyterian Directory, join in union with the Scots, and come to a settlement with the king.[63] *A word in season* was Walwyn's well-timed answer to "The City Petition" in which the Common Council finally urged Parliament to accede to the wishes of the Presbyterians. On May 26 this City Petition was presented to Parliament; on the same day Lilburne was also at Westminster handing out copies of *A word in season*, toward the printing of which John Goodwin's Independent congregation had contributed fifty shillings.[64]

The fact that Walwyn's pamphlet had this combined support and that it quickly ran through 10,000 copies is explained both by its timing and by its content.[65] It is a brief, tempered, and cogent appeal for unity. Warning that "to be innocent as doves" is dangerous in a time of national peril, Walwyn goes on to plead for harmony among the Puritan forces, which, he says, are on the brink of self-destruction. Indeed, because the world is full of wolves and serpents, the Puritan coalition must beware of both its external and internal enemies, particularly of those who are attempting to split it by asking Parliament to curtail religious freedom. None the less, the strength and safeguard of the Puritan cause, as well as the true preserver of English liberties, is Parliament. The bulk of *A word in season* therefore consists of praise of Parliament, and Walwyn at some length reiterates his faith in its wisdom. This pamphlet thus marks the high point of radical confidence in the Long Parliament, and, largely as a result of this, the zenith of cordiality between the Independents and the Levellers-to-be.

At the very end of May, when the Presbyterian faction in the House of Commons was bending every effort to convince the temporary Independent majority to concur with the Lords and the London Council in accepting Charles's recent overtures, the second part of Edwards' *Gangraena* added its bit to the din of debate. Many of its 212 pages were devoted to the strident refutation of Walwyn, John Goodwin, and the fervent mystic John Saltmarsh. But Walwyn had his answer ready, *An Antidote Against Master Edwards His Old and New Poyson: Intended To Preserve This long-distempered Nation from a most dangerous relapse. Which his former, his later, and next Gangrenous Book is likely to occasion, if not timely prevented.*

In this extremely readable tract Walwyn does not bother to reply to Edwards' specific slanders against him; instead, he analyzes Edwards' lying and divisive technique, a technique which is particularly dangerous in its immediate historical context. Revealing a keen understanding of Machiavelli, Walwyn proceeds to show how Edwards has taken advantage of the innate decency of most people to prey upon their fears and delusions, and he exposes Edwards' use of such tricks as mud-slinging and rumor-mongering, even the devices of the whispering campaign and the big lie, or any and all of them in combination:

If you observe any man to be of a publique and active spirit . . . you are to give him out to be as strongly suspected of whoredom, or drunkenesse, prophanesse, an irreligious person, or an Atheist, and that by godly and religious persons he was seen and heard blaspheming the holy Scriptures, and making a mock of the Ordinances of Christ, or say he is suspected to hold intelligence with Oxford, or any thing no matter what, somewhat will be beleeved.[66]

Next, after several times warning Edwards' readers to be wary, Walwyn tells the Presbyterians point-blank that they need the help and protection of the Independents. Moreover, all the parties of the Puritan coalition must continue to have faith in Parliament — "the terror of the wicked and comfort of the just" — and must continue to work through Parliament to defeat their common enemies. Finally, in a postscript entitled "A Graine More," Walwyn reaffirms his belief in a God of love and in the need for love and charity in the affairs of men, and with a note of comic sadness he thus refers to his own efforts in behalf of Edwards:

Observing by some passages and occurences of late that all the labour bestowed towards the conversion and reducing of Master Edwards into a truly charitable and Christian disposition hath proved to be no other then as the washing of a Blackamoore; and thereupon daily expecting a poysonous issue from his infectious braine: To prevent the mischiefe that might ensue, I prepared this little Antidote.[67]

Though it involves some distortion of the approximately chronological treatment of the Levellers' development, Walwyn's two final tracts in reply to Edwards can best be considered at this point, for Edwards, despite Walwyn's prodding, did not cease to be a spiritual "Blackamoore." Aware that a third part to *Gangraena* was in preparation (it appeared in December 1646, with the climactic subtitle *a new and higher Discovery of the Errors, Heresies and insolent Proceedings of the Sectaries of these times*), Walwyn first anticipated it in mid-August with his delightfully serio-comic *A Prediction of Master Edwards His Conversion and Recantation.*[68]

Walwyn begins by informing the reader that Edwards' condition is even worse than Paul's before his conversion, but that there is still hope because often, "in cases so desperate as this . . . when things are at the worst, they are nearest to an amendment." The fact that Edwards, by his persecutions, has made himself a heretic, the fact that he is presumptuous in his ignorance, and the fact that he can "rayle, revile, reproach, backbite, slander, or despise men and women for their weaknesses: their means of trade and callings, or poverty," are all indications that he can sink no lower. And so, Walwyn again suggests, he will repent, hoping to gain for himself many of the better qualities of those whom he has so severely castigated, hoping to absorb, that is, the virtues of the Independents, Brownists, Anabaptists, Seekers, and members of the Family of Love. Then, for eleven pages, Edwards recants. His alleged repentance ranges from abject self-abnegation to a lyrical celebration of God's universal love, from the opening

Where have I been! Into what strange and uncouth pathes have I run myself! I have long time walked in the counsell of the ungodly, stood in the way of sinners, and too too long sate in the seat of the scornfull [69]

to the concluding

farewell for ever all old things, as pride, envy, covetousness, reviling, and the like, and welcome love, that maketh all things new, even so let love possess me, let love dwell in me, and me in love.[70]

In the course of this supposed confessional, Edwards damns himself in a manner suggestive of *A Modest Proposal*, for in disclaiming his former pride and vanity, his ignorance and greed, Edwards is made to denounce Presbyterian pretensions with the mordant vigor of Swift — or Overton. Moreover, when Edwards repines at "how fowle . . . and filthy" he has been, his self-description gives a fuller insight into the largeness of Walwyn's "Puritanism":

Yea I strictly observed order in such things as . . . the wearing of my cloak of at least a Clergy-mans length, my Hat of a due breadth and bignesse, both for brim and crown, somewhat different from lay men, my band also of a peculiar straine, and my clothes all black. . . . I had a care to be sadder in countenance and more sollemne in discourse. . . .[71]

Nor does Walwyn neglect to point out the class conflict implicit in the struggle for religious liberty. Here, again, is Edwards: "I have been a great respecter of persons for outward respects, the man in fine rayment, and with the gold ring, I have ever preferred, whilst the poore and needy have beene low in my esteeme." [72] Finally, Walwyn's parody shows that its author believed strongly in that true simplicity of worship which Milton describes in Book IV of *Paradise Lost*. No "learned man in a carved pulpit," no "neate and black formalities," no richly clad audience or "stately, high and stone-built Church" is necessary to "pure religion and undefiled." [73] Perhaps better than any other polemical tract of the time, *A Prediction of Master Edwards His Conversion and Recantation* italicizes the fact that the seventeenth-century "Puritan" need have no resemblance to the twentieth-century cartoonist's conception of Andrew Volstead.

In a similar broad and essentially comic spirit, but not so effective, is the final anti-Edwards tract from Walwyn's pen, *A Parable, or Consultation of Physitians Upon Master Edwards*, which appeared late in October 1646. Since by this date Overton and Walwyn almost certainly knew each other and had probably worked together, it is not surprising that Walwyn's *Parable* shows the direct stylistic influence of Overton. Its allegory, like that of *The Araignement of Mr. Persecution*, is generally heavy-handed and obvious, though in both tracts the irony is often corrosive. Walwyn has Love, Justice, Patience, and Truth serve as the doctors on Edwards' case. These personifications have been called in to remove the gangrenous and infectious bladder which has poisoned and disfigured his head. They are watched by Conscience, Hope, Piety, Superstition, and Policie, the last two of whom try to prevent the surgeons from performing the operation necessary to restore their patient to decency, sense, and tolerance. But, in the end, Edwards is cured; he at last realizes that the "Touch-stone of Christianity" is love, and he shows his newly attained spiritual health by a lengthy eulogy of God's universal beneficence.

Unfortunately, however, the third part of *Gangraena* revealed no signs of either repentance or effective surgery. But by early 1647 Walwyn had become too busy in a larger conflict, against more formidable opponents, to concern himself any longer with direct answers to the indefatigable Master Thomas Edwards.[74] By then, with Overton and Lilburne, he was coöperating in the birth of the Leveller party.

The Genesis of The Leveller Party

I. June to October 1646: Conception

Lilburne, since his release from prison in the autumn of 1645, had remained relatively quiet,[1] and in February 1646, when Edwards was readying the first part of *Gangraena* for the press, the House of Lords finally joined in voiding Lilburne's Star Chamber sentence, declaring it to have been "unjust, illegal, and contrary to the liberty of the subject." The matter of any reparations due him, however, was again postponed, a repeated process which contributed to Lilburne's growing bitterness against both Houses of Parliament.[2] But it was with the Lords that he first came into conflict. On the larger outcome of this conflict Sir Charles Firth comments:

It was in the exercise of its judicial powers that the House of Lords first came into collision with this democratic spirit, and was exposed to an attack which began as a denial of its claim to exercise judicial rights, became next a denial of its claim to a share in legislation, and ended as a demand for the abolition of hereditary authority in general.[3]

Lilburne, as one of the more articulate voices of this new "democratic spirit," was the first actively to battle the Lords' claim to judicial rights.

The preliminary skirmishes began in April, when Colonel King brought charges against Lilburne in the Court of Common Pleas.[4] To these charges Lilburne, the man whom Prynne had labelled an "upstart monstrous lawyer," objected, since, as he claimed, a witness to a charge of high treason pending before the House of Commons should not have to answer for his testimony to any lower court.[5] This argument Lilburne published in June in a tract called *The Just Mans Justification*.[6] The major portion of this pamphlet is a letter to Justice Reeves, head of the Court of Common Pleas, in which Lilburne questions the legality of King's charge, recapitulates his own case against King, and ends with a lengthy dissertation against the needless complexities of the common law. Lilburne was even more tactless in the concluding section of *The Just Mans Justification*, a petition to Parliament requesting that King promptly be brought to trial, and listing twenty-two counts against the Colonel; for here, in a marginal note, Lilburne refers to the Earl of Manchester as the man "who was since impeached of Treason, by L.G.C. [Lt. General Cromwell] for being false to his trust, and had undoubtedly lost his head therefore, if L.G.C. had followed it as he should." [7]

Unfortunately Manchester was then speaker of the House of Lords, a body which, as it grew smaller and revolutionary ideas loomed larger, was becoming ever more sensitive about its own prestige, rights, and privileges. On June 10, therefore, Lilburne was summoned to appear before the Lords to answer for *The Just Mans Justification*, and at six o'clock the next morning an officer of the Upper House routed Lilburne from his bed. By that evening Lilburne was in Newgate.[8] The main bout had begun.

Five days later Lilburne published *The Free-Mans Freedome Vindicated*, an account of the events of the previous week which stressed his reluctance to join battle with the Lords. Since, however, that battle had now been joined, Lilburne here reprinted the "Protestation" he had attempted personally to hand the Lords during their interrogation of him. The core of this "Protestation," and the theoretical basis for Lilburne's intransigence before them, was the belief that the Lords had no jurisdiction in the case of a commoner — an immunity guaranteed Lilburne and every free-born Englishman by both the Twenty-ninth Chapter of Magna Carta and the crucial statement in the *Book of Declarations* that "all betrusted powers must and ought to be for the good of the trusters." [9]

On the same day that *The Free-Mans Freedome Vindicated* appeared, Lilburne also petitioned the House of Commons for his release, again pleading the Lords' lack of jurisdiction. The petition was, of course, publicly circulated.[10] That it undercut the authority of the House of Lords, and, further, that it addressed the House of Commons "as the chosen and betrusted Commissioners of all the Commons of England, in whome alone (by right) resides the formall and legall supreame power of England," resulted in Lilburne's recall to the bar of the Upper House. Thus largely through his own activity the issues had become larger, the contestants more incensed.

On receipt of the order to reappear, Lilburne wrote a note, also promptly published, to the Keeper of Newgate.[11] Its concluding paragraph speaks for itself:

> Sir, I am a free-man of England, and therefore I am not to be used as a slave or vassell by the Lords. . . . I also am a man of peace and quietnes, and desire not to molest any if I be not forced there unto, therefore I desire you as you tender my good and your owne, take this for an answer, that I cannot without turning traitor to my liberties, dance attendance to their Lordships Bar, being bound in conscience, duty to God, my selfe, myne, and my country, to oppose their incroachments to the death, which by the strength of God I am resolved to doe. Sir you may or cause to be exercised upon me some force or violence to pull or drag me out of my chamber . . . and therefore I desire you, in a friendly way, to be wise and considerate before you doe that which it may be you can never undoe.

But notwithstanding his threats, Lilburne was surprised in his prison and forcefully carried before the Lords.[12] Defiant, he refused to kneel to them, and was recommitted to Newgate, there "to be kept close prisoner without pen, inke or paper, the accesse of . . . wife or any other friend." [13]

Lilburne, however, was now no longer alone in his fight. Someone, in all probability Walwyn, at the time of Lilburne's recommittal praised the prisoner and castigated the Lords in two compact pamphlets, *The Just Man in Bonds* and *A Pearle in a Dounghill*.[14] The first of these opens with the author's emphasis on Lilburne's case as a test case for all Englishmen:

> Since this worthy gentlemans case is mine, and everymans, who though we be at liberty to day may be in Newgate to morrow, if the House of Lords so please, doth it not equally and alike concerne all the people

of England to lay it to heart, and either fit both our minds and necks to undergoe this slavery, or otherwise thinke of some speedy and effectuall means to free our selves and our posterity there from?

Thence *The Just Man in Bonds* goes on to say of Lilburne's valor, "Let us rather blame our selves for want of fortitude, then accuse him, as having too much." [15] But the author still has confidence in the House of Commons, as shown by his hopeful exhortation to them to free Lilburne, since by failing to do so they would be unexpectedly remiss in their duty and would lose the favor of God.

A Pearle in a Dounghill amplifies these points in a manner which also suggests the hand of Walwyn. The author again lauds Lilburne's efforts, contrasting them to the presumptuous and reactionary tyranny of the Lords. Indeed, it is in large part their responsibility that the "quiet people" are now persecuted for matters of conscience and that the press has been restricted, and that a man like Lilburne, "a man so faithfull in all his waies, should be so lyable to trouble as he hath been." Hence, if one searches for the real cause of Lilburne's imprisonment, he will find that "the faithfulnesse of his heart toward God and all good people, and the freenesse of his tongue against all kinde of injustice or unworthinesse . . . is the only cause and no other." [16] *A Pearle* then ends with a reaffirmation of faith in Parliament, but it is a Parliament now symbolized solely by the "Worthyes" of the House of Commons. These men, because it is their acknowledged function to serve the people's liberties, will put an end to oppression, and in the process "reduce the Lords to a condition suitable to the freedome of the People, and consistent with the freedome of Parliaments." Yet the tract's final sentence qualifies this hope; and — if *A Pearle* is by Walwyn — it marks the beginning of his open shift in confidence from Parliament to people:

The People are become a Knowing and Judicious People; Affliction hath made them wise, now Opression maketh wise men mad; ther's no deluding wise men; it is all one to them who oppresseth them; and if Parliaments do in truth and deed really deliver them, they will love Parliaments, . . . otherwise they will abominate them, because for a People to be made slaves by or in time of Parliament is like as for a man to be betrayed or murthered by his own father. [17]

This same shift found a resonant voice in Overton. Early in July he came to Lilburne's aid with a militant tract which clearly set forth his untraditional belief in the power of the people effectively and directly to mold and control their government. The full title of this pamphlet was itself a battle cry, *A Remonstrance of Many Thousand Citizens, and other Free-born People of England, To their owne House of Commons. Occasioned through the Illegall and Barbarous Imprisonment of the Famous and Worthy Sufferer for his Countries Freedoms, Lieutenant Col. John Lilburne. Wherein their just Demands in behalf of themselves and the whole Kingdome, concerning their Publike Safety, Peace and Freedome, is Express'd; calling those their Commissioners in Parliament to an Account, how they (since the beginning of their Session, to this present) have discharged their Duties to the Universallity of the People, their Soveraigne Lord, from whom their Power and Strength is derived, and by whom (ad bene placitum,) it is continued.*[18]

Between the preceding January, the date of his final Mar-Priest tract, and *A Remonstrance* Overton had written little or nothing.[19] But now Lilburne's imprisonment helped to cement the informal alliance between Lilburne, Walwyn, and Overton, and to convert that alliance into the caucus of a disciplined political movement.[20] *A Remonstrance* itself was not only an incitement to revolutionary ardor, but also the platform, in rough, of such a movement. Far better than *Englands Birth-Right* it expressed the principles and the propositions which were to form the bulk of the Leveller program, and it did so with that mixture of threatening belligerence and optimistic idealism which seems to be typical of embryonic radical crusades.

As a political platform, *A Remonstrance* in large part anticipates the Agreements of the People; it also foreshadows much of the American Declaration of Independence and Constitution. Its basic premise is that all power rests in the people. A second premise, though implicit, is equally relevant to the documents it helped to father: that the direct exercise of power corrupts him who exercises it. Therefore, in order to ascertain that government will function for the good of the people, *A Remonstrance* makes clear that a proper government must be one of laws, not of men; and that these laws, rather than being grants of power, must be restrictive on the governors. Like that of the American Bill of Rights, Overton's political theory is based on a combination of faith in the people and suspicion of their rulers.

As a result, the specific proposals of *A Remonstrance* are largely negative or limiting. The monarchy is to be ended, and the House of Lords, if it is alowed to survive, must lose its veto power and become, to all intents, a social figurehead. Once England is thus made a republic, all men are to become equal in the eyes of the law, while the laws are to be reformed in the direction of equity and simplicity. The House of Commons, the representative body of the people, is also to be limited; in the near future the present Parliament should disband, to be replaced by an annually and freely elected group. Though Overton is a little vague on the nature of these elections, his use of such phrases as "our free choice of Parliament once every year," and his unqualified use of "we" as the electors, strongly suggest that he already believed in the right of all Englishmen to have an equal voice in choosing their "Agents."[21] These "Agents" of the people are, in turn, to be prevented forever from interfering with religious freedom. In addition, Overton instructs them that it will be their duty to curb monopolies, including those relating to the press, and to put an end to imprisonment for debt and to impressment for military service.

Overton's full-fledged republicanism was grounded ultimately in his skepticism and his rationalism, but one of the immediate causes for his republican outburst was political expediency. Overton's anger against the House of Lords had obviously been heightened by Lilburne's imprisonment. Moreover, resentment against Charles was building up among the Puritans of the center and left. As early as 1643 Henry Marten was said to have urged the King's deposition,[22] and by the beginning of 1644 a Royalist newspaper was able to report that sixteen people had "publikely beene noted" for saying that they would be glad to kill the King.[23] The pro-Presbyterian "Propositions of Newcastle" which had just been dispatched to Charles did nothing to curb this slowly growing antimonarchical fire.

A less immediate impetus to Overton's republicanism was the intellectual influence on him of William Walwyn, whose recent pamphlets against Edwards had probably helped to reinforce certain of the egalitarian ideas with which Overton, as a General Baptist, had for a long time been familiar. A third proximate cause of Overton's present political views was almost certainly a relatively new concept of English history. *A Remonstrance* contains several references to the "Norman yoke" and to the "Norman bondage." In this respect Overton was again giving voice, and a radical twist, to an idea very much in the air of 1646. Anti-Normanism, the idealization of the Saxon past, was in fact the chief manifestation of that amorphous primitivism to which most Interregnum groups at one time or another appealed. It had already played a small part in Walwyn's tributes to "natural" man and in his suspicions of formal learning, and it soon reached its most extreme form in Winstanley's agrarian communism which regarded private property as a "Norman innovation."

Among the Elizabethan chroniclers, Holinshed, Speed, and Daniel had all tended to glorify the pre-Norman past; so, on occasion, had Coke. As early as 1616 one of the readers at the Inns of Court had enunciated the doctrine that William the Conquerer was responsible for introducing absolutism into England.[24] More recently, Henry Parker had suggested an anti-Norman interpretation of English history in support of his theory of an ancient social contract.[25] Indeed, as Woodhouse points out, some form of historiographical primitivism was common to all the anti-Royalist parties in that they all adhered to the "mythical presumption that there had once been a free constitution in England which it was the purpose of the Civil War to restore." [26]

Probably the most articulate contemporary exponent of historical primitivism was John Hare, a man of some learning who by 1648 became a staunch supporter of the king. In a pamphlet written in 1642, though not printed until 1647, he gave rather violent expression to a racist and romantic view of English history. *St. Edward's Ghost: or, Anti-Normanisme* depicts England as a nation conquered in the eleventh century by foreigners, and one still fettered by foreign laws, names, titles, and customs. This is doubly an evil, for the English themselves are descended from heroic Teutonic stock, a racial group which, says Hare, can be directly traced back to the Tower of Babel. It was, he continues, the flower of German youth who first settled England; nor until the time of William was the country's development marred by any stain of Latin degeneracy. Unfortunately, however, Edward was the last good and rightful king, and the Civil War is now being fought to recover from "Gallic" corruption the ancient rights and traditional forms for which he stood.[27]

Overton's *Remonstrance*, however, modifies Hare's line of reasoning in order to point up the evils of arbitrary government: "The history of our Fore-fathers since they were Conquered by the Normans doth manifest that this Nation hath been held in bondage . . . ever since by the policies and force of the Officers of Trust." [28] To Overton, the "Norman yoke" is both the symbol for and the alleged source of "all unreasonable lawes made ever since that unhappy conquest." But unlike Hare he makes of this primitivistic view of history a slogan for revolutionary reform, not for the reestablishment of any *status quo ante.* Thus Overton took a current popular idea, embedded it in a series of constructive political proprosals, and by so doing gave his program, his radicalism, a nationalistic and traditional aura. A little more than a year later, during the debate at Putney, the myth of historical rights was more fully fused with the myth of inherent natural rights, until, in combination, they became the most powerful weapon in the Leveller propaganda arsenal.

A Remonstrance, then, not only foreshadows some of the later Leveller proposals and techniques, but by its revolutionary tone it anticipates the violence of both arguments and events between late 1647 and early 1649. Overton, for instance, thoroughly flays the king; Charles is unnecessary, evil, the source of iniquity, and the "originall of all Oppressions." Overton asks Parliament, "have you shoke this Nation like an Earth-quake" in order to restore it to a bad king? And he answers:

Wee doe expect . . . that yee should . . . declare and set forth King Charles his wickednesse openly before the world, and withall, to shew the intollerable inconveniences of having a Kingly Government, declare King Charles an enemy, and to publish your resolution never to have any more, but to acquite us of so great a charge and trouble for ever.[29]

About the House of Commons itself Overton makes a similarly inflammatory and "levelling" comment:

For wee must deale plainly with you, yee have long time acted more like the House of Peers then the House of Commons: We can scarcely approach your door with a Request or motion . . . but yee hold long debates, whether wee break not your Priviledges; the Kings or the Lords pretended Prerogatives never made a greater noise, nor was made more dreadful then the Name of Priviledge of the House of Commons.[30]

And, toward the end of *A Remonstrance*, he explicitly warns the House that they must expect to hear more frequently from the common people: "nor will it be your wisdome to take these Admonitions and Cautions in evill part." In a similarly belligerent tone Overton stiffens Walwyn's view of Magna Carta: "It self being but a beggarly thing, containing many marks of intollerable bondage."[31] But the most revolutionary sentiment expressed in *A Remonstrance* is Overton's contention that the Civil War has been improperly prosecuted because Parliament has been afraid to arm the people.[32]

A Remonstrance in both matter and manner was an explosive document. The House of Lords promptly realized this and took steps to deal with its author. But first they had to finish with the equally dangerous Lilburne. On July 10, 1646, three days after the appearance of *A Remonstrance*, he was recalled before the Lords, who voted his two most recent pamphlets and his Protestation "a high breach of the privilege of Parliament, and high offenses against the laws and statutes of this kingdom."[33] The next day Lilburne was brought back to answer to this charge. Not only did he refuse to kneel to the Peers, but he stopped his ears in order to avoid hearing the charge; twice he went through this performance, each time telling the Lords that they had no jurisdiction in his case.[34] The result of this behavior was inevitable: Lilburne was fined £2,000, sentenced to seven years' imprisonment in the Tower of London, and barred forever from holding "any office or place, in Military or Civill Government, in Church or Commonwealth"; further, *The Just Mans Justification* and *The Freemans Freedome Vindicated* were ordered burnt by the common hangman.[35] From mid-July to mid-September, when conditions were somewhat relaxed, Lilburne remained a close prisoner in the Tower, under the watchful surveillance of a keeper apparently especially delegated to him.[36] Even so, neither he nor his colleagues were effectually silenced.

Lilburne's renewed persecution stimulated Overton to voice another violent protest. Though he had managed to escape detection as the author of *A Remonstrance* — a skill which he had no doubt acquired as Martin Mar-Priest — his defense of Lilburne at the end of July, *An Alarum To the House of Lords*, eventuated in his arrest. Like *The Just Man in Bonds* and *A Pearle in a Doung-hill*, this pamphlet both commends Lilburne as "Defendour . . . of his countries Freedome" and assails the tyranny of the Lords. Though there are no new or significant ideas in *An Alarum*, it is a vigorous work, one which alternates between threats and cajolery, between sardonic skepticism and fervent hopes. The tract begins with a loaded question to the Lords: why do they not refer to Lilburne as Lieutenant Colonel, considering his brave efforts in the Parliamentary cause? Then, in a biting passage which names names, Overton discusses how Lords get to be Lords, a brief history of the English nobility which suggest Swift's Glubdubdribbian chronicle. Overton's bitterness increases as he describes Lilburne's newest prison sufferings and as he answers the Lords' charges against Lilburne. "Is it seditious," Overton asks, "For a Free-man unjustly imprisoned, to publish the same to all the World?" From here Overton moves to a defense of Lilburne's writings, characterizing them as dangerous only to those who wield arbitrary power — the persecuting clergy, the lawyers and monopolists. Thence *An Alarum* suddenly shifts to a note of confidence, to the assurance that ultimately the forces of freedom will triumph, because "the people are now quick-sighted, and not easily deluded." On this key the pamphlet ends; for, utilizing the language of Revelation, Overton predicts a dire judgment for all those who go against God.[37]

Judgment, however, first fell on Richard Overton. On August 11, 1646, he was brought before a committee of the House of Lords, which therewith committed him to Newgate. His account of his arrest and conviction, written a week later though not published until early September, is one of the most enjoyable of the polemical pamphlets of the Interregnum. *A Defiance Against all Arbitrary Usurpations* combines the broad humor of Dickens, the suspense of a good detective story, the indignation of Lilburne, and the insight of Walwyn; like many of Milton's prose works, though on a less exalted level, *A Defiance* is a work of art.

Overton tells how early in the morning one Robert Eeles, a printer employed by the Lords to suppress seditious books and sufficiently unpopular to be disliked even by the competing agents of the Stationers' Company, broke into Overton's house. Eeles awoke Overton by announcing in "a loud menacing voice," "W—w—w—we will have him in his bed." Thereupon the very pregnant Mrs. Overton started to faint, despite which Eeles commanded Overton to get dressed, prefacing his order with "Tut, tut, tut." During the dressing process, Eeles and his assistant proceeded to pick the pockets of various garments lying about the room.

Then, shifting in part to the mock-heroic, Overton describes his seizure by the large group of armed men who had by now surrounded the house: first his futile resistance, next his arguments with them concerning the legality of his arrest, and finally his exhortation to his neighbors, who had flocked to the scene, to take notice of this warlike invasion of English liberty. Overton then tells how he was dragged from his house to a tavern, where he resumed the argument with his captors; thence to Westminster, with Overton again being carried bodily through the streets, this time all the while announcing to the onlookers that he was not "apprehended by any Magesteriall Authority, but by violence and force of Arms."

Overton's actions before the Lords were largely a replica of Lilburne's. He refused to answer their interrogatories and denied their jurisdiction. At one point Eeles broke in to ask if Overton was one of "Lilburne's Bastards," to which Overton merely replied that he was "free-born." After declaring that he would appeal to the House of Commons, Overton was ordered to wait in an adjoining room. There he was joined by the Earl of Essex, whom Overton infuriated by a device that can only be called the hat-game: he kept taking off his hat to Essex as a gentleman, then putting it back on to Essex as a Lord, until Essex ordered it snatched from Overton's head. Finally, Overton was recalled to the committee bar, where he again refused to answer any questions, was mocked by the Peers for his intransigence, and committed to Newgate "untill the pleasure of this House be further signified." [38]

His first act in jail was to write this account of his apprehension and arraignment; but *A Defiance* is more than a provocative personal story, for Overton supports his narrative with a sturdy scaffolding of theory and precedent. Despite his own vicissitudes, he is still confident in the wisdom of the people, though he qualifies the optimism expressed in such a work as Milton's *Areopagetica* by assuming that the people must be deliberately roused from their lengthy and benighted lethargy:

Yea, such hath been the misterious mischievous subtilty from generation to generation of those cunning usurpers [Kings, Lords, and Clergymen] . . . that the poore deceived people are even (in a manner) bestiallized in their understandings, become so stupid, and grossly ignorant of themselves, and of their own natural immunities . . . that they are even degenerated from being men . . . being void of the use of Reason for want of capacitie to discern whereof and how far God by nature hath made them free, if none have so much magnanimity as to ingage betwixt them and their deceivers, as not only Religion, and Reason, but even Nature itself doth bind every man to do according to his power . . . whatever perill or danger shall ensue, though of liberty, estate, or life . . . because no man is born for himself.[39]

To come between the people and their deceivers is Overton's view of his own mission.

The external sanction for such a mission he finds in Magna Carta, in the *Book of Declarations*, and in a strange source now to be cited by the Levellers, Prynne's *Sovereigne Power of Parliaments and Kingdomes* of 1643. But Overton also relies on the common argument that "Reason is the life of the Law," and that reason, as well as nature, confirms man's inherent right to life, liberty, and the pursuit of happiness. To secure and maintain this inherent right, he continues, the people of England must "stand close to their own House of Commons." It is their bulwark of strength and their tribunal of last resort. Thus, Overton concludes, both he and Lilburne are fighting a personal and legal battle in behalf of the safety and liberty of all Englishmen, including that of the House of Commons.

Nor did Lilburne, despite the restrictive regulations of imprisonment in the Tower, fail to point out again that he stood at Overton's side in fighting the good fight. In August *Liberty Vindicated against Slavery*, notwithstanding its third-person technique, presented Lilburne's defense of Lilburne to the tribunal of public opinion. The pamphlet gets under way with a lengthy paraphrase of Coke on Magna Carta to show that the rights this document guarantees are never to be superseded. Now, however, not only are certain government officials abusing these rights, but the cruelty of jailers and the exorbitant fees they exact are symptomatic of a growing disregard for the traditional legal privileges of Englishmen. Moreover, imprisonment for debt, legalistic delays, and unduly cruel punishments are contraventions of that merciful spirit basic to the common law. Then, after the citation of many statutes, after several appeals to an idealized past, and after an itemized list of some of the money Lilburne has been forced to disburse within the Tower, *Liberty Vindicated against Slavery* shifts into an undisguised appeal to class-consciousness. For instance, the poor have the added burden of not being able to hire those now necessary "Horsleeches" the lawyers; the fees extracted from unfortunate prisoners are in sharp contrast to the income of certain wealthy members of Parliament; and a rich Royalist delinquent is treated far better than an impecunious patriot, for graft has made the jails of London a refuge and den of immorality for the rich, a torture chamber for the poor. Here again, in his appeal to the public, Lilburne has used his own sufferings as a test case for broad social issues and as a conspicuous sample of social injustice.

But in the years immediately preceding the establishment of the Commonwealth probably the most effective means, with the exception of the pulpit, for educating and arousing the public was not the pamphlet but the petition. It had many advantages: it was sanctified as ancient custom; it was a relatively easy method of evading restrictions on the press; its signature provided a means of expression to an often otherwise inarticulate public opinion; and its circulation helped to crystallize public discontent and to serve as a vital preliminary to the organization of large-scale popular demonstrations.[40] The future leaders of the Levellers were becoming increasingly adept in their utilization of the device of the petition, a device which grew progressively more important to them as their belief in democracy solidified and as the opposition to democratic ideas began to close ranks. Hence in September 1646 Lilburne, who had had the most experience with petitions, circulated two in his own behalf. The first, ostensibly from his wife,[41] addresses the House of Commons as "the high and supream Court of Parliament," reiterates the doctrine of the legal equality of all subjects, and underlines Lilburne's sufferings by what she is given to say about her own and her children's destitution. Less than a month later Lilburne repeated these themes in a petition signed by himself.[42] With the probable assistance of Walwyn, certainly the first and very possibly both of the petitions were given prompt circulation.

Lilburne did not confine himself to polemical autobiography and petitionary appeal. At the end of October he utilized a somewhat new approach in *Londons Liberty in Chains discovered*, a tract designed to play on certain well-defined public fears and desires. As such, it epitomizes the mixture of traditionalism and expediency which characterizes most seventeenth-century radicalism; and in particular it points up Lilburne's dependence on ideas which were traditional but which he modified pragmatically in the light of popular currents of opinion and his own involvement in the rough and tumble of politics.

One of the characteristics of the Civil War period was the people's time-hallowed local pride, as opposed to national patriotism. Accounts of the Interregnum are full of incidents which reveal that among the large majority of Englishmen a man's loyalty to his town or his county stood higher than did his loyalty to country or to one side or the other in the constitutional and religious conflict.[43] It was to this feeling of local pride that the Levellers were soon to appeal by their emphasis on greater local self-government and by their insistence on safeguards against centralized power. *Londons Liberty* represents a forerunner to this appeal in that it advocates the practical application of this sentiment of localism to the metropolis.

A second strand in *Londons Liberty*, though of lesser importance, is its response to the incipient trade-union movement which was just then beginning to manifest itself, particularly in London.[44] The years immediately before the Civil War had witnessed an acceleration of the process by which individual guilds tended increasingly to be controlled by the richer masters; hence, despite the fact that there was no industrial proletariat, the ferment of the war itself produced some democratic agitation within the guilds.[45] Among the depressed urban working class, whose ranks were daily augmented by the military dislocations and concomitant economic stagnation of 1640–1650, there was a potentially large audience, concentrated in London, ready to listen to democratic propaganda.

Closely connected to the problem of guild organization was that of the government of London, involving as it did many of the same top personnel and constitutional devices. As early as the twelfth century the citizens of London had been recognized as a corporation; subsequently their rights, like those of the country at large, were theoretically defined and strengthened by such statutes as Magna Carta and its confirmations. But during the seventeenth century the same process which curtailed democracy within the guilds hastened the development of an oligarchy in the government of the city. Thus the leaders of the Livery Companies had by the mid-1640's pretty well excluded the ordinary citizen from participation in the election of Lord Mayor.[46] These same wealthy men controlled the aldermen, a group which, in turn, wielded an effective veto over any acts of the subservient though potentially democratic London Common Council. Finally, this metropolitan oligarchy, Parliament's chief source of large loans, was generally conservative and Presbyterian.

In addition to local pride, incipient trade-unionism, and the increasingly democratic pressure for reform of the government of London, Lilburne probably also had even more immediate considerations in mind when he wrote *Londons Liberties*. His personal resentment against monopolies was partly directed against the Court of Aldermen, which he often said was instrumental in promoting various oppressive restraints of trade. Further, his current opponents among the Lords and the Presbyterians were closely allied with the ruling powers in the city. On all these counts, then, he was ready to take advantage of an issue which was very much alive. When, at the end of September, he heard that a protesting citizen had been kept by force from attending the meeting at which the Lord Mayor was elected, Lilburne sent for some books on London history, and immediately began writing, with obvious haste and vehemence, *Londons Liberty in Chains discovered*.[47]

He was already familiar with this new crusade. In *Englands Birth-Right* of the preceding year, one of the many issues he had touched on was the lack of democracy in the government of London.[48] Also, Overton in his recent *Remonstrance* had noted the "exorbitances in the Cities Government, and the strivings about Prerogatives in the Mayor and Aldermen, against the Freedoms of the Commons." [49] Even so, *Londons Liberty* is not a lucid expansion of the grievances of the city, for again Lilburne's writing is discursive, rambling, and, on the surface, illogical. His topics seem to have been selected by association rather than plan, and they are connected largely by his histrionic self-consciousness.

Lilburne's starting point and basic premise is the ubiquitous *salus populi suprema lex*. But now, with Walwyn and Overton, he amplifies this loose principle to include the proviso that "all lawful powers reside in the people." To secure their "good, welfare and happinesse," both local and national administrations should be elected annually and freely. Such free elections, in so far as London is concerned, go back to the time of Alfred and have been reaffirmed by Magna Carta. However, he goes on, London has lately fallen into a "Bastard Norman Bondage," a condition which is proved by the undemocratic elections of recent Lord Mayors and by numerous current encroachments on the rights of the citizen. Monopolies, depression, illegal taxes, injustices in law, and cruel edicts are among the dire consequences of this drift toward oligarchy.

To dramatize this decline Lilburne then tells the story of the citizen who had been ejected from the mayoralty election in September. Though Lilburne, for a change, is not the central character, his identification with the embattled Londoner is close, and, as he points out here and elsewhere, freedom, wherever it is assaulted, is theoretically everyone's responsibility. Hence he too felt that it was his mission to rouse and sensitize the people to accept that responsibility. Nor, he continues, is the problem in this case merely local: the "Masters" of London are closely allied to those evil men who are violating the true laws of the land on a national scale. Moreover, the basic laws of both London and the country as a whole are "true" because they consist of "the ancient constitutions and modern acts of Parliament . . . but of these onely such as are agreeable to the Word of God, the Law of Nature, and sound Reason." [50] In short, any law to be just (or "true") must conform to four criteria: history, God, nature, and reason. Since, however, the Leveller view of history was both flexible and anachronistic, God, nature, and reason became their primary means of judging the validity of a law; history could be adjusted to confirm whatever God, nature, and reason indicated.

But Lilburne, in the steps of his colleagues, was moving closer to another traditional, if now largely non-Calvinistic, pattern of thought. This intellectual current can be seen in Walwyn's emphasis on man's God-given rationalism, and in Overton's contention in *Mans Mortallitie* that nature, specifically all natural processes, is the manifestation of God. In other words, proper human reason corresponds to that of God, and "natural" processes are in keeping with the divine plan. Therefore, since the Levellers never devised any full constitutional system of judicial review to ascertain if a law was godly, natural, and rational, the three criteria became not only almost synonymous but a matter of individual decision. As in *Paradise Lost*, the ultimate sanction was each individual's right reason. The fact that this ultimate court was potentially within the mind of every man does much to explain the philosophic rationale behind democratic radicalism, as it does to account in part for Lilburne's constant recourse to the events of his own life to support his social views.

From his analysis of the nature of law, Lilburne shifts his focus to the abuses of economic monopoly. Though he seldom approached the astuteness of Harrington, Lilburne had gradually become acutely aware that political and economic power were interlinked. This awareness also helps to explain some of the literary and intellectual leaps in his writings. For instance, into the midst of *Londons Liberty's* class-conscious onslaught against restraints on the right to petition, Lilburne inserts this plea to the disenfranchised of London:

I know no reason (unlesse it can be proved that you are all slaves & vassals) why you should be concluded by the determinations, orders, and decrees of those that you have no vote in chusing: (for it is a true and just maxim in nature, no man can binde me but by my own consent) neither do I see how in reason or conscience it can be expected from you to pay any taxes &c. But that the whole charge that is layd upon this City should totally be borne by the Aldermen and the Livery

men till you be actually put in possession, and injoy your equall share
in the lawes, liberties, and freedoms thereof; as by the law of nature,
reason, God and the land, yea, and your own antient and originall
Charters, the meanest of you ought to do, as fully and largely in every
particular, as the greatest of them.[51]

A year later, at Putney, Rainsborough dramatically repeated this
plea in terms of and for the entire country; and in the following
century the issue of taxation without representation played a major
role in the American Revolution.

Nor did Lilburne miss the obvious extension of his plea for passive disobedience: *Londons Liberty* progresses from its attack on
economic and local "Prerogative Charters" to an attack on the rot-
ten-borough system of Parliamentary representation. In its stead
Lilburne demands the free and equal franchise for all men, thereby
restoring "every free-man of England to his native legall rights and
freedomes." Undemocratic elections, he goes on, will increase the
corruption of Parliament; the corruption of Parliament, in turn,
will lead to a second civil war. And Lilburne italicizes the evil inherent in this chain of events by stressing the already existing contrast between wealthy members of Parliament and poor soldiers'
widows begging on the streets of London. But despite the underlying logic of his radicalism, Lilburne here again reveals his almost
complete lack of any artistic or structural sense, particularly in the
conclusion of *Londons Liberty* where he is concerned with an excessively documented personal dispute between himself and one of the
warders. His final apology, based on the exigencies of composing in
jail, was from a literary point of view well warranted.

Two months later Lilburne repeated his charges and reforms in
*The Charters of London; or, the Second Part of Londons Liberty in
Chaines discovered*.[52] Three years later many of the citizens of London showed their approval of their "champion" by supporting him
during his 1649 trial and electing him to a seat on the Common
Council. The immediate result of Lilburne's attack on political and
economic monopoly, however, was probably to strengthen his position as one of the chief spokesmen for the *petite bourgeoisie*, a group
from whom the Leveller party was soon to draw its major organized
support.

To measure the size of this group or, more specifically, the size of the audience directly reached by such a pamphlet as *Londons Liberty*, is a highly conjectural process. One contemporary source states that the normal impression of a pamphlet was 1500 copies,[53] though, as in the case of Walwyn's *A word in season*, it might go as high as 10,000. Samuel Chidley, later one of the printers used by the Levellers and for a short period their treasurer, estimated in 1652 that each copy of a pamphlet might well have ten readers.[54] Because of Lilburne's flair for self-publicity, it is highly probable that many of his pamphlets had a somewhat larger circulation than the average political tract of the day.[55]

It is an even more conjectural process to try to estimate the cumulative impact of the various forces exerting pressure from the left, of which the radical pamphlets were only a part. Included in this impact were most sectarian and some Independent preaching, many localized and specialized movements for specific reforms, the growing political consciousness of the New Model, the increasing number of partisan newspapers, and the economic dislocations incident to a period of violence. In addition, it is obvious that the various currents of opinion, of all political shades, were reciprocally influential, often indeed becoming inextricably blended.

This is certainly true, on a small scale, of the mutual borrowing between Lilburne, Overton, and Walwyn on the eve of the Leveller party's formal birth, though in such borrowing, Lilburne, despite the fact that of the three he received by far the most public attention, was more often the debtor than the creditor. Much of the philosophical underpinning of *Londons Liberty* was, in fact, probably strongly influenced by a concurrent pamphlet by Overton.

On October 12, 1646, *An Arrow Against All Tyrants and Tyrany, shot from the Prison of New-gate into the Prerogative Bowels of the Arbitrary House of Lords and all other Usurpers and Tyrants Whatsoever*, signed by Richard Overton, appeared. It was addressed to Henry Marten, probably the member of Parliament most sympathetic to radical republicanism, who had just been appointed the head of a committee of the House of Commons to investigate the Lords' actions against Lilburne and Overton.[56] Aware of Marten's analytic mind and democratic leanings, Overton wrote *An Arrow* in a humorless, legalistic, and closely reasoned manner which lacks the zest but not the intensity of most of his earlier works. Its opening paragraph both establishes this tone and effectively asserts Overton's view of the innate dignity of the individual. Moreover, it shows succinctly how the Calvinist insistence on the individual's private responsibility to God could be transformed to a secular insistence on the individual's economic and political rights and on his implicit responsibilities to society:

To every Individuall in nature is given an individual property by nature, not to be invaded or usurped by any. . . . No man hath power over my rights and liberties, and I over no mans; I may be but an Individuall, enjoy my selfe and my selfe propriety, and may write my selfe no more then my selfe, or presume any further; if I doe, I am an encroacher & an invader upon an other Mans Right. . . . For by naturall birth, all men are equally and alike borne to like propriety, liberty, and freedome, and as we are delivered of God by the hand of nature into this world, every one with a naturall, innate freedome and propriety (as it were writ in the table of every mans heart, never to be obliterated) even so are we to live, every one equally and alike to enjoy his Birth-right and priviledge.

The individual, Overton continues, may of course delegate certain powers to his chosen political representative, but these powers are, and must be, severely restricted. "Every man by nature being a King, Priest and Prophet in his own naturall circuite and compasse, whereof no second may partake, but by deputation, commission, and free consent from him," each man can delegate only those powers which will not undercut his inherent rights or involve him in self-injury. The function of the House of Commons, the delegates of the people, is therefore to preserve the freedom of themselves and those whom they represent. In addition, English constitutional history substantiates the view that the House of Commons is the only truly representative body of the people, and the highest court of judicature in the land. But behind this interpretation of history is Overton's only partially articulated belief in a mythical social contract whereby every member of the sovereign people both delegated certain rights to his chosen representatives and reserved other, more important rights to himself.

The greatest threats to the fruition of this more detailed concept of *salus populi suprema lex* have been "the encroachments of Lords . . . and the barberous, inhumane, blood-thirsty desires and endevors of the Presbyterian Clergy"; but it is on the Lords that Overton concentrates his attack, his present concern being with political rather than religious freedom. He reaches back into history for examples to show that his own oppression by the Lords is by no means unique, that his own case is merely indicative that now "in their ambitious careere . . . they soar higher & higher." The king does not have power of his own to delegate to the Lords, nor do he or his minions have a veto power over laws passed by the delegates of the people, the House of Commons. There is, indeed, no just or legal sovereignty beyond those limited powers which the "Represented extend to the Representors."

Overton, in short, has here taken another step in setting forth a clear, if still loosely defined, republican system. The House of Commons exercises both legislative and judicial power, limited only by the implied contract that it will not transgress certain inviolable individual rights, and made responsive because its selection is to be democratic — hence the king or his equivalent may have restricted executive powers, but only as the agent of the House. Yet despite Overton's ostensible fervor in behalf of the House of Commons as his own refuge, as the keystone of his republicanism, and as the institutional repository of the people's collective wisdom, he was no superficial optimist; like Lilburne, Overton asserts that, should it prove remiss, the people of England will become the final court of appeal, the means to a new revolution. Near the end of *An Arrow* Overton warns Marten:

Therefore now step in or never, and discharge your duties to God and to us, and tell us no longer that such motions are not yet seasonable, and wee must still waite; for have we not waited on your pleasures many faire seasons and precious occasions and opportunities these six yeares, even till the Halters are ready to be tyed to the Gallows; and now must wee hold our peace, and waite till wee be all imprisoned, hang'd, burnt and confounded? . . . For shame, let never such things be spoken, far lesse recorded to future generations.[57]

Thus both he and Lilburne, impelled by their own predicaments and by their belief in individual rights, were moving out of the traditional channel of appeal to the House of Commons into the more turbulent waters of direct popular action.

II. *November 1646 to March 1647: Gestation*

The six months between *An Arrow* and the "Large Petition" of the Levellers marked the irregular approach of Overton and Lilburne to their first full plunge into large-scale and organized democratic action. Though Walwyn during this period largely remained in the background, his encouragement of this decision was evident in his readiness, in March 1647, to officiate at the birth of the Leveller party.

During the winter of 1646–1647, however, the party was still in its period of gestation. On November 6 Lilburne was called from the Tower to testify before Henry Marten's committee. Three days later he published his testimony under the title of *An Anatomy of the Lords Tyranny and Injustice*. Except for the threat to bring pressure on the House of Commons by means of a "grand petition" in his own behalf, Lilburne's tone is comparatively plaintive and submissive, and he concluded his reported interrogation by telling the committee:

I shall with all willingnesse and cheerfulnesse submit to what punishment shall be just for them [the House of Commons] to inflict upon me; and I hope that by this faire offer you will be provoked with the strength of resolution to deal impartially betwixt the Lords and me.[58]

Lilburne's offer had at least one positive result. On November 19 Thomason entered a lengthy unsigned pamphlet, *Vox Plebis, or the Peoples Out-cry against Oppression, Injustice and Tyranny*, very probably the work of Henry Marten, who here came to Lilburne's support with an elaborate analysis of constitutional and common law.[59] Laws are good if they preserve the people's liberties, and Magna Carta is the specific law most basic to resisting arbitrary encroachments. On it rests a series of statutes whose major concern is with due process of law, which itself secures many individual rights, among them trial by a jury of one's peers. Then, like Lilburne and Overton, Marten defines true law in its larger sense as that which is customary, rational, godly, and natural; but he differs from the Levellers in his greater emphasis on documented historical precedent. It is to this precedent that he appeals in showing that the Lords lack jurisdiction over a commoner, and that therefore

Lilburne's imprisonment is a threat to English liberties. However, both Lilburne and the people should retain their confidence in the House of Commons, England's true "trustees" and "tribunes," for as long as the House of Commons adheres to the known laws of the land the government cannot become oppressive, weak, or rotten.

Marten, whether or not he wrote *Vox Plebis*, was typical of an expanding group in Parliament and among the London Independents. Apprehensive about the increased sentiment for a restoration of the king and fearful of an open rupture between England and Scotland, this predominantly centrist group began to rally to the aid of its more radical potential allies.[60] It was partly to speed this process by appealing to English nationalism against a combination of Scottish and Presbyterian Royalism, and specifically to answer certain recent Scottish propositions in support of Charles, that Overton wrote his next pamphlet, the inflammatory *An Unhappy Game at Scotch and English.*[61]

With heavy-handed irony and a great deal of vituperation Overton answers the Scottish claims. But the most significant aspect of *An Unhappy Game*, and that which made it so galling to most members of Parliament, was its profusion of explicit and intemperate antimonarchial statements. The main contention of the "Scotch Papers" had been that Scotland did not have to deliver the king to the English Parliament; to this allegation Overton replies that the king is willful, scheming, and dangerous, and that to exalt his whims over the public desires of two kingdoms is to make "the greater take the wall of the lesse." Charles, in fact, has been to a large extent personally guilty of the war against Parliament and the people of England.

In the manner of many of his earlier tracts, Overton's style includes much zestful mockery. Of the Scottish dilemma of having a political white elephant in the person of Charles, Overton writes:

Whither now Jockie? Hoyt — Hoe — Haufe — Ree — Gee — Hoe — Jockie: What: neither backwards nor forwards, one side nor the other? Riddle me, what's this? You'll neither have him, nor be without him; neither keep him nor deliver him; a pritty paradox! [62]

But underneath the passages of raucous derision and blunt irony, there is a grimmer tone to *An Unhappy Game*. Overton's appeal to

English nationalism, as well as his denigration of Charles Stuart, is stated in such a way that it foreshadows the mood of that small coalition which bitterly prosecuted the Second Civil War and beheaded a king. "Advance Southward," Overton tells the Scots, "and then you may expect greater broyles and troubles then ever." He was correct.

More broadly prophetic, though more garbled, was a book (108 pages complete with index is no pamphlet), *Regall Tyrannie Discovered*, which was begun in September, completed two months later, and published in the first days of 1647.[63] Though almost certainly by Lilburne, there are passages which suggest that Overton in Newgate may have had some access to Lilburne in the Tower. In any case, *Regall Tyrannie*, in its very profusion and confusion, offers a synthesis of Leveller philosophy, historiography, and political theory as they had developed during 1646, and just before they were incorporated into the formal platform of an organized political party.

Lilburne is the book's central character.[64] But in addition to his dramatic role as chief witness and victim, he makes his own story the point of departure for an expansion of the left-wing concept of the social contract. This concept, here buttressed by the voluminous citation of ancient laws which allegedly curbed the power of kings and Lords, is now used as a guarantee of popular rights against an undemocratic House of Commons — if and when such a guarantee becomes necessary. Even more pronounced in its antimonarchical views than *A Remonstrance* or *An Unhappy Game*, *Regall Tyrannie* displays Overton's touch in its concentrated bitterness against Charles. His influence is also apparent in Lilburne's now more secular analysis of political problems, as evidenced, for instance, by his greater effectiveness in using historical sources and current events rather than God and the Bible to substantiate his premises and his prophecies. Consequently, though *Regall Tyrannie* is largely a self-centered narrative of Lilburne's recent oppressions, it is also an analytic and far-reaching assault on the judicial presumptions of king and Lords.

Lilburne's starting point in this respect is Scripture: God's Word and His practices in Jewish history both show that "all government whatsoever ought to be by mutual consent and agreement." Therefore no mere man like Charles Stuart can make his will law nor violate the preëxisting contract between himself and his subjects. Such is God's law, which is also "engraven in Nature, and demonstrated by Reason." Further, the Bible, instinct, and logic support the Golden Rule and the universal urge for self-preservation. When combined, this rule and this urge also lead to a godly society based on a mutual agreement between governor and governed. Then, still avoiding precise definition, Lilburne restates the case for a social contract in a different manner. Man, since he is made in God's image, is rational. It follows that to exercise his rationality he must have freedom. In addition, no man can compete with God in ruling the destinies of other men. On two counts, then, such an office as that of king "is not in the least of God's initiation" or in keeping with His plan.

None the less, according to the contract theory, it might still be possible for a king to rule by implicit popular consent. Lilburne's next step was, therefore, to prove that Charles had violated any such tacit agreement. In support of this charge Lilburne reviews English history in the expedient and idealized manner he had recently learned to utilize. Glorifying the Saxon past and stressing a wide variety of ancient democratic signposts, Lilburne shows that Charles's personal and political ancestry bears the taint of the tyrannical bastard, William the Conqueror; and with the help of Speed and Daniel, Lilburne traces this taint down through William's successors to Charles Stuart. Moreover, such documents as Magna Carta have attempted to reassert English liberties in the face of Norman corruptions and to clarify the doctrine of contract between king and people. Turning to more recent history, Lilburne then uses the *Book of Declarations* to prove that the king is limited by law, and that he can only remain king so long as he observes his contractual obligations to the people. Parliament, "as the Representative Body of the Kingdome," is the judge of when the king breaks his trust. Because of the oath taken by members of Parliament which acknowledges that "His Majesty is Supream Head and Governour," the king may legitimately serve as the country's highest officer, but he is not the highest power in the land. That highest power is the people, who, in turn, may delegate part of their authority to Parliament.

Lilburne's next step was to show that Parliament is essentially the House of Commons, that the Lords are usurpers, not representatives, of the people's rights. This he does by pointing out that the Lords' title is only by blood, much of which is corrupt, "not by the common consent or choyce of the people." Further, the Lords are the king's "creatures," and by their recent tyrannies they have forfeited what few rights they may have had as advisers to the executive.

Having thus disposed of the Lords' claim to legislative and judicial powers, Lilburne, after another emphatic account of his tribulations at their "prerogative hands," comes to the political climax of *Regall Tyrannie*: the explicit accusation of treason against Charles for repeated and deliberate violation of the social contract. No longer does Lilburne attach the blame to the king's evil advisers; he now proclaims that Charles Stuart, "one of the monsters of the earth," should be deposed and punished. The laws of God, nature, and reason override all royal pretensions and confirm the people's innate and contractual right to preserve their own liberties.[65]

Despite the fact that Lilburne's reasoning is obviously circular, for his premise and his conclusion are basically identical, and despite the traditional surface quality of his arguments, *Regall Tyrannie* did contribute to Leveller political theory a fuller emphasis on known historical precedent and a more explicit legal denunciation of Charles, whatever the merits of that denunciation. At the same time, *Regall Tyrannie* also shows that Lilburne, at the end of 1646, still believed that the present House of Comons was the institution which best reflected the will of the people. However, toward the end of his "book" he qualifies this belief when he gives an affirmative answer to this query concerning the House of Commons: "Whether or not they have . . . done and acted some things prejudicial and mischevious to the generality of the Kingdome, and destructive to the fundamental Lawes and Liberties thereof?"[66] His "yes," already anticipated by Overton, further foreshadows the imminent Leveller assertion that because England has returned to a state of nature a radically new and explicit social contract has become necessary.

But three more tracts, one by Lilburne, one by Overton, and one by the two men together, predated the organization of the Leveller party in March 1647. Each enlarges Overton's threat and Lilburne's hint that the radicals will soon appeal directly to the people, and now also to the army, should the House of Commons fail in its duty to the nation.

To Lilburne, his own plight continued to be the principal test of whether that duty was being fulfilled. Angered at the Commons' delay in releasing him from the Tower and partly inspired by the third part of *Gangraena* which dealt roughly with him, Lilburne, at the end of January 1647, published *The Oppressed Mans Oppressions declared*.[67] Now a stronger note of disillusion permeates his text. For instance, though he had "always sided with Parliament," the cruelty, graft, and petty tyrannies of prison life have brought him to the point where he can say of the House of Commons:

They will not and have not done all this long Parliament any man any effectual justice that . . . has complained of them, but every man is crushed, and in manner destroyed that meddles anything to the purpose with them.[68]

In refuting Edwards' charges, Lilburne denies that he has been politically fickle, though he does admit — with no hint of irony — that his views have become more consonant with true English traditions during the past six years. It is, he goes on, the Presbyterians who have been the tyrannical and unprincipled turncoats. However, in answer to Edwards' claims for the Presbyterian discipline, Lilburne reveals his comparative religious consistency by extensively citing the *Answer to Nine Arguments* which he had written in 1638. Yet though he still speaks of toleration largely in its reference to the Saints, his political development has brought him very close to Walwyn's and Overton's belief in full liberty of conscience. Lilburne, in fact, now denies the magistrate any power in matters of conscience, for "Tyranny is tyranny, exercised by whomsoever." But the high point of his attack on Presbyterianism and the Long Parliament comes at the end of *The Oppressed Mans Oppressions*. With righteous indignation Lilburne thus announces his new court of highest appeal and his new technique of appealing to it; at the same time, he illustrates how a revolution engenders its own momentum:

I am now determined, by the strength of God, if I speedily have not that Justice, which the Law of England affords me, which is all I crave, or stand in need of, no longer to wait upon the destructive seasons of prudentiall men: but forthwith to make a Formall Appeale to all the Commons of the Kingdome of England, and Dominion of Wales, and set my credit upon the tenters to get money to print 20000 of them [petitions], and send them gratis to all the counties thereof; the ingredients of which shall be filled with the Parliaments owne Declarations and Arguments against the King, turned upon themselves, and their present practise, and with a little narrative of my . . . tyrannical sufferings.[69]

Within a few days Overton played an even more effective variation on the theme of Parliamentary tyranny and the consequent justification of an appeal to the people. *The Commoners Complaint: Or, A Dreadful Warning from Newgate, to the Commons of England* [70] has all the personalized zeal of *The Oppressed Mans Oppressions,* but Overton injects into his "Complaint" a note of humor and a sense of proportion which give it greater cogency. The core of Overton's narrative, like Lilburne's, is the author's misfortunes. He begins his present story in November 1646, when for a second time he was faced with the problem of whether or not to obey the order of the Lords and thereby walk to jail — as he puts it:

whether I should be so base to my Country, and to my self in particular, as to yeeld these Arbitrary Lords so much Villain-service as to become their Lordships Prerogative-Porter, to carry my self to the stinking, lowsie, barbarous Gaol of Newgate; I resolved . . . that as in heart I defied all injustice, cruelty, tyrannie, and oppression . . . I would not be so treacherous to my owne self, to my wife and children, and especially to this Nation . . . as personally to yeeld my active submission of any limbe that was mine.[71]

Then follows a seriocomic account of how Overton had to be carried back to Newgate, for "the law of our land makes no man his own executioner." He further supports his intransigence by affirming that the letter of the law is always subordinate to its equity; and, since reason is the criterion by which to judge the applicability of a given precedent (in this case, walking), "therefore as their Lordships . . . found warrants, so should their Lordships find Leggs to obey them." Overton's final point in this connection is that he is free of the Lords' jurisdiction from the top of his head to the soles of his feet.

As a result of his logic, Overton was forcibly carried from Westminster to Newgate, "just as if the John of all Sir Johns had got little Martin by the feathers." En route, in a manner reminiscent of Lilburne's trip to the pillory of a decade earlier, Overton attracted much public sympathy. Lilburnian, too, was Overton's lament back in prison when his copy of the Second Part of Coke's *Institutes* was taken from him: "My armour of proof, the Charter of my legall Rights, Freedoms, and Liberties!" But unlike Lilburne in manner, though not in content, is Overton's conclusion to the first section of *The Commoners Complaint.* Describing the "Trained Bands of Newgate," the thousands of well-disciplined lice which infest the place, he warns the House of Commons that these prison "soldiers" may soon be guarding them if they are not more "active, vigilant, and faithfull" in behalf of their real friends.

Overton and Lilburne had wives who shared and fought for their husbands' views. In January Mrs. Overton had also refused to walk to prison; despite the fact that she was pregnant, she had forced her captors to drag her bodily to Bridewell.[72] Overton's account of her fortitude in the face of brutal and arbitrary assault shows him at his stylistic best. In this section of *The Commoners Complaint* he combines effective ridicule, achieved by well-placed mock-epic touches descriptive of the "battle" between the fainting woman and the "puissant forces" of the Lords, with a moving strain of pathos and anger. "This is the honour," he asserts, "that their Lordships are pleased to confer on the free Commoners wives who stand for their Freedoms and Liberties," and he makes the fact that his wife was dragged through the streets of London a stirringly explicit symbol of the suppression of English rights. Returning then to his own and Lilburne's predicament, Overton concludes by telling Marten, to whom *The Commoners Complaint* is addressed: "Let our doom be proclaimed to the whole world that the commons of England may know what to trust to," for the time is now fast approaching when "we may lose our labours no longer in petitioning, complaining, and seeking for reliefe at your hands."

In keeping with this threat was *The out-cryes of oppressed Commons,* the joint work of Overton and Lilburne, which was directed

to "all the Rationall and understanding men in the Kingdome
. . . that have not resolved with themselves to be Vassells and
Slaves unto the lusts and wills of Tyrants." A month had passed
without the House doing anything to rectify the lot of either man.
Their tone, therefore, is more belligerent, their willingness to turn
to the New Model Army as the only effective agent of the people
more apparent. But the heart of *The out-cryes* is the point which
Lilburne had already hinted at in his *Regall Tyrannie*: that England, because it has returned to a state of nature, now stands in
need of a new social contract. Since the pamphlet is intent on
proving this, the authors' emphasis is largely negative; they stress
the betrayal of the people by their representative institutions, not
the creation of new institutions or the precise definition of a new
social contract.

Overton and Lilburne, however, begin by skillfully reiterating
their respect for law and tradition to show that they are neither
anarchists nor subversives. Next follows a review of the Lords' encroachments, first against Lilburne and Overton, then, through
them, against all freeborn Englishmen. By the failure of the
House of Commons to curb such tyranny, by its failure to uphold
the trust reposed in it, the House has vitiated its former patriotic
"protestations, imprecations, and just Declarations." At this point
an evident note of regret enters *The out-cryes*: what was recently the
repository of the people's hopes has now become largely a body
of corrupt men who have departed from the known and fundamental laws of the land.[73] As a result of this dereliction, Overton
and Lilburne must now "tread in Parliaments steps" by appealing
directly to the people. It is not the authors who have "dissolved
the whole frame and constitution of the civill pollicy and government of the Kingdome"; it is the House of Commons which by
allowing the Lords to subvert the law of the land has given England
its final push into a state of nature. Parliament, in fact, is now permitting "will and lust but not law to rule and governe" the people
of England, and the people themselves are now thrown back onto
"the originall law of nature, for every man to preserve and defend
himselfe the best he can." [74]

Overton and Lilburne then restate the logic behind their belief in
the right of both the individual and the nation now to preserve

themselves. All power is for the good of the "betrusters," the people; but when their trustees have forfeited the trust which the people have reposed in them, then "the people are disobliged from their obedience and subjection, and may lawfully doe the best they can for their owne preservation." That best, *The out-cryes* urges, has now become the potential right and active duty of the people to take up arms against a corrupt Parliament, as Parliament did against a corrupt king.

Shorn of its profusion of legal and historical allusions, such is the immediately revolutionary message of *The out-cryes of oppressed Commons*. But that a new period of civil war and violent change would be no easy and pleasant transition to a better world, Overton and Lilburne make clear by the undercurrent of lament which runs through their inflammatory appeal and which counterpoints the threat with which it ends. "Woe, woe, unto poor England!" is their concluding exclamation. The actual birth pangs of the Leveller party had begun.

The Party Comes of Age

I. March to June 1647: The "Large Petition" of the Levellers

The efforts of Lilburne, Overton, and Walwyn in 1645 and 1646 had done much to prepare for the official arrival of the Leveller party. But in the spring of 1647 three factors were still necessary to mold their scattered and potential followers into a disciplined group and to shape the recent impassioned outcries of Lilburne and Overton into a feasible political program. These three factors were a more cohesive, receptive, and politically energetic audience, an effective whipping boy, and a guiding hand. To a large extent, the army supplied the first, Parliament the second, and Walwyn the third.

The first major phase of the Civil War had come to an end early in 1646. During the two years of comparative peace which followed, the soldiers of the New Model had the leisure to become more political, and the motivation, because of the increasing uncertainty of a stable national settlement, to devote that leisure to political discussion and activity. This situation was fully satisfactory to the radicals. As early as 1644 the Royalist newspaper, *Mercurius Aulicus*, had gone out of its way to warn against sectarian agitation in the army; [1] and in 1646 the violently anti-Parliament *Mercurius Rusticus* had a brief revival when it devoted itself almost entirely to the "barbarous Out-rages," both spiritual and physical, committed by the radicals in and on the New Model.

But the best testimony to the receptivity of the soldiers to new ideas is the much-cited section from Richard Baxter's autobiography which deals with his services as a chaplain in the New Model. Baxter had much to say, in a tone of subdued shock, about the disputatiousness of the soldiers, particularly those who belonged to the more extreme sects. Not only did he hear "plotting heads very hot upon that which intimated their intention to subvert both church and state," but he listened with horror to the rising tide of antimonarchism among the soldiers: " 'What were the Lords of England,' said they, 'but William the Conqueror's colonels; or the barons, but his majors; or the knights, but his captains.' " [2]

By late 1646, according to Baxter, radical propaganda had already won many military adherents "who had been seduced into a disputing vein." "State democracy and . . . church democracy," he goes on, were common topics of discussion, "but their most frequent and vehement disputes were for liberty of conscience." The direct influence of the Levellers can also be seen in Baxter's explanation that

a great part of the mischief was done among the soldiers by pamphlets, which were abundantly dispersed, such as Overton, Martin Mar-Priest, and more of his, and some of J. Lilburne's . . . and divers against the King, and against the ministry, and for liberty of conscience, &c. The soldiers being usually dispersed in quarters, they had such books to read when they had none to contradict them.[3]

Indeed, says Baxter, concluding this section of his life story, the most dangerous, the most freethinking, the most "Jesuitical" faction in the army was the same group of men "that afterwards were called Levellers."

Even among those soldiers who were indifferent to politics, a seedbed for radical ideas was being prepared. Gardiner thus describes the New Model in March 1647:

Large numbers of the soldiers cared little for politics or religion. On a question of the pocket they were ready to stand up as one man, and the question of the pocket was, in a very real sense, a pressing one. The pay of the foot-soldiers was now eighteen weeks in arrear, and that of the horse and dragoons no less than forty-three.[4]

Besides this issue, of which Overton and Lilburne had already made some political capital, that of indemnity for injuries to life

or property done during the war was not yet settled. The appointment of army Agitators in April, *The Declaration of the Army*
and the scattered mutinies in May, and Joyce's seizure of Charles
in June were all, in large part, the combined result of radical propaganda and military discontent.

This discontent was greatly augmented by the actions of both
Houses of Parliament. Not only were they delinquent in the matter
of arrears and indemnity, but their dickerings with the king at
Holmby were neither secret nor, among the soldiers, popular. Parliament, in fact, was busy making itself a suitable whipping boy
for the Levellers and the New Model. In February 1647 both
Houses came under the control of a Presbyterian majority. This
conservative leadership, disturbed by high taxes and by the growing independence and Independency of the army, besieged, too, by
several weighty pro-Presbyterian petitions from the City, and under
considerable if diffuse pressure for a peaceful settlement, sought to
solve its problems by, in effect, disbanding the New Model. Fairfax and Cromwell also came under sharp Parliamentary attack. By
April the conservatives, after they had secured command of the
powerful, anti-Independent London militia, began to conduct negotiations with the Scottish army in reference to its possible intervention in support of English Presbyterianism.[5] Parliament had, in
short, done much to alienate not only the civilian radicals but both
the top leaders and the rank and file of the army.

That Walwyn supplied the guiding hand in the organization of
radical propaganda and acted as chief midwife at the birth of the
Leveller party is extremely probable. Since October 1646, when he
had written the last of his pamphlets against Edwards, he had published nothing. This did not mean that he was politically inactive.
He had gained further practical experience in the summer and fall
of that year in his petitionary and organizational efforts in connection with his support of Lilburne and his attendance at Salter's
Hall; [6] and this experience, as well as his long-range shrewdness, is
evident in both the pronouncements and the tactics employed by
the Levellers in the spring of 1647. By then, too, Walwyn apparently was eager to apply his personal method of proselytizing to
the whole kingdom — to play the part of "compassionate Samari-
tan on a larger scale and with more far-reaching effect than he had

yet attained." [7] Moreover, by this time Lilburne and Overton had
so persistently offered the House of Commons the choice of releasing them or of facing the potential consequences of their threats
that Parliament, by choosing the second alternative, had helped
to win the radicals an even more receptive hearing in the New
Model. Such, in brief, was the background for the first party manifesto issued by the Levellers.

This manifesto took the form of a petition, almost certainly from
the hand of William Walwyn.[8] On March 15, 1647, when the work
of getting signatures to it had just begun, an agent of the House
of Commons secured a copy and turned it over to his employers.
It was immediately voted "a seditious paper." Two days later the
Lord Mayor of London and his oligarchical associates asked the
House of Lords to suppress the Leveller petition. Its supporters, in
turn, promptly countered this request with a certificate presented to
the Parliamentary Committee for the Suppression of Unlicensed
Printing which stated that their petition was genuine and patriotic.
On March 19, one of the Leveller followers, reading this certificate
to a group of bystanders outside Westminster, was arrested and
committed to jail. That afternoon another of the Leveller adherents was accused of disorderly conduct and also jailed. The day
following, the nonjailed Levellers prepared a second petition, demanding the release of these two men and taking Parliament to
task for its arbitrary and hasty actions.[9] Then, after a brief lull, the
House rejected this second petition, at the same time arresting a
third person for being overzealous in asking why they had not replied sooner.[10] Early in May the original Walwyn petition, now
somewhat strengthened, was at last formally presented to Parliament. On May 20 Parliament formally replied by ordering it burnt
by the common hangman. A few days later Parliament bluntly rejected a third version of the March Petition. On May 31 Lilburne
told this story fully and angrily in *Rash Oaths Unwarrantable*, and
two weeks later Walwyn repeated it, much more briefly, in *Gold
tried in the fire*.[11]

This dramatic petitionary parry and thrust, and the attendant
popular demonstrations and widespread publicity, indicate in themselves at least a rudimentary party organization. But, in addition,
the wide circulation of petitions for signature, the presumably

well-planned meetings near Westminster and in and around London, the speed with which circulars were printed and distributed, and the evident fund-raising efforts behind these various activities, all reveal a political organization that was already functioning. It is very likely, in fact, that the ward-by-ward setup of London and the establishment of branches in other parts of England, both of which the Levellers completed by the end of the year, were well under way in the spring of 1647.[12]

Besides demonstrating at least a fledgling political organization, the adventures of the March Petition point to a concerted plan of action on the part of the radicals. This plan certainly involved securing a maximum of publicity; and in view of Parliament's immediate violent reaction, it apparently promptly included provoking the House of Commons to an extreme of repression which would both further alienate Parliament from the army and add validity to the Leveller theory of the need for a direct appeal to the people. Tactically as well as strategically the Levellers were using the device of the petition to its fullest extent.

In all this maneuvering Walwyn probably received help from Lilburne in the Tower and from Overton in Newgate. He was also assisted by a few of the London Independents.[13] In all likelihood, too, this period marks the beginning of John Wildman's activities as a Leveller. Twenty-four years old in 1647, Wildman had been educated at Cambridge, had studied law in London, and had already, perhaps through a friendship with Lilburne, become a staunch republican.[14] Since within six months he became one of the most diligent of the intermediaries between the London Levellers and the army Agitators, it is almost certain that he concluded his political apprenticeship as a member of the radical board of strategy in the early months of 1647.

The "Large Petition," the focal point of all this maneuvering, was a party platform consisting of a preamble and thirteen specific planks.[15] As such, it was mainly a compendium of the ideas of Overton and Lilburne, polished and moderated by Walwyn, with perhaps a few legal emendations from Wildman. It was addressed to the House of Commons as "the supreme Authority of This Nation," for the denial of the Lords' legislative and judicial power had become standard radical doctrine; and the preamble, which outlined the political philosophy of the "many thousands" who supported the petition, was likewise a summary of the now almost fully developed social theory of the Puritan Revolution's nonmystical left wing.

The petition's opening phrase states the republican premise which had become accepted by the political radicals of many shades: "That no Government is more just in the Constitution than that of Parliament, having its foundation in the free choice of the People." Indeed, the people of England have traditionally turned to Parliament for "the most proper remedies of their grievances." Yet, the preamble continues, those in power have always, "either by disuse or abuse of Parliaments, deprived the people of their hopes." At the start of the Civil War, however, the present Parliament had power "sufficient to deliver the whole Nation from all kind of oppression and grievance . . . and make it the most . . . free nation in the world." To this end it at first accomplished much: the petitioners congratulate Parliament, for instance, for abolishing Star Chamber and Episcopacy. But, alas, much more remains to be done. The preamble then lists these necessary reforms, and concludes with this somewhat conciliatory hope:

After so long a Session of so powerful and so free a Parliament . . . made and maintained by the abundant love, and liberall effusion of the blood of the people, and therefore knowing no danger nor thraldome like unto our being left in this so sad a condition . . . and observing that you are now drawing the great and weighty affaires of this Nation to some conclusion, . . . whilest we yet have time to hope, and you power to helpe, and lest by our silence we might be guilty of that ruine and slavery, which without your speedy help is like to fall upon us . . . we have presumed to spread our cause thus plainly . . . before you, and doe most earnestly intreat that you will stir up your affections to a zealous love and tender regard of the people, who have chosen and trusted you, that you will seriously consider that the end of your trust was freedome and deliverance from all kind of grievances and oppressions.[16]

Despite the relatively propitiatory tone of the preamble, the reforms which it suggests would probably have been enough, both in themselves and because of the political disrepute of the petitioners, to cause Parliament to react as strongly as it did. But such a

reaction was doubly ensured by the specific proposals which constitute the remainder of the March Petition. These fall into four
loose categories: political, religious, economic, and legal.

The first and last points are essentially political. The first, and
historically the most important, urges the House of Commons "to
preserve . . . [their] just Authority from all prejudices of a Negative voice in any person or persons whatsoever." England is thus,
in fact if not in name, to be a republic. The final proposal advocates
that no man be barred from political office because of his religious
belief — a plea which Macaulay substantially reiterated two centuries later.

Three proposals come under the general head of religion. Point
four demands the repeal of "all Statutes, Oathes, and Covenants"
which in any way interfere with the free exercise of religion or
penalize a man for his spiritual beliefs. The fifth proposal, which
gets to the heart of democratic rationalism, turned out to be a special bone of contention in the Army Debates at Putney and Whitehall and during the troubled years of the Commonwealth and
Protectorate. It asserts:

No man for preaching or publishing his opinion in Religion, in a
peacable way, may be punished or persecuted as hereticall by Judges
that are not infallible, but may be mistaken as well as other men in their
judgements, lest upon pretense of suppressing errors, Sects, or Schismes,
the most necessary truths and sincere professions thereof may be suppressed, as upon the like pretense it hath been in all ages.[17]

Point nine completes the Leveller scheme for full religious liberty.
It demands the end of tithes and of all other compulsory methods of
clerical maintenance, and states that ministers are to be paid "only
by those who voluntarily choose them, and contract with them for
their labours."

Of the economic reforms which the petition advocates, the sixth
plank, which asks for the dissolution of the Merchant Adventurers
and the prohibition of similar monopolies, is the most central.[18]
The tenth urges an end to imprisonment for debt; and the twelfth,
in somewhat vague terms, asks Parliament to curtail the widespread
and shameful practice of begging.

The proposals which come within the legal category show the

Leveller propensity, which crops up again in the Agreements of the People, to mix general and, in a sense, personal issues. The seventh and eighth points advocate fundamental reforms in the law. The first of these, in particular, anticipates most of the demands implicit in *Bleak House*: "a just, speedy, plain, and unburdensome way for deciding of Controversies and suits in Law"; the reduction of all laws to an agreement with Christianity — in this case a synonym for "equity" as it had so often been used by Lilburne and Overton; the translation of all laws into simple and ordinary English, including the proviso that abbreviations be prohibited; and the setting forth clearly of both the fees and the duties of those connected with the law. Point eight reiterates the demand for speedy legal procedures, asserts that one witness should be insufficient in capital cases, and stresses the long-standing radical conviction that the law should be merciful, and that, in a non-Mikadoan manner, the punishment should fit the crime.

The three remaining propositions are more directly the outcome of the Levellers' personal experience with the law. One of these asks that any sentence imposed on a commoner without due process of law be revoked, that reparations be paid that commoner, and that any such encroachments in the future be considered capital offenses: in short, that Lilburne and Overton be vindicated against the House of Lords. The second sets up safeguards against self-incrimination in a court of law, a reform which Lilburne had advocated since his appearance before Star Chamber almost ten years earlier; and the third, again the product of the Levellers' individual suffering, urges that prison keepers be only men of "approved honesty," and that prison graft and cruelty be ended.

Thus the March Petition succinctly set forth the planks in the first formal platform of the Leveller party, giving it a program from which it was not to deviate significantly, except for the move from republicanism to democracy, for the remaining two years of the party's active political life. Obviously, despite its deliberately noninflammatory language, this platform was such that it alienated most of the vested interests in mid-seventeenth-century England. King and Lords, prelatists and Presbyterians, even the majority of the Independents, could view with alarm the political and religious changes advocated by this document. On the economic front, both the petition's larger implications and its specific clauses against monopoly and imprisonment for debt must have frightened the conservative business man of the day — this despite the fact that its laissez-faire economic philosophy proved in the long run conducive to the rapid growth of capitalism. Similarly, the legal reforms put forward by the Levellers not only hit directly at the powerful profession of the law, but their program might well open the gates to an even wider flood of actively prosecuted revolutionary ideas. Thus the Large Petition of the Levellers was more than republican, it was dangerous. Its history and that of its close supporters in the spring of 1647 merely serves to underline the revolutionary impact of the reforms it advanced.

Probably in the period immediately following the drawing up of this petition, Walwyn took the time to compose a pamphlet which, on the surface, appears to be quite different from this party manifesto.[19] *A Still and Soft Voice From the Scriptures, Witnessing them to be the Word of God* is Walwyn's most complete religious self-portrait. For this reason it is one of the more attractive theological works of the seventeenth century. In all likelihood it was written mainly to convince those members of the Independent congregations who were wavering between approval and disapproval of the Leveller platform that Walwyn, its chief architect, was neither politically nor morally non-Christian. *A Still and Soft Voice*, besides being a spiritual autobiography, is therefore a judicious self-vindication and a shrewd political apologia.[20]

The distinction between "true Religion and Superstition" is Walwyn's central topic, and he approaches it in a pragmatic and rational manner:

Experience making the best Schoole-master in things naturall and morall . . . so is it in Religion, he only can best judge, advise and counsell others, who hath observed and most seriously considered the severall passages and progresse of his owne knowledge in things divine.[21]

On the basis of his own careful self-scrutiny and his experience with such men as Edwards, Walwyn then proceeds to characterize those whose religion is essentially false and superstitious. These men are not only "zealous of the traditions of the times," but they deliberately pursue the opinion of the majority. They are, in addition, antirational, and their favorite weapons are therefore slander, distortion, and evasion. Further, these "worldly Pollititians" have found that "superstition is the easiest means to lead a multitude," and, incidentally, the best way to line their own pockets. Then, with keen psychological insight, Walwyn describes the man intoxicated with a false god:

A superstitious man suffereth neither God nor man to live in peace, . . . he apprehendeth God as one anxious, spiteful, hardly contented, easily moved, with difficulty appeased, examining our actions after the human fashion of a severe Judge that watcheth our steps, which hee proveth true by his manner of serving him: he trembleth for feare, is never secure, fearing he never doth well, and that he hath left some thing undone, by omission whereof all is worth nothing that he hath done.[22]

It is such a man, Walwyn continues, who now instead of helping the poor spends his time persecuting all those who hold opinions differing from his and the accepted point of view, for he is not half so moved by the sight of poverty and oppression as he is by the sight of someone going into a church of which he does not fully approve. This sort of man's inner disturbance and the national discontent which he occasions are both the result of "educated, customary or superstitious Religion."

In sharp contrast is Walwyn's "true religion," the outward characteristics of which are "good Workes" rather than public displays of faith, and an abiding concern, regardless of contumely and persecution, for full political and religious liberty — in short, "more of the deeds of Christians, and fewer of the arguments." It is in his praise of the deep-lying spiritual satisfaction which such a religion conveys that Walwyn most clearly reveals the inner sources of his political idealism. In a mood reminiscent of the ecstatic Lilburne of 1638, Walwyn refutes the allegation that he has denied God and slandered Scripture. His faith in God, and in the Bible as God's Word, is, he says, the result of "an unexpressable power . . . an irresistible perswasive power . . . from within" that carries with it a "Peace which passeth all utterance or expression . . . [and an] abundance of joy and gladnesse."[23] Hence, unlike the unhappy man whose religion is based on fear and worldly considerations, Walwyn's rational-mystical certitude that God is a God of love has endowed him with true spiritual tranquility and happiness, as well as with an active and undying devotion to the cause of human brotherhood.

This spiritual certitude can therefore be seen as one of the factors which determined the underlying rationale of the March Petition: Walwyn's antinomianism, along with Lilburne's long experience with martyrdom, and Overton's reformist secularism, had helped to shape and articulate the radical traditions of their era. The spirit of love and tolerance which permeated Walwyn's religion in particular, along with his own and his colleagues' optimism in regard to the democratic potentialities of human reason, were thus carried over into the hurly-burly of politics by means of the specific reforms advocated by the Levellers.

Yet, even at this early stage, the brave new world envisioned by the Levellers was surrounded by and contributed to the national turmoil; and from this turmoil a military state, not a democratic utopia, emerged. But such a result might have been predicted: by early April the Levellers had already begun to shift their appeal from the House of Commons and the amorphous populace to the disciplined New Model Army, and the first printed evidence of this shift was a pamphlet almost certainly by Richard Overton.

On April 4 the London Presbyterians sent a petition to the county of Essex, there to be circulated by the "godly" ministers. It asked Parliament to disband the army, and it arranged for the petition's subscribers to meet at Westminster on April 18 to present it, en masse, to Parliament. Between these two dates, Overton's pamphlet, *A New Found Stratagem*, was distributed in Essex, and also "scattered abroad" in the army on the very day that the Parliamentary Commissioners were on hand to discuss the disbanding of the New Model.

Though primarily addressed to the people of Essex, Overton's tract was also intended to appeal to the soldiers. The army, it says, is "the principall meanes, as things now stand, to defend and maintain your [the people's] liberties, and to keep you and yours from sudden vasalage and slavery." [24] Against this threat — against the attempts of Parliament to become the "Absolute Masters" of England — Overton is aggressively articulate. All the people, he declares, should beware of that "Presbyterian yoake" which will turn the freeborn Englishman into a slave physically lower than the peasant of France, and spiritually more circumscribed than the follower of Mohammed. The present danger from the "trayterous party" in control of Parliament has, in fact, made the army indispensable to the safety and freedom of England.

Overton also astutely diagnoses the "Machiavilisme" of those "pretended friends," the Presbyterians. For instance, the lower taxes which they claim will result when the army is disbanded are a snare and a delusion, for the armies which they will have to muster will be more expensive, and, in contrast to the New Model, such forces will not be dedicated to the cause of justice. Indeed, the attempt on the part of the conservative majority in Parliament to entrap the citizens of Essex is merely symptomatic of this group's scheme to ensnare the whole nation. The crisis, therefore, is urgent, the kingdom at the "pit brinke." The people's only sure recourse is to turn to the army "to have justice speedily and impartially executed, and . . . Lawes and liberties established." Once this has been done, Overton predicts, the army will "of its own accord" disband and lay down its arms, for then "the wheels of state would go easily . . . and dividing spirits would be utterly disappointed." [25] Such is the note of optimism on which *A New Found Stratagem* concludes. It soon turned to disillusion: unfortunately Lord Acton was not around to remind Overton of the latter's own conviction that, under the circumstances, such disillusion was inevitable.

But during the spring of 1647 the political activities undertaken by certain segments of the army probably encouraged the belief that the wheels of state would soon go easily and in the direction of democracy. In the middle of April each of eight cavalry regiments elected two representatives from their own rank and file. These so-called "Agitators" immediately provided a democratic means of exerting pressure on the military high command, on Parliament, and, by means of judicious publicity, on public opinion at large. By the end of the month every regiment had selected its own Agitators.[26] On April 30, three of them appeared before the House of Commons to present the grievances of the soldiers. Under stiff cross-examination they conducted themselves with the legalistic assurance of Lilburne and Overton.[27] Then on May 4 they drew up a plan which, by implication at least, would make the New Model the

instrument for a national reform along Leveller lines.[28] Finally, by
the middle of May, not only had the Agitators completed setting up
an elaborate organization of their own but they had fully outlined
a radical national program for the army to present to Parliament.[29]
In view of these rapid developments, all of which reflected the
direct influence of the Levellers, and in view of Parliament's continued deaf ear to the legitimate demands of the army, the concluding note of optimism of *A New Found Stratagem* is not surprising.

During this hectic period Lilburne from the Tower of London
was helping to direct the civilian efforts in behalf of the March
Petition and contributing his advice to the army Agitators; [30] and
twice he wrote Cromwell warning him not to be false to his
soldiers and his country.[31] At the end of April Lilburne supplemented these public letters by publishing *The resolved mans Resolution*, a work which represents him at his long-winded and personally embittered worst.[32] Manchester, Colonel King, and Prynne
continue to be the objects of his vituperation, but to this list he now
adds the "sluggish" Henry Marten and some of the leading Independents who are allowing Lilburne to rot in the Tower.[33] In a
series of scattered passages he also makes it clear that the real cancer
in the body politic is the present Parliament, and that this growth
must be cut out. This can be done, says Lilburne, only by a return
to those "historical" principles whereby Parliament was once freely
elected and its members did not have as their sole aim the increase
of their private emoluments. Now, however, since the people need
a new "Bul-warke to preserve them from being swallowed up by
unlimited prerogative & unknown priviledges," Parliament must
be dissolved forthwith — possibly by the army — and replaced by a
truly representative and patriotic assembly.

By late May some of the more radical members of the New Model
were ready to engage in armed conspiracy to dissolve Parliament
and to set up a new bulwark for the soldiers' and the people's
liberty.[34] The danger of mutiny in the army and the continued
leftist pressure from the London Levellers, of which Lilburne's
strident cries were only a part, added to the alarm of the more conservative forces in Parliament and the New Model, and contributed
further to the growing split between radical and Independent.[35] A

symptom of this alarm, as well as of this split, was a clever tract
called *The Recantation . . . Of John Lilburne . . . Opening all the
Machinations of the Independent Partie*. In an obvious attempt to
alienate Lilburne from Overton, and Independent from Leveller,
this pamphlet, after straightfacedly narrating Lilburne's chronic
tribulations, attacks Overton as a greedy heretic. The Independents
are asked to help the needy Lilburne, not the "profane Martin." *The
Recantation* concludes, in Walwynian fashion, with an avowal of
Lilburne's alleged new creed, a six-point program which is Royalist,
Episcopal, and reactionary.

At the end of May, Lilburne in his next pamphlet, the long but
almost brilliant *Rash Oaths unwarrantable*, paused only momentarily
to attack the anonymous author of *The Recantation*. Lilburne was
too intent on reviewing the fate of the March Petition and on
launching his fullest, most sustained, and most penetrating attack
on the House of Commons to bother with any Royalist opponent.

Rash Oaths begins with praise of Henry Marten, to whom it is
addressed. Marten has been "for a long time . . . one of the great
pillars of the Liberties of the Commons of England." But his and
his committee's continuing delays in attending to Lilburne's vindication have been betrayals of English history and English rights.
Then Lilburne shifts his tone from injured faith to aggressive indignation. "Cost what it will," he writes, "I can no longer forbeare,"
and he launches into a heavy attack on Marten and his colleagues
in the Lower House. These men have "degenerated from a just
House of Parliament" to "betrayers of their trust." Hence Lilburne
can justify his appeal to force to remove them from office, for Parliament is now

a conspiracy and confederacy of lawlesse, unlimited, and unbounded
men, that have actually destroyed the Lawes and Liberties of England,
and that will have no rule to walke by but their owne corrupted and
bloody wills, and thereby have set up the highest Tyranny that can be
set up in the world, against which, by your owne principles, the Kingdome may justly rise up in Armes as one man, and destroy all the
fore-said conspirators without mercy or compassion, . . . for take away
Law . . . and deny us justice and right, . . . and what are we now better then the brute beasts of the field? [36]

The remainder of *Rash Oaths* is mainly an effective history of

Parliament's recent treachery and an amplification of the people's revolutionary alternatives in the face of that treachery. The most significant landmark to Lilburne in his account of Parliament's perfidy is their approval of the Solemn League and Covenant — the worst of their rash and unwarrantable oaths. Since then, Lilburne continues, Parliament has proceeded to violate its own ancient constitution and legitimate declarations and to tamper with the basic right to freedom of conscience. Does Parliament, Lilburne then asks, have the right to impose any sort of oath on those whom it supposedly represents? Three centuries have not lessened the effectiveness of his answer:

Oathes . . . now are become nothing else but cloaks of knavery, and breeders of strife and mischief. Therefore for shame lay them all down and presse them no more upon any man whatsoever, for he that consciensiously makes nothing of an Oath, will make as little of breaking his Oath, whensoever it shall make for his profit, ease, or preferment, whereas to him that conscienciously scruples an Oath, his bare word, promise, or ingagement is the sincerest tye in the world, which he would not willingly violate for all the earth.[37]

Lilburne goes on to suggest to Marten that perhaps the Revolution has lost its momentum, that the "House hath already done the last Act of Justice that ever they intended to doe." In fact, guided by fear of the Lords, of the rich, and of the lawyers who infest the land, Parliament has not only halted the march of progress, but it has substituted reaction for progress. This retrogression should be a signal to the people that, if they still believe in the real aims for which the war has been fought, they must set up a new Parliament. As clinching proof of this urgent need Lilburne then goes into a detailed history of the March Petition. Moreover, he shows how the people's right to appeal to force has been strengthened in direct proportion to Parliament's increasingly repressive response to the efforts of the radicals, until now

this poore distracted Kingdome . . . have no other course to take but to remonstrate and justly to declare to all the Commons of England, and the Army, the unparaleled, illegall and tyrannicall dealing of the House of Commons . . . and . . . by force of Armes to root up and destroy these tyrants.[38]

Lilburne, however, is here preaching more than an anarchical return to a state of nature. He appeals to history, God, and reason to justify his call to revolution and to assist in charting that revolution's course. The course at which he then arrives is similar to that given in the March Petition: England is to be governed by a legal system which is simple and equitable, and the country's new Parliament is to be annually elected by all men. But in his appeal for universal manhood suffrage and in his ensuing analysis of the need for a fair redistribution of Parliamentary seats, Lilburne goes beyond the formally stated Leveller demands. For instance, he thus amplifies the rather loose republicanism of the preamble and first proposal of the Large Petition:

Each County equally and proportionably, by the common consent of the people [is] to divide it selfe into Divisions, Hundreds, or Weapontacks, that so all the people (without confusion or tumult) may meet together in their severall divisions, and every free man of England, as well poore as rich . . . may have a Vote in chusing those that are to make the law, it being a maxim in nature that no man justly can be bound without his own consent.[39]

Rash Oaths is Lilburne's most logical and in many ways his most functional political pamphlet. Though he begins and ends with his own plight, his analysis of Parliament's defection and his relatively nonpersonal narrative of the violent rejection of Leveller demands do eventuate in a broad avowal of democracy — democracy brought into the world by revolution, but having its roots in history, and nourished by every godly, natural, and rational principle. The radical doctrine of the social contract thus comes to some sort of intellectual fruition in this pamphlet; for it shows, if sometimes indirectly, how Parliament, partly as a result of Leveller tactics, has allegedly returned the country to a state of nature, and how out of that theoretical and actual chaos a new society can grow.

Two weeks after the appearance of *Rash Oaths*, Walwyn's *Gold tried in the fire, or the burnt Petitions revived* told the story of the March Petition with brevity, restraint, and regret. At no point in its few pages does Walwyn become obviously inflammatory, but the sorrowful tone of the pamphlet is by no means one of submission. The people, he says, will hence forth conclude, that as there is little good to be hoped from such Parliaments as need to be Petitioned, so there is none at all to be expected from those that burn such Petitions as these.[40]

Since Parliament, therefore, was no longer the effective instrument of the popular will, the radicals now pinned their hopes on the only other body which could implement their program and revive their burnt petitions, the New Model Army.

II. *July to October 1647: Prelude to Putney*

Ten days before *Gold tried in the fire* appeared, on June 4, 1647, Cornet Joyce, with his commission in the form of a body of New Model troopers, abducted the King from Holmby, an escapade almost certainly undertaken with the collusion of the Agitators.[41] The following day the army at a general rendezvous accepted the *Solemn Engagement*, itself a rough sort of covenant between the soldiers and the nation.[42] It declared that the army would not disband until a General Council should decide that certain specified military demands, as well as certain general conditions for the settlement of the kingdom, had been met. Within a few days this General Council, consisting of two Agitators and two commissioned officers from each regiment, but weighted in a conservative direction by the addition of a few of the highest officers, was established.[43] These moves in themselves indicated the influence of the Levellers, as did *A Representation from . . . the Army*, which appeared in mid-June.[44]

In this document the comparatively conservative Ireton, on behalf of the whole army, set forth the soldiers' immediate grievances and tried to justify the New Model's interference in helping to effect a decent national settlement. "We were not," he states in words that were to be repeatedly quoted,

a mere mercenary army, hired to serve any arbitrary power of a state, but called forth and conjured by the several declarations of Parliament to the defense of our own and the people's just rights and liberties.[45]

In temporary agreement with the Levellers, Ireton goes on to assert that the political intervention of the New Model is also supported by the "law of nature and nations," as well as by the law of God.

A Representation concludes by advocating certain familiar reforms, among them a purge of Parliament, electoral and legal democratization, and a strengthening of the guarantees of religious freedom and of the right to petition. When these rights are secured, says Ireton, then the army will trust itself fully to Parliament and even be willing to restore the king.

Ireton's modified echo of Overton's optimism soon faded away. In the latter days of June the army moved closer to London. The Presbyterian faction in Parliament and the City, in response to this military pressure, temporarily capitulated to some of the more limited demands of *A Representation*.[46] But the Agitators, at the instigation of the Levellers, were not satisfied and urged an immediate march on London. Caught between the soldier's demands and the refractory policies and tactics of the Presbyterians, the high command of the army delayed an immediate decision by holding a debate at Reading in mid-July on some of the radicals' proposals.[47] Then on July 26 a London mob, organized in large part by the city oligarchy, terrorized Parliament into submitting to the Presbyterians; momentarily civilian coercion replaced military coercion. But only momentarily: early in August the army, escorting the expelled Independent members of Parliament, entered London.[48] Along with them, the army also brought its own constitutional scheme for settling the kingdom, *The Heads of the Proposals*, a compromise plan again largely the work of Ireton.[49] But despite this scheme's attempt to please almost all factions, the political pressure continued dangerously to mount during the summer of 1647.

Besides their behind-the-scenes activities in London and the army, the Levellers contributed to this pressure by means of the popular press.[50] Thus, concurrently with the debate in the General Council of the Army at Reading, Overton issued *An Appeale from the Degenerate Representative Body of the Commons of England Assembled at Westminster*.[51] In stirring language Overton now addressed his message directly to the New Model, convinced that it was, for the present, the only instrument potentially willing and able to execute the will of the people. Yet in spite of this unfounded hope, *An Appeale* is the most philosophical of his political works, his most sustained and serious exposition of social thought.

Overton's thinking had been given a slightly new turn by a tract which appeared two weeks before his *Appeale*, a tract titled *Plain Truth without Feare or Flattery*, written by a political moderate for the "benefit of the poore, oppressed, betrayed, and almost destroyed commons of England." [52] It received high praise from Overton and apparently reinforced his conviction that "extream danger driveth to extream means." Steeped in Leveller terminology, *Plain Truth* was a strong attack on the Presbyterians, a vindication of Fairfax and his army, and a call to militant action against the corrupt leadership of Parliament. So vehement, in fact, was its anti-Presbyterianism that the anonymous author betrayed his Royalism by concluding with a partial defense of Charles and a plea for reconciliation between king and people. Hence it pointed up the fact that a growing number of people in the center and on the right were relying increasingly on the New Model as the answer to England's problems — and that the army was assuming a position to serve as the nucleus for a strange and unstable political coalition.

The possibility of some such anti-Presbyterian coalition, but under radical leadership, was probably the chief cause for Overton's elaborate defense of the propriety of the Levellers' appeal direct to the people and soldiers rather than to Parliament. Overton begins *An Appeale* with the frank statement that English history affords no precedent for any such direct call to popular action, nor is there traditional support for it anywhere in the letter of English law. But, the pamphlet continues, lest its author be condemned as "an open and desperate enemy to Parliaments and Magistracy, a subverter and destroyer of all Nationall Lawes and Government," he will prove that this course of action was and is fully justified. Overton then, on the basis of principle, of personal experience, and of national emergency, sets up his careful justification of the Leveller strategy, making it seem whenever possible in keeping with English tradition.

His first principle, as when he refused to walk to Newgate, is that "Reason is the fountaine of all just presidents [precedents]." From there, after celebrating the divinity of reason in a manner strongly suggestive of Walwyn, Overton moves to his second point: "right reason" can warrant and legalize a direct appeal to the people under certain conditions. These conditions, in turn, may apply either to a single person or to an entire nation. In either case an unprec-

edented move can only become warranted and legal if it conforms
to the instinct for self-preservation, the demands of urgent necessity,
the equity rather than the letter of the law, and the concept that all
political power resides in the people.

Overton then reinforces this intellectual analysis of the right of a
nation to appeal over the head of its government by a dynamic account of his own and his family's personal tribulations. Self-preservation, urgent necessity, the spirit of equity, and the traditional
rights of the individual have, he says, all been so flagrantly violated
in his case that now, at long last, he is compelled to appeal formally
against his persecutors:

[I] doe by these presents Actually and formally APPEALE from and
against the Members Representative . . . assembled at Westminster
unto the Body Represented, (the true originall Soveraigne Authority of
Parliaments) the free borne commoners . . . for protection and relief
against those obstructors of Justice and Judgement . . . in the House of
Commons. . . . I shall and do from henceforth utterly disclaime and
renounce all triall and Judgement by the degenerate Members Assembled
therein, & shall hold all Orders and Ordinances whatsoever proceeding
from them . . . as altogether invallid, and void of all Parliamentary
authority and power, not obligatory or binding at all to the people, but
to be opposed and resisted to the death.[53]

"As one man . . . rise up in the cause of the Army," he therefore
exhorts his readers, so that the citizens of England may finally be
allowed to live "in peace and tranquility."

In telling of his own injuries Overton gradually and skillfully
merges them with the grievances of his country. His account of
Parliament's treatment of the March Petition serves to cement this
merger. The House of Commons, "contrary to their many Oathes,
Covenants, Declarations, Vowes, and Protestations," contrary also
to the traditions and principles of justice and freedom, now reject
and crush the people's petitions, "call the Petitioners Rogues," and
imprison those individuals most active in the service of their country. Overton's climax is the statement that Parliament, by having
had the common hangman burn the March Petition, has "essentially
. . . burnt the Great Charter of England."

The perpetrators of this indignity, Overton continues, deserve

"Halters and Gallowes . . . [rather] than places in Parliament, . . . for . . . hee that oppresseth for complaining of oppression must needs be a Tyrant in the highest measure." Against such tyranny, the "mighty and puissant vertuous Army" now seems the best recourse, for in the face of oppression common citizen and common soldier have become one. But again the serious nature of *An Appeale* and Overton's awareness of the possibilities of an anti-Presbyterian coalition induce him to qualify his inflammatory remarks. He does this by emphasizing the distinction between the man and the office. Of the present leadership of the House of Commons, he says, for instance, "The rejection, disobedience, and resistance of their personall commands is no rejection, disobedience, or resistance of their Parliamentary Authority." [54] He then tries to support this distinction between the individual and the official, between "personnall commands" and legitimate law, by saying that this same distinction was made by Parliament in the early days of the Civil War. At that time they officially declared their aim of liberating the man Charles from his evil advisers so that he could properly perform his kingly office. On the same basis the Levellers have appealed directly to the people to "free" themselves from the present evil Parliament.

Overton's republicanism is brightly manifest in the picture he goes on to paint of religious and political freedom under the rejuvenated and democratic Parliament which will be set up. However, in order to achieve this freedom, the army, "now the only formall and visible Head that is left unto the people," must put into effect what he calls the "Defensive principle of resistance," the prerequisite, that is, to a better world. But *An Appeale* does not conclude with a Shelleyan picture of utopia; rather, it ends with a threat to the New Model. Be firm and faithful, Overton tells the Agitators; beware of your officers, and remember that the people, already irritated by the burdens of maintaining an army, can easily turn against it:

for our affection and concurrence with you is but for our safety and protection, expecting more faire and honest dealing from you then ever we could obtaine from the hands of our false Trustees at Westminster; have a care therefore how you interpose your owne light, and follow their [the Officers'] Ignis fatuis into their delusions and delayes, for if you doe not timely beware, your friends will become your enemies.[55]

Attached to the end of *An Appeale* is a supplement containing "Certaine Articles for the good of the Commonwealth," also addressed to Fairfax and the New Model. These largely duplicate the thirteen proposals of the March Petition, though the differences between it and Overton's supplement indicate the range of his secularized and pragmatic humanism. Thus his four articles "Concerning Parliaments" echo the republicanism of the earlier Leveller petition, but they implement its belief in political decentralization by giving each county full control over the impeachment of its own representatives. Overton further promotes this tendency toward the decentralization of power in his articles on law reform: unnecessary national laws and courts are to be abolished, but the number of purely local courts increased; in addition, mayors, sheriffs, and justices of the peace are to be locally elected. Overton's articles for making law and penology more equitable and more merciful, for the reform of judicial procedures, and for the elimination of monopoly and tithes parallel, though they often implement, the March proposals of himself and his colleagues. But three of the four final points in his supplement are unique among the formal demands of the Levellers during this period. The first of these is inherent in Leveller democratic rationalism: it urges the spread of public education so that "few or none of the free men of England may for the future be ignorant of reading and writing." The second, anticipating Beveridge and Blue Cross, advocates some form of nation-wide hospital plan, supported by a tax on church lands, for the relief and maintenance of "poore . . . aged and impotent persons." The third asks that enclosed land be restored "to the free and common use and benefit of the poore." [56]

An Appeale sets forth Overton's mature political philosophy and his program to implement it. That both are still in the process of being realized is a tribute to the fact that he was farsighted, not a symptom that he was softheaded. Though neither he nor Walwyn published any works which were not the products of collaboration until the summer of 1649, both men continued active in the efforts to secure a radical national settlement. The March Petition, Walwyn's *A Still and Soft Voice*, and Overton's *An Appeale* had supplied the people of England with a program and a philosophy for such a settlement. The next move was up to the army.

From June through September 1647 Lilburne attempted to prod the army into making the proper move by means of a spate of published letters, some addressed directly to Cromwell and Fairfax or to the common soldiers, others working on the army indirectly through open appeals to Henry Marten and the House of Commons.[57] By the middle of August the lot of Lilburne and Overton had, in fact, become one of the more controversial issues not only in the broad dispute between radicals and Independents but within the group of mainly Independent officers who controlled the destiny of the army. Since the reiterated identification of the people's rights with those of Lilburne and Overton had been accepted as valid by a large segment of the New Model rank and file, the leading officers, divided on the problem of a second march on London and aware of the incipient breach between Cromwell and Fairfax, reacted promptly to new accusations from Lilburne that Cromwell had become his chief destroyer.[58]

This reaction first took the form of a suggestion to Lilburne that he petition the House of Lords for release, in which case the officers would then bring pressure to bear to see that his petition was granted. Lilburne's reply, in a public letter to Fairfax, was an indignant refusal.[59] Then early in September, Cromwell, after he had secured the Independent control of Parliament by a display of force, visited Lilburne in the Tower. There Lilburne told him that he would stop his agitation in the army and leave England, "so long as the present troubles lasted," if the House of Lords would only deny the fact that they had any jurisdiction over him.[60] But Cromwell apparently did not concur in this arrangement, for Lilburne continued his vehement appeals to citizens and soldiers, even warning the latter to check up on their Agitators, who, Lilburne implies, have been corrupted by their general officers, particularly Cromwell and Ireton.[61]

Early in October, under Leveller prodding, most of the regiments did select new Agitators.[62] Meanwhile Lilburne had ended his flurry of letter-writing with three additional public letters to Marten, in which he supported the election of new Agitators, repeated a variety of charges against Cromwell, and again proclaimed that the House of Commons was no longer a legal body.[63] As his final effective propaganda thrust of this period, Lilburne published with these letters a lengthy list of all of Cromwell's relatives who held high positions in the army.

During October Lilburne shifted his operational emphasis from letter and press to behind-the-scenes collaboration with the radicals in the army, especially with the newly elected Agitators,[64] though he managed to see that his own predicament continued to receive the limelight of publicity. On October 2 he addressed a proposition to both Houses of Parliament challenging any member of the Lords to a debate on the issue of their jurisdiction over a commoner.[65] On October 20, in *The Grand Plea of Lieut. Col. John Lilburne*, he returned to an appeal to the House of Commons, asking it to preserve the rights of a freeborn Englishman against the arbitrary encroachments of Lords and Grandees.[66] As Overton had done in *An Appeale*, Lilburne here justifies his own and his party's actions by attempting to show that those who have persecuted the Levellers are really the anarchists; that the Lords, and not the new Agitators, are the apostates from tradition and law, as well as the truly dangerous revolutionaries.

A week later, on the day that the Putney Debate began, he followed a similar course in his *Additional Plea*, for he again equates Cromwell, his "now grand adversarie," with the subversive Lords of England. In fact, the Upper House, Lilburne charges, now consists of Cromwell's "white boyes"; and, if the House of Commons is not careful, Oliver, by his "Hocus Pocus dealing," will succeed in subduing its members too.[67]

In his proposition and two pleas it is evident that Lilburne was coördinating his personal propaganda with the combined efforts of the civilian Levellers and the army Agitators. His increasing animosity against Cromwell and the Grandees, as well as his denial that either he or his colleagues are out of step with English traditions, were parts of a broader campaign. The intense partisanship and complex maneuvering aroused by this campaign can be seen in the increased frenzy displayed by the contemporary newspapers of various political shades. *Mercurius Anti-Pragmaticus*, for instance, which reflected the now dominant views of the middle-of-the-road Independents, promptly made Lilburne its symbol of radical destructiveness. Its second issue thus plays on the fears of its London readers:

For John Lilburne hath new designes on foot to split all in pieces, for he is resolved to appeale to all the Commons of England . . . to set them to cutting throats again, and to see what the private souldiers of the Army, the hobnails and clouted shoes will do for him; for this grand incendiary finding not his wishes accomplished, will attempt with Cataline to fire the city about our ears, and to give his undertakings the fairer glosse, he furbisheth them continually with exclamations against the Parliament and the Officers of the Army.[68]

The pro-Royalist *Mercurius Melancholicus,* typical of that segment of the press which was both delighted by any dissension within the antimonarchy ranks and alarmed at the leftist direction in which events seemed to be moving, alternated its praise of the Levellers for attacking Cromwell and the Independents with such items as this ditty on the Agitators:

> No more a beggar under bush.
> No more a lowzie-Varlet,
> The Pedler now shall praunce in Plush
> And Scoundrel march in Scarlet.[69]

The keystone in this broad campaign of the Levellers, as well as a pamphlet which itself generated intense and immediate partisan excitement, was *The Case of the Armie Truly Stated,* for this manifesto both provided the point of departure for the Putney Debate and served as the proximate source of the first Agreement of the People.[70] Though written largely by Wildman, it was essentially the offspring of all the London Levellers — and, to a far lesser degree, of the recently elected Agitators.[71] On October 9, 1647, it was signed by the eleven Agitators who ostensibly wrote it; it appeared in London on October 15; and it was reprinted and circulated throughout the army a day or two after its formal presentation to Fairfax on October 18. These few days also produced a flood of radical-inspired rumors that Cromwell had sold out to Charles; nor was the mutinous atmosphere in the army lessened by Cromwell's elaborate defense of the monarchy at Westminster on October 20.[72]

The Case of the Armie is suffused with Leveller principles, stated and restated in the words and phrases made commonplace by Lilburne, Overton, and Walwyn. It begins by announcing that, "without some more speedy and vigorous actings," nothing is likely to be done for either the soldiers or the "poore oppressed people." The burdens of both groups are then listed in a melange of specific military complaints and generalized proposals for constitutional reform. Lilburne's experienced technique of identifying his own tribulations with those of the kingdom is thus repeated on a larger scale in behalf of the New Model: for instance, the demand that England be made a democratic republic is contiguous to the Agitators' resentment at the fact that certain deserters have received three months' back pay.

Running through *The Case* is the refrain from *A Representation from . . . the Army* of the previous June that "we are not as mere mercenary soldiers, hired to serve an arbitrary power of the State." Accompanying this refrain is the often expressed fear that various sinister forces are trying to disrupt the army by dividing soldier from officer, by casting doubts on the good faith of the Agitators, and by slandering and persecuting those civilian radicals who are the true friends of both common man and common soldier. Moreover, if "the strength and sinewes of the Army be broken," the people will have no effectual instrument of reform; and if no national settlement is soon forthcoming, the continued burden of the army on the people will, of itself, alienate soldier from civilian. Hence, *The Case* continues, it is urgent that the New Model both adhere to the democratic principles of its earlier "Engagements" and speedily implement them.[73] The technique and nature of such implementation then follows. It is almost the complete program of the Levellers, including the various recent additions of Lilburne and Overton; and it is prefaced by a scriptural lament which suggests a naïve version of Walwyn's antinomianism.

The Case's first specific proposal is that a definite and near date be set for the dissolution of Parliament; in the interim, the House of Commons must be forcibly purged. Despite this undemocratic opening, the tract proceeds to incorporate the March Petition as modified by six months of turmoil. A constitutional democracy, including universal manhood suffrage, is insisted upon, and anything which interferes with a system of equal representation, such as "Pattents, Charters, or usurpations by pretended customes," is outlawed. In the field of economics, *The Case* demands that taxes be made more equitable, that a decentralized arrangement for public accounting be set up, that monopolies be curtailed, and that imprisonment for debt be abolished. Typical of the blend of Calvinist morality and secular radicalism which characterizes much of Lilburne's writing is the suggestion that "all those large sums of money that were alowed to needlesse pretended Officers of the Court which did but increase wickedness and phophaneness" be diverted to national defense.

The Case also largely duplicates the earlier Leveller proposals to safeguard religious liberty and the people's judicial rights, but it goes beyond even Lilburne in its demand for simplification of the law: the laws of England are to be reduced to fit into one volume! It repeats Overton's recent plea that enclosed common lands be returned "to the antient publique use and service of the poore." Finally, such reforms as the abolition of tithes and oaths, the guarantee of the right to petition freely, and the mitigation of unjust court and prison procedures are stated in terms almost identical to those in which Walwyn first framed them. In fact, the major differences between the actual articles of the two documents lie in the less logical and compact arrangement of *The Case*, and in its addition of certain clauses which pertain to the misuse of public funds and to military matters. Among these military matters, it advocates that, once the country's government has been settled, England maintain only a small but well-paid army, one that will be "no burthen to the Nation." The last article advanced by Wildman and the Agitators, the result of the rapidly shifting political alignments of the day, is also new: that mercy be shown both financially and politically to a large class of relatively inactive Royalist delinquents.

Fairfax replied to these proposals in a brief note which said that "he thought it meet" they be presented to the General Council of the Army. On October 28, 1647, in an enlarged Council which included representatives from the civilian Levellers, these proposals became the first topic of discussion. *The Case of the Army*, itself the result of active collaboration between Leveller and soldier, was thus the wedge by which Lilburne, Walwyn, and Overton finally entered those councils where national policy was actually determined. For a moment the Levellers stood on the threshold of political power. During that moment at Putney the calendar of English history was, at least theoretically, in a position to skip two centuries.

From Putney to Whitehall:
The Zenith of The Leveller Party

I. November and December 1647: Frustration at Putney

John Wildman, not Lilburne, Overton, or Walwyn, was the leading spokesman for the Levellers in the debate which took place in and near Putney Church during the last days of October and the first days of November 1647. The point of departure for these debates was the controversial *Case of the Armie*, in particular a condensed vresion of it which was presented to Fairfax on October 18 as "Propositions from the Adjutators of five Regiments of Horse." [1] These propositions, which actually constituted the first formal Leveller proposal for an Agreement of the People to set up a new constitution, were then discussed in a small military committee. [2] Now this program was the point at issue in the meeting of the General Council of the Army.

The first day's debate occurred on October 28. It is unnecessary to review in detail this day's proceedings, or those that followed on October 29 and November 1, since these events have been fully treated by Woodhouse and discussed by many other writers. [3] However, certain tendencies which are directly relevant to the writings of the Levellers should be pointed out. Thus on the first day Wildman, who early labeled himself as the "mouth" of the recently elected Agitators, repeatedly stated what was by now the standard radical thesis that reason and the law of nature justified an immediate constitutional revolution inasmuch as the national emergency had returned England to an anarchical condition. Cromwell and Ireton, particularly the latter, countered this doctrine. Cromwell emphasized the impracticability of new and visionary schemes. "How do we know," he asked, "if, whilst we are disputing these things, another company of men shall [not] gather together, and put out a paper as plausible perhaps as this?"[4] And Ireton stressed the immorality, illegality, and chaos incident upon breaking the army's announced commitments to Parliament and king. Hence the underlying issue seemed to be whether the Civil War would result in a radical revolution or in only a gradual shift within the traditional balance of political and economic power. Ireton's emphasis on the army's prior engagements was therefore a sign of his and Cromwell's relative conservatism on this issue. Indeed, Ireton said, to break a covenant or to fall back on a vague law of nature is not only to call all contracts in question, but, what is more important, such bad faith invalidates all law, all property rights.

It is, however, an oversimplification to think of Cromwell and Ireton as conservatives in nineteenth-century terms, or of the Levellers as liberals or radicals. Cromwell was no Disraeli; Lilburne no Cobden. In one sense, in fact, Cromwell was far more radical than the Levellers in that, despite his many rationalizations and reluctances, he ended by supplanting traditional institutions with military expedients; whereas the Levellers persistently advocated the establishment of a democratic Parliament that would be in accord with their own reading of English history and which would, they hoped, develop into the normal constitutional channel for English progress. The settlements of 1660 and 1689, and the reforms of the nineteenth century, indicate that the Levellers were more "conservative" in the literal sense that their projection of history was more accurate than Cromwell's. None the less, in terms of the late 1640's, the Levellers were the radicals, the Grandees the middle-of-the-roaders. First, because that is how both groups, in spite of occasional statements to the contrary, viewed themselves. Second, because that is how their contemporaries viewed them: the wealthy, the press, the legal and business interests in general preferred the Independents to the Levellers; the dispossessed, the persecuted, the visionaries, if and when they made the choice, tended to line up with the Levellers. Since, of course, "liberal" and "conservative" are relative terms — the states'-righter being the radical of one generation and the reactionary of the next — it is probably best to accept each age's pragmatic definition of these terms. Consequently, despite the events of the 1650's or the 1950's, the Levellers at Putney carried the banner of radicalism, while Cromwell and Ireton manned the barricades of conservatism. And in 1647 the split between radical and middle-of-the-roader, between disgruntled soldier and worried general, between optimistic idealist and practical policy-maker, precluded any satisfactory compromise.

The evidence for this split was obvious not only in the arguments advanced by both sides, but in the noticeable difference in their political vocabularies: whereas Ireton often fell back on the phraseology of contract law; the sweeping affirmative slogans made familiar by Lilburne, Overton, and Walwyn were now the commonplaces of the radicals. Colonel Rainsborough, probably the most effective and certainly the most dramatic of the Leveller speakers, often echoed the words of such a work as Overton's *Remonstrance*, as did the less literate Agitators. At the same time, Leveller secularism, if in slightly disguised form, was also evident. During the first day of debate, when one of Cromwell's colonels suggested a prayer meeting, both Wildman and an ally of his implied that to call on God at this time was more in the nature of a tactical filibuster than a sincere search for divine guidance, that the business in hand was not prayer but a vital political debate.[5]

Manifestations of this cleavage within the General Council of the Army also appeared outside the walls of Putney Church. On the first day of debate at least two letters which denied that the Agitators were acting divisively were circulated among the soldiers.[6] On the next day a pamphlet, almost certainly by Wildman, exhorted the army to stand firm for democracy.[7] Warning the rank and file not to be misled by such masters of deception as Cromwell and Ireton, it explicitly urges the soldiers not to be frightened by the word "Anarchy" into supporting the monarchy or denying their true friends the Levellers. Wildman concludes his exhortation with the plea that the New Model, "the instrument of God," adhere to its democratic principles, even, if necessary, to the extent of choosing new officers and establishing a more responsive General Council.

The second day of debate, on October 29, served to confirm Wild-man's fear that the present Council would not prove pliant to the demands of the Levellers.

The discussion of this day was more explicit, for it centered on what is probably the shortest formal national constitution on record. This constitution, a still further condensation of those underlying propositions brought together in *The Case of the Armie*, was entitled *An Agreement of the People for a firme Peace*.[8] There is no positive evidence to prove that Lilburne, Overton, or Walwyn had a hand in this document, and it is so worded that it appears to be by the Agitators newly elected by five regiments. Nevertheless it is extremely probable that the three leading civilian Levellers were, along with Wildman, responsible for this ostensibly practicable but essentially visionary set of proposals:[9] *An Agreement* represents not only the culmination of the first major bid by the Levellers to super-impose their scheme on the nation, but it is a condensation of those ideas which they had developed in the course of three years of political maturation.

The preamble to *An Agreement* indirectly sums up the vicissi-tudes suffered by the radicals in their growth toward a cohesive party, and it gives voice to the optimistic and democratic rationalism which had become fundamental to their social philosophy. An in-telligent people, operating through a responsive body of representa-tives, could, the Levellers thought, be at once the product of and the answer to a destructive civil war. Consequently the opening state-ment of the preamble looks both forward and backward in time:

Having by our late labours and hazards made it appear to the world at how high a rate we value our just freedoms, and God having so far owned our cause as to deliver the enemies thereof into our hands, we do now hold ourselves bound in mutual duty to each other to take the best care we can for the future to avoid both the danger of returning into a slavish condition and the chargeable remedy of another war; for, as it cannot be imagined that so many of our countrymen would have opposed us in this quarrel if they had understood their own good, so may we safely promise to ourselves that, when our common rights and liberties shall be cleared, their endeavours will be disappointed that seek to make themselves our masters. Since, therefore, our former oppressions and scarce-yet-ended troubles have been occasioned either by want of frequent national meetings in Council, or by rendering those meetings ineffectual, we are fully agreed and resolved to provide that hereafter our representatives be neither left to an uncertainty for the time nor made useless to the ends for which they are intended.[10]

To implement this large aim the Levellers set up four key proposals: first, that a more democratic system of representation be established; second, that the present obstructive Parliament be dissolved within a year; third, that future Parliaments be biennial; and fourth, that the people reserve to themselves certain inalienable rights. These rights, which reflect the Levellers' suspicions of any type of arbitrary government, prohibit Parliament from interfering with freedom of conscience,[11] from impressing citizens for military service, and from prosecuting anyone for his part in the Civil War (such prosecutions presumably having been taken care of by the present Parliament.) Further, *An Agreement* concludes, all people are to be equal before the law, and, "as the laws ought to be equal, so they must be good, and not evidently destructive to the safety and well-being of the people." The final paragraph then declares that all the foregoing rights are "native," and that the peace and freedom which are inherent in them ought to eventuate from "a cruel war" as the only alternative to the continued national indecision, bloodshed, and tyranny.

The debate on October 29 quickly turned to this *Agreement*, particularly to its first article, the demand for equal and, by implication, universal suffrage.[12] This demand for political equality rather than the problem of religious liberty was now at the heart of the dispute between Leveller and Independent. Since the former intended that the *Agreement* be accepted by the people, who were actually to assent to this new and explicit social contract by affixing their names to it, and since much of the subsequent discussion of freedom of conscience veered from spiritual consequences to an analysis of the political jurisdiction of the magistrate, the fulcrum of debate was literally whether or not the people, as a whole, were to be their own rulers. Rainsborough, in a much quoted sentence, tersely put the radical case:

For really I think that the poorest he that is in England hath a life to live as the greatest he; and therefore truly, sir, I think it is clear that every man that is to live under a government ought first by his own consent to put himself under that government.[13]

Ireton immediately replied:

I think that no person hath a right to an interest or share in the disposing of the affairs of the kingdom, and in determining or choosing those that shall determine what laws we shall be ruled by — no person hath a right to this that hath not a permanent fixed interest in this kingdom, and those persons together are properly the represented of this kingdom, and consequently are to make up the representers of this kingdom.[14]

Such a "permanent fixed interest," Ireton went on, lies only in the possession of land or of a certain income: "All the main things that I speak for is because I would have an eye to property." [15]

Against this argument Rainsborough appealed to the dictates of human reason and to the laws of God and nature. Wildman backed him up by saying that the history of England had been a record of the slavery of her people, while Sexby, citing Ireton, claimed that the army had not served as "mere mercenary soldiers," but as men who were battling for their proper birthright: not for property, but for their "privileges as Englishmen." [16] The intense tone which characterized the speakers on both sides was heightened by the dramatic threat on Cromwell's part to withdraw from public affairs, by the vehement charge and equally vehement denial that the radicals were preaching anarchy, and by several covert allusions by Ireton to the divisive and dangerous activities of the civilian Levellers. The mutual respect of the opposing sides for each other and the sense of urgency behind every speech were not great enough, however, to narrow the breach between those who wished essentially to preserve the traditional balance of power and those who wished to establish a democratic republic in England.

On the next day, therefore, a committee of officers and Agitators, not including Wildman, attempted to reconcile *An Agreement* with the army's previous engagements.[17] Largely avoiding the central issue of the day before, this group, under the dominance of Cromwell and Ireton, achieved a temporary compromise. It agreed to the dissolution of the Long Parliament and to the establishment of future biennial parliaments, but on the question of the franchise the committee merely resolved that

the election of Members for the House of Commons . . . shall be . . . according to some rule of equality of proportion, soe as to render the House of Commons as neere as may bee an equall representative of the whole body of the people that are to elect.[18]

To the Levellers was conceded the principle that all those who had assisted the side of Parliament in the wars should be allowed to vote. In return for this concession the radicals presumably agreed to permit the erection of a Council of State as envisioned in *The Heads of the Proposals*, and, as later committee meetings indicated, to impose any new constitutional scheme only by an understanding between army, king, and Parliament.[19] Cromwell's power and Ireton's skill in debate were thus winning the battle against Rainsborough's oratory and the visionary plans of the Levellers.

The third day of full debate was in a sense anticlimactic. After an effective statement by Cromwell that the New Model depended for its being solely on the authority of Parliament, the discussion turned to the problem, left almost untouched by the preceding day's committee meeting, of the future of the king and House of Lords. Wildman not only castigated the Lords, but at one point demanded the death of Charles — a proposal which received no recorded second. From Clarke's somewhat garbled reporting of the discussion it seems evident that a property qualification of £20 a year was temporarily agreed on as the minimum necessary to qualify a man to be elected to Parliament;[20] otherwise the problem of the franchise continued to be glossed over. But recurrent in this final day of debate was the issue of practicability, of the public safety. Near the end of that long Monday afternoon, when Wildman was attempting to bring the argument back to *An Agreement*, Ireton begged the radicals that,

unless they will produce some kind of evidence of history upon record by law . . . they will forbear arguments of that nature [in particular, the Leveller glorification of a democratic Anglo-Saxon past] . . . and rather insist upon things of common safety.[21]

And Wildman, a few moments later, audibly wished that the argument would return to "principles and maxims of just government." Apparently then as now practicability and principle seemed irreconcilable.

During the following week the committee of officers and Agitators again attempted to bring the conflicting parties closer together.[22] But after certain ostensible concessions to the Levellers had been made, after much discussion of the franchise and of how best to establish any new constitution had proved fruitless, and after the debate on what to do about Charles had grown dangerously hot, Cromwell, increasingly aware of the breakdown of discipline taking place in the New Model, on November 8 purged the committee of its more radical elements.[23] At a rendezvous of part of the army on November 15, notwithstanding the exhortations of Rainsborough to the soldiers to defy their commanders and to stand by *An Agreement of the People*, Cromwell was able to assert the full weight of his military authority. Four days later, when the few scattered attempts at resistance had been quelled, the New Model formally agreed to obey its proper leaders, and on that same day Cromwell received the official thanks of the House of Commons for the services he had just rendered.[24] Thus the Putney Debate ended in a brief flurry of mutiny, then in the apparent restoration of harmony in the army — after much talk of democracy, military discipline again held full sway.[25]

The civilian Levellers had fought against this contingency. On November 1 Cromwell and Fairfax were presented with a petition from Hertfordshire which backed up the demands of the Agitators.[26] Appended to *An Agreement* in circulation of November 3 were two letters from the more radical Agitators which implored citizen and soldier to follow the lead of the Levellers in establishing a just peace, and to signify their opposition to anarchy, communism, and tyranny by signing the *Agreement*.[27] Thus by means of their now widely publicized *Agreement*, the Levellers were again using the device of the petition to its fullest extent: in this case as an attempt at constitutional revolution by an informal and extragovernmental plebiscite.[28]

Lilburne during this period was holding almost daily meetings with certain of the Agitators, and he probably was in regular contact with Walwyn and Overton.[29] By mid-November Wildman, too, was back in London helping to organize a concerted campaign against the leaders of the army and against both Houses of Parliament.[30] On November 23 Lilburne sent forth his inaptly titled *A new complaint of an old grievance* — new only in its more concentrated personal bitterness.[31] The hand of Walwyn is evident in an event of the same day: the presentation to Parliament of a petition asking that body to limit its own powers by ratifying *An Agreement of the People*.[32] But this was more than an ironic gesture: during the three weeks before the presentation of this petition, the party organization of the Levellers, which had grown up mainly to further the Large Petition of March 1647, had again expanded its activities, particularly in regard to circulating *An Agreement of the People* for signature; and by the end of November "many thousands" had signed it. In all probability it was Walwyn who was again the chief architect of this campaign of democratic pressure.

Among Walwyn's assistants were three men who continued to be active in the Leveller party: Samuel Chidley, who had known Lilburne since the late 1630's; William Larner, who had been associated with the publication of Lilburne's earliest tracts; and Thomas Prince, a successful London cheese merchant.[33] The nature of their campaign was largely determined by Cromwell's reassumption of a tight control over the army, for the New Model was thus at least temporarily eliminated as a propitious ground for Leveller activity. Moreover, on November 9 Parliament had voted, without debate, that *An Agreement* was not worthy of discussion.[34] This action served again to underline the oft-repeated Leveller contention that neither House could serve as the means of implementing their radical program; hence it was once more directly to the people, who could be activated by the device of the petition, that Walwyn and his allies turned. Asking the House of Commons to back their *Agreement* was only part of that Leveller publicity campaign by which the people were to be aroused into demanding the democratic republic for which Wildman and Rainsborough had pleaded at Putney. So it was that on November 23, 1647, five of the more respectable Levellers, including Chidley, Larner, and Prince, presented the above petition to Parliament and were promptly jailed.[35]

Two days later a second petition was presented to the House of Commons.[36] Its first half, the concise phraseology and moderate tone of which suggest the authorship of Walwyn, declares that the army has failed the people because its leaders have prevented the New Model from implementing the popular will. Then, after denying that the Levellers have either plotted to murder the king or "to levell all mens estates, and subvert all government," the petition asks Parliament to back *An Agreement* in order that the people of England "may expect the blessing of peace and prosperity." The stylistic impetuosity of the second half of this document indicates the work of Lilburne. In the main, it is a blunt attack on Parliament. The House of Commons is reviled because it has represented the Leveller Petition of November 23 "as contempt of them [Parliament] when they [the petitioners] rendered them the highest honour"; and, the author continues, in a passage that is still painfully relevant, "observe their iniustice in committing these your brethren without laying any crime to their charge; by the law, sedition nor faction is no crime, for no man knows what is sedition or faction." [37]

During December the Levellers, in addition to continuing their build-up of an effective party organization, opened a new line of propaganda: an explicit assault on the Grandees' restoration of discipline in the New Model by means of martial law and courts martial. Early in the month Lilburne started to write *A Defiance to Tyrants*, one of the many items he reprinted in *The peoples Prerogative and Priviledges* in February 1648.[38] The *Defiance*, in defending the London Levellers against arbitrary arrest, profusely and with a maximum of legalistic substructure reiterates Lilburne's long-held belief that any law which does not conform to the basic law of the land is tyrannical, and, on moral, legal, and rational grounds, to be resisted. Even before this, at the end of November, someone (probably Lilburne) wrote a tract known as the "Plea for the Late Agents." [39] This tract contends that the army has not really been subject to martial law since its Engagement of June 1647, whereby the soldiers voluntarily agreed not to disband until their grievances had been met; consequently, the New Model remains an aggregation of free men, not a "mere mercenary Army." Further, the "Plea" continues, the organization of such a body as the General Council of the Army was itself proof that this has been no ordinary army subject to ordinary military laws. The new Leveller attempt to override Cromwell's discipline is already explicit in the final statement of the "Plea": "all Agents and soldiers now accused of mutiny . . . shall unworthily betray their owne and their Countryes Liberty if they shall submit to be tryed in any other way then by the knowne Lawes and statutes of the Land." [40]

In mid-December *Englands Freedome, Souldiers Rights* appeared, a pamphlet which, though signed by William Thompson, was also almost certainly by John Lilburne.[41] To the reasons advanced against martial law in the earlier plea, this tract adds two points: now a soldier is illegally subject to the double jeopardy of civil and military law; and Parliament cannot delegate its law-making or judicial functions to any group of military leaders. The pamphlet also enlarges on the argument mentioned in the "Plea" that, since the country is now at peace, such arbitrary and emergency procedures as martial law and courts martial should be abrogated.

Then at the very end of December, when Charles's overtures to the Scots were finally alienating Cromwell and the Independents from almost any support of the monarchy, Wildman published his *Putney Projects. Or the Old Serpent In a new Forme.*[42] Ironically, much of this pamphlet is a diatribe against Cromwell and Ireton for adhering to that king whom they were in the very process of deserting. In vehement language, interlarded with frequent displays of Biblical, classical, and legal learning, Wildman cleverly lays bare what he considers the dishonest and unpatriotic aims and techniques of the army leaders, particularly those evidenced between June and December 1647. *Putney Projects* is thus a manipulated disrobing of the Grandees, an attempt to "spread abroad the cloak of their promises, wherewith they have covered themselves . . . [and] to present them naked in their actions." [43]

With this intention Wildman first skillfully builds up the characters of those "pretended patriots" Ireton and Cromwell, men who, he says, seemed to disdain all private interests. Then, with a deft mixture of fact and alarmist speculation, he goes on to detail their various negotiations with the king, including the charge that Ireton was working for and with Charles during the Putney Debate. From here Wildman moves to a scathing attack not only on Charles but on the institution of the monarchy, as well as on those largely hereditary and anachronistic bodies — such as the House of

Lords or the tithe-supported clergy or the associations of obscurantist lawyers — which support the throne. "O my once honoured Cromwell," Wildman asks rhetorically,

can that breast of yours, which was the quondam royall pallace of principles of freedome and justice, can that breast harbour such a monster of wickednesse as this regall principle? can you . . . plead for a pattent for the King to make a Monopoly of injustice? [44]

Next, in depicting Cromwell's apostasy, Wildman, with all the vigor of Overton, performs the most thorough anatomization of the evils inherent in the kingship yet to come from any Leveller pen. Though he adds nothing new to Leveller political theory, Wildman marshals the arguments which all the Parliamentary parties, but especially those on the left, had developed against Charles since 1640. By portraying Cromwell and Ireton as the willing dupes of the throne, Wildman, however, gives to these arguments a more revolutionary twist than ever Prynne had dreamed of in his philosophy.

Continuing to use the device of the loaded rhetorical question, Wildman devotes the final pages of *Putney Projects* to asking Cromwell, Ireton, and their adherents whether or not they realize the true nature of that slavery which they are trying so hard to introduce, and the inevitable dangers consequent on the reëstablishment of any sort of arbitrary government, particularly a monarchy; whether or not they are aware of their own dishonesty and the falseness of their earlier promises; and whether or not they honestly acknowledge the ultimate political fact that all just human power resides in the people. Wildman's climactic final sentence then proclaims the growing sense of urgency felt by the Levellers — a sense of urgency which, though almost always present in their writings, had since Putney become more strident:

O then suffer not your Representors in Parliament to sit any longer like so many Plovers pricked down for stales, . . . free them from all contradictions and obstructions . . . in succouring and relieving you: if they be negligent, joyne together speedily, vigorously, with courage and resolution, and cry to them, cry aloud . . . Let us not be consumed by delayes, Let us either be saved or perish.[45]

Ten weeks earlier the Levellers had held high hopes of being the intellectual leaders of a strong and just and democratic army and of helping to set up a truly republican constitution in England. Now, however, the process of disillusion had set in. Consequently, they turned again directly to the people, for "the people," because it was undefined and for all practical purposes politically weak and incoherent, was a body which could not explicitly denounce its self-appointed saviours. Lilburne's continued complaints, the petitionary activities of Walwyn, the concerted attack on martial law, and Wildman's bitter review of recent events were all parts of a campaign to enlist the people in a powerful and cohesive political movement. Once this movement was under way, the Leveller party, now on the threshold of its organizational maturity, would, its leaders hoped, continue to be the driving and directing force of this massive forward march.

II. January to March 1648: The Organization of the Party

The person most conspicuous in the mobilization of the Levellers as a national political party was John Lilburne; next in importance was John Wildman, and in the background the guiding hand of William Walwyn often seems evident. In the early months of 1648 the Levellers achieved their highest point of party organization, in many ways a surprisingly modern and democratic apparatus for political action. This apparatus was obviously founded on the Levellers' fundamental beliefs, but its operation was improved by the lessons they had learned since Putney.

Since the autumn of 1647 Lilburne had been allowed a measure of freedom from the Tower. With the other civilian Levellers he had actively backed the Agitators at Putney, had helped to inspire the attacks on the Grandees, and by a variety of means had supported an Agreement of the People. In addition, by the beginning of 1648 the Levellers were busily getting ready to promote a new mass petition that would supplement and partially replace *An Agreement of the People* of the previous November.[46] It was specifically in support of this newer document that they now directed their organizational efforts, though, again, this abortive petition was merely part of a larger program of constitutional reform and of a wider struggle for political power.

Thus, on January 17, 1648, at a private house in the Smithfield district of London, the civilian Levellers held one of several organizational meetings. This meeting is of particular importance because it was attended by one George Masterson, a disciple of Thomas Edwards and a rabid opponent of the radicals, who immediately sent in a full report of it to Parliament. This report at once became the grounds for further prosecution of Lilburne — and now of Wildman, both of whom replied voluminously to its charges. A month later, Walter Frost, the secretary of the Parliamentary Committee of Both Houses, summarized the meeting and the charges resulting from it in a full and government-sponsored pamphlet, a pamphlet to which, again, both Lilburne and Wildman responded.[47] All this ample documentation not only supplies a detailed picture of the Leveller party at work, but it presents that picture from two widely divergent angles. The result, particularly in those areas in which all the reports essentially agree, is a reliable and relatively intimate portrait of a growing party organization.

The first step necessary to such growth was organizational meetings. Here, then, is Masterson paraphrasing Lilburne, the chairman and chief speaker at the Smithfield gathering:

[The leading Levellers] had their constant meetings on Mondays, Wednesdays, and Fridays in the evening at the Whalebone; and the other three days at Southwark, Wapping, and other places, with their friends; and . . . upon the next Lords day they were to meet at Dartford in Kent, to receive an account of their Agents (from Gravesend, Maidstone, and most of the choice townes in that County) how they promoted the business there.[48]

These agents were mainly the self-appointed men most active among the civilian Levellers, and one of their chief functions was to enlist other sympathizers to aid in spreading their gospel to the entire country. Particularly after their failure with the New Model, the leaders of the Leveller party felt the need to "send out Agents into every City, Town, and Parish (if they could possibly) of every County of the Kingdome, to inform the people of their Liberties and Priviledges." [49]

As in the past, the chief means of thus informing and arousing the people was the mass petition. Masterson's report strongly emphasizes the use of this device as a revolutionary tactic; Lilburne and Wildman stress its informative role and traditional legality; and all three men agree that it was central to Leveller strategy.[50] But holding meetings, securing agents, and printing and circulating public petitions all required money. Again Masterson quotes Lilburne:

because the business must needs be a work of charge (there being thirty thousand Petitions to come forth in print to morrow,[51] and it would cost money to send their Agents abroad, though the honest souldiers now at White Hall would save them something in scattering them up and down in the Counties),[52] they had therefore appointed Treasurers, namely Mr. Prince, Mr. Chidley, and others, and Collectors . . . who should gather up from those that acted with them, of some two pence, three pence, six pence, a shilling, two shillings, half a crown a week.[53]

London was the hub of the Levellers' activities, the rest of the country their orbit. That their organization was now financially and structurally ready to take decisive political action on a national scale is indicated by the prefatory remarks which Lilburne, Wildman, and two of their colleagues addressed to the people of Kent in a public letter dated January 9, 1648 — one of several similar letters:

There is a Method and Order setled in all the Wards in London, and the out Parishes and Suburbs; they have appointed severall active men in every Ward and Division to be a Committee to take the speciall care of the businesse, and to appoint active men in every Parish to read the Petition at set meetings for that purpose, and to take Subscriptions, and to move as many as can possibly to goe in person when the day of delivering it shall be appointed; and they intend to give notice of that time to all the adjacent Counties, that as many of them as possibly can may also joyne with them the same day.[54]

Among the counties then listed are Hertfordshire, Buckinghamshire, Oxford, and Cambridge; and each county is urged to follow the same organizational procedure as that of the London branch of the party. The divisions within each county are further urged to

select faithfull men of publick spirits to take care that the Petition be sent to the hands of the most active men in every Town to unite the Town in those desires of common right, and to take their subscriptions.[55]

To complete the picture, the Levellers also planned a series of re-
gional meetings; for example, the "well-affected" in Kent are invited
to assemble at Dartford in mid-January, and to bring along as many
potential allies as they can find.

The complexity and scope of such a party organization was the
result of the Levellers' year-long experience with the mass petition
and of the intensification of their propaganda activities since mid-
November 1647, when they had begun rapidly to expand the civilian
functions of the party.[56] Now, in January 1648, when the king was
openly dealing with the Scots, the possibility of renewed civil war
increased the pressure for some sort of quick national settlement.[57]
The Levellers' prompt response to this new opportunity was both
the development of a widespread organization and the modifica-
tion of their program along lines designed to save it from the defeat
it had suffered at Putney. The same pamphlets which depict the
expanded party set-up of the Levellers also make clear this somewhat altered program.

The central document of this modified program was the petition
to which the party workers were to secure signatures, and which
was to be presented to Parliament sometime at the end of January
by a large number of delegates.[58] The differences between this
petition and *An Agreement of the People* are striking. The petition is considerably longer and it is underpinned by citations from
an imposing variety of documents; its tone is angrier, less hopeful,
than that of November 1647; and its emphasis on economic grievances partially replaces the stress on constitutional reform of the
earlier program. Lacking both the compactness and order of *An
Agreement*, the January Petition seems largely the work of an
increasingly embittered Lilburne. The last paragraph of the preamble, for instance, thus sets the tone for the sixteen proposals
which follow it:

That though our Petitions have been burned, and our persons imprisoned, reviled, and abused only for petitioning, yet we cannot despair
absolutely of all bowels of compassion in this Honourable house [of
Commons] to an inslaved perishing people. We still nourish some hopes
that you wil at last consider that our estates are expended, the whole
trade of the Nation decayed, thousands of families impoverished, and
merciless Famine is entered into our Gates, and therefore we cannot

but once more assay to pierce your eares with our dolefull cries for Justice and Freedom, before your delays wholly consume the Nation.[59]

The first two articles then request the House of Commons to declare themselves the "Supream power," and to make it clear in the process whether they are the servants of the people or self-appointed tyrants. Obviously, the number of names which the Levellers hoped to secure in support of this petition was intended to influence Parliament's answer. However, instead of proceeding to outline a political program, the petition shifts, in article three, to the problem of judicial reform: the jurisdiction of each court is to be clearly demarcated; all unnecessary courts are to be abolished; Parliament is not to usurp judicial functions; and that reminder of "Slavery to a Norman Conqueror," law French, is to be replaced by simple English in all laws and statutes. In addition, the Leveller belief that power corrupts — a belief now still further reinforced by their recent experiences with those in power — is evident in the provisos that no judge be allowed to hold office for more than three years, and that any alleged criminal be given a prompt trial at which he be either condemned or acquitted.

Thence the petition moves to the correction of economic grievances. Monopolies are to be prohibited, and a system of local and national accounting is proposed whereby each month the public can be informed of government receipts and expenditures. The excise is also attacked as a burden to the poor and a handicap to trade. As a substitute for it the Levellers advocate a form of proportional taxation, and they accompany this suggestion with a plea that the wages of those who perform common labor be raised.[60]

The only major proposal which corresponds closely to the constitutional aims of *An Agreement* is the demand for universal suffrage and for a more equal arrangement of electoral districts. With this, the Levellers again urge their system of rotation in office, now with the provision that no local official concerned with the administration of justice, except for judges, be allowed to serve more than a year. Essentially political, too, are the petition's seventh and twelfth proposals: that bribery and barratry be declared capital offenses; and that all oaths, including any of those which interfere with liberty of conscience, be annulled.

But the two final planks of this petition are particularly indicative of a shift in Leveller strategy and emphasis. One asks that all who have suffered at the hands of Parliament, either before or since the start of the Civil War, receive full reparation: among the names of those who have so suffered, that of John Lilburne follows those of Bastwick and Prynne! Underlining this implicit bid for a new popular front against the Grandees is the final proposition, an involved arrangement whereby the temporary Independent majority in Parliament might be circumvented.

The attempt to unite those forces hostile to or disappointed with the leadership of Cromwell and the Independents is further clarified by the omissions in this petition. The power of the people directly to impose constitutional change is ignored, the power of a responsive House of Commons stressed. Freedom of conscience is touched on only lightly, and there is no mention of tithes or of any restrictions to be imposed on a tolerant established church. One can therefore view this document as a calculated rallying point for any liberal faction in the Presbyterian group, for lukewarm Royalists, for those Independents disgruntled with Cromwell's shifts, for those whom the unprosperous war years were pushing into political activity, and, of course, for the radicals both in and out of the New Model. Coupled with the maturity of the Leveller organization, the somewhat amorphous nature of this petition made it seem, in the disturbed context of early 1648, particularly dangerous to those men who were getting ready to fight a second civil war.[61]

This attempt of the Levellers to broaden their appeal is also exemplified in a strangely naïve pamphlet which they circulated near the end of January, *The mournfull Cryes of many thousand poor Tradesmen, who are ready to famish through decay of Trade*.[62] Probably written by some new adherent to the cause, it is a repetitious and breast-beating lament, in which the cries of starving widows and orphans are counterpointed by the clinking of the gold of nefarious embezzlers, and in which frequent appeals for the adoption of the January Petition are haphazardly interspersed. Though it probably won the Levellers few new allies, it might well have added to the threat which the army leaders and Parliament saw in this fresh burst of agitation and activity.

Parliament met this threat directly. Two days after the Smithfield meeting, on January 19, 1648, Lilburne was called to the bar of the House of Commons; the following day he was recommitted to the Tower, this time as a close prisoner; and Wildman was sentenced to an indefinite stay in the Fleet.[63] At this time, too, most of the activities in behalf of the January Petition came to an end, for it soon ceased to be central to the Leveller program. However, the Smithfield meeting had involved more than the promotion of this petition, and it was partly against these other aspects of Leveller agitation that Parliament was also stimulated to react directly and vigorously.

Besides reporting on Leveller methods and strategy, Masterson had informed his employers in the House of Commons of certain speeches made at Smithfield — speeches which were undoubtedly typical of other Leveller exhortations of this period. Lilburne, closely followed by Wildman, was, Masterson stated, the chief offender; and it was Lilburne who played up the revolutionary aims of his group. "We must," Masterson quoted Lilburne as saying,

own some visible Authority for the present, or else we shall be brought to Ruine and Confusion: but when we have raised up the spirits of the people through the whole Kingdome (whether it be nine dayes hence, or a moneth, or three moneths, when the House shall be fit to receive an Impression of Justice) We shall force them to grant us those things we desire.[64]

When, according to Masterson, one of Lilburne's listeners then questioned him about the dangers of future violence, Lilburne replied, "He that hath this Petition in his hand, and a Blue Ribband in his Hat, need not fear his throat cutting." Lilburne, continued Masterson, next went on to tell of an agreement between Cromwell and the king whereby Cromwell had been successfully bribed to turn traitor by the offer of an earldom. To confirm this story Lilburne alleged that he could prove that a member of Parliament had sworn to murder Cromwell, a story which Wildman corroborated by stating that he knew of three other men who had independently arrived at the same resolution.[65] Finally, still according to Masterson, Lilburne and Wildman contrasted the worth of their petition to the wickedness of their opponents by declaring that certain Lords had offered them a large bribe (£30,000) and some political concessions if they would only cease their efforts in behalf of constitutional reform.[66]

Thus when Lilburne and Wildman were called before Parliament they faced a heavy barrage of charges. Nor was the case against the Levellers mitigated by the fact that there were mass meetings held to protest Lilburne's rearrest, and that there was a small riot at Parliament's door provoked by Lilburne's so persuasively pleading his innocence to the soldiers guarding him that a new detachment had to be sent for.[67] Ironically, then, one of the immediate results of such Leveller meetings as the one at Smithfield was to add to the turbulence accompanying the break between the king and Cromwell.

The first significant literary offspring of these meetings was a pamphlet by Wildman which appeared on or about February 1, 1648, *Truths Triumph, Or Treachery Anatomized*. Largely devoted to his testimony before the House concerning the Smithfield meeting and his subsequent arrest, this tract also attempts to depict Wildman's views in a broad and relatively traditional manner. Thus he emphasizes the urgent need for national unity in order to reëstablish justice and freedom. (It is in this connection that he mentions that certain items were deliberately omitted from the January Petition to avoid further "distractions.") Thence he shifts to proving that his own arrest has been arbitrary and illegal. But his words and his argument remain conciliatory, and it is with a great deal of expert legal documentation that he makes his own case a plea against any misuse by Parliament of its power to make law, against any ex post facto judgments, and against any unwarranted extension of the House's limited judicial functions. Consequently he can devote the remainder of his pamphlet to demonstrating the nontreasonable, nondivisive nature of the Leveller petition, and the traditional, legal, and moral right of the people freely to petition their chosen representatives.

The moderate tone of *Truths triumph* is interrupted several times, however, by pointed slurs against Masterson. When, therefore, on February 10, Masterson issued his *The Triumph stain'd*, much of it was a direct reply to Wildman's tract. In addition to reprinting his own report of the Smithfield meeting, Masterson derogates the honor and trustworthiness of the Leveller leaders, reiterates his alarm at their incendiarism, and ends with the advice to Wildman that he return to the safe and comfortable bosom of true Presbyterianism.

Four days later a far more formidable tract took the Levellers to task. This was *A Declaration of Some Proceedings*, written by Walter Frost, but probably with the help of some of his fellow members of the Parliamentary Committee of Both Houses. Inasmuch as *A Declaration* is one of the few point-by-point answers to a major Leveller scheme, and since Frost's attitude is neither reactionary nor irrationally alarmist, his pamphlet warrants analysis as one of the more convincing refutations of Leveller practices and program.

Frost begins with a brief antimonarchical examination of the causes of the Civil War. From there he moves to an attack on the Levellers by showing how their subversive tactics and "Anarchicall levelling" have played into the hands of Charles.[68] Parliament cannot tolerate such attempts to undermine its authority and defeat its war aims; and, in particular, it cannot tolerate the activities of the presumptuous John Lilburne, notably his contemptuous dealings with both Houses of Parliament. For corroboration of these assertions Frost then reprints Masterson's report, the Leveller letter to Kent, and the January Petition.

The polemical core of *A Declaration* is its analysis of this petition. First, says Frost, it is "nothing else but a Calumnie against those they seem to petition," an attempt "to render Parliament odious to the People." Moreover, he continues, it fails to "descend . . . to particulars"; and it fails to recognize Parliament's right "to repeale, as well as to make Lawes," a right which, in turn, refutes the Leveller claim that Parliament must be bound by "precedent Lawes." Before turning to his scrutiny of the sixteen proposals of the Leveller petition, Frost concludes his over-all attack on the radical program with a statement that effectively points up the problem of where political power actually resides:

a Petition may well deserve to be burned and the Petitioners punished, if the matter be unjust, false, scandalous, seditious. . . . 'Tis true, it is your liberty to Petition, and it is also your duty to acquiesce in the Parliaments jugement upon it; a Petition is to set forth your grievances, and not to give a rule to the Legislative Power; if you mean it shall be an Edict, which you must compose, and the Parliament must verifie, call it no more a Petition.[69]

Many of Frost's answers to the specific planks of the January Petition which follow his broad analysis are a mixture of quibbling and recrimination. Throughout he is less pessimistic than the Levellers about the plight of England; and he recurrently falls back on the theory that any further major political changes would be impracticable. The echo of Ireton's speeches at Putney can, in fact, be distinctly heard in *A Declaration*. But three of Frost's explicit rejoinders to the Leveller platform are significant in the light they cast on middle-of-the-road thinking shortly before the start of the Second Civil War. First, also reflecting the suspicion long held by the Levellers that political power is corrupting, Frost supports the House of Lords as a check or balance against the House of Commons.[70] Second, he defends Parliament's right to arrest those whom the good of the Commonwealth — the traditional *salus populi* — requires to be restrained. And third, he countenances excise taxes as a spur to frugality and as a stimulus to a more moral way of life. Like Masterson, Frost then winds up his generally effective counterattack with the suggestion that the Leveller leaders mind their own business until they have better learned the "art of Statizing," leaving "the publique affairs to those to whom God and the Kingdome hath committed them."

The next tract from Lilburne's pen, *The peoples Prerogative and Priviledges*, which appeared a few days after *A Declaration*, is not an answer to Frost. Instead, it is a hodgepodge of documents, petitions, pleas, and interjections, with only a smattering of asides in behalf of the charges and aims of the January Petition.[71] Its only importance lies, therefore, in that it represented an attempt to make certain declarations and statutes which the Levellers considered charters of English liberty readily available to their followers — though it also bears witness to Lilburne's propensity for getting himself violently involved in a variety of liberal causes.

At the end of February, however, Lilburne replied directly and angrily to the charges of Frost, and of those for whom Frost was speaking, in *A Whip for the Present House of Lords*. This pamphlet concentrates its attack on Cromwell and the House of Lords, but because Lilburne here keeps himself under better control, *A Whip* achieves more than histrionic invective. In addition, it is significant both as a denial of economic radicalism on the part of the Levellers and as an only partially concealed bid for broader support for them in the House of Commons.

Lilburne opens with an assault on Frost's accuracy and motives, after which he repeats the year-old claim that the Levellers are the true defenders of liberty and property, that they are neither communists nor anarchists: "those that you nickname Levellers [are] the supporters and defenders of Liberty and propriety, or Anti-Grandees, Anti-Imposters, Anti-Monopolists, Anti-Apostates, Anti-Arbitrarians, and Anti-[economic] Levellers." [72] As an example of the sort of treason which the Levellers have long opposed, Lilburne then exposes the recent efforts of the Independents to curtail freedom of the press; and to such restraints he contrasts his own lifelong adherence to truly democratic and patriotic principles, in spite of eleven years of "thundring shakings, pearcing trials." [73] Thus, blending dramatic autobiography and political vituperation, Lilburne builds up the contention that it has been he who has consistently played the part of "a faithfull Englishman, in maintaining and justifying . . . [his] liberties and freedomes, and sticking close to the law of the land," while his opponents and persecutors, now in particular Cromwell and Ireton, have been the "usurping tyrants, and destroyers of law and liberty." But the keystone of Lilburne's argument, as it moves to a less personal level, is the charge that much of England's turmoil is due to the fact that Parliament has kept the people in the dark as to its ultimate war aims, and that this confusion has been increased because Parliament has proved apostate and inconsistent in pursuing those few objectives it had made relatively clear. Still, he concludes, this lack of policy has been largely the fault of the Lords — whose subversive acts have been the chief cause of the war, of the present apparent aimlessness in national policy, and of Parliament's persecution of Lilburne.

Early in March, a pamphlet by John Wildman, *The Laws Subversion*, partially supplemented *A Whip*, and, in so doing, it also indicated the temporarily negative nature of Leveller policy in the early spring of 1648. [74] The major concern of the party was, for the time being, the plight of its leaders, and the consequent need for a stronger public protest in their behalf. As a result, Wildman's pamphlet presents the case of one of Lilburne's fellow prisoners in the Tower, Sir John Maynard, a Presbyterian and a man by no means unsympathetic to the cause of Charles.[75] In pointing out that Maynard, like Lilburne, has been illegally and arbitrarily jailed, Wildman attempts to show how far along the path to tyranny the Grandees and their dupes are leading England. "Who is a patriot?" and "Are the Leveller leaders rebels or patriots?" are the rhetorical questions obvious in this support of one of the Levellers' strangest political bedfellows.

In keeping with this temporary lull in Leveller activities was a brief pamphlet which appeared in mid-March, *A Plea, or Protest, made by William Prynne*. Though it is tempting to see in this parody the hand of either Walwyn or Overton, its heavy-handed technique and a marginal note by Thomason both indicate that it was the work of Lilburne.[76] Prynne was fair game; in February he had blasted at the radicals in *The Levellers Levell'd to the Very Ground*, and he had just published a defense of the Upper House entitled *A Plea for the Lords*. His alleged "Protest" against the encroachments of the Lords and their presumed supporters among the army leaders was therefore an evident forgery to discredit Prynne by making him seem a conspicuous turncoat. At best, therefore, *A Plea, or Protest* can be considered only an indirect and clumsy bid for the support of those conservatives who had continued to object to the army's purge of Maynard and ten of his colleagues from Parliament in June 1647.

Despite this hiatus in the organizational and intellectual growth of the Leveller party, the increasing threat of renewed civil war was beginning to push the Levellers into a relatively strong bargaining position. Indeed, Lilburne soon found himself in the uncommon situation of being wooed by his former enemies — not because of his and Wildman's bid for wide support against Cromwell but because the Leveller leaders might help to swing the balance of power either to the Presbyterians or to the Independents. Moreover, the march of events was rapidly producing a national dilemma that might call for a radical constitutional solution. Thus by April 1648 the Levellers were in a position to reap the fruits of a new harvest, but of a harvest they had had little direct part in sowing.

III. April to November 1648: The Second Civil War and Its Immediate Aftermath

The Second Civil War lasted from May to October 1648. During these five months many of the splits between the various political groups in England became chasms, many of the amorphous political alignments grew into solidified, though generally smaller, unified factions. The axe which decapitated Charles early in 1649 was, in a very real sense, honed on the bitter conflicts of the summer and fall of 1648. Yet in April Lilburne was still busily attacking Cromwell, still groping for his own vindication — apparently almost indifferent to what quarter it came from. Ironically, it was Charles, not Lilburne, who was pushing Cromwell and his followers to the left, pushing them closer to the Levellers.

Though Lilburne had often remarked on the dire consequences of renewed civil war, *The Prisoners Plea for a Habeas Corpus*, which he published early in April 1648, was largely an unrestrained and bitter attack on Cromwell. As such, much of it is retrospective, and it illustrates Lilburne's expedient rather than theoretical turn of mind, his flair for self-dramatization rather than for profound political analysis. The pamphlet begins by equating Cromwell with the bishops who, in 1639, had attempted to "murder" Lilburne; it concludes by reprinting the plea Lilburne had addressed to his fellow apprentices nine years earlier. In between, *The Prisoners Plea* devotes its energies to supporting the supremacy of law against any inroads made in the name of military necessity or of legislative and judicial prerogative. Yet events were already undercutting the effectiveness of Lilburne's defense of the traditional and legal right to habeas corpus, for his opening argument states that, since the war has long been ended, the excuse of a national emergency — and hence military rule — no longer applies.

At the same time, a potentially profound and major concept, one almost entirely new to the radical thought of the day, appears in rough outline in the nature of the appeal which Lilburne threatens to address to the people of London if his demand for habeas corpus is not allowed. In that event he will request the people of London to deliver a short petition to the judges of the King's Bench, asking them to review his case in open court. Whether or not this was merely the recourse of a desperate man, it does foreshadow Lilburne's defense of himself in 1649 and 1653, and, in larger terms, it foreshadows the American system of judicial review of legislative action; for here, explicitly and as part of a quasi-logical argument, Lilburne states that on such basic issues as the legality of ex post facto laws or the abrogation of the right to habeas corpus the judges of the common, or more fundamental, law are empowered to review, and to supersede, acts of Parliament.[77] But that Lilburne was by no means fully aware of the implications of his own plea is indicated by his prompt shift in the pamphlet to the most violent of his attacks on Cromwell, an attack in which Cromwell is accused of murder, robbery, lying, and usurpation, and which Lilburne climaxes with the demand that Cromwell and Ireton be impeached.

Three days later Lilburne issued a similar epistolary tract, *The oppressed mans importunate and mournfull cryes to be brought to the Barre of Justice*. Its opening sentence declares that the "Law of the Land . . . [is] the common birthright and inheritance" of all the people, to which "the meanest man in England is as much intituled and intaled . . . as the greatest Subject." Then, citing Coke, Lilburne goes on to show that, if any person or any agency departs from this principle, anarchy is loosed, "and all liberty and property of meum and tuum is thereby totally levelled, destroyed, and confounded." Three times, with almost identical wording, Lilburne repeats this sweeping prediction, amplifying it with autobiographical, historical, and religious *exempla*. In the course of this amplification he goes out of his way to attack those Independents who, instead of being vigilant for the rights of all, "care for no more but to get liberty to meet freely together, and to prate and discourse of religion, and will let others without cause perish, rot, and be destroyed in prison." [78] Since, Lilburne continues, he himself is thus perishing and rotting, and since he has long been appealing for justice in every "Formall, magesteriall way" possible, now, in order to vindicate the law of the land, he must get a hearing before the proper judges of that law, "the ordinary judges in Westminster Hall" — hence his petitionary pressure in behalf of habeas corpus for himself.

The second half of *The oppressed mans importunate and mournfull cryes* then displays Lilburne the effective political organizer, in this case arranging for a well-publicized review of Parliament's dealings with John Lilburne. He exhorts his readers to assemble together to present his appended petition to the judges of the King's Bench, and to advertise this event by having it publicly read aloud, preferably to local mass meetings organized especially for that purpose. There is, however, no evidence to indicate that these appeals occasioned the response Lilburne desired. Yet, largely as a result of Presbyterian maneuvering to gain his support — and certainly not because the majority of Parliament was convinced by his new exegesis of constitutional rights — Lilburne in mid-April was granted a weekly allowance of forty shillings by the House of Commons.[79] At about this time, too, the cross-party dickering which eventuated in his release from the Tower four months later probably got under way.

Despite omens of better treatment to come, Lilburne continued to turn to the judges of the common law for relief from persecution at the hands of Parliament. Early in May he published *The Prisoners mournfull cry, against the Judges of the Kings Bench,* a brief epistle to one of these judges which laments that the court has not yet granted his plea for habeas corpus. But still at no point in this pamphlet or in the four petitions which it reprints does Lilburne clearly set forth the broader implications of the fact that he is formally and publicly seeking recourse in the courts of common law against administrative or legislative tyranny.

The Lawes Funerall, which appeared on May 15, 1648, somewhat atones for this neglect. On May 8, partly as a result of the activities of his allies in his behalf and partly because of the shifting party alignments within Parliament, Lilburne was finally brought before the judges of the King's Bench.[80] *The Lawes Funerall* is mainly devoted to transcribing Lilburne's carefully prepared defense of himself, a defense which drew some of the more obvious conclusions from his resort to judicial review: in particular, an elementary definition of those areas in which the legislature and judiciary were to operate, and a clearer statement of a theory of political checks and balances.

After having been granted permission to serve as his own lawyer, Lilburne made his first basic point: that Parliament is the lawmaker of the nation, but that the judiciary, from the Westminster judges in front of him to local justices of the peace, are "the sole and only executors" of the law. In other words, still reflecting the Leveller suspicion of centralized power, Lilburne claimed that it is the function of the judicial branch of the government to take over many of those duties which are today, in England and the United States, the responsibility of the executive branch.

Lilburne's second main point was a reaffirmation of the much-cited contention from Coke that Parliament has no right to try any commoner. On the contrary, every commoner is guaranteed trial by a jury of his peers. The encroachments of Parliament upon this basic and traditional right have been, Lilburne told the court, particularly heinous when performed by the "prerogative" House of Lords. Notwithstanding a series of reprimands from the judges, Lilburne then proceeded to castigate the Lords, citing among other relevant cases that of Richard Overton, and of course linking the Lords to Cromwell's alleged megalomania. In analyzing Parliament's aggressions into the judicial realm Lilburne also attacked the attempts of both Houses to stretch their power by administering unlawful oaths, by accusing their opponents of general rather than specific crimes, and by often assuming in their warrants and charges that their intended victims have already been proved guilty.

Fervidly appealing to his judges to do something about Parliament's departures from its legitimate legislative role, Lilburne then claimed that his own case was fundamental to the preservation of English laws, English rights, English property, and even English lives; that his recent period in jail had been

that which strikes the Fatall Stroke through the heart-Roote of Freedome, and Justice; yea it overturnes the Foundations of the Kingdome; this very single act, if drawne into president hath a seminall vertue in it whereby is contained in its selfe all the distinct species of injustice whereof the Sun was ever yet spectator.[81]

Hence the judges before whom he is pleading have the duty of declaring the illegality of his treatment at the hands of Parliament —thereby reasserting their own proper role and vindicating traditional English liberties. Thus, in essence, Lilburne was using his own case to build up a system of checks and balances in which the courts of common law were to serve as a corrective to any unwarranted extension of Parliament's power, and as a bulwark for the citizen against any despotic actions on the part of his government.

Lilburne's grandiose plea inspired only some negative questions from his judges; and to these questions Lilburne responded by reviewing the many misfortunes he had accumulated in fighting the good fight. That afternoon he was recommitted to the Tower of London, there to languish in relative silence until his release three months later. Neither his oratory before the judges of the King's Bench nor the publication of *The Lawes Funerall* made any apparent dent in the pragmatic concept that Parliament, particularly in a temporarily kingless land, was a court which had no legal superior.

In these ensuing three months, while the undubious battles of the Second Civil War were being fought, there was little sign of Leveller activity, though at the end of June a single pamphlet, *Englands weeping Spectacle*, portrayed the "sad condition of . . . John Lilburne." [82] This short tract, possibly the work of Walwyn, tells the story of Lilburne's life in terms of his continuous battle for righteousness, presenting its hero as a Puritan Saint who has long waged war against evil in the form of Lords, clergymen, lawyers, military leaders, and judges. Then, a month later, Sir John Maynard, the man whom Wildman had previously defended, delivered a speech in the House of Commons in support of Lilburne.[83] Maynard had, the year before, also unsuccessfully demanded a trial by jury against the actions of Parliament; now, recently released from the Tower where he had become acqainted with Lilburne, he stated to the House that Lilburne's sufferings were both excessive and illegal, and that they should immediately be rectified. Not because Maynard's rhetoric or logic was effective, but because he was speaking as a member of the Presbyterian majority which was at the moment in control of Parliament, Lilburne within a week became a free man.[84]

A further indication of the jockeying for political position in the summer of 1648 is a moderately worded pro-Lilburne petition, signed by 10,000 persons, which was published on August 1.[85] Both Houses of Parliament promptly and almost unanimously concurred in the petitioners' request that Lilburne be released, and preliminary steps were taken to see that he might receive proper reparations.[86] It is obvious from this solicitude that the Presbyterians expected an unshackled Lilburne to be a greater thorn than ever in Cromwell's flesh.[87]

The Presbyterians were wrong. On the second day of his freedom Lilburne sent Cromwell a note which is a revealing mixture of presumption and idealism:

Sir. What my Comrade hath written by our trusty Bearer might be sufficient for us both; but to demonstrate unto you that I am no stag-gerer from my first principles that I engaged my life upon, nor from you, if you are what you ought to be, and what you are strongly re-ported to be; although, if I prosecuted or desired revenge for an hard and almost sterving imprisonment, I could have had of late the choice of twenty opportunities to have payd you to the purpose; but I scorn it, especially when you are low: and this assure your self, that if ever my hand be upon you, it shall be when you are in full glory, if then you shall decline from the righteous wayes of Truth and Justice: Which, if you will fixedly and impartially prosecute, I am Yours, to the last drop of my heart bloud (for all your late severe hand towards me).[88]

As further proof that the Levellers had no liking for the cause of Charles and the Scots, on August 15, 1648, two days before the Battle of Preston, a group of Levellers and Independents jointly petitioned Parliament to find a common basis on which to unite all the well-intentioned elements in England against the threat from the north.[89] A week later, Walwyn in a trenchant pamphlet, *The Bloody Project*, set forth the ingredients which the Levellers thought essential to any such victorious popular front — a mixture of in-gredients which was not to the taste of either Charles or the In-dependents.[90]

The Bloody Project begins with a discussion of the horror and futility of unnecessary war; then it moves to the correlation of an unnecessary war with one whose aims have not been properly defined:

But especially let men pretending conscience take heed how they either engage themselves or perswade others to engage to fight and kill men for a cause not rightly stated or not thoroughly understood to be just.[91]

Thence Walwyn proceeds to anatomize recent history in order to show that thousands have died in the cause of king or Parliament without knowing in precise terms for what they were fighting and without having had any specific war aims placed before them. A typical paragraph in this analysis can reveal the penetrating and slightly ironic manner in which he characterizes the years since 1642:

Or was it sufficient thinke you now, that the Parliament invited you at first upon generall terms to fight for the maintenance of the true Protestant Religion, the Libertyes of the People, and Priviledges of Parliament; when neither themselves knew, for ought is yet seen, nor you, nor any body else, what they meant by the true Protestant Religion, or what the Liberties of the People were, or what those Priviledges of Parliament were, for which yet nevertheless thousands of men have been slain, and thousands of Familyes destroyed.[92]

Next, in summing up the fruitlessness of seven years of intermittent war, Walwyn graphically calls attention to the existing oppressions under which the people are groaning, a far cry from that liberty for which they have presumably been fighting. He goes on to italicize this disillusion by examining some of the forces which seemed dominant to him at that moment when Charles and his allies were on the verge of defeat: the army leaders who brand certain soldiers as "Mutineers, or Incendiaries"; the magistrates of London who wield arbitrary power and who are limited only by their own selfish whims; the "present Ruling Party of Presbyterians" whose aim is tyranny and usurpation — in short,

all the quarrell we have at this day in the Kingdome is no other than a quarrel of Interests, and Partyes, a pulling down of one Tyrant to set up another, and instead of Liberty, heaping upon our selves a greater slavery then what we fought against.[93]

Because such is the present predicament, Walwyn continues, the basic political problem is to define some kind of "Supream Authority," some single power which can put an end to quarrels and help to erect a solid future for the nation. The history of England has shown, and recent events have confirmed, the corollary fact "that there should be either three or two distinct Estates equally supream is an absurd nullity in government." Besides,

If by all your endeavors you cannot prevail to have the supream author-

ity declared and proved, how can you lawfully fight, or upon what
grounds with a good conscience can you engage your selves or perswade others to engage in killing and slaying of men? . . . Therefore
as you are to forbear till you see the supream Authority distinctly and
rationally stated, so also you are not to engage till the Cause be ex-
pressly declared. . . . For by experience you now find you may be
made slaves as effectually by a Parliament as by any other kind of government.[94]

And Walwyn concludes this section of negative analysis and warning with the advice to his readers to "hold your hands till you
know what you fight for, and be sure that you have the truth of
Freedom in it, or never meddle, but desist, and let who will both
fight and pay."

But from here Walwyn moves first to a positive definition of the
supreme authority, then to the setting up of a program which can
serve as a basic meeting ground for the "well-intentioned" of the
nation. In regard to the former, Walwyn states that a new and
representative House of Commons must be the central agency of
political power. In regard to the program, he briefly outlines the
constitutional reforms for which the Levellers had long been
pleading. This is, he says, the minimum program. To it the people
of England must agree in order to avoid the continued futile shed-
ding of blood, in order to avoid national enslavement under king
or Parliament or army, and in order to bring about "the establishment of such equal rules of government for the future, as shall lay a
firm foundation of peace and happiness to all the people without
partiallity."

Walwyn's sense of history is particularly evident in a short postscript which repeats his plea for national unity based on the program
of the Levellers. "If," he declares, "the Peace of the Nation cannot
be secured without the Restauration of the King, let it be done
speedily and honorably; and [to] provide against his misgovern-
ment for the future, let his power be declared and limited by Law."
Thus Walwyn in part anticipated the form which the "revolutions"
of 1660 and 1689 were to take. But, more immediately, *The Bloody
Project* was the opening salvo in the Leveller campaign of the next
six months to make the aim of the Second Civil War only incidentally the defeat of Charles and "the Scotch interest," and pri-

marily the establishment of a progressive and constitutional democracy in England. At the same time, this pamphlet also announced, if somewhat obliquely, that any political coalition formed to achieve this positive aim ought to be under the leadership of the Levellers.

This intention was made explicit in a lengthy petition which the Levellers presented to the House of Commons on September 11, 1648, at a moment when the war was coming to an end in the complete victory of Cromwell and his disciplined army.[95] This petition, written mainly by Walwyn and Lilburne, represented the full program which the Levellers tried to get Cromwell to accept during the remaining months of 1648. Like both the March Petition and the first *Agreement of the People*, it temporarily formed the hub for Leveller organizational and intellectual activities — until, in December, it was partially supplanted by a new *Agreement of the People*.[96]

The Levellers had begun work on this petition in August, utilizing *The Bloody Project* as a sort of generalized introduction to it, and preparing their party organization actively to push the program it presented. By September 13 it was reported that the Levellers had already secured 40,000 signatures to this petition, and they had also arranged for a crowd to gather at Westminster, there vociferously to urge its favorable consideration.[97]

The petition itself is one of the more eclectic manifestoes of the Levellers, much of it representing those grievances which the party had accumulated in the last year and a half, but part of it reflecting such comparatively incidental circumstances as the fact that, for the time being, all the Leveller leaders were out of jail, and that an anti-Cromwell group was now holding sway in the House of Commons. Even so, the petition's preamble follows standard Leveller political philosophy and, at the same time, supplements *The Bloody Project*. It addresses the House of Commons as the "supream Authority of England" because it is the only agency that can be historically considered in any way representative of the people. Further, the actions of Parliament early in the war were "real Demonstrations" that the House of Commons considered itself to be a self-sufficient instrument of government; nor, as the war has proved, can it "consist with either the safety or freedom of the

Nation, to be governed by 3. or 2. Supreams." And yet, the preamble concludes, the political future of England is now more uncertain than ever; and the national futility and turmoil, instead of being ended, are about to be enhanced by the reopening of negotiations with Charles — by, that is, the reëstablishment of competing and arbitrary sovereignties. It is in the light of this frustration that the twenty-seven proposals which constitute the body of *The Humble Petition* are then presented.

The petition's first three articles are political. Without mentioning manhood suffrage, they eliminate the negative voice of king and Lords, dissolve the present Parliament, and arrange for automatically annual Parliaments in the future. The next two articles prohibit the "new Representative" from interfering with freedom of conscience and from impressing men for the armed forces, while articles six through nine repeat the now stock Leveller demands for reform of the law in the direction of simplicity and equality. The next ten proposals are largely concerned with economic matters. Excise and monopoly are of course excoriated, beggary condemned "in so fruitful a Nation," and the abolition of tithes again brought forward as an essential prerequisite to true religious liberty. However, two relatively new proposals are advanced: first, that only those enclosures of fens and commons which have directly benefited the poor be permitted to survive; and second, that, if the kingship is retained, the king be granted a fixed revenue "past increase or diminution." That this battery of economic reforms, though tending to raise the level of the poor, was not to be considered revolutionary is made abundantly clear in article eighteen, which prohibits this and all future Parliaments from "abolishing propriety, levelling mens Estats, or making all things common."

Of the final eight articles, five represent, in one way or another, additions to the formal Leveller program. One supplements the proposal establishing the king's revenue by its demand that the power of king and Lords be rigidly defined. Another asks for a restoration of democracy to the government of London and the guilds. A third is a strong statement in behalf of full freedom of speech as the chief antidote to corruption and tyranny. And two of the three final proposals recommend that Charles be brought to trial for his part in "all the abundance of innocent bloud that hath been spilt, and the infinite spoil and havock that hath been made of peacable harmlesse people."

By and large, the emphasis of *The Humble Petition* was political, and many of its articles looked forward to the imminent establishment of the Commonwealth. Moreover, except for its slightly premature demand that the king be brought to trial, it was less out of line with the actual march of events than previous major Leveller documents. None the less, the House of Commons ignored this petition as it busily selected its commissioners to negotiate with Charles at Newport.[98] Within two months, however, Charles had finally arranged that his sobriquet should be martyr, not king, and by November 1648 the foundations both for Charles's scaffold and for the Commonwealth had been laid.[99]

The extent of the Levellers' contribution to these two achievements is hard to assess. In one way it was considerable, for two years of active propaganda on their part had certainly helped to prepare the ground for the ostensibly republican harvest of 1649. Perhaps less important was the fact that the Leveller leaders, once more on the threshold of actual political responsibility, were again about to participate in the councils of the mighty. Indeed, the relative conformity of *The Humble Petition* can be accounted for by the supposition that Lilburne and Walwyn were aware that they might soon be asked to confer with the Independents concerning some sort of constitutional settlement for a kingless England.

Evidence of the temporarily significant role the Levellers were about to play can be seen in the pages of *The Moderate*, the newspaper which since July 1648 had reflected their point of view, and which by September had become the semiofficial organ of the party.[100] In addition to weekly editorials and slanted news articles in favor of various Leveller proposals, *The Moderate* called attention to a succession of pro-Leveller petitions; for, as the party with the most democratic platform, the Levellers were again using the device of the petition to display their growing strength and to bring pressure on Parliament and army to implement their program. During October, for instance, *The Moderate* cited a radical anti-Charles petition from Oxford, quoted from letters from four different army units in support of *The Humble Petition*, mentioned petitions from York and Newcastle which pleaded for a republic, and publicized a variety of left-wing, antimonarchial letters, informal petitions, and public pleas. *The Moderate* continued this supporting campaign in November, but with its emphasis now on the grievances and proposals emanating from the army, and with the murder of Colonel Rainsborough as the lurid focus for its political militancy.

The operations of the pro-king, anti-"heresy" faction still in control of Parliament help to explain this renewed recourse to the New Model on the part of the Levellers, as well as on the part of the Independents. The tactics of the Presbyterians, Charles's inept evasiveness, and the reawakened controversy over a national religious settlement all contributed to the revival of that republican sentiment which the Levellers had tried to stir up a year earlier at Putney. Now, too, the demand for the king's death had become, particularly to the more radical elements in the army, the first pre-requisite to the establishment of any secure peace; and with Ireton as a convert to this attitude, the New Model once again seemed the most appropriate sword of the Lord and the Levellers.[101]

Thus, early in November, Fairfax, alarmed at the rising chorus of voices asking that the king be tried, called a meeting of the Council of Officers — not of the full Council of the Army, a group which would have included some of the Agitators. During a week of argument and compromise, the leaders of the army decided not to sanction the trial of Charles, but instead to intervene in the negotiations between him and Parliament for the sake of securing a firmer and less Pyrrhic peace.[102] Ireton, apparently dissatisfied with the partial rejection of his plans and unwilling to work too closely with the mystically inclined, radical millenarians in the army, therefore turned, if reluctantly, to Lilburne and the Levellers in order to strengthen the hand of the now relatively left-wing group of Independents for whom he was the chief spokesman.

Lilburne, meanwhile, had travelled north, where he had spoken to Cromwell. There Cromwell had told the skeptical Lilburne that he believed in, and would work for the establishment of, freedom and justice.[103] Back in London, Lilburne received a message from Cromwell reaffirming this statement and suggesting a meeting between certain Levellers and Independents to discuss the settlement of the kingdom.[104] It was thus with the apparent blessing of their two strongest opponents at Putney that the Levellers reëntered the councils of those who were to determine the immediate future of England.

The first official meeting between Leveller and Independent occurred early in November 1648. Present for the Levellers were Lilburne and Wildman. Wildman, in the course of "a large debate of things . . . exactly laid open," reports Lilburne, the war aims of the Levellers. To the declaration of these aims the Independents, both civilian and military, responded that the first step must be, instead, "to cut off the Kings head, &c. and force and thoroughly purge, if not dissolve the Parliament." Lilburne's answer shows that the Levellers had become sufficiently disillusioned, or realistic, to have lost much of their political naïveté, for he told the meeting:

I look upon the King as an evill man . . . but the Army has couzened us the last year, and fallen from all their Promises and Declarations, and therefore could not rationally any more be trusted by us without good cautions and security: In which regard, although we should judge the king as arrant a Tyrant as they supposed him . . . and the Parliament as bad as they could make them; yet there being no other balancing power in the Kingdome against the Army but the King and Parliament, it was our interest to keep up one Tyrant to balance another, till we certainly knew what the Tyrant that pretended fairest would give us as our freedoms.[105]

He wound up his remarks by saying that rule by the sword might well be the country's greatest danger, and that the first and only properly rational step for the meeting to advocate was a constitutional settlement via an Agreement of the People.

In retrospect it seems very likely that the Levellers' reluctance to go along in the condemnation of the king at this time was largely a bargaining point, many of the pages of *The Moderate* being then devoted to whipping up anger against Charles. Moreover, the Levellers probably realized that Royalist sentiment in the country was growing, and they were certainly aware that the Independents now needed radical support to outface both Fairfax and Parliament. Lilburne's statement that the king might well counterbalance the army was therefore not an entirely straightforward expression of Leveller opinion, a fact which goes a long way to explain the "desperately cholerick" reaction to it of the Independents at the meeting. None the less, it was decided that a second session should be held, in which four Levellers and four Independents should "debate and conclude of some Heads towards the accomplishment of an Agreement of the People." One of the four Levellers selected was William Walwyn, but when John Price objected to his inclusion, Lilburne angrily agreed to reduce the total number of conferees to six.[106]

On November 15, 1648, these six men, again including Lilburne and Wildman, met at the Nag's Head Tavern in London.[107] At this meeting, "after some debate," it was unanimously resolved that a convention should be called of representatives of army and people to draw up an Agreement of the People, which agreement would then be personally ratified by all the well-affected of the nation; that, in the meantime, Parliament should not be dissolved; and that these two decisions, and certain of the matters raised in *The Humble Petition*, should be dealt with in the "Remonstrance of the Army" then under discussion by the Council of Officers at St. Albans. This resolution was promptly forwarded to Ireton and his colleagues. They, in turn, along with one or more representatives of the Levellers, at once proceeded to modify the "Remonstrance," which, in a revised version, was presented to the House of Commons on November 20.[108]

These emendations took the form of some additional paragraphs which mark both a clear break in the continuity of the "Remonstrance" and an obvious shift in it toward the Leveller point of view.[109] Among the more vital modifications are the declarations that, after Parliament is dissolved, future biennial Parliaments will be set up which will be fully responsive to the wishes of the people, as well as uncurbed by the negative voice of king or Lords; and that

these matters of general settlement . . . [will be] established by a general contract or agreement of the people, with their subscriptions thereunto, and . . . none may be capable of any benefit by the agreement who shall not consent and subscribe thereunto; nor any King be admitted to the crown, or other person to any office or place of public trust, without express accord and subscription to the same.[110]

But when, a week later, Parliament postponed consideration of the "Remonstrance," when the rumors concerning Charles's chances of escape were mounting, and when the Levellers, despite or because of their recent display of power, were becoming suspicious of Ireton's good intentions, Lilburne, Wildman, and two associates rode to Windsor, there to urge the New Model officers to accept a modified Agreement of the People as the only safe barrier to either kingly or military despotism.

The negotiations of these two days, November 28 and 29, 1648, between the Levellers and army officers at Windsor mark the high point of actual Leveller power. But, strangely enough, the Levellers attained this height in a few semiprivate and informal talks, of which the most important took place late at night between Lilburne and Colonel Harrison, at the moment acting as intermediary between Ireton and the radicals.[111] In fact, this conversation between Lilburne and Harrison on November 28 represents the only occasion on which those in power made any major concession — major in the sense that they intended actually to implement it — to that party which had long asserted that power must reside in and come from the people.

That afternoon there had been an acrimonious debate between Lilburne and Ireton. The main point at issue had been Lilburne's charge that certain of the Independents were "too strict [in] restraining liberty of conscience, and in keeping a power in the Parliament to punish where no visible Law is transgressed." Lilburne's reaction to Ireton's vigorous countercharge had been the threat to return to London, there to arouse a public clamor against the leaders of the New Model. To forestall this display of radical power, Harrison returned that night for a conference with Lilburne and Wildman. Harrison informed them of the army's plan "to destroy the King . . . and also totally to root up the Parliament"; after which, he avowed, the generals and the coöperative members of Parliament would then set up an Agreement of the People which would guarantee an equitable and responsive Parliament. When Lilburne replied that the Levellers could not trust the promises of the military, Harrison countered their renewed threat to return to London by setting forth the plight of the army now that the king and the Presbyterian majority in the House were ready to sign a treaty which would eventuate in the destruction of the New Model and the return of the nation to that form of arbitrary government and religious restriction against which the war had mainly been fought. For a moment at least, the Grandees needed the support of the Levellers; nor could the Levellers stomach a Presbyterian-Royalist coalition which would not be counterbalanced by a potentially democratic army. The result was a compromise. Shortly before midnight the Levellers proposed the following scheme, to which Harrison immediately agreed, and in which Ireton the next morning, so Lilburne alleges, verbally concurred: [112]

That if their honest friends in the Parliament . . . would chuse four from amongst themselves, and the Army four from amongst themselves, and the Independents four from amongst themselves; we that were nicknamed Levellers would chuse four from among our selves; and these sixteen should draw up the Agreement finally, without any more appeal to any other; and we for our part . . . would be willing to acquiesce in and submit to the determination of them 16, or the major part of them.[113]

So it was that Lilburne on the next afternoon, riding back to London with a group of civilian Independents, was a "joyfull" man; the chances of establishing a democracy by a caucus of sixteen men, almost all of them assuredly anti-Royalist at the least, seemed for the moment excellent. Thus at the end of November 1648 it appeared possible that the victorious military power wielded by Cromwell and Ireton might be wedded to the political theory of the Levellers, and so produce a nineteenth-century constitutional settlement for seventeenth-century England. If so, a new Agreement of the People was to be the major article in that marriage ceremony.[114]

IV. *December 1648 and January 1649: The Second Agreement of the People*

On the day after Lilburne left Windsor, the Council of Officers presented an ultimatum to Parliament demanding "the impartial administration of justice, the regular payment of the soldiers . . . and the speedy enactment of salutary laws." [115] To secure these ends the army was to enter London, and on the next day it started to march. On that same day, November 30, 1648, it issued a *Declara-*

tion which assumed that the officers' three demands would be turned down, and that therefore the present Parliament would have to be dissolved.[116] On December 2 the army arrived in London, and four days later Colonel Pride stood at the door of the House of Commons and permitted only those members favorable to the leaders of the New Model to take their seats. Two weeks later Charles started on his journey from Hurst Castle to London and the scaffold.

The compromise arranged between Lilburne and Harrison had helped to strengthen the hand of the army leaders, but as that hand rapidly came more and more to resemble a fist, so the high hopes of the Levellers began to crack and crumble. While the preliminaries to Pride's Purge were being taken care of, Lilburne assembled thirteen of his sixteen-man committee back at Windsor to draw up their "Agreement."[117] There, after "a large discourse about . . . [its] foundations," Lilburne, Wildman, Walwyn, and Maximillian Petty,[118] the four representatives of the Levellers, and Henry Marten, the only one of the Parliamentary group who appeared, "lockt" themselves up and hurriedly drafted a new Agreement of the People.

Early in December this draft was placed before the now thirteen-man committee, a majority of whom accepted it in amended form.[119] But on the next day, much to the chagrin of the Levellers, this amended draft was sent to the Council of Officers for further debate. It was thus not accepted as a national charter which would immediately be signed by the Grandees, the soldiers, and then the people. The discussion in the Officers' Council at the headquarters of the army at Whitehall, a discussion in which the Levellers at first participated, lasted on and off until January 13, 1649, less than three weeks before Charles lost his head. However, except for the final flurry of Leveller activity in the spring of 1649, the opening days of the Whitehall Debate signified the swan song of the Levellers as a cohesive and potentially epoch-making political party. Indeed, during this month the few printed manifestoes of the Levellers diverged more and more from the decisions being hammered out by the leading officers of the New Model, until, by mid-January, the actual power of the Levellers, though still magnified by their adherents, had become negligible.

As early as December 11, 1648, Lilburne called a party meeting at which he reported on how the army leaders, "especially the cunningest of Machiavilians . . . Ireton," had "couzened and deceived" the Levellers.[120] It was there and then apparently decided to publish the Agreement of the People which had been approved by the thirteen-man committee before it was inevitably further modified by the Grandees now debating it at Whitehall. On December 15, therefore, *Foundations of Freedom; or an Agreement of the People* appeared,[121] that constitutional contract which, if Lilburne's understanding of Harrison's commitment at the end of November had been correct, might well have become the basic law of the land. Because the agreement was drawn up with this in mind, and because various points of view contributed to its final form, it is the most practicable of the major Leveller programs. But both its content and its harsh treatment at the hands of the army officers show that, essentially, it was by no means a middle-of-the-road compromise.

Its preamble, harking back to the rational analysis of *The Bloody Project*, calls attention to the dangers of continued war and of a return to tyranny, dangers which can be avoided only if specific, constructive action is taken:

For as it cannot be imagined that so many of our Countrymen would have opposed us in this quarrel if they had understood their own good, so may we safely promise to our selves, that when our common Rights and Liberties shall be cleared, their endevors will be disappointed that seek to make themselves our Masters.[122]

To this end, the dissolution of the present Parliament is ordered, and a new representative, consisting of 300 persons "more indifferently proportioned," is set up. But that this agreement was intended to be no mere visionary program is proved by the two sections which come next: first, the breakdown by county and town of these 300 representatives; and second, a series of detailed paragraphs on the actual election procedures. These precise instructions, in turn, indicate one area of Leveller compromise; for, no longer insisting on universal manhood suffrage, the Levellers had assented to the definition of the electors as

[those] Natives or Denizens of England . . . [who] have subscribed to this Agreement, not persons receiving Alms, but such as are assessed

ordinarily toward the relief of the poor; not servants to or receiving wages from any particular person: And in all Elections (except for the Universities) they shall be men of one and twenty yeers old, or upwards, and Housekeepers, dwelling within the Division for which the Election is.[123]

A second area of Leveller compromise can be seen in the provision that a "Councel of State" manage the affairs of the nation between meetings of Parliament.[124] (This council, however, was not to be the equivalent of a modern English cabinet, for none of its members were to be members of Parliament. Also intended as a device against the rise of political "factions," though not necessarily a compromise, was the clause that no one on the public payroll could serve as a representative.) [125]

But the influence of the Levellers is far more obvious in the next section of the agreement: the explicit reservations on the power of the new "peoples Representative." The first of these reservations, and that which occasioned the hottest debate at Whitehall, is the guarantee of full religious liberty, though the government will be permitted to set up a noncompulsive, non-Catholic method of "publick Worship." Impressment is prohibited, as is the future questioning of citizens and soldiers for their part in the civil wars. Three other reservations make it clear that the laws are to be equitably administered, regardless of the persons involved; nor is Parliament ever to "intermeddle . . . with the execution of Laws." Finally, the House of Commons of the future is barred from taking away any of the "foundations of Common Right, Liberty or Safety contained in this Agreement"; and it is never to "levell mens Estates, destroy Propriety, or make all things common."

Besides these broad reservations and restrictions, the thirteen-man committee, almost certainly at the insistence of the Levellers, added a list of "Particulars which were offered to be inserted in the Agreement, but [which were] judged fit as the most eminent grievances to be redressed by the next Representative." This list of particulars is a medley of legal and economic reforms from which it would almost be possible to deduce the biographies of those middle-class men who led the radical wing of the Puritan Revolution. The next House of Commons is instructed to enact legislation which will simplify and put into English all laws; further, such laws are to

preclude self-incrimination, excessive delays, and capital punishment — except in cases of murder or the attempt forcibly to upset
this agreement. At the same time, the right to proper witnesses and
to trial by jury is to be clearly strengthened, while punishments are
to be generally alleviated and made more appropriate to the crime.
In the field of economics, the future representative is advised to
establish free trade and to eliminate the excise. This body is also
to work out some system of proportional taxation, from which
those having an income of less than £30 a year are, on the whole, to
be exempted. Two corollary recommendations involve the end of
imprisonment for debt, and the setting up of a maximum interest
rate of 6 per cent. Lastly, the future House of Commons is urged to
discontinue tithes and to declare that no person will ever be prohibited from holding any public office because of his religious
opinions.[126]

It was this largely eclectic program — a program mainly devoted,
despite its list of particulars, to establishing the constitutionally
limited supremacy of a more representative House of Commons —
that was the subject of a month's intermittent debate at Whitehall.
As in the case of the Putney Debate, Woodhouse's account of these
proceedings requires little amplification.[127] However, the session on
December 14, 1648 — the only meeting of the Council of Officers
for which there is a comparatively full transcript — is important to
an understanding of both the strength and the weakness of the
Levellers at that moment when their political power had crested
and was already starting to break. The major question under debate concerned the agreement's first reservation on future Parliaments: "Whether the magistrate have, or ought to have, any compulsive and restrictive powers in matters of religion?" This problem, which for the next decade remained a major stumbling block
to any stable national settlement, was also one around which other
issues tended to gravitate; hence the debate on that day emphasized
the political as well as the religious differences which separated
Leveller from Independent.

John Goodwin, speaking for the London Independents, remarked
that, since religion is a matter of conscience, it is a mistake to
"intermeddle" with it by even mentioning any limitation on the
power of the magistrate in affairs of the spirit;[128] and the more

conservative Nye strongly implied that the magistrate, like his Old Testament archetype, should exercise his power to curb sin and evil, that, indeed, such power is vital to his proper performance as a magistrate.[129] There was now a distinct echo of Thomas Edwards in the words of these two men whom Edwards had once castigated as heretics and freethinkers.

Ireton, the most effective spokesman for the majority of the officers on the Council, agreed with the London Independents' contention that any restriction on the magistrate need not appear in the agreement. His first major point in their support was based on his confidence in the government that was to be established, and it reveals the gulf that divided his political thought from the Leveller belief that power necessarily corrupts him who wields it. "Let us go on to make an agreement for our civil rights upon those things wherein we are agreed," Ireton urged,

and let us not make such a thing necessary to the agreement as will inevitably exclude one of us from the agreement, but let us make such a distribution of the public trust in such hands as shall give every man an equal share, an equal interest and possibility; and let us submit ourselves to these future Representatives, and if we be not satisfied in one Representative, it may be [we shall be] satisfied in the next.[130]

Therefore, he concluded, let the future House of Commons be allowed to decide for itself what "power of determining as to the outward man . . . they will allow or suffer in matters of religion."

Ireton's second major point against any religious restriction on the new representative was a mixture of theology and politics. It rested on the traditional distinction between the inner and the outer man, translated into almost equally traditional political terms as the distinction between the compulsive and the restrictive power of the magistrate in affairs of the spirit. That is, a magistrate should be unable to enforce a set of beliefs, for that would be compulsion; on the other hand, he ought, said Ireton, to be able to restrict a man from performing certain rites or uttering profanities which are "blasphemous."

Colonel Harrison and Joshua Sprigge, speaking for the millenarians, opposed the Independents and Ireton. They suggested that it was the mission of Christ, not of the magistrate, to "root up and destroy . . . heresies." [131] But the chief voices raised in behalf of a permanent and constitutional guarantee of full religious toleration came from Lilburne, Overton, and Wildman. Overton,[132] suspecting the distinction between compulsive and restrictive power which Ireton was about to make, declared that the magistrate who had power over his body had power also to keep him at home when, for instance, he desired to "go abroad to serve God." [133] Wildman explicitly pointed out that, from the Leveller point of view, the real problem was not what power to give to the magistrate but what power to withhold from him: that the war had been fought to determine what power should be given to, or retained by, the people. Then, toward the end of that long day of debate, he effectively summed up the pragmatic rationalism that was at the heart of Leveller doctrine:

Matters of religion or the worship of God are not a thing trustable, so that either a restrictive or a compulsive power should make a man to sin. . . . It is not easily determinable what is sin by the light of nature. . . . It is not easy by the light of nature to determine [more than that] there is a God. The sun may be that God. The moon may be that God. . . . Indeed, if a man consider there is a will of the Supreme Cause, it is an hard thing for [him by] the light of nature to conceive how there can be any sin committed. And therefore the magistrate cannot easily determine what sins are against the light of nature, and what not. . . . [But] because the magistrate must be conceived to be as erroneous as the people whom he is to restrain, and more probable to err than the people that have no power in their hands, the probability is greater that he will destroy what is good than prevent what is evil.[134]

Ultimately, though the army leaders and some of the London Independents had moved closer to the Leveller position, the same issues which determined the over-all political alignments of the mid-1640's still divided radical from Independent and Grandee. Consequently the problem of properly wording any article on religious freedom was turned over to a military subcommittee, while Lilburne and Overton, conscious of the fate of their agreement, withdrew from any further participation in the Whitehall Debate.[135] Walwyn and Wildman, after being on hand for the discussion of Parliament's future instructions to equalize the law, soon followed their two colleagues.[136] Thus, despite the fact that the Leveller-dominated agreement had skirted the touchy problem of what to do with king and Lords other than to secure their constitutional subordination, and despite the fact that their program was, in part, the outcome of a series of compromises, still the agreement's underlying philosophy was sufficiently revolutionary to force the leaders of the New Model first to water down and then by and large to discard this plan for an altered England.

A possible factor contributing to the emasculation of the agreement was a four-page pamphlet which appeared on December 21, 1648, *No Papist nor Presbyterian*.[137] This plea for full and unlimited toleration indicates either that the Levellers, with all the adroitness of their matured publicity techniques, were bidding for Catholic and prelatical support, or that some moderate Catholic was trying to attach his cause to that of the Levellers. Since the former hypothesis seems more likely, *No Papist nor Presbyterian* may well have been the work of Walwyn.[138]

It begins by asserting the Golden Rule as its basic principle, a principle which, says the author, necessitates "Liberty of Conscience without exception." To this end, and with an implied nod in the direction of Whitehall, the tract propounds that "all penall Statutes against non-conformists in Religion," but with particular attention to those against Popery, be revoked; that all oaths be "declared against, and taken away"; that tithes be abolished; that the sequestration of Catholic property be greatly mitigated; that Catholics who have helped the cause of Charles be no more harshly dealt with than other Royalists; and that there be no bars whatsoever to a "free and unmolested exercise of religion." [139]

But on the same day that *No Papist nor Presbyterian* appeared, the Council of Officers arrived at their own solution to the religious question: the future representative was to be forbidden from interfering with the "worship of such Christian societies as do not disturb the public peace," with the wide exception of those addicted to "Popery and Prelacy." [140] Many of the historically daring ideas of the Levellers were thus being relegated to the limbo of premature theory and impractical radicalism, as the leaders of the New Model, their strength temporarily insurmountable, began to draw up their plans for the trial of Charles.

This impending forcible interruption of the Stuart dynasty helped to determine the treatment which the Council of Officers accorded to the Second Agreement of the People.[141] Not only was the religious reservation weakened, but the clause outlawing special legal privileges was dropped. Further, subscription to the agreement was eliminated as a prerequisite to voting, the article against impressment was made more flexible, and the list of eleven particulars for the consideration of the new House of Commons was entirely omitted from the final document of the officers. Finally, while certain sections of this revised agreement were declared "fundamental," others were described as "for convenience," and therefore subject to change by future Parliaments; moreover, the entire amended agreement was turned over to the House of Commons for appropriate action. As Lilburne later sadly remarked,

Alas, an Agreement of the People is not proper to come from the Parliament, because it comes from thence rather with a command then any thing else. . . . Besides, that which is done by one Parliament, as a Parliament, may be undone by the next Parliament: but an Agreement of the People begun and ended amongst the People can never come justly within the Parliaments cognizance to destroy.[142]

Instead of destroying this diluted agreement, Parliament shelved it. Completed by the Council of Officers by the middle of January 1649, it was presented to the House on January 20. In the excitement attendant on the trial of Charles, the agreement, as Cromwell and Ireton no doubt anticipated, was tabled, there to remain until February, at which time it was supplanted by the act appointing a Council of State to govern England.[143]

Despite its predictable official fate, the original version of the Second Agreement of the People also occasioned several unofficial responses. One of these, *Reasons against . . . The Agreement of the People*, which appeared on December 26, 1648, presented the point of view of a conservative supporter of the Independents, William Ashurst. In conjunction with the remarks of Goodwin, Nye, and Ireton at Whitehall, Ashurst's pamphlet supplies a valid résumé of the contemporary middle-of-the-road position. Ashurst first attacks the Levellers for failing in their agreement to define "the People," and for invoking too extreme and untried a national step. Then he criticizes them for grossly underestimating the disturbance that would follow any such major political changes: among other charges, he makes the point that the people of England might well be split between those who would subscribe to the agreement and those who would refuse to assent to its provisions. Furthermore, he indicates the constitutional weakness of the Leveller scheme by showing that it envisages no supreme judicial body to determine future disputes concerning the agreement itself. Finally, the argeement would not only open the gates to Popery and to atheism, but it would violate the whole structure of commitments made by Parliament and the army. Hence, Ashurst concludes, it would lead to "a Government without authority, a Magistrate without power . . . and a People left to be of any Religion, of all Religions, or of no Religion." [144]

A considerably less negative reaction to the Second Agreement had already appeared on December 22, 1648, *Several Proposals for Peace & Freedom, By an Agreement of the People*.[145] This self-styled "Great Agreement" had been laid before Ireton on December 11 by certain Independent citizens of London; [146] shortly thereafter it was published, in an attempt to unite many of the anti-Royalist groups around an acceptable platform. Its chief author, John Jubbes, who had worked with the Levellers at Putney, therefore steered a course somewhat to the right of the Levellers, though one far to the left of Ashurst.[147]

Several Proposals inclines toward Ireton's views in that its program is first to be presented to Parliament, and only then circulated for popular subscription. It also achieves a middle position by stressing the guilt of the king, but at the same time permitting the continuance of the kingship, even under Charles, provided that the monarch make no claims to a negative voice. Its arrangements for biennial Parliaments and its property limitations on the suffrage are also quite close to those finally recommended by the Council of Officers. But Leveller are Jubbes's demands for full equality before the law, poor relief, the abolition of impressment, more equal taxes, the end of the excise, a more equitable distribution of enclosed land and drained fens, and an end to "inslaving Tenures." Jubbes's two most interesting compromise suggestions concern religion and the temporary government of England pending the full acceptance of his agreement. First, *Several Proposals* stands for complete religious toleration, including explicitly Popery and prelacy, though it does permit a noncompulsive but tithe-supported state church. Second, the "Great Agreement" proposes that a nonpermanent committee govern the country until the new representative is ready to take over. Jubbes then lists the names for this proposed thirty-man group. It is a diverse list, which includes Cromwell and Ireton, Lilburne and Wildman, such representatives of the Presbyterians and millenarians as Maynard and Harrison, and a smattering of London Independents, Parliamentary "Republicans," and aristocratic neutrals.

Unlike Ashurst's alarm or Jubbes's somewhat protean compromise was a third unofficial reaction to the Leveller agreement: a ringing pamphlet by John Goodwin, *Right and Might well met*, which appeared on January 2, 1649. Here the learned Independent divine vigorously affirms the rectitude of Pride's Purge and contends that the New Model has only followed the law of nature in "freeing" the House of Commons from its evil and potentially evil tyrants. Goodwin was therefore able to conclude his tract with the statement that a new day is dawning for England because the army has restored the nation's liberty. It was clearly not the new day planned by the Levellers.

The final weeks of debate by the Council of Officers on what to do with the Second Agreement and the First Charles were thus counterpointed by the rumblings of the end of a dynasty and by the spate of violent pamphlets pouring from the city's presses.[148] The Levellers, however, after they withdrew from the Whitehall Debate, directly contributed little to this din. Though the pages of *The Moderate* continued to be filled with radical petitions, only two Leveller tracts were published between mid-December and the death of the king.

The first of these, *A Plea for Common-Right and Freedom*, appeared on December 28, 1648.[149] Addressed to Fairfax and his officers, it was personally delivered to the General on that date by Lilburne, Overton, and a large group of civilian Levellers.[150] It begins by recounting the history of Leveller coöperation with the New Model for the purpose of securing a firm and just victory; then it shifts to a brief account of how the new Agreement of the People, is being frustrated by those who have, "for politick ends, become pleasers of unreasonable men." As a final recourse against such treason and apostasy, *A Plea* recommends four revisions in the make-up and procedure of the Council of Officers. These are intended to lessen the power of the higher officers, and, not surprisingly, to curb Ireton's opportunity for oratory. If these reforms are adopted, and if representatives of the Levellers are permitted to attend the Council's meeting, then, *A Plea* concludes, "the Army . . . and the worthy Officers thereof may be the joy and the rejoycing of this Nation to all future generations."

The second Leveller tract of these weeks is more significant — the "Areopagitica" of the party, it was an appeal that the Leveller propaganda campaign be allowed full freedom of the press in order to secure the ultimate victory of truth. This *humble Petition*,[151] signed like *A Plea* by the "presenters and Promoters of the Large Petition of September 11," was addressed to the House of Commons, to which body it was formally presented on January 18, 1649. The House responded by promptly relegating it to a subcommittee for, at best, possible consideration.[152] This brusque treatment can mainly be explained by the fact that a week earlier Parliament had authorized Fairfax to use the army to help enforce various restraints on the press which, though previously enacted into law, had largely been honored in the breach.[153] Hence Parliament's reaction to this petition; for now journalists and pamphleteers of all shades of political opinion were responding to this new threat with a variety of outcries, the most effective of which was this Leveller petition, itself probably largely the work of Overton.

It is at once a terse, self-congratulating history of the Leveller movement and a battle cry of democratic philosophy. After vividly calling attention to the rise and fall of the hopes of the nation, the petition points out how instrumental the writings of the radicals have been to those defeats which "Tyrannie" has suffered. Indeed, for at least a decade such men as Lilburne and Overton have been martyrs in the cause of freedom, and it has only been through their efforts and the efforts of others like them to educate the public that any progress at all has been possible:

And if you [Parliament] and your Army shall be pleased to look a little back upon your affairs, you will find that you have bin very much strengthened all along by unlicensed Printing; yea, that it hath done (with greatest danger to the doers) what it could to preserve you, when licensed [printing] did its utmost to destroy you.[154]

The author supports this statement by showing that tyranny cannot grow where there is knowledge and freedom:

For what-ever specious pretences of good to the Common-wealth have been devised to over-aw the Press, yet all times fore-gone will manifest, it hath ever ushered in a tyrannie; mens mouth[s] being to be kept from making noise, whilst they are robd of their liberties. . . . Nor did anything beget these oppressions so much opposition as unlicensed Books and Pamphlets.[155]

Both the efforts and aims of the Levellers and the course of history can therefore provide a central maxim of government: freedom of the press is essential "to preserve any Nation from being liable to the worst of bondage." *The humble Petition*'s saturation in democratic and rational ideas is made even clearer when, just before warning the country against the perils of a new "military jurisdiction," it thus concludes its relatively lengthy preamble:

As for any prejudice to Government . . . [by unlicensed printing], if Government be just in its Constitution and equal in its distributions, it will be good if not absolutely necessary for them to hear all voices and judgements, which they can never do but by giving freedom to the Press; and in case any abuse their authority by scandalous Pamphlets, they [the Government] will never want able Advocates to vindicate their innocency.[156]

But despite its provocative and timely message, *The humble Petition* went unheeded. Two days after it was presented to the House, the charge against the king was completed; a week later Charles was sentenced. Pending his execution, the government worked diligently to see that only those journals and pamphlets favorable to the actions of the army and the purged Parliament saw the light of circulation.[157] Thus January 1649 came to a tense and foreboding end. Lilburne had by this time gone to Newcastle, there to withdraw temporarily into the obscurity of private affairs.[158] Walwyn and Overton had also briefly stepped out of the political arena, as, probably, had Wildman. The republic which the Levellers had long advocated was about to be born; but this new child was to bear little or no resemblance to its spiritual parents — instead, it resembled the surgeons who performed the Caesarean.

The End of The Leveller Party

I. February to April 1649: Prelude to the Final Agreement of the People

Charles lost his head on January 30, 1649. During the next two weeks the House of Lords and the kingship were abolished by the Rump, and a Council of State was set up.[1] Then, in mid-February, the Levellers showed signs of renewed political activity. By this time, however, Wildman had withdrawn from the party,[2] and Lilburne was still "in a kind of deep muse . . . being like an old weather-beaten ship that would fain be in some harbour of ease and rest."[3] Back in London, and having turned down the offer of a job with the Cromwell-dominated government, he considered the prospects of going into business or moving to Holland.[4] Instead, he got ready to reënter politics, motivated in part by what he felt was the unfair prosecution of certain Royalist leaders who were receiving the same sort of justice before a special high court which had caused him to oppose the manner, though not the fact, of the king's death.[5]

But in all likelihood the major stimulus to the revival of Leveller activities came not from Lilburne but from a few common soldiers. Sometime in the middle of February there was a flurry of activity in the ranks for the appointment of new Agitators and the recreation of the potentially democratic but long unused General Council of the Army.[6] To this brief stir, the Officers' Council promptly responded by setting up rules which required that all petitions emanat-

ing from the army go through proper military channels, and by
requesting Parliament to draw up an act for the severe punishment of any civilians who might attempt to arouse discontent within
the army.[7] It was this last request that pulled Lilburne, and with
him his colleagues, out of political semiretirement. In Lilburne's
angry words,

[When] I heard . . . of . . . [the Officers' Council's decision] to procure by Cromwels means a Law at their Pleasure to dispatch me and
my honest friends . . . my spirit was all on fire . . . to consider with
my self that all our Liberties and so large expectations must Center in
this, "That now our lives must be at the absolute wil and pleasure of a
company of bloudy and inhumane Butcherers of men, that had served
seven yeers apprentiship to that bloudy and wicked trade of cutting
mens throats for money, and nothing else; who never had kept faith
or troth with any sorts of men they dealt with, and yet must now become
our Accusers, Prosecutors, Witnesses, Parties, Jury, Judges, and Execu-
tioners." [8]

Thus, on February 26, 1649, Lilburne wholeheartedly returned to
the political wars. He announced this return in a short address to
the House of Commons and in a paper for their consideration,
both immediately published as *Englands New Chains Discovered*.[9]

Turning again to Parliament as a refuge against tyranny, this
time the tyranny of the high officers of the army, Lilburne, on behalf of the Levellers who accompanied him, pleaded the case of his
party cogently and dramatically. Anticipating Nathan Hale, he at
one point told the Speaker, "I am sorry I have but one life to lose
in maintaining the Truth, Justice, and Righteousness of so gallant a
piece." [10] The "gallant piece" which he then presented to the rem-
nant of the House of Commons, though it was flattering to its re-
cipients, was doomed to legislative oblivion. The reason is obvious:
it first supports the theory behind an Agreement of the People and
then goes on to point out the deficiencies in the revised agreement
presented to the House in January by the Council of Officers. Much
of it, therefore, is a review of those points made in *Foundations of
Freedom* and in the first days of the Whitehall Debate, though there
is some shift in emphasis occasioned by the rapid parade of events
between mid-December and the end of February.

Now, in addition to their expected program, the Levellers ask for a firmer reserve against the reëstablishment of king or House of Lords, and they show considerable alarm concerning the powers of any administrative group that is to govern England between the sittings of biennial Parliaments. Consequently, to cut down on the power of any such Council of State, Lilburne here declares that there should be a maximum period of six months between Parliamentary sessions, that the Rump should not dissolve until the new representative is ready to take over, and — perhaps the most modern of the Leveller proposals — that, after an adjournment, a committee of members of Parliament, "limited and bounded with express instructions, and accountable to the next Session," should rule the country [11] — in short, a politically responsible cabinet.

Then, in order to stress the dangers inherent in such an agency as the present Council of State, *Englands New Chains* proceeds to list the abuses which have already marred republican England: Parliament not only serves as a court of law but coöperates in the establishment of arbitrary special courts of justice; there is new evidence of religious restraint; sailors have been impressed, printing curtailed, and petitions handled in a despotic manner; few if any legal reforms have been undertaken; the Council itself daily grows more powerful; and now the officers are trying to get Parliament to legislate against the Levellers. Thus, continues the pamphlet, he who runs may see the apostasy and Machiavellianism of the Grandees. It is particularly alarming, too, that there should have been such a falling off, for, as Lilburne optimistically proclaims,

our Cause and principles do through their own natural truth and lustre get ground in mens understandings, so that where there was one, twelve moneths since, that owned our principles, we beleeve there are now hundreds, so that though we fail, our Truths prosper.[12]

However, to take advantage of this public enlightenment and to secure the prospering of Leveller truth, *Englands New Chains* concludes with a series of specific requests to the Rump: that it not yield its power to the Council of State, but only to the new representative; that the strength of the army leaders be severely curtailed; that a committee of Parliament examine conditions in the army, with particular regard to any abuses of martial law; that the press be immediately opened to all; that the Council of State be dissolved; and that action be taken to lower government salaries, abolish tithes, settle up arrears, and arrange that future petitioners be better received. The Levellers were very much back in politics — and a note to the reader at the end of *Englands New Chains* announces that the party is getting ready to support its demands by a mass petition which may help to arouse an apparently indifferent House of Commons.

In anticipation of this need for greater political pressure, the Levellers also tightened and extended their collaboration with the radical elements in the New Model. On March 1, 1649, five soldiers, very possibly with the aid of Overton, presented a petition to Fairfax and the Council of Officers in which the signers attacked, among other abuses, the growing power of the Council of State and the recently decreed limitation on the soldiers' right freely to petition.[13] Two days later, when the five soldiers were being court-martialed, Overton petitioned the House for reparations for himself and for those others who had suffered from the "Prerogative Jurisdiction" of the Lords and who were now in danger of new, if similar, oppression.[14] During these early days of March, too, both he and Lilburne were busy, along with their military and civilian allies, organizing anew the Leveller forces in the army, in London, and throughout England.

Meanwhile, sometime between February 23 and March 12, 1649, appeared Walwyn's final printed statement of his religious position, a timely and provocative pamphlet entitled *The Vanitie of the Present Churches*.[15] This pamphlet, though still markedly antinomian in its point of view, is largely an attack on the Independents rather than the affirmation of a creed. At the same time, Walwyn's democratic conviction that free grace is the heritage of all men saturates his pages.

The timeliness of this pamphlet lay in its attempt to define what its author considered a true church, and to show the extent of the Independents' departure from the proper path to God. Thus *The Vanitie of the Present Churches* opens by telling how the Independents, like the Presbyterians before them, have practised persecution, have "belyed the Spirit of God," and how, by so doing, the Independents have gained temporary material power; for "they are increased in numbers and have as it were, scumm'd the Parish

Congregations of most of their wealthy and zealous members." [16] Opposed to their "fals presence of a Spirit" is the true religion of "practicall Christianity," which, though it emphasizes good works, is founded on a literal faith in the "word" of the Bible.[17]

But that such a concept led neither to strict fundamentalism nor, ultimately, to Milton's church of a single right believer, Walwyn indicates by the incipient Quakerism of his "practicall Christianity." Like the contemporary views of George Fox and his followers, those of Walwyn in this tract are a mixture of obscurantism and rationalism. Obscurantist, for instance, is his blast at the sophistication of the Independents, "the iniquity of [whose] learning . . . is impudent," and who now "make a gain of Godlynesse, . . . a trade of religion." [18] In contrast to the Independent way, the reader is admonished to "Study the Scriptures," to find, that is, the road to truth without the aid of misleading learned men or opinionated fanatics. Yet even this process need not be private or contemplative, for Walwyn goes on to suggest that the path to truth can best be gained

not by preaching or long set speeches: which are apt to deceive; but by conferences and mutuall debates, one with another (the best way for attaining a right understanding) far excelling that which is called preaching.[19]

And he concludes his pamphlet by underlining the "meeting house" aspect of his religious philosophy:

and therefore it would be happy that all wel-meaning people would seriously set themselves to procure frequent and full meetings, for increase of knowledg in all sorts of people, and no longer to depend either on publique or congregationall Sermons for information of their understandings.[20]

Under the duress of the 1640's Walwyn's antinomianism had become more explicitly social; and the underlying doctrines of his creed were now less mystical, if not at their source, at least in their manifestations. Five years before, Walwyn could well have written this sentence from *The Vanitie of the Present Churches*:

It is the bloud of Christ which cleanseth us from all sinne; this evangelicall truth of its own nature would instantly set man on work to do the will of him that hath so loved him, and constrain him to walk in love as Christ hath loved: so that after this, all the care would be how to advance the Gospel, by making our light to shine forth before men that others seeing our good works may glorifie our Father which is in Heaven.[21]

But to this paean to love and good works Walwyn now twice feels compelled to add an itemized list of the ways in which the good man's light is to shine forth:

By . . . feeding the Hungry, Cloathing the naked, visiting and conforting of the sicke, releeving the aged, weake, and impotent, . . . delivering of Prisoners, supporting of poor families, or . . . freeing a Common wealth from all Tyrants, oppressors, and deceivers.[22]

Only in such fashion, he repeatedly states, can the love which is at the heart of the Bible, and therefore at the heart of any true religion, be expressed. Thus Walwyn had joined in the battle against the Independent faction ruling England; while Lilburne hurled his defiance at the Council of State, Walwyn in this tract disparaged such of its pulpit supporters as Nye and Goodwin. In political terms, however, neither attack was effective.[23]

During the spring of 1649 Walwyn withdrew from Leveller activities,[24] his place as one of the spokesmen of the party being partially and momentarily filled by Captain William Bray. Bray had been so stirred by Leveller propaganda at the end of 1647 that he had participated in the brief mutiny against Cromwell which followed the Putney Debate. Then, early in March 1649, as a member of the Council of Officers, he protested so vigorously against the treatment of the soldier petitioners that he was promptly cashiered.[25] Immediately thereafter he issued two militant "Appeals," both of which indicate that the cause of the Levellers was well along the road to complete defeat;[26] for Bray, in stressing his own and his military colleagues' grievances, was no longer expressing the complaints of a large segment of the army, but only those of a small and ineffectual group of dissidents — a group shortly thereafter suppressed as mutineers. In fact, the disillusionment evident in these appeals, despite their external Lilburnesque air of defiance, was corroborated by Bray's prompt commitment to jail.

This disillusionment was made more manifest in one of Overton's final pamphlets, the violently class-conscious *The Hunting of the Foxes from New-Market and Triploe-Heaths to Whitehall, By five small Beagles (late of the Armie.),* which appeared on March 21.[27] The five small beagles who allegedly penned this tract were the same soldiers who the month before had written Fairfax attacking the Council of State and protesting the curtailment of their right to petition, and who, therefore, had been immediately court-martialed. Writing in their names, Overton came to their defense in this stinging attack on the Grandees, filling it with all the bitter irony and invective of which he was capable. *The Hunting of the Foxes* is thus a masterpiece of angrily distorted history, one which traces the footsteps of Cromwell and Ireton from their first apparent wickedness in 1647 to their present "Master Den, where you may finde the whole litter . . . in conspiracy."

According to Overton, these two years have been marked by the continued conflict between the forces of good and evil, and he begins his vivid oversimplification by identifying the soldiers with good, the officers with evil: "for . . . there is no more difference between them than betwixt Christ and Belial, light and darknesse." [28] Then, after telling how Charles had purportedly bribed Cromwell with the offer of an earldom, Overton summarizes the events of the second half of 1647:

They [Cromwell and Ireton] cast off those robes of Royalty with which they had rendred themselves acceptable with the King's adherents, and laid aside the King and them; finding the way of an Agreement of the People to be much affected and endeavored after among the souldiery, they also invest themselves with that Robe, to hide their deformity from the Army; and the better to allay all motions after the same, they confess and acknowledge the excellency and goodness of the premises, they only find the same unseasonable; and this was drest out in such taking Saint-like language, as the religious people might best be surprised, not suspecting any venomous thing to be lurking under the leaf of their holy and sacred pretences: they call Fasts (a certain fore-runner of mischief with them), cry, and howl, and bedew their cheeks with the tears of hypocrisie and deceit, confess their iniquity and abomination in declining the cause of the people and tampering with the King; and humbly, as in the presence of the all-seeing God, acknowledge the way of an Agreement of the People to be the way to our Peace and Freedom; and even then, as soon as they had wiped their eyes and their mouths, they proceed even to death, imprisonment or cashierment of all such in the Army as promoted or owned the Agreement . . . by which the honest party of the Souldiery was very much weakned, and all the promoters of Freedom discouraged, and the people struck into desperation; which gave rise unto the second war amongst our selves, and invasion of the Scots.[29]

So, too, Overton continues, have been the dealings of the Grandees with the Second Agreement of the People, and their present "usurpation of the civil Authority." But these actions are not surprising, for ever since the Engagement of June 1647 the Grandees have considered the soldiers as "meer mercenary slaves." Nor have Cromwell and Ireton stopped there; now even the Parliament "is no Parliament, but a Representative of Cromwell, Ireton, and Harrison." [30] Consequently England, which before the war was "ruled by King, Lords, and Commons," is now ruled by "a General, a Court Martial, and [an impotent] House of Commons." "What," Overton asks, "is the difference?"

In this way *The Hunting of the Foxes* provides a vitriolic background for its presentation of the case of the five soldiers who had just been cashiered for demanding their democratic rights. Overton's detailed abstract of their military cross-examinations was not calculated to evoke any sympathy for Cromwell and the Officers' Council. Each of the five defendants is here reported to have stood up for the liberties of England against the Machiavellian and brutal browbeating of the officers who interrogated them. Like Lilburne, each of the five often played the part of the accuser rather than the accused, and the last soldier to be examined charged the Grandees with being the "real Levellers," for it is they who have "levelled to the ground" the faith and confidence of the nation.[31] After this, *The Hunting of the Foxes* comes to an abrupt end with a petition presumably prepared by some of the New Model soldiers: addressed to the House of Commons, it asks that the right of the rank and file to petition be fully restored, that the power of the high officers be curbed, and that the apprehensions expressed by Lilburne in *Englands New Chains* "be speedily taken into consideration, and effectually accomplished."

The very stridency of *The Hunting of the Foxes* — its aggressively loaded language and twisted evidence — is perhaps another indica-

tion of the Levellers' growing realization that the wall of Cromwell's power against which they were butting (and wailing) was
made of stone.[32] Indeed, it seemed to be, for within three days of
the appearance of Overton's pamphlet the Independents in Parliament and army had their pretext for jailing the London Levellers: on March 24, 1649, Lilburne presented to the House of Commons *The Second Part of Englands New-Chaines discovered*, the
mass petition promised, or threatened, at the end of *Englands New
Chaines*.[33] Already signed by many hands,[34] it asked all who approved its program to bring their written assent to an agent of the
Levellers.[35] For almost the last time their party organization was
functioning throughout England, and in all probability the Grandees' quick reaction to this pamphlet was occasioned more by the
activities in its support than by its seemingly inflammatory message.[36]

Basically, this message was inconsistent. The pamphlet begins
by attacking the Rump for its subservience and degeneracy, and it
concludes by asking the Rump to make arrangements for its own
dissolution, for curbing the Grandees, and for instituting a democratic Agreement of the People. Despite this inconsistency, Lilburne
manages to make the intervening story of Cromwell's allegedly
calculated megalomania seem brutally undeviating: from Cromwell's "false" Engagement of June 1647, through his deceits practiced at Putney, his selfish and hypocritical negotiations with the
king, his tricking of the Levellers, his defamation of all true patriots, his rigged murder of Rainsborough, his enslavement of the
army; until now, by means of the Council of State, he and the
Grandees have finally arrived at the power they long "aimed at
and intended," the only remaining step being the elevation of
Cromwell to the throne so that he can continue to exercise the military dictatorship that has been his contribution to the welfare of
England. At this stage of the desperate game of history, Lilburne
continues, the only hope against these tyrants lies in the fact that
"they have already lost the Affections of all People, and are onely
supported by their present strength"; therefore the Levellers, by a
campaign of public enlightenment and minor civil disobedience,
may be able to induce Parliament to take urgently needed action.

This somewhat hysterical assault on the Grandees differs from

The Hunting of the Foxes in three respects: first, its tone is a little sadder, its style less acid; second, it is less concerned with the plight of the common soldiers, more concerned with the country as a whole; and third, it is more aware of the economic dislocations which were then causing trade to stagnate and adding to the poverty of the English masses.[37] Much of Lilburne's build-up to the accusation that the Grandees are even worse than the Royalists or Presbyterians is, in fact, devoted to an emphasis on these economic ills, ills about which the government has done nothing "except the setting [of] fresh hungry flyes upon the old sores of the People."

Alive to this national economic discontent, alive to the Leveller agitation against the excise and the free quartering of soldiers, and alive to the dangers implicit in the active circulation of this so-called petition, the military leaders, through the Rump, acted quickly and decisively. On March 27, three days after *The Second Part of Englands New-Chaines* was laid before the House, its supposed authors were declared traitors.[38] The next day Lilburne, along with Walwyn, Overton, and Thomas Prince, was haled before the Council of State.

The narrative of their arrest and examination is told in *The Picture of the Councel of State*, which consists of statements by Lilburne, Overton, and Prince, signed by them between the first and fourth of April;[39] and in Walwyn's *The Fountain of Slaunder Discovered*, in which, at the end of May, he published his own story.[40] Each man tells how, early in the morning, he was routed from bed, then escorted by armed guards to Whitehall, and there interrogated by the Council of State. Each of the four dramatic accounts is essentially similar, yet each reveals certain differences in the personalities, though not in the social ideals, of these Leveller leaders.

As might be expected, Lilburne's narrative is the longest. Because he was the principal author of *The Second Part of Englands New-Chaines*, and because he was the first to be cross-examined, his answers to the Council established the pattern followed by Overton, Prince, and Walwyn. After detailing the horror of his rough and sudden arrest, Lilburne tells of his initial appearance before Bradshaw and his colleagues, and how he introduced himself to them by refusing to take off his hat until he recognized certain members of Parliament on the bench. Then followed his interrogation: "What was Lilburne's part in this recent scandalous pamphlet?" and his lengthy reply to the effect that the Council had no judicial power, and that, if Parliament had granted it any such power, that grant was illegal, for Parliament could make but could not execute the law. Moreover, continued the fiery Lilburne, the Council was proceeding against him in a manner unknown to declared law, and with all the accoutrements of military tyranny — as if he were "some monstrous man."

To Lilburne's long speech Bradshaw replied that the Council was acting as a board of inquiry, not as a judicial tribunal; therefore, had Lilburne had any part in *The Second Part of Englands New-Chaines?* Again Lilburne refused to answer, now basing his refusal on the fact that by responding he would acknowledge the Council's legal jurisdiction over him and thus "betray the Liberties of England"; further, any answer would be self-incriminating. He therefore concluded his testimony with this defiant assertion:

But Sir, This I will say to you, my late Actions have not bin done in a hole, or a corner, but on the house top, in the face of the Sun, before hundreds and some thousands of people; and therefore why ask you me any questions? Go to those that have heard me, and seen me, and it is possible you may find some hundreds of witnesses to tell you what I have said and done; for I hate holes and corners: My late Actions need no covers nor hidings, they have bin more honest than so, and I am not sorry for what I have done, for I did look well about me before I did what I did, and I am ready to lay down my life to justifie what I have done; and so much in answer to your question.[41]

Then, specifically addressing Cromwell, Lilburne told the Council that if he were turned over to military arrest he would burn the prison to the ground, though "he be burnt to ashes with the flames thereof."

After the other three men had returned similar answers, Lilburne, his ear to the door of the Council chamber, overheard Cromwell say that there was "no other way to deale with these men, but to break them in pieces; . . . if you do not breake them, they will break you."[42] The Council chose the first alternative: on the next day the four men, having been denied bail, were committed to the

Tower — to which, with a rare touch of humor, Lilburne refers as his "old and contented Lodging." There an Independent minister promptly came to try to win the four men over to the cause of Cromwell. Lilburne's response to his inducements was a challenge to the Grandees: either amend the Officers' Agreement of the People to conform to most of the Leveller expectations and then implement it, or let four Levellers and four members of the government, including Cromwell and Ireton, work out a new agreement. Then, says Lilburne, he and his party will be content!

Lilburne's total performance was thus amazingly like his first appearance before Star Chamber twelve years earlier. His final remarks in his section of *The Picture of the Councel of State* specifically attest to the fact that, in a sense, his ideological wheel had come full circle: [43]

I know before God none is righteous . . . but only he that is clothed with the glorious righteousness of Jesus Christ, which I assuredly know my soul hath bin, and now is clothed with, in the strength of which I have walked for above 12 yeers together, and through the strength of which I have bin able at any time in al that time to lay down my life in a quarter of an hours warning.[44]

Overton's testimony was briefer, harder hitting, and the graphic circumstances of his arrest lost none of their color in the telling. Unlike Lilburne, Overton was able to sprinkle his indignation with many touches of irony and satire, though his answers to Bradshaw almost repeated Lilburne's words. His concluding remarks in his portion of *The Picture of the Councel of State* also echo Lilburne's in that both men took this opportunity to reaffirm their personal integrity. But Overton's tone is more secular. After telling his readers that, unless they realize that his case is theirs, they will find themselves "new fettered in chaines such as England never knew or tasted before," and after justifying his career against an assortment of calumnies, Overton thus ends his peroration with this incisive statement:

So that the businesse is, not how great a sinner I am, but how faithful and reall to the Common-wealth; that's the matter concerneth my neighbor, and whereof my neighbor is only in this publick Controversie to take notice; and for my personall sins that are not of Civill cognizance or wrong unto him, to leave them to God, whose judgment is righteous and just.[45]

Prince's narrative is short and colorless, and it merely repeats the sentiments of Lilburne and Overton. Nor does Walwyn's brief though later account add much except a note of surprise at being linked to a manifesto in which, for a change, he had had no hand.[46] But in spite of Walwyn's innocence, all four men were able to behave in almost identical fashion, and with Lilburne in this case calling the tune they defied the Council in concert. Together they were committed to the Tower, there to await trial before the judges of the Upper Bench at Westminster.[47]

Though its leaders were in jail, the Leveller party, in its final struggle with entrenched authority, sprang into immediate petitionary activity. On April 2, 1649, a petition bearing 10,000 signatures was presented to the House by a group of eighty men.[48] Two weeks later a similar petition, demanding that the government adhere to the declared law and traditional legal procedures of the land and also signed by 10,000, was presented to the Rump.[49] And, on April 23, a *Petition of divers wel-affected Women* was brought to the House of Commons by a crowd of women.[50] Calling attention to their own grievances, among them the high cost of living, these women proclaimed their intimate identification with the cause of the Levellers. Moreover, their activity in circulating and promoting this petition illustrates the ferment occasioned by the democratic propaganda of the Levellers: for almost the first time in English history, and much to the ribald amusement of certain contemporary journalists, women were asserting that they had some political rights, not excluding the right to participate in the actual rough and tumble of politics.[51] This flurry of party activity, which extended well into the month of May, also included at least one petition circulated among the soldiers.[52] As a result, the plight of the four prisoners was given enough publicity, if not to cause their release and vindication, at least to prod Parliament into promising them a speedy trial.[53]

From the Tower, on April 14, the prisoners themselves issued their own impressive vindication, *A Manifestation.*[54] Though signed by all four men, this moderate, succinct, and by no means subliterary document was almost certainly written by Walwyn alone.[55] Since it

represents a final summary, along with the last Agreement of the
People which appeared two weeks later, of fully matured Leveller
philosophy, program, and aspirations, and since it is in reality the
history of a lost cause, its message is at once exciting and plaintive.
Hence it is not surprising that the opening paragraph is both traditional in its devout humility and visionary in its underlying optimism — an optimism which becomes far less subdued as the pamphlet moves forward:

Since no man is born for himself only, but obliged by the Laws of
Nature (which reaches all), of Christianity (which ingages us as Christians), and of Public Societie and Government, to employ our endeavours
for the advancement of a communitive Happinesse, of equall concern-
ment to others as our selves: here have we (according to that measure
of understanding God hath dispensed unto us) laboured with much
weaknesse indeed, but with integrity of heart, to produce out of the
Common Calamaties such a proportion of Freedom and good to the
Nation as might somewhat compensate its many grievances and lasting
sufferings: And although in doing thereof we have hitherto reaped only
Reproach and hatred for our good Will, and been faine to wrestle with
the violent passions of Powers and Principalities; yet since it is nothing
so much as our blessed Master and his Followers suffered before us, and
but what at first we reckoned upon, we cannot be thereby any whit dis-
mayed in the performance of our duties, supported inwardly by the
Innocency and evennesse of our Consciences.

A Manifestation then goes on to show that, in spite of the "abundant Calamaties" that have "overspread all quarters of the Land,"
the only changes wrought have been "Notionall, Nominall, Cir-
cumstantiall, whilst the reall burdens, Grievances, and Bondages
be continued, even when the Monarchy is changed into a Repub-
like."[56] One of the main reasons for this evident lack of national
progress has been the deliberate attempt by those in power so to
traduce the Levellers that they will be "uselesse and unserviceable
to the Common-wealth." Walwyn thus summarizes this campaign
of rumors, before answering them one by one in the remaining
pages of his tract:

In all places they [these rumors] are spread and industriously propo-
gated, . . . the first being . . . that there is more in our designs
then appears, that there is something of danger in the bottom of

our hearts, not yet discovered; that we are driven on by others, that we are even discontented and irresolved, that no body yet knowes what we would have, or where our desires will end; whilst they that know us not are made believe any strange conceit of us, that we would Levell all mens estates, that we would have no distinction of Orders and Dignities amongst men, that we are indeed for no government, but a Popular confusion; and then againe that we have bin Agents for the King, and now for the Queen; That we are Atheists, Antiscripturists, Jesuites, and indeed any thing that is hatefull and of evill repute amongst men.[57]

Walwyn first turns to the charge that the Levellers are "levellers" — in other words, that they are blood brothers to the scorned Diggers who were at that moment attempting to communize a hill-top in Surrey. The truth is, Walwyn affirms, that his party is against communism, and it has long and explicitly advocated a clause in its various manifestoes to restrain Parliament for ever from "an equall-ling of mens estates." Such an equality, he implies, might be de-sirable if, as was the case among certain "primitive Christians," it were entirely voluntary; but for the present the political Levellers are only working to establish a state in which "every man may, with as much security as may be, enjoy his propriety."

To the accusation that he and his fellow prisoners are anarchists Walwyn gives vigorous denial:

That we are for Government and against Popular Confusion, we con-ceive all our actions declare, . . . our aim having bin all along to reduce it as near as might be to perfection, and certainly we know very well the pravity and corruption of mans heart is such that there could be no living without it; and though Tyranny is so excessively bad, yet of the two extreames, Confusion is the worst: Tis somewhat a strange consequence to infer that because we have laboured so earnestly for a good Government, therefore we would have none at all, because we would have the dead and exorbitant Branches pruned . . . therefore we would pluck the Tree up by the roots.[58]

Shifting next to the allegation that the Levellers are agents of the king, Walwyn points out that "those Principles and Maxims . . . which are most fundamentally opposite to the Prerogative, and the Kings interest" had their "first rise and originall" within his party; at the same time, Walwyn also claims that the Levellers have always worked for the conversion, not the destruction, of the Royalists.

A Manifestation illuminates the rationalism and the belief in progress implicit in the entire Leveller program when it comes to answer the charge that the leaders of the party are in any way corrupt: "the things we promote," Walwyn says,

are not good onely in appearance, but sensibly so: not moulded nor contrived by the subtill or politick Principles of the World, but plainly produced and nakedly sent, without any insinuating arts, relying wholly upon the apparent and universall beleefe they carry in themselves; and that is it which convinces and engages us in the promotion thereof.[59]

This optimism, in turn, has a religious basis, for the Levellers, Walwyn continues, are not Jesuits or atheists or antiscripturists. Though he and his friends may not be too strict "upon the formall and Ceremoniall part" of service to God, they firmly believe that He is eternal and omnipotent, and that to His "will and direction . . . [they] ought to square their actions and conversations."

Finally, combining the Calvinist's sense of sin with the radical's vision of potential perfectibility, Walwyn answers the last in this imposing list of anti-Leveller innuendoes:

And whereas 'tis urged, That if we were in power we would bear our selves as Tyranically as others have done: We confesse indeed that the experimentall defections of so many men as have succeeded in Authority, and the exceeding difference we have hitherto found in the same men in low and in an exalted condition, make us even mistrust our own hearts, and hardly beleeve our own Resolutions to the contrary. And therefore we have proposed such an Establishment, as supposing men to be too flexible and yeelding to worldly Temptations, they should not yet have a means or opportunity either to injure particulars, or preju- dice the Publick, without extreme hazard and apparent danger to themselves. Besides . . . we aim not at power in our selves, our Principles and Desires being in no measure of self-concernment: nor do we relie for obtaining the same upon strength, or a forcible obstruction; but solely upon that inbred and perswasive power that is in all good and just things to make their own way in the hearts of men, and so to procure their own Establishment.[60]

Firm in this last conviction, the four prisoners are now busy, so

A Manifestation reports, preparing their final Agreement of the People, "the standard and ultimate scope" of their designs. It is only by means of such an agreement, Walwyn concludes, that the Commonwealth can secure "the fairest probabilities of a lasting Peace, and contentfull Establishment." But from the Tower it was probably difficult to assess the troubles Cromwell's junta was having in curbing a widespread Royalist reaction, in fighting a war in Ireland, and in putting down a variety of antirepublican demonstrations throughout the land.[61] Wolfe aptly sums up the limitations of Walwyn's *A Manifestation* when he notes that the political idealism of the Levellers was at once their major ideological strength and their chief weakness: "they were last-ditch idealists, born centuries too soon, impatient, impulsive, unwilling or unable to gauge the barriers that barred the way to their utopian England." [62] Presumably then as now extreme farsightedness was not a political asset: the fate of the final Leveller Agreement was already written on the wall of Whitehall.

II. May 1649: The Final Agreement of the People

The visionary idealism of *A Manifestation* received a prompt reply. At the end of April 1649 appeared *Walwins Wiles*, largely the work of John Price, an associate of John Goodwin's and the man who the previous November had objected to Walwyn's participation in the negotiations for an Agreement of the People.[63] Among the seven Independent and Baptist ministers who signed the dedication to *Walwins Wiles* were William Kiffin and Edmund Rozer, two of Lilburne's closest colleagues in the days when he first admired John Bastwick. That the Levellers had travelled far from their former friends is further shown by the contents of this elaborately derogatory pamphlet, the material for which the alarmed Independents had been accumulating for almost three years, and which, on the eve of the final Agreement of the People, they now flung at Walwyn and his fellow prisoners in one concentrated package.[64]

In order effectively to accomplish its major purpose, the vilification of Walwyn, *Walwins Wiles* first gives high praise to the powers ruling England; then it goes on to show that Walwyn is the real leader of the Levellers, with Lilburne, Overton, and Prince functioning mainly as his misled tools. Therefore the subversion and revolution preached by the Leveller party is the responsibility of its wily intellectual leader, the "deluding, cozening, . . . deceiving, . . . destructive" William Walwyn. The case against him is carefully built up: his political Machiavellianism, his agnosticism and scepticism, his mockery of the orthodox, his class-conscious communism, his demagogic radicalism. The lavish evidence in support of these accusations takes two forms: anecdotes (for instance, the story that Walwyn once induced a woman to commit suicide), and selections from Leveller manifestoes, particularly from recent petitions which, the tract avers, reveal the clever and incendiary hand of Walwyn. Price, with his Independent and Baptist allies, thus attempts to show that this man, so active against the *status quo*, no longer has a place among the fellowship of the righteous, for he is a man who can smile and smile and be a villain, and whose soul will never go to Heaven. Hence the charges against Walwyn are chiefly personal and religious; Walwyn's political derelictions merely substantiate the wickedness of his ways.

One of the most flagrant as well as one of the most illustrative of these political derelictions, says Price repeatedly, has been the recent Leveller opposition to sending troops to Ireland for the suppression of the anti-Protestant, anti-Commonwealth rebels. Shortly before the publication of *Walwins Wiles* certain regiments had been chosen by lot for service in Ireland; yet many of the New Model soldiers to whom arrears were still owed were ready to resist their officers.[65] Therefore Price's charge that the Levellers were attempting to "divide the Army" seemed particularly cogent, and it throws more light on Cromwell's threat that the Levellers had to be broken. On April 24 there was a minor mutiny in one of the regiments stationed in London. The next day it was easily put down and two days later its ringleader, Robert Lockyer, for two years an active supporter of the Levellers, was executed.[66] The murmur of discontent in the army consequently provided an ominous background for the shocked outcries of the Independent and Baptist ministers.

On the day that Lockyer stood before a firing squad, Lilburne and Overton released *The Copie of a Letter* addressed to Fairfax. This

one-page denunciation of the Grandees proclaims that they have
subverted the glory of a democratic army and the basis of English
law by their tyrannical abuse of military power, and that Cromwell, like Strafford, will "meet the revenge visited upon . . . illegal
usurpers." Lockyer's impressive funeral two days later, though it
did not fulfill this threat, probably did mark the high point of
Leveller popularity — but not of Leveller power. In a manner
tain to appeal to the antimilitary sentiment prevalent in
the corpse of the "Army's Martyr" was led through   a
slow procession, while thousands of the mourners   llowed
the hearse wore a green ribbon to show their sympathy for the
cause of the Levellers.[67] It was to the echo of the mournful trumpets
of this funeral and to the preliminary rumblings of the scattered
New Model mutinies of early May that the final Leveller Agreement of the People was published.[68]

May 1, 1649, was not a propitious moment to issue a revolutionary manifesto. Moreover, *An Agreement of the Free People of
England* was the most fully developed program ever put forward
by the Levellers. The four authors, Lilburne, Overton, Walwyn, and
Prince, had, as *A Manifestation* declared, been working on the
Agreement for at least two weeks — and in the Tower these men
were not in a position where they had to compromise with any
group of officers, nor did they have to worry about being arrested
for issuing anything "scandalous" to the government. As a result,
this *Agreement*, coming at the end of more than two years of organized party activity, and at the end of a decade of intense social
thinking on the part of its framers, exhibited a synthesis of the
accumulated political wisdom of the Levellers. Though this document contained little that was new, the fully ripened conviction
held by its authors that power corrupts made it the most revolutionary of the Leveller constitutions — this despite the fact that the
program itself was presented as a "Peace-Offering to the . . .
Nation." Further, as the Levellers had learned by personal experience increasingly to distrust those in power, so their apparent confidence in "the wisdom of the People" had grown. The radicalism
of this final *Agreement* lay, therefore, in its attempt to set up as
broad and enduring a democracy as its imprisoned authors could
envision.

An Agreement of the Free People of England begins with the optimistic claim that the idea of such an agreement has "made its own way into the understanding, and taken root in most mens hearts and affections," and that, consequently, the majority of the people, God willing, can expect the blessings of true democracy.

The thirty articles which constitute the program for that democracy follow this brief "Preparative." Their over-all purpose is to establish a government which will "abolish all arbitrary power, . . . set bounds and limits both to . . . [the] Supreme, and all Subordinate Authority, and remove all known grievances." The fulcrum of the Leveller scheme, the supreme authority, is the "Representative of the People." It is to consist of 400 persons, elected by all men over the age of twenty-one who are not servants or paupers.[69] No officer of the army or paid civil servant can be a member of this new House of Commons, and lawyers are again barred from practicing their profession while serving as its members. The next five articles set up further barriers to the concentration of power in the hands of any person or faction: no man can serve in two successive Parliaments; Parliaments are to be annual and are to sit for at least four months; in the interval between sessions England is to be run by a Parliamentary committee, not by a Council of State; the Rump is to be dissolved in August 1649; and, in case it has not made arrangements for a new representative to take over, the people are to proceed to elect one of their own.[70]

The *Agreement*, after briefly listing the general powers of this future supreme authority, next itemizes those reservations which the Levellers had long declared necessary to preserve the native rights of the people. Thus freedom of religion is guaranteed, limited only by the very negligible restriction that a person who maintains the political supremacy of the Pope can be barred from holding public office. Several articles are devoted to securing that equalization of the law which had long been a staple of radical propaganda, and, collectively, they form an effective assertion of the liberty and dignity of the common man. No man is to be exempted from normal legal procedures because of privilege, grant, or birth; no magistrate or court is to invade the domain of individual rights by means of ex post facto laws; self-incrimination, long legal delays, and the need to rely on professional lawyers are all done away with—

instead, the law is to be simplified and put into English, trials are to take place before local and freely chosen juries, the right to proper witnesses is to be made absolute, and capital punishment, except in cases of murder and subversion of the agreement itself, is to be eliminated, along with other cruel and unusual punishments.

The limitations placed on Parliament's power in the field of economics are essentially the result of a similar mixture of personal experience and historical foresight, of the traditional grievances of the lower middle class and the incipient rugged individualism of forum and market place. Therefore, in addition to its predictable denunciations of communism and tithes, the *Agreement* declares against any restrictions on foreign trade, against the excise, against imprisonment for debt, and in favor of a system of taxation based on real and personal property.

The chief new points in this final *Agreement* are those which go beyond the Levellers' usual laissez-faire attitude in politics and economics for the sake of securing a maximum decentralization of power. Among these added provisions is the right given each parish to choose its own minister "upon such terms, and for such reward, as themselves shall be willing to contribute, or shall contract for." Moreover, the people of any recognized local entity ("Counties, Hundreds, Cities, Towns, or Boroughs") are now annually to choose their own public officers.[71] Then too, because the Levellers had learned that "nothing threateneth greater danger to the Common wealth then that the Military power should . . . come to be superior to the Civil Authority," they inserted this supplemental rule concerning the raising of future armed forces:

That they [the new representatives] allot to each particular County, City, Town, and Borrough, the raising, furnishing, agreeing, and paying of a due proportion [of the armed forces], . . . and . . . the Electors of Representatives in each respective place . . . [shall have] Free liberty to nominate and appoint all Officers . . . and to remove them as they shall see cause, reserving to the Representative the nominating and appointing onely of the General, and all General-Officers.[72]

To their suspicions of king and Lords, of prelate and presbyter, of Parliament unpurged and purged, the Levellers thus added their

legitimate doubts about the trustworthiness of the New Model.
Hence, to make sure that common people of England would retain
their extensive democratic rights in perpetuity, the last clause of
An Agreement of the Free People of England specifies that no
future House of Commons can "take away any part of this Agreement," and that "all laws made, or that shall be made contrary to
any part of . . . [it] are hereby made null and void." In short,
this final Leveller "Peace-Offering" was intended to settle the
Commonwealth in prosperity, peace, and freedom for untold generations.

Posterity was given no chance to put the Leveller program to
the test, for despite its allegedly benign aims and the moderateness
of its language, this new *Agreement* threatened almost all the
vested interests in England; and, what is more important, it explicitly asked those men in the Rump and in the army now running the country to step down and allow "the People" to take
over. But the Rump did not dissolve itself, and Cromwell did not
retire from public affairs; instead, the restrictions on the four prisoners were tightened.[73] The popular response to Lockyer's funeral,
the signs of sporadic mutiny in the army, and the wide circulation
of this *Agreement* had all helped to convince the government that
precautions were necessary. In addition, an apparently prearranged
outpouring of petitions in behalf of the prisoners and their program now increased the pressure on the Grandees to view the
Levellers as a real and immediate threat to England's stability.

On May 2, 1649, two separate delegations petitioned the House
of Commons to free Lilburne, Overton, Walwyn, and Prince, and
to provide for Parliament's speedy dissolution.[74] Three days later
the female branch of the Leveller party returned to Westminster
with a second *Petition of Women*, in which they both asserted that
they had "an equal interest with the men of this nation in . . .
[its] liberties and securities" and demanded that the rights of
their husbands and protectors be restored.[75] On the following day
the apprentices of Cripplegate published their thanks to the prisoners in the Tower for the efforts of these men in behalf of "this
poor distressed and miserably wasted nation";[76] and a week later
probably the same group of apprentices issued a similar manifesto —
one which likewise indicates the potentially revolutionary appeal

the Levellers had built up among their economically depressed urban adherents.[77] Finally, during this first half of May, in the last truly concerted campaign of the party, the radical agents outside London were also busy, and at least two petitions, one from Essex and one from Buckinghamshire, were brought to Westminster.[78] Thus were the Grandees under pressure to view with alarm.

But more dangerous to the authorities than these vehement petitions was the response to *An Agreement of the Free People of England* of two small and disaffected groups within the New Model — a response which was quickly and effectively suppressed: the Levellers' "Peace-Offering" and the final surge of party activity which it occasioned thus resulted directly in only the aimless and historically insignificant violence of two minor mutinies.[79] But by the middle of the month full military discipline once again held sway. The apparent harmony and stability of the new government were given official sanction on May 19, 1649: Oxford granted honorary degrees to Cromwell, Fairfax, and others of the Grandees, and Parliament passed "An Act Declaring England to be a Commonwealth." [80] It was a Commonwealth that had room neither for king and House of Lords nor for the Levellers and their disturbing schemes. But for the moment it was stable: Charles was dead; the Leveller party was rapidly dying.

III. *May to November 1649: The Death of the Leveller Party*

The *rigor mortis* of the Levellers as a political party manifested itself in two forms: first, disillusionment; second, personal vindication by the still imprisoned leaders of what had recently been a cohesive and widespread revolutionary organization. The disillusion is particularly evident in two pamphlets of the end of May 1649. On May 24 Henry Denne, one of the army mutineers, published his recantation, *The Levellers Designe Discovered: Or the Anatomie of the late unhappie Mutinie.*[81] Though this pamphlet is primarily an open confession of sin, it is also a testimony to the quick shattering of Leveller hopes. Denne tells how the mutineers were convinced by the Levellers that the vast bulk of the army would join them; how the violence of the radicals' aspersions on the Grandees, combined with the New Model's irritations at Parliament's failure to meet the soldiers' material demands, seemed to assure the success of any such violent social revolution. Denne ends his tract with a sorrowful and shamefaced apology for his own participation in this deluded and vicious undertaking, and with a warning to others not to be similarly misled.

The following day a short pamphlet entitled *A Discourse Betwixt . . . Lilburne . . . and Mr. Hugh Peters* appeared.[82] This presumably authentic report of the interview between the two men is another example of Leveller disillusionment, for despite Lilburne's proud and aggressive language, and despite his impassioned defense of a government of laws, it shows his willingness to shift to the cause of the Royalists as an alternative to military dictatorship or an undemocratic Commonwealth.

The first of several pamphlets devoted to vindicating the characters and actions of the four prisoners appeared at the end of May. This work, *The Charity of Church-men*, written by Walwyn's son-in-law Humphrey Brooke, was a direct reply to *Walwins Wiles*.[83] Valuable largely as a spiritual biography of Walwyn, Brooke's tract emphasizes its subject's "Christian fortitude" in the face of the nefarious and calculated calumnies of the Independents, though it implies that the cause for which Walwyn has so long fought is on the verge of defeat.

Brooke's pamphlet was promptly followed by Walwyn's publication of *The Fountain of Slaunder Discovered*.[84] Like the narratives of the three other prisoners in *The Picture of the Councel of State*, *The Fountain* is largely concerned with the story of Walwyn's arrest and cross-examination. But now, two months after the event, he brings his account to an end with the remark that he and his colleagues are still languishing in the Tower, "to the great rejoycing of all that hate us, [and] whose longing desires are so far satisfied" — and whose satisfaction, he implies, is unlikely to be thwarted.

Early in June, Walwyn supplemented this vindication of his own conduct and morals by *Walwyns Just Defence*.[85] A far more effective reply to *Walwins Wiles* than Brooke's *Charity of Church-men*, it represented almost two years of thought on Walwyn's part about how best to answer the charges which he knew the Independents were marshaling against him. As a result, his *Just Defence* is both closely reasoned and retrospective. Much of it is devoted to a detailed history of the alleged double-dealing practiced since late 1646 by the mud-slinging Independents, and with an imposing array of names, incidents, and conversations Walwyn lays bare the story of the growing breach between the followers of John Goodwin and those who believed in the cause of the Levellers, a breach which has culminated in Price's outrageous attack and in the present plight of Walwyn and his associates. The remainder is largely concerned with picturing Walwyn's own development: his reading and discourse, the growth of his antinomianism, his efforts in behalf of a better Commonwealth. In drawing this picture Walwyn continues to use the device of contrast to point up the gulf between himself and his opponents. At one point, for example, he notes that the Independents (like Emerson) are not in jail, for "it seems . . . [their] Congregation is of a near relation to those that hold prosperity a mark of the true Church," while the Levellers, because they have supported the ideal of a fairer Commonwealth, have met only with affliction.

Walwyn's sense of regret may well have been confirmed by an officially sponsored attack on the Levellers which came out early in June 1649. This answer to *The Second Part of Englands New-Chaines, The Discoverer,* was composed partly by the chief secretary of the Council of State, Robert Frost, but principally by a Baptist minister named John Canne.[86] Between them, Frost and Canne here add little that is new to the case against the Levellers — except the statement that to keep them in check is now costing the government £100,000 a year.[87] *The Discoverer* does reveal, however, that the publicity campaign against them has further shifted from the political polemics of an Ireton to the moral indignation of a John Price. Thus the Levellers are compared to the incendiaries who fired Munster; they are accused of hypocrisy and of using scurrilous language; they are called atheists who believe in rationalism and mortalism, who attack ministers of the Gospel, and who ignore true religion. Moreover, their atheism is close to the ungodly beliefs of the Diggers, just as the Leveller attacks on the vested interests of the nation are akin to the threats in Digger communism.[88] Finally, the Levellers have addressed themselves to the "vulgar and poor" in an attempt to subvert both Parliament and army; consequently their writings and actions have been divisive, dangerous, and depraved. In short, say Frost and Canne, Parliament and the Council of State have acted wisely and patriotically in putting these men behind bars.

In the seventy-five pages of *The Legall Fundamentall Liberties of the People of England*, which appeared a week later, Lilburne only mentions *The Discoverer* once.[89] Yet this mainly autobiographical work is, like Walwyn's *Just Defence*, devoted to justifying the life, the actions, and the moral views of one of the leaders of the Leveller party. In so doing, *Legall Fundamentall Liberties* also attempts to show that the Leveller movement has been intent on peace, freedom, and righteousness, not on power, self-interest, and wealth. Lilburne is here both wrathful and long-winded, but at the same time he is extremely intense about his own, and indirectly his party's, vindication. As a result, this pamphlet is a rich mine of information on the life of the most active and most articulate of the Levellers, but it is a mine that contains a great deal of slag.

Lilburne gets under way with a voluminous attack on the present Parliament, for under the leadership of Cromwell it is now an illegal body which is persecuting the true defenders of England in the same manner formerly employed by the House of Lords. Now, too, his former friends are hunting him down "like a partridge upon the mountains." This present martyrdom is Lilburne's cue to tell the saga of his vicissitudes in fighting the good fight. He therefore starts his autobiography with his coming to London as a young apprentice in the early 1630's, and concludes it with his "causeless Captivity" of June 1649. Like his own misfortunes, he goes on, are the economic depression and the terror gripping the nation — themselves further symptoms of the decline of England's hopes. Depression is bringing misery to the people and, augmented by official restraints on trade, it is preventing such honest and industrious men as Lilburne from setting up in business. Governmental terror is manifesting itself in the illegal acts perpetrated by the sword of the military, a sword wielded in special courts and effecting cruel and arbitrary punishments. Thus, Lilburne concludes, the convictions and experience he has acquired during his adult life have forced him again to warn his countrymen of their plight; the two parts of *Englands New Chains* and now *Legall Fundamentall*

Liberties have constituted that warning, while the Tower has symbolized the reaction of the Grandees.

Thomas Prince's retort to *Walwins Wiles* and indirectly to *The Discoverer*, *The Silken Independents Snare Broken*, came out on June 20, 1649. He too denies that he is a "younger brother" misled into the councils of the Levellers, and he berates the authors of the recent attacks on himself and his colleagues as liars, slanderers, and upholders of a "New England design." Further, it is they, the self-righteous Independents, who have emasculated Parliament and abused and divided the people of England, whereas his own life, like the lives of his fellow prisoners, has been devoted to patriotism and decency; and Prince therewith lists all the contributions, both personal and financial in nature, which for seven years he has been making to the godly cause of peace and freedom.

Finally, at the end of June, the last in this series of personal vindications appeared, Humphrey Brooke's *The Crafts-mens Craft. Or The Wiles of the Discoverers*. Here Brooke shifts his counterattack from Price and Goodwin to Frost and Canne, though he accuses both groups for which these men spoke of maliciously spreading false reports. To their attempts to identify the Levellers with the Diggers, Brooke responds by comparing Walwyn and his party to the martyrs of the Bible, and their present tormentors to Biblical tyrants. Brooke also answers *The Discoverer's* three major charges against the Levellers as a political movement: atheism, communism, and sedition. By means of illustrations from current history and citations from Leveller texts, Brooke shows that these "crimes" cannot be laid at the feet of the party with which he now explicitly allies himself, but rather that they belong to those self-interested men who are ruling England by martial law.

In contrast to these somewhat defensive justifications of the Leveller leaders was Overton's printed reaction to calumny and imprisonment, *Overton's Defyance of the Act of Pardon*. Overton delayed his own response until early July, but when it was published it was a call to arms, not a personalized apologia. Addressing himself to his London comrades of the political wars, Overton attributes his relatively long silence only to his intense dedication to the cause of the final Agreement of the People, for he has been waiting to see what or who might come to the rescue of that cause:

that Agreement I will have, or else Ile dye at their [the "Tyrants'"] feet; Ile have no accord or peace with them at all till they have yeelded that: whether at liberty or in prison, it is all one to me.[90]

But alas, he goes on, despite his own integrity and zeal and that of his co-prisoners, they are "no more but four men," and the problem of liberating England is as much the responsibility of the people to whom he is writing as it is of the inmates of the Tower. Therefore he feels compelled to reprimand those summer patriots who once seemed to adhere to the creed of the Levellers:

Upon all occasions you expect vigorous actings from us, while you look over your selves: I cannot see but that a Prison, the Gallows or halter would become the best of you as well as any of us, to vindicate or assert that Agreement of the People. But you spit in our mouthes, and clap us on the backs like Dogs, and cry, ha-looe a-looe, and turn us loose upon all the Bulls, Bears, Wolves, Lyons and Dragons of the times, which are thousands to one, (I confesse I love the sport) while you shrink, and skulk into your holes.[91]

Then, referring to himself as "Martin," Overton exhorts all the well-affected who will listen to "strike now . . . [unless] your spirits [have] sunk into your heels, or your wits into the napes of your necks." His own spirit, he announces, is still roused, and he will not turn his back on the Agreement of the People for any bribe from the government of "a little dirty liberty."

A week later Overton followed up this challenge to the government and his own quondam supporters with *The Baiting of the Great Bull of Bashan unfolded*.[92] Except for the revised edition of *Mans Mortallitie*, this pamphlet was probably the last work from his pen. Strangely enough, it is a medley of stylistic as well as of political opinions. Apparently the forceful language of his *Defyance* had antagonized certain of its readers, for Overton begins *The Baiting of the Great Bull* with an apology for his use of vivid metaphors and strong expletives: such, he says, were the only means he knew to arouse his audience, to provoke them to their duties. Moving on to politics, Overton then restates his devotion to the cause of the Agreement, and a note of optimism, absent from Leveller writings for more than a month, appears when he attempts to re-kindle his audience to action. Again and again he repeats the theme that, despite all persecution, the true patriot must work and suffer to establish a democratic commonwealth in England. That is why he has continued to "presse . . . forward to the good work of the people"; that is why the final creative paragraph from the pen of Richard Overton has that ring of sincerity which only an intelligently dedicated life could provide:

And if I have been a little too sharp in my advice and admonishment, impute it I pray you to the heat of my zeal and ardent affections to the promotion of that Cause; for truly to me it is as the life of my life; without it I'm nothing, with it I live.

There is no evidence to indicate that Overton's stirring words evoked any positive response from those citizens of London who had supported the Leveller petitions of the preceding year. Instead, at the same time that Overton's farewell tract appeared, the government issued a new blast at the Levellers, John Canne's *The Discoverer . . . the second part discovered*. This lengthy supplement to the original *Discoverer* is largely concerned with answering *The Second Part of Englands New-Chaines*, though it also acknowledges certain of the pamphlets vindicating the Leveller leaders. For the most part it is a repetition of the cumulative charges against the Levellers and a justification of the actions of Cromwell and Fairfax. Typical of the author's technique is his definition of "Leveller" as the "Name ordinarily given unto any . . . as hold dangerous and destructive Principles, tending to the ruine of Church and Commonwealth." Throughout, when replying to the charges that Lilburne had directed at the present government, Canne contrasts the stability of the Commonwealth to the disruptive efforts of the Levellers, now adding to his evidence the allegation that Levellers and Royalists are actively working together to undermine Parliament's victory in the Civil War. In fact, he concludes, the very steps being taken to suppress the rebels in Ireland have been made necessary by Leveller-Royalist sedition. Here, in full, detailed, and ostensibly scholarly panoply, the government temporarily rested its case against the four prisoners in the Tower and their quiescent followers outside of it.

Lilburne, however, was not content to let matters rest there. In mid-July he prepared a blistering attack on the Grandees, but delayed its publication in order not to jeopardize the partial liberty he then had to visit his small-pox-stricken family.[93] Immediately after the deaths of two of his sons, Lilburne returned to his pamphlet war on the government. Either because he had become more violent as a result of personal affliction or because his was now the only voice loudly raised in behalf of Leveller principles, his tracts of August are the most bitter of his career.

On August 10 Lilburne published the delayed *An Impeachment of High Treason against Oliver Cromwell and his Son in Law Henry Ireton*, a concatenation of vehement attacks on Cromwell.[94] Once again Lilburne urges the Levellers in and around London to choose agents to promote their cause at Westminster; and he adds that if the popular desire is now for a king then Prince Charles might be a far better choice than the "pretended, false Saint Oliver."

A few days later Lilburne let loose with an even more intemperate polemic, *A Preparative To An Hue and Cry After Sir Arthur Haslerig*. In addition to his other provocations, he was now motivated to write this tract because Haslerig had apparently retained some of Lilburne's rents from Durham, as well as because rumor had connected him with certain wild plots on Lilburne's life.[95] *A Preparative* therefore charges Haslerig with personally conspiring against the Leveller leaders and with stooping to rob Lilburne of his few property rights. In the course of these charges Lilburne calls Haslerig, the Governor of Newcastle, a variety of names, of which "Pole Cat" is typical. Moreover, the very violence of Lilburne's language proves that he could be as aggressive in defense of what he considered his own property as he could in defense of English liberties.

Two days after the appearance of *A Preparative*, the Council of State, which had recently been permitting Lilburne to go in and out of the Tower almost at will, ordered his close confinement; but he momentarily so intimidated the guard sent to rearrest him that for a short period he was allowed to remain at large.[96] Despite this relatively lenient treatment, Lilburne on or just before September 1, 1649, issued a short and incendiary manifesto, *An Outcry*

of the Young Men and Apprentices of London.[97] It calls, even
screams, to those citizens and soldiers sympathetic to the Leveller
cause to rise up and forcibly assert the principles of an Agreement
of the People, for "the very persons, . . . lives and properties" of the
people are now being mangled by the "raging lawless sword" of
military compulsion — a sword which is "drenched in the precious
blood of the people." *An Outcry* was obviously more than a plea for
passive disobedience, and it bore prompt if withered fruit.

On September 8 a small group of pro-Leveller soldiers, very possibly prodded by the Royalists as well as by Lilburne's *Outcry*,
mutinied at Oxford.[98] Though this abortive uprising was quickly
and easily quelled, it did push the Council of State into taking new
action against the seemingly irrepressible Lilburne. On September
11 Parliament ordered the author or authors of *An Outcry* prosecuted; three days later Lilburne was brought before the Attorney
General; and on September 19 an order was issued recommitting
him to the Tower.[99] In mid-October the Council of State informed
Parliament that it had enough evidence to convict the prisoner of
treason, and the date for his trial was set for October 24. Thus
though the party he led was to all intents and purposes dead, Lilburne was still very much alive, and his life rather than his cause
was now at stake.

Lilburne's campaign of militant noncoöperation had been momentarily echoed in one of the final mass petitions associated with
the Levellers, *The Remonstrance of many thousands of the Free-
People of England*, which appeared on September 21. This *Remonstrance*, the postscript to which claims that it has already been
signed by "98,064 hands," announces that disobedience, passive
or active, against the arbitrary government at Westminster is justified, is in fact obligatory, until the greedy and unrepresentative
Rump is replaced by a supreme authority based on Leveller principles. In retrospect, however, this clamorous call for action marks
the death rattle of the Leveller party at that moment when the
government had decided finally to crush its most vociferous opponent.

In mid-October, when the Council of State was informing Parliament that there was now sufficient evidence to convict and be-
head Lilburne, the decision to eliminate him and the remnants

of his party was reflected in *An Anatomy of . . . Lilburne's Spirits and Pamphlets*, a tract probably written at the instigation of the government. The work of a Puritan divine, Cuthbert Sydenham,[100] it takes Lilburne to task for being a chronic incendiary, slanderer, demagogue, malignant, anarchist, etc. He has, says Sydenham, been the worst of a group of communistic and licentious radicals whose chief aim has been to "scandalize" Parliament; and Lilburne's pamphlets, particularly his *Impeachment of High Treason against Cromwell* and his *Preparative*, represent the nadir of Leveller libels. Consequently the House of Commons has the legal right and the moral obligation to convict Lilburne as a traitor.

Three days after this blast, Lilburne published *Strength out of Weaknesse. Or, The finall and absolute Plea of . . . Lilburne . . . against the present Ruling Power sitting at Westminster*. Its major concern is to narrate Lilburne's interview with Attorney General Prideaux which had taken place a month earlier. In so doing it reveals how Lilburne's defiant but well-founded suspicions of the government's intentions overshadowed the ostensible amenities of this conversation. Beneath the surface one can sense the dramatic struggle between the humorless, self-centered, loquacious Lilburne and the quiet, urbane, and slightly mocking Prideaux.

Lilburne began the interview by again asserting that the present Parliament, because it has been the puppet of the false and power-hungry Grandees, has no real constitutional authority, and that, therefore, the country has temporarily been returned to the "Law of Nature." Though, Lilburne continued, he has resisted this Parliament with words only, never with physical force, and though his life has been dedicated to upholding the power of a true Parliament, yet the Rump is no such body: Pride's Purge, the manner of the king's trial, and the recurrent interposition of the army leaders are all proof that it has outlived its "trust." A government based on freedom, reason, justice, and equity, not a Commonwealth superimposed on the people by military force, is the only proper way to settle the problems of the nation. It is for this reason, Lilburne went on, that he now denies the right of Parliament or Council of State to question him, for neither their threats nor his own fear of what Cromwell may do to him will force him to go against his conscience and bow before the "false powers" he has so long fought. Lilburne then terminated the discussion with a threat of his own: if he is killed in this struggle with the Grandees, may his account of this interview be published and, if necessary, distributed free, so that all the people of England can see how John Lilburne has upheld their liberties in his battle against arbitrary and selfish interests.[101]

Four days before his trial began, Lilburne, back in the Tower and increasingly desperate at the apparently inexorable forces arrayed against him, published the relatively subdued *Innocent Man's First Proffer*. This challenge to his adversaries, in particular to Haslerig, to accept an open and fair trial before two judges was ignored. Two days later, on October 22, 1649, Lilburne therefore issued *The Innocent Man's second-Proffer*.[102] Here he proposes that he be allowed to go to the West Indies, far away from the Rump and the Council of State, provided, however, that three conditions be met: that all who want to, be permitted to accompany him; that these people first be paid any monies owed them by the government; and that any very poor people who desire to join his expedition be subsidized by the state. To this *second-Proffer* Lilburne added "the names of the severall Bookes and Papers" which he had written "since his first Contest with the Bishops in the yeare 1637." [103] But despite this impressive testimonial to his twelve-year devotion to the cause of England's freedom, and despite his request that his trial might be delayed so he could have more time to consider the lawfulness of the Commonwealth government, his *second-Proffer* was also ignored. Whether lawful or not, that government was in no mood to compromise. Nor did a last-minute and voluminous petition to the House from a scattering of Levellers in and about London on the next day do anything to change that mood.[104]

On October 24, in the well-guarded Guildhall in London, the trial of John Lilburne opened.[105] In large part it was an almost theatrical struggle: Lilburne, backed by a sympathetic crowd, versus thirty-nine special commissioners. At one point in the proceedings Lilburne interrupted the court to proclaim that he was on trial for his life; to which the presiding judge, Keble, replied, "We are upon our lives too as well as you." [106] In the context of Clement Walker's exciting transcript of this case it indeed often seems that the question at issue was Lilburne's life versus the continued existence of the Commonwealth.[107]

On the first day of the trial the grand jury presented its indictment. On the next day Lilburne, the aggressive and voluble amateur lawyer, concluded hours of argument by pleading not guilty to a modified form of this indictment. At many times during this second day the court was more on the defensive than its litigious defendant. Anxious to undercut Lilburne's claims that they constituted an illegal body, the judges bent over backwards to allow several of Lilburne's demands and to countenance his disrespectful interruptions. Moreover, because the court permitted the doors to be opened, Lilburne was provided with a sympathetic audience to which he could, and did, appeal for vociferous support.[108] Throughout this second day, therefore, Lilburne fought and stalled the court on a variety of issues, some massive, others quibbling. He stated, for instance, that his own case was a test of the historical liberties of the people of England; that the court trying him was neither traditional nor legal; that his arrest had been improperly conducted and the warrant difficult to read; that he needed legal counsel; and that the "Law of God" supported his array of contentions.

The third and last day of the trial saw the jury empaneled and the full indictment read. Lilburne was charged with treason because his recent pamphlets had been patently intended to subvert the government.[109] To prove Lilburne's "scandalous poisonous and traitorous" aims, the clerk then read certain passages from *An Impeachment of High Treason* and from *An Outcry of the Young Men and Apprentices*. To this full charge Lilburne responded with two types of strategy. First, by a series of legalistic quibbles and oblique denials Lilburne tried to punch holes in the court's assumption that these works were by him, and thus he attempted to point out the inefficiency of the court before which, as he kept suggesting, he had allowed himself to be tried. Second, he did his best to impress on the jury and the crowd that what the government considered treason was merely the traditional right of the common people to state their grievances. Turning to the jury, he at last concluded more than ten hours of wrangling cross-examination with this peroration:

My honest jury and fellow citizens, who I again declare by the law of England are the conservators and sole judges of my life, having . . . alone the judicial power of the law, as well as fact; you judges that sit there being no more . . . but ciphers to pronounce the sentence, . . . being at the best . . . but the Norman Conqueror's intruders; and therefore you gentlemen of the jury, my sole judges, the keepers of my life, at whose hands the Lord will require my blood in case you leave any part of my indictment to the cruel and bloody men: . . . therefore I desire you to know your power and consider your duty both to God, to me, to your own selves, and to your country.[110]

To this plea "the People with a loud voyce, cried Amen, Amen," and more soldiers were rushed in to guard the court.[111] By his sturdy defiance — by his sudden shifts from daring inquisitor to victimized martyr, by playing the part of underdog with a courage and shrewdness and tenacity that would appeal to his common hearers, and by incorporating in his own plight the accumulated and traditional grievances against military power and an increasingly restrictive government — Lilburne not only capitalized on his successful demands for trial by jury, but won his case. To the "Amen" of the crowd, the jury, some two hours later, added their verdict of not guilty.[112] With this announcement,

immediately the whole multitude of People in the Hall, for joy at the Prisoners acquittall, gave such a loud and unanimous shout, as is beleeved was never heard in Yeeld-hall, which lasted about halfe an hour without intermission: which made the Judges for fear turne pale, and hange down their heads; but the Prisoner stood silent at the Barre, rather more sad in countenance than he was before.[113]

That night there were bonfires in the streets of London; [114] and two weeks later, on November 8, 1649, after a vague threat of court-martialing the latest public hero, the government released Lilburne and his three fellow-prisoners.[115] But the party they had led no longer had any real existence, while the government they had opposed and recently discomfited was still very much in the saddle.[116] The story of the Leveller leaders and their now dispersed party during the decade remaining to the Interregnum is thus largely an obituary: physically free, the Levellers were politically moribund. Perhaps that is why Lilburne, at his moment of triumph, was "rather more sad in countenance than he was before."

Aftermath: November 1649 to May 1660

Though the part which the Levellers had played in the political drama was almost finished, the rest was not silence. Yet except for Lilburne, who long continued to be a self-advertised thorn in the flesh of the Commonwealth, the other Leveller leaders quickly subsided into obscurity or into ineffectual conspiracy. Thus Prince, after his release from the Tower in November 1649, probably returned to his wife and his profitable cheese business. At the end of that year he almost certainly took the Engagement to the Commonwealth, a brief pledge for all citizens to sign which stated that they would be "true and faithful to the Commonwealth of England, as it is now established without a King or House of Lords." [1] Thereafter, except to note that he stood by Lilburne at the time of his trial in 1653, the newspapers and pamphlets of the day fail to mention the name of Thomas Prince.

Walwyn's life, after the disintegration of the Leveller party and his own release from prison, closely follows the pattern of Prince's career.[2] Walwyn almost certainly took the Engagement, and then sank back into the domesticity of his large family and his prosperous linen trade. Yet his removal from the national political scene was not quite as complete as that of Prince. It is quite possible that Walwyn maintained some sort of contact with a localized group of Levellers in his native Worcestershire, a group which managed to keep its political identity alive into the period of the Restoration; and in 1659 Harrington included his name among a list of those who were to meet and discuss some of Harrington's proposals.[3] In addition, Walwyn twice spoke out publicly on issues that were potentially national in scope.

The first occasion was in a pamphlet which appeared early in 1651. In November 1650 Henry Robinson had published *Certain Considerations In order to a more speedy, cheap, and equall distribution of Justice*. Among the considerations he had advanced was the suggestion that trial juries be supplanted by local judges appointed by Parliament. Walwyn's answer, *Juries Justified*, reasserts its author's continued faith in the common man. Claiming that his friend Robinson has shown himself to be a "William the Conqueror" in his tract, Walwyn goes on to say that trial by jury is a "fundamental right" of the people of England. In fact, the law should be to the common people as the Bible is to good Protestants: a simple and easily knowable means to a better life. Hence, Walwyn concludes, juries, though they may irritate unscrupulous lawyers, are basic to English traditions and to social justice.

The second and probably last time Walwyn spoke out publicly was in a speech in support of free trade which, sometime in 1652, he delivered before a governmental "Committee for Trade." [4] His remarks in this instance also point to the longevity of his basically democratic convictions; for a "generall freedome of Trade" is, he said, a "right" that is at once traditional and essential to the common good. Further, it is only under conditions of free trade that the majority of men will be able to flourish in a "moderately contentful" condition. Apparently Walwyn himself so flourished; he died in 1680, a respected and well-established member of the London community.[5]

Such was not the case with Richard Overton, the time and place of whose death are now unknown, and whose biography after his release from the Tower suggests the plot of an adventure novel. That he took the Engagement is verified by a comment in the Royalist *The Man in the Moon* to the effect that he signed it with the proviso that he would adhere to it as faithfully as most members of the Council of State had kept their oath to support the Solemn League and Covenant.[6] In mid-1653, at the time of Lilburne's second major trial, Overton turns up again; standing up for his former comrade, he at one point personally delivered a letter from Lilburne to one of the judges in charge of the proceedings.[7] Then, sometime in 1654, Overton offered his services to Thurloe as a spy for the Protectorate, but in the following year he was in Flanders with the now notorious Colonel Sexby, busy with arrangements to enlist Spanish support for the overthrow of Cromwell and for the restoration of Charles II.[8] In that same year Overton published *Man Wholly Mortal*, a second edition of *Mans Mortallitie*, "by the author corrected and enlarged." But this work, though somewhat longer and subdivided in a more orderly fashion than the original tract, shows little change either in Overton's ideas or in his manner of expressing them.[9] Four years later, in the midst of the turbulence of 1659, Overton found himself back in a London jail; and again in 1663 he was arrested, this time for printing an attack on the Restoration government.[10] After that he drops out of sight, probably to go on fighting for what he considered the ideals of an Agreement of the People.

Whereas Overton's story is murky, that of John Wildman is lurid. Because he had withdrawn from the councils of the Levellers early in 1649, he was able during that summer to make some sort of compromise arrangement with the Grandees, probably receiving as a reward the position of major in a cavalry regiment.[11] The following year, and for the ensuing five years, he engaged in a series of rather shady but usually extremely profitable real estate speculations, becoming sufficiently rich and respectable to be elected, though not admitted, to Cromwell's first Parliament under the Instrument of Government in 1654.[12]

Meanwhile, at the very end of 1650, Wildman returned briefly to the public hustings as a spokesman for Leveller principles. In 1649 a group of London citizens had petitioned the Common Council to investigate the undemocratic manner in which the Lord Mayor and London sheriffs were elected. A committee of the Common Council had then recommended that the local franchise be considerably broadened, a suggestion to which the entrenched Livery Companies reacted vigorously.[13] In December 1650 at the Guildhall where Lilburne had been tried, Wildman, assisted by John Price, the chief author of *Walwins Wiles*, answered the objections of the Livery Companies — objections which were mainly delivered by another ex-inmate of the Tower, Sir John Maynard. To complete this composite picture, much of Wildman's plea for an extension of democracy to the municipal affairs of London echoed the arguments Lilburne had advanced in 1646 in *Londons Liberty in Chains Discovered.*[14]

Wildman's own version of *Londons Liberties*, his rebuttal, that is, of Maynard's case, concentrates on two major points, both of which reflect the central issues which had underlain the Leveller-Grandee debates at Putney and Whitehall. His first major contention is that human rights are more important than property rights; for "certainly men's titles to land and to a power of government are, or ought to be, of a different nature." [15] From here he moves to his second main argument: because "all just power . . . is from the people," the magistrate can derive his power only by the explicit assent of the people. This principle, Wildman continues, overrides any laws or traditions or customs which seem to go against it; and the democracy which it avows is heartening, not frightening, because the collective wisdom of the common people is superior to that of any small and prerogative-conscious group. "It is strange," he concludes, "to hear that the fear of popularity, or of giving away so much to the liberty of the people, is so much insisted on." [16]

Even stranger, however, was the remainder of Wildman's life. From 1654 to the Restoration he engaged in a series of plots and conspiracies. Most of this time, along with Sexby and Overton, he worked behind the scenes for the overthrow of Cromwell, but intermittently he also served as one of Thurloe's spies. Apparently trusted neither by the Royalists nor by the agents of the Protectorate, he spent much of 1655 and part of 1656 in several jails, but after his release he continued to plot and to make money in land speculations.[17] At this time, too, Wildman became a convert to those theories which, in October 1656, Harrington set forth in *Oceana*.[18] As a result, early in 1659 Wildman, who had presumably participated in the informal discussions which preceded the founding of the Rota Club, almost certainly helped to write a pamphlet called *The Leveller*.

Though this latest model "Leveller" is in many ways more Harringtonian than Lilburnian, it is also an effective if retrospective justification of the party for which Wildman had formerly exercised his talents. *The Leveller* first defends its exponents against the old

charge of economic levelling; then it proceeds to plead for a government of laws, not of men, and for a system of "successive" and
popularly elected parliaments. But Parliament, as in the Kingdom of
Oceana, is to consist of two houses: one chamber to propose the laws,
the other to "resolve" these proposals. Like its ancestral Agreements
of the People, however, this new *Leveller* demands full equality before the law. Further, continuing to reflect the troubled history of the
Interregnum, it asks that England never again have a "mercenary
Army," but that the defense of the nation be placed solely in the
hands of a democratic militia. The final "fundamental" with which
The Leveller concerns itself — leaving the "circumstantials" of its
program to be decided by Parliament — is the demand for almost
complete religious toleration. Throughout, Wildman's pamphlet
maintains a moderate and rational tone, and it concludes with the
declaration that it has been written to avoid animosities and to promote peace, harmony, and justice. No call to arms, it suggests the
cause long lost, and the comfortable study rather than the agitated
street corner.

Even so, the thirty-four years remaining to Wildman's life were
neither nostalgic nor sheltered. Immediately after the Restoration,
Wildman, despite his support of the brief "second republic" of 1659,
became a figure of importance in the Royal Postal Service. Again,
however, his conspiratorial bent and his political principles got him
in trouble, and he spent the years from 1661 to 1667 in one of
Charles II's prisons. Thereafter, Wildman's story is a skein of successful financial operations and of unsuccessful political plots, further tangled by his intermittent involvement in the affairs of George
Villiers, the second Duke of Buckingham.[19] In 1681, with Algernon
Sidney, Wildman intrigued for the reëstablishment of a republic.
Two years later he was back in the Tower because of his efforts in
connection with the Rye House conspiracy, and in 1685, having advocated the assassination of James, he was forced to flee to Holland.
He returned to England in time for the "Glorious Revolution," and
the next year was elected to the "Convention Parliament."[20] In
1692 he was knighted by King William III — a monarch against
whom he had also conspired — for his services as an Alderman of
London, as a member of Parliament, and as a key man in organizing a national postal system. Sir John Wildman died a quiet death

at the age of seventy in June 1693, at a moment when, as far as is known, he was not engaged in any movement to overthrow or reform the government in power.

The short remainder of Lilburne's career had neither the chameleon-like quality nor the financial and civic rewards which distinguish Wildman's biography. Yet whatever spark of life was left in the original Leveller party manifested itself almost entirely in the unsuppressible reflexes, both personal and political, of John Lilburne. Thus despite his recent narrow escape at the Guildhall, one of his first acts after being released from the Tower was to supervise the publication of Clement Walker's full and dramatic account of the trial. Three days later, on December 1, 1649, Lilburne again growled back at the momentarily sleeping dogs of the Commonwealth, in the *Second Part of the Triall of . . . Lilburne,* a pamphlet in which he and Walker set forth additional reasons why the trial was illegal and why the defendant should have been acquitted. However, Lilburne's growl promptly subsided in a letter to the Speaker of the House which he added to the end of this tract, for here Lilburne says that he is now weighing the relative merits of self-exile from England and of taking up some quiet and noncontroversial vocation.

Neither of these alternatives turned out to be an entirely accurate prediction. On December 21 Lilburne, who had taken up residence within the City of London, was elected to the Common Council.[21] Ordered to take the Engagement to the Commonwealth, he complied, but diluted his oath of allegiance by explaining that he defined the Commonwealth as the people and the basic laws of the land, not as the system set up by the Council of State and the army.[22] As a result of this evasion, Parliament nullified Lilburne's election and imprisoned one of his most active supporters.[23] But Lilburne did not rise up in wrath or rush into print; instead, he took up the trade of soap-boiling. Commented *Mercurius Politicus*: "this [trade] he hath need of; for . . . the last Bout he scapt a Scouring." [24] Lilburne agreed, and by early 1650 he had settled down to a trade, reconciled himself with Cromwell, and explicitly refused to take any part in politics.[25]

Lilburne remained steadfast in this refusal for more than a year, despite the fact that in June 1650 Henry Parker published a *Letter of Due Censure . . . to . . . Lilburne* which assailed the prolixity, ignorance, and subversion which Lilburne had displayed at his trial the preceding October, and despite the fact that during the summer of 1650 certain remnants of the Leveller party established negotiations with Charles II and even circulated one petition attacking the Commonwealth.[26] But in July the Rump paid Lilburne the reparations owed him, and soap-boiling if unexciting was not unprosperous.[27] Even so, toward the end of 1650 Lilburne began to stir. Though blocked from entering the Temple, he decided to take up the part-time career of practicing law, thus gratifying a desire he had long had and one which he had only partly satisfied in his own encounters with the law.[28]

Lilburne's first important case as an amateur attorney involved him in a queer and tumultuous suit. In the autumn of 1650, he, with Wildman, went to Lincolnshire to represent certain tenants of the Manor of Epworth who were being threatened with displacement by the efforts of a large company to enclose and drain the lands which, these tenants claimed, traditionally belonged to them.[29] The two former leaders of the Leveller party took the side of human rights as opposed to agricultural progress; in fact, they took this side so vigorously that, in addition to their legal briefs and pleadings, Lilburne and Wildman participated in a barn-burning riot intended to frighten off the company which had purchased the disputed land. Not long afterwards, while this case was pursuing its slow and complicated course,[30] Lilburne engaged in his second — and final — action as a lawyer; for in the process of defending his uncle George Lilburne, John succeeded in bringing to an end his brief career as a part-time attorney, his apparent harmony with the government, and his residence in England.

The object of the Lilburnes' wrath in this legal melee was Sir Arthur Haslerig, the man whom Lilburne had already accused, in 1649, of attempted murder and of actual robbery. Since then, Lilburne charged, Haslerig had continued to persecute his family by retaining or seizing certain properties and rents in and around Durham which belonged to them.[31] For Lilburne, only one of the many lawyers entangled in this legal net, the case began to reach its climax in the summer of 1651. On July 30 he published *A Just Reproof to Haberdashers-Hall*, which, in support of the property claims of his family, accuses Haslerig of greed, extortion, cruelty, and bribery. In a postscript Lilburne adds the statement that he is not trying to disturb the public peace in any way, but the tone and the vocabulary of *A Just Reproof* reflect the same bitterness and anger which Lilburne had displayed in his earlier attacks on Cromwell. Then, on December 23, 1651, George Primate, the Lilburnes' chief business associate, presented a petition to Parliament asking it to overrule the decision of a local agency and to reward the disputed properties to himself and his partners. This petition, signed by Primate and Lilburne, repeated many of the angry and defamatory accusations of *A Just Reproof*; instead of a request for Parliamentary action, it read like a libel on Haslerig.

Parliament chose so to read it. Though Cromwell and Lilburne had recently had a friendly conversation,[32] Parliament, on January 15, 1652, fined Primate and Lilburne a total of almost £7,000, jailed Primate, and ordered Lilburne banished from England, pronouncing a sentence of death on him if he should ever return.[33] Because Primate's petition had allegedly "scandalized" a member of the House, as well as certain members of Haberdashers' Hall, Lilburne, its cosigner, was treated as if he had committed a major overt act of treason. Going far beyond the law, Parliament made him at once a scapegoat and a felon, in the hope of thereby strengthening its own position and that of the Council of State.[34] That this position needed little strengthening is indicated by the fact that only one petition publicly denounced the action of the Rump.[35]

Five days after he was sentenced, Lilburne, in *A Declaration. . . To the Free-born People of England*, tried to make clear that Parliament's vindictive and illegal actions against himself proved the justice of his earlier attacks on Cromwell and his government.[36] Comparing himself to Christ and proclaiming that his conscience is still unbowed, Lilburne here explains why he refused to kneel before the bar of the House when sentence was passed; why, following the example of Overton, he would never physically or symbolically bend his knee to tyranny. Parliament reacted to this declaration by reducing the period of grace before Lilburne's exile from thirty to twenty days; and early in February 1652 he crossed the Channel to Holland.

Later that month one of the correspondents for *Mercurius Po-*

liticus reported from Amsterdam that Lilburne was quietly lodging there.[37] Probably he was engaged in making preliminary private contact with the Royalists and in writing the first of two lengthy tracts in vindication of himself, *his Apologetical Narration, in reference to his late illegall and unjust banishment, directed to the people of the united Provinces.* This largely autobiographical pamphlet, published in April, suggests that its author's life has been and continues to be mainly a journey through a vale of tears, but a journey sustained by God and ennobled by persecution.[38] More subdued in tone than most of his writing, the *Apologetical Narration* also conveys the impression that Lilburne's religious faith has moved back toward his dominant spiritual mood of the late 1630's; again his faith, though now more resigned, is pervasive and sustaining.[39]

The second of Lilburne's self-vindications of this period appeared in May 1652, under the retrospective title of *As You Were.* Most of it consists of a letter to Kiffin, dated April 2, 1652 — a strange mixture of nostalgia and bravado, of sorrow at his own exile and wild threats of what he will accomplish on his return to England. Now less subdued, Lilburne begins by telling Kiffin that his banishment was Cromwell's doing. He then denies having had any direct dealings with Charles, thought he does admit to having discussed his position with certain Royalists. Indeed, he goes on, the youthful Charles is a man of shallow judgment and an advocate of violence; and violence, as Lilburne himself has learned, is a two-edged sword. If nothing else, the events of the past decade have taught him the lesson that social change, to be permanent, must take place democratically and constitutionally — not as the outcome of violence, but as the product of a liberal and inviolable Agreement of the People. Little good, he adds, has emerged from that series of bright promises and bitter fulfilments which have constituted the war years. At this point in *As You Were* Lilburne suddenly extols the Latin Secretary of Cromwell's Council of State, for he quotes in English, and with high praise, the concluding lines of Milton's *First Defence* in order to show that it is the actions of the English people themselves which must refute the charges of the adversaries of their present government.[40] Lilburne then ends his letter with the exhortation that the well-affected in England therefore bring pressure on Cromwell to revive and implement an Agreement of the People; if not, Lilburne concludes, he, the most conspicuous victim of governmental tyranny, will dedicate his pen and his life to the overthrow of the Commonwealth. He follows this threat by reprinting a letter to Cromwell, the postscript of which announces that, should Cromwell continue in his ways of "Atheisme and Machiavellisme," then he, Lilburne, will do all in his power to return to England, there to work personally for a true republic.

A year intervened, however, before Lilburne felt that his return from banishment could have any chance of success. During that year he probably published only one pamphlet;[41] instead of writing, he busied himself in a variety of ineffectual and complicated intrigues with the Royalists.[42] As early as April 1, 1652, Sir Edward Nicholas was able to report that Lilburne had assured Charles that, if the King would raise a certain sum of money and make certain democratic guarantees, then Lilburne and the 40,000 Levellers who he claimed would follow him would restore Charles to his father's throne.[43] By May, Lilburne was already discussing plans with the Duke of Buckingham and the exiled Bishop of Londonderry for the overthrow of Cromwell and the establishment of a limited monarchy in England.[44] But Lilburne's lines of intrigue were snarled by several factors: many Royalists suspected him of being a spy for Cromwell;[45] he himself was under constant surveillance by agents of the Council of State;[46] and Buckingham, the member of Charles's retinue whom he most admired, was willing to reconcile himself to the Commonwealth for the sake of getting back to England.[47] To add to the strain of Lilburne's exile and to the growing frustration of his cloak-and-dagger activities, he had little money, and at home his family was on the verge of extreme poverty.[48]

In the spring of 1653 Lilburne began a campaign to extricate himself from this morass. A few months before, a Captain Wendy Oxford, an agent for both the Royalists and the Council of State, had publicly accused Lilburne of receiving money from the English Levellers and of fabricating a chain of malicious tales against some of the Royalists with whom he had been dealing.[49] At the end of March, Lilburne issued his angry reply, *L. Colonel John Lilburne revived*.[50] Two of the three letters which constitute this reply concentrate on reaffirming Lilburne's patriotism, particularly in so far as the manifestations of that patriotism refute the canards of "alchemy St. Oliver's . . . rotten Secretary," Wendy Oxford. Partly as a result of these accusations and denials, further charges and countercharges, intensified by Cromwell's dissolution of the Long Parliament at the end of April, continued to swirl around Lilburne's head.[51] In May, Lilburne's wife arrived at Bruges to work with him in behalf of his return to England, both of them apparently certain that Cromwell might now summon the free Parliament for which the Levellers had pleaded.[52] On May 4, therefore, Lilburne wrote to Cromwell and the Council of State requesting permission to end his exile.[53] A few weeks later he was in Dunkirk, there to await notification that the sentence of the Rump had been revoked. He waited in vain. On June 13, despite the fact that his wife had returned to France to dissuade him, Lilburne, without a pass and without any form of even covert permission from the Council of State, crossed the Channel to England.[54] The next day the Council of State informed the authorities of London to be on their guard; accordingly, on June 16, the Sheriff of London placed Lilburne behind the familiar bars of Newgate prison.[55]

Lilburne's return to England had not been surreptitious. On June 4 he had written the Council of State from Calais an extensive and in part threatening request for a pass.[56] On June 6 he had petitioned Cromwell for permission to return.[57] Then, on June 14, immediately after landing, he forwarded to Cromwell *The Banished Mans suit for Protection.* Here he announces his decision to come to London with the intention of settling down to a quiet life of service to the Commonwealth and his family.[58] Two days later, probably already in the custody of the Sheriff of London, Lilburne issued *A Second Address . . . to . . . Cromwell and the Council of State,*[59] where he again avows his desire not to offend the authorities: all he wants of them is to suspend the obviously unjust sentence of the now discredited Rump. On June 20 Lilburne sent forth from Newgate his *Third Address . . . to . . . Cromwell and the Councell of State.* Submissive and redolent of an air of injured innocence, this appeal recapitulates the illegalities and vicissitudes of his exile, again expressing its author's desire to lead a peaceful, private, and domestic life. Will permission for Lilburne to breathe English air, a *Third Address* plaintively asks, endanger the Commonwealth? Though Cromwell had by now assured him of a fair trial,[60] Lilburne no doubt feared an affirmative answer, for within two days he published the most humble work of his articulate life, the aptly-titled *A Defensive Declaration*. With a rare strain of apology Lilburne here stresses his occasionally good relations with Cromwell, denies that he has ever worked actively for or with the Royalists, and concludes with the assertion that he now only desires to prove his loyalty to the Commonwealth.

During the three weeks remaining before his inevitable trial as a returned felon — a delay granted him by the government — Lilburne did not stand unsupported. On the same day that *A Defensive Declaration* appeared, Samuel Chidley, the pious onetime treasurer of the Leveller party, published *An Additional Remonstrance To the Valiant and wel-deserving Souldiers . . . with a little friendly touch to . . . Lilburne*, though his "touch" was that of an admonitory finger rather than a helping hand. Far more effective was another pamphlet which came out on June 22, 1653, *A Jury-Man's Judgment Upon the Case of . . . Lilburne*. Its anonymous author looks back to Lilburne's trial in 1649 and ahead to his imminent ordeal in order to make a point equally applicable and equally central to both of Lilburne's legal self-defenses: that the jury can judge of law as well as of fact. Further, this "Jury-Man" continues, juries are the true guardians of England's fundamental rights, and should this coming jury acquit Lilburne it will have taken an important step in reasserting these rights for all citizens. Nor was Lilburne's original offense felonious; in fact, the supposed breach of privilege of his attack on Haslerig was partially justified by Haslerig's own actions, and under no circumstances could it have warranted Parliament's excessive and illegal reaction. If anything, therefore, Lilburne's present plight testifies to his zealousness, not to any subversive intention or "turbulency of spirit" on his part.

Somewhat similar in its anticipation of Lilburne's own defense was a petition of June 24 from "divers well-affected People" in and around London.[61] Stating that the actions against him have run counter to all the aims of the Civil War, it asks that Lilburne be pardoned; that, if this is impossible, he be given a fair trial; and that trial by jury be guaranteed in all future cases which might otherwise result in cruel and arbitrary sentences. On the next day Elizabeth Lilburne, with other "afflicted women," begged the Parliament that

was to open on July 4 to see that the prisoner was dealt with merci-
fully and justly.[62] And during the first weeks of July two other
petitions appealed to the new House of Commons in the same
vein.[63]

Since, however, these petitions were the scattered protests of only
a few people, not the manifestations of a revitalized party, Lilburne
was himself especially active in supplementing their demands. On
July 1 he issued *The Prisoner's Most mournful Cry*, a bitter lament
against his oppression by the Council of State. Addressed to John
Fowke, the Lord Mayor of London, the *mournful Cry* resumes the
attack on Cromwell and his subordinates. Not only have these officials refused to heed the petitions in Lilburne's behalf, but they
have confiscated "divers thousands" of papers which he had just had
printed. With a flash of his earlier self, Lilburne concludes his
lament by announcing that he will appeal directly to the people if
his miseries continue to accumulate.

Among these confiscated "divers thousands" of papers had been
many copies of *A Jury-Man's Judgment* and of a tract "penned by
a faithful lover of the fundamental laws and liberties of the free
people of England," *Lilburne's Plea in Law, Against an Act of
Parliament*. Immediately after Lilburne's supply of this latter pamphlet had been seized by agents of the Council of State, a new edition, "much enlarged," was brought out. Whether or not Lilburne
wrote or supervised either or both editions, the *Plea in Law* accurately foretells his line of defense in his forthcoming trial.[64] In
the first place, it questions the fact that the Lilburne named by the
act of banishment is legally the same Lilburne who has now returned to England. In the second place, relying heavily on Coke and
the Bible, it challenges the validity of that act: Lilburne had not
been adjudged guilty by a court of common law; Parliament had
acted illegally, irrationally, and immorally; and, most telling, Cromwell and the Council of State were now in the position of trying to
enforce the decision of a Parliament which a few months before they
had forcibly dissolved and officially discredited.

By attempting to suppress this able defense of Lilburne, the Council of State had only temporarily interfered with his publicity campaign in his own behalf; but the government had also impeded his
possible acquittal by refusing to allow him to question witnesses

before the grand jury which had recently indicted him. Consequently, in a *Second Letter . . . To . . . John Fowke*, Lilburne, on
July 10, aired this grievance and pleaded that he be allowed professional counsel.[65] Finally, on July 12, the day before his trial began,
Lilburne humbly petitioned the Nominated Parliament to abrogate
his sentence at the hands of their disesteemed predecessors.[66]

The Nominated Parliament, however, did nothing to mitigate
Lilburne's plight or to interfere in his trial. Thus, on July 13, 1653,
the prisoner was brought before the regular sessions at Old Bailey.[67]
On that same day the government, in a shrewd move to counter the
popularity that Lilburne had been building up for himself, published *Severall Informations and Examinations Taken concerning
. . . Lilburne, His Apostasy to the Party of Charles Stuart.* This
compilation, by reprinting the testimony of five agents of the Commonwealth, erects an impressive array of evidence to show that Lilburne had actively and underhandedly plotted the overthrow of the
government. Nor did Lilburne's immediate reply, *Malice Detected*,
do much to dispel these charges; instead, its chief message is that he
has become wearied by the cumulative weight of affliction.

But there was little rest for the weary. On the first day of the
trial Lilburne refused to plead to the indictment, making instead the
unprecedented demand that he be allowed to see a copy of it.[68] Two
days later, after much wrangling, the court granted this request,
and gave Lilburne until the following morning to draw up his exceptions.[69] These exceptions, already outlined in the *Plea in Law*,
he presented on July 16. This was the signal for a loud dispute, in
which Lilburne thundered imprecations at Cromwell and which
was silenced only when the armed soldiers surrounding Old Bailey
moved in to quiet the crowd that was vigorously expressing its sympathy for the prisoner at the bar.[70] Amid these "furious hurleys
burleys," the court, then in the last day of its session, adjourned the
case until August 10.[71]

Lilburne did his part to keep the hurly-burly going. On or just
after July 16, in addition to publishing his *Exceptions* to the indictment, he issued *A Conference with the Souldiers*, a brief description
of his harangue to the troops who had entered the courtroom to restore order. At this time, too, he wrote a short tract, *Oyes, Oyes,
Oyes*, to justify his overt appeal to the people crowding Old Bailey.

Finally, within a few days of the court's adjournment, the first version of Part I of *The Tryall of . . . Lilburne* was abroad in print.

Supplementing these pamphlets by Lilburne was the concurrent *A Caveat to those that shall resolve . . . to destroy J.L.*, an able and objective statement of the primacy of law. To its anonymous author, Lilburne is the symbol of man under unjust persecution:

But it may be objected that J.L. is such a man that an age produceth not the like: he is never well but when fishing in troubled waters; he is a busie body meddling with other mens matters; picking holes where he finds them; . . . but if J.L. hath offended the Law, let him be tryed by the Law, and not by Arbitrary Judgement.[72]

Regardless of his personality, *A Caveat* ends, if Lilburne should die as a result of the wishes of strong men, not at the hands of merciful law, then only evil will result to the nation.

In the last days of July and the early days of August several petitions also helped to keep Lilburne's plight before the public eye. On July 29 the "afflicted Women" reasserted their political rights and their durable patriotism — both of which, they claim, justify them again to plead for the prisoner.[73] On August 2 they were seconded by a group of "Young Men and Apprentices." [74] And on August 10, the day Lilburne's trial resumed, *A Voyce from the Heavenly word of God*, in pious and respectful language, begged Parliament to see that the defendant was acquitted.

During these three weeks of close imprisonment Lilburne too continued to dramatize his danger. On August 1 he issued *The Upright Mans Vindication*, a long and jumbled compilation of personal asides, addresses, letters, and petitions. It contrasts sharply to his next tract, which, though not published until the end of the month, was almost certainly written early in August, *The Just Defence of John Lilburne, Against Such as charge him with Turbulency of Spirit*.[75] Probably the most effective of all Lilburne's tracts, it is his apologia pro vita sua, his own political obituary.

Lilburne's chief purpose in *The Just Defence* is to answer the charge that he is a chronic dissident, a man of unregenerate turbulence. Mocking at this accusation, Lilburne says that his adversaries have built up the case against him to the point where, "if there were none other in the world but John Lilburne, rather than want one to

strive withall, forsooth, John would certainly quarrel with Lilburne." [76] Then, in order to refute this calumny, he outlines his political autobiography, introducing it by showing how the martyrs in
the Bible and history have consistently been accused of "Turbulency
of Spirit," and how such accusations have always come "from those
that do the injury . . . purposely to fit and prepare such for destruction as oppose their unjust designs." Consequently Lilburne's life of
affliction, like Paul's, is a testimony to his own righteousness and to
the wickedness of his opponents. As further proof of this righteousness Lilburne briefly narrates the story of his fifteen-year battle for
"the ancient laws and ancient rights of England," a story which he
breaks down into eleven major episodes. These episodes give, in
capsule form, the history of left-wing Puritanism during the Civil
War period: Lilburne's battle against king and bishops "for the
freedom of mens persons against arbitrary and illegal imprison-
ments"; his concomitant fight against self-incrimination and close
confinement; his efforts in the cause of religious freedom; his war-
time services on the side of Parliament, culminating in his standing
with Cromwell against the Earl of Manchester; his assault on the
"usurped and innovated powers" of the House of Lords; his opposition to the Grandees in behalf of "the restauration of the Fundamental Laws and Rights of the Nation"; his sacrifices to secure for
all citizens the inalienable right of trial by jury, accompanied by his
fight against the Council of State and entrenched economic privilege;
and finally, his present struggle against Cromwell and against Cromwell's agents in Parliament, in the Council of State, and on the
bench.

Though the emphasis in this narrative is of course vehemently
autobiographical, Lilburne's vanity, even his egocentricity, are often
counteracted by the pervasive conviction that the bell which has
tolled for him has also tolled for all men, that his life has been dedicated to a cause which really does transcend individual privation:

for what is done to any one may be done to every one: besides, being
all members of one body . . . one man should not suffer wrongfully,
but all should be sensible, and endeavour his preservation; otherwise
they give way to an inlet of the sea of will and power upon all their
laws and liberties, which are the boundaries to keep out tyranny and
oppression; and who assists not in such cases betrayes his own rights,

and is over-run, and of a free man made a slave when he thinks not of it, or regards it not, and so shunning the censure of turbulency, incurs the guilt of treachery to the present and future generations.[77]

Hence, though his "words and actions . . . have been scanned with the spirit of Jobs comforters," now at the moment of his "deepest distress and danger" he will still go on doing battle against those who are treading "the laws and rights of the Nation . . . under foot." If such be turbulency of spirit, then and only then, he concludes, is John Lilburne guilty of the Cromwell-inspired charge against him.

But Lilburne's "turbulency" continued to be the most prominent feature of his trial when it reopened on August 10, 1653. For nine days it made almost no progress. Lilburne devoted his talents to picking out minor flaws in the indictment, to which he still refused to plead, and to filling in the picture of himself as a dedicated martyr.[78] Though he persistently played to the crowd, the court treated him with fairness and did little to accelerate the leisurely pace of the proceedings.[79]

During this period three pamphlets did their part to keep the cause of the defendant extremely alive. On August 11 one of Lilburne's devout sectarian followers exhorted jury, populace, and soldiers to heed the warning of Revelation by standing firm for John Lilburne.[80] On August 13 Lilburne issued his own *humble and further Demand*, largely a transcript of some of his remarks to the court on the illegalities, small and large, of his indictment. And three days later, in the far more effective *More Light to Mr. John Lilburnes Jury*, he attempted to make his own case the test of each juror's conscience and patriotism.

Then, at the end of nine days, the court took decisive action: Lilburne was told that if he still refused to plead to the indictment he would be executed.[81] On the next day he finally entered a plea of not guilty, the cue promptly to empanel a jury.[82] But Lilburne had profited by the delay, for on the preceding night he had finished and arranged for the immediate publication of a letter which set forth the rationale behind his final appeal to the jury. The gist of Lilburne's public epistle, *The Afflicted Mans Out-Cry*, is his long-held conviction that freedom and "right Reason" are inseparable, and that what is contrary to reason is contrary to basic law. It is in the light of this belief that Lilburne then proceeds to anatomize Parliament's act of banishment against himself to show how it was at once irrational and illegal. The trinity on which all earthly laws rest, he goes on, consists of life, liberty, and property; however, since most lawmakers presume that all men are evil, it is the mission of the judges to assume the innocence of any man accused of violating life, liberty, or property until that man is proved guilty. That is why he, Lilburne, has long fought for the division into separate and distinct bodies of those who make the law and those who enforce it; and that is why the traditional safeguards of the defendant are so vital to the preservation of liberty and, if to a lesser degree, of life and property.

These basic ideas can perhaps justify his quibbling fault-finding with the letter of his indictment, even his repeated legalistic assertions on the trial's final day that he was not the John Lilburne intended by the act of banishment because he had ceased to be the Lieutenant Colonel named therein.[83] Moreover, as in 1649, Lilburne told the jurors that they were, indeed that they had to be, judges of law as well as of fact. But now he placed his major overt emphasis on the logical argument that, if Cromwell had rightfully dissolved the Rump, then its unjust decisions ought not to be upheld; if Cromwell had been wrong in that action, then Cromwell and not Lilburne ought to be punished. Again, as he had done four years earlier, Lilburne ended his plea to the jury — and to the courtroom — with a stirring and at the same time pathetic declaration that his case was their case, that by showing mercy to him they would be showing mercy to themselves and their posterity.[84]

Despite the prosecution's well-documented claim that the act of banishment was legal and proper, the jury, after a long absence, returned with its verdict: the prisoner was "not guilty of any crime worthy of death." [85] Again Lilburne's histrionic effectiveness in the role of underdog and his skill in stretching legal technicalities until they became a declaration of the dignity of man had won the day. Again there was rejoicing in London — in which even the soldiers guarding Old Bailey joined.[86] Thus the self-proclaimed victim of tyranny was once more the hero of the hour: the Venetian ambassador reported that cries of "Long live Lilburne" filled the metropolis.[87]

Yet the immediate effect of Lilburne's acquittal was to draw Cromwell and his Nominated Parliament closer together.[88] Further, though Lilburne may have been a public hero, the government which he had ostensibly outfaced was strong; and it was unwilling to allow its confirmed antagonist to take advantage of the popular turmoil in his favor to agitate either for the overthrow or the constitutional reform of the Commonwealth. On August 28, therefore, the Council of State, after summoning the members of Lilburne's jury to examine them on their motives for acquitting the defendant,[89] ordered Lilburne removed from Newgate to the Tower, where for six months he was kept in close confinement. A victor in law, Lilburne was in fact a prisoner, and a prisoner he remained until his death in 1657.

Lilburne must then have realized that his political career, and perhaps his life, was drawing to an end. His relative silence is at least partial proof of his new spirit of resignation. Though late in August he saw to the publication of the three parts of *The Tryall of Mr. John Lilburne*, in September he neglected to reply to a public letter which accused him of having been angry, intemperate, conceited, demagogic, and incendiary.[90] On November 21 he applied to the Upper Bench for a writ of habeas corpus, but when, five days later, Parliament declared that his imprisonment was to continue indefinitely, there was no published reply from John Lilburne.[91]

During these final months of 1653 Thomason entered only one pamphlet which explicitly protested against this state of affairs. Cautiously signed by "Anonimus" but bravely entitled *An Hue and Cry after the Fundamental Lawes and Liberties of England*, this tract claims that the nation has sunk into a condition of tyranny, and that her jewels, the laws of the land, have become sadly besmirched.[92] Lilburne's story, from his arbitrary banishment to his continued illegal imprisonment, is merely evidence of this tragic and ugly decline. In contrast to "Anonimus," John Canne, speaking for the government, in November reiterated the full case against the prisoner in the 164 pages of *John Lilb. Tryed and Cast*.[93] To show that Lilburne has long been a dangerous tumor in the body politic and a threat to the *salus populi*, Canne depicts Lilburne's many years of incendiary activity, and, in particular, his career since 1649: his riotous interference as an amateur lawyer with the drainage of the fens, his intemperate dispute with Haslerig, and finally his factious performance at his recent trial. Thus, the author concludes, the jury was wrong, the government right, and the only fit place for the "worldly" Lilburne is the safe seclusion of a prison.

So thought the government. Lilburne remained in the Tower until March 1654, when Cromwell, anxious for the stability of the new Protectorate, arranged for Lilburne's removal from England.[94] He was therefore transferred to an isolated prison on the Isle of Jersey — where, long before, William Prynne had spent three years.[95] There Lilburne remained, in steadily declining health, until the autumn of 1655, though both his wife and his father issued several appeals to the Protector for his release.[96] From the Isle of Jersey Lilburne himself sent forth only one pamphlet, the tired and subdued *Declaration to the Freeborn People of England*, which appeared in May 1654.[97] A restrained plea for a government of just laws, it ends with a routine request for habeas corpus and the hope that perhaps, at long last, "the Law and Courts of Justice . . . [will] be the Keys for opening of prison doors."

The doors opened only very briefly. In October 1655 Lilburne was moved to a cell in Dover Castle.[98] But shortly before, like many of his former fellow radicals, he had been converted to Quakerism. Consequently on his arrival at Dover Lilburne was able to write his wife in praise of the new religious peace he had found, telling her not to worry about his outward liberty, for he had acquired inner light and inner security.[99] Then, in the spring of 1656, after his wife and children had moved to Dover, he published an account of his conversion, *The Resurrection of John Lilburne*. In addition to reprinting certain letters which tell of his progressive inner revelation, this pamphlet describes his new-found, otherworldly peace; and Lilburne closes it with the signature,

From my innocent and every way causeless captivity, . . . the place of my souls contentful abode, where I have really and substantially found that which my soul hath diligently sought after, and with unsatisfied longingness thirsted to enjoy.

Therefore, in a sense, Lilburne's spiritual wheel had also come full circle: the religious exaltation of his *Resurrection* echoes the mood of *Come out of her my people*, as its style, overloaded with Biblical citations and suggestive of self-induced assurance, harks back to the earlier pamphlet. Even a concluding letter, printed in an appendix to the second edition of *The Resurrection* and probably the last published product of Lilburne's pen, is reminiscent, for it brings in a note of theological quibbling and bold recrimination.[100]

Yet the year of life left to Lilburne was relatively tranquil. He was allowed brief periods of liberty to be with his family and to engage in a few local and nonpolitical activities with the Quakers in Dover. In August 1657 he was permitted to accompany his pregnant wife to Kent.[101] Though ordered to return to prison from there, Lilburne was "too sick and weak" to comply; and on August 29, at the age of forty-three, he died.[102] Worn out by many years of struggle, Lilburne even then did not find full peace until the grave, for *Mercurius Politicus* was able thus to describe the incipient turbulence of his funeral:

[His] Corps [was] conveyed to the house, called the Mouth at Aldersgate, which is the usual meeting-place of the people called Quakers. . . . At this place . . . assembled a medley of people, among whom the Quakers were most eminent for number. And within the house a Controversie was, Whether the ceremony of a Herse-Cloth should be cast over his Coffin; but the major part being Quakers not assenting, the Coffin was about five a clock in the evening brought forth into the street. At its coming out, there stood a man on purpose to cast a Velvet-herse [cloth] over the Coffin, and he endeavoured to do it; but the croud of Quakers not permitting it, and having gotten the body upon their shoulders, they carried it away without further ceremony.[103]

Two years later, on the eve of the Restoration, a more fitting epitaph appeared — with the appropriate title of *Lilburns Ghost*.[104] Addressing the people as the source of all political power, this militant Ghost calls on them to make certain that, for the future, church and state are completely separated, the monarchy never restored, and themselves so trained in the ways of democracy that they can fully and capably exercise their just rights. Far better than Lilburne's physically and mentally tired escape into the refuge of Quaker mysticism, this "whip . . . to scourge tyrants out of authority" epitomizes his durable battle for the ideals of an Agreement of the People.

The Contribution of the Leveller Party

The seventeenth-century battle for an Agreement of the People was lost in 1649, a date which signifies the temporary solidification of the Puritan Revolution. A degree of stagnation inevitably accompanied this solidification. For instance, during the eight years before 1650 Thomason collected over 12,000 items; in the period from 1650 through 1657 he collected less than half that number.[1] The Nominated Parliament, purportedly consisting only of "godly" men — none of whom were Levellers — marked the high point of normative Puritanism in power. Yet the excessive zeal of this Parliament in attempting the reform of church and state led to its prompt replacement by the Protectorate, established at the end of 1653 under the Instrument of Government.[2] This document was no Agreement of the People. Despite the fact that it reflected the Grandees' long and intimate contact with Leveller constitutional theories, it was based on the undemocratic premise that a written national charter was the proper foundation for government mainly because the people would then have less power and opportunity to alter their government. Having lost confidence in the "fickle multitude," Cromwell and his chief aides thus sought to freeze the revolution by erecting an authority superior to, not derived from, the people. The brief rule of the major generals in 1655 and 1656 was further proof that the administration distrusted its subjects, for the generals functioned largely as the agents by which a centralized government tried to enforce that moral discipline which had previously been the hortatory function of the church.

The establishment of the Protectorate also contributed to the growth in size and violence of the last of the large-scale revolutionary movements of the Interregnum, that of the Fifth Monarchy.[3] Unlike the remnants of the Leveller party, however, the Fifth Monarchists objected to the Protectorate not because it was authoritarian but because its chief executive was Cromwell rather than Christ. But by 1656 the then only slightly less militant Quakers had absorbed many of these radical "Saints," along with Lilburne and other frustrated left-wingers. In fact, it is one of the many anomalies of this period that Cromwell, perhaps the man of his age most effective in the defense of religious liberty, died while under attack from the Baptists and Quakers, the two sectarian groups which were in the forefront of the fight for full freedom of conscience.[4]

But as the death of Charles had marked the end of the first phase of the Puritan Revolution, its period of ferment and change, so the return of his son brought to an end the second phase, its period of solidification and then of disintegration. In the field of religion, the post-Restoration established church became mainly a lever of respectability rather than a fulcrum of conflict, and protest-ant Puritanism gradually but appropriately changed its name to nonconformity. In politics and economics, Locke's emphasis on property rights reflected that search for stability in theory and practice which was central to the reaction against the turbulence of the Interregnum. The Revolution of 1688 was neither revolutionary nor republican, and it is significant that France, not England, became the theater for revolutionary radicalism in the eighteenth century.[5] Thus within a short space even Lilburne's ghost was laid, and in the first year of the Restoration a Royalist author could write a pamphlet, *The Tales and Jests of Mr. Hugh Peters*, in which the Good Old Cause had already become a joke, and a vulgar joke at that.[6]

Yet despite the fact that the "back-to-normalcy" impact of the Restoration helped to relegate the Leveller movement to almost total oblivion, it had lived long enough to generate certain ideological pressures which did not entirely disappear. To some extent these pressures were the symptoms of a revolutionary age rather than the intended results of party activity. Further, in many cases it is impossible to separate the Levellers' contribution to the history of ideas from that of their contemporaries. None the less, it is probably

true that if Lilburne, Overton, and Walwyn had not joined together to establish a distinct political movement the history of
Western democratic ideas would have been somewhat different.

The central purpose of the Leveller party was to establish a constitutional democracy in England. In the seventeenth century that
purpose failed. When in the nineteenth and twentieth centuries
it was at least partially realized, the Levellers had long been for-
gotten. Yet they formed a link in the chain of England's evolution
toward democracy: by helping to channel the nascent and amorphous democratic sentiment of the seventeenth century in the direction of those ideological way stations through which it moved in the
three following centuries, the Levellers made their major contribution to the history of modern ideas. When examined from the van-
tage point of these three centuries, this contribution can be broken
down into four constituent elements, which, though overlapping
and interlinked, can be labeled optimism, secularism, rationalism,
and pragmatism.

The philosophy on which democracy rests must be optimistic.
It is no coincidence that the achievements of nineteenth-century
liberalism paralleled the increased acceptance of the idea of human
progress, for the despair of a Schopenhauer or the cynicism of an
Alexander Hamilton are both hostile to that faith in majority
rule which is basic to practicable democracy. But the Levellers
neither invented optimism nor directly stressed an optimistic philosophy. The millenarians of their day were far more sanguine in
their expectations; the rule of the Saints which they advocated
was merely preliminary to the imminent second coming of Christ.
On the political right such a confirmed supporter of the Royalist
cause as Dudley Digges viewed the monarchy as the means whereby
confusion could be averted and the nation given the stability necessary to achieve its potentially glorious destiny.[7] How, then, did
the Levellers specifically contribute to the development of an optimistic philosophy which was directly relevant to the growth of
democracy?

Primarily in two ways. First, the Levellers were the motive power
in establishing a series of coalitions composed largely of those
forces who were theologically united in their tendency toward
antinomianism and those forces politically united in their oppo-

sition to religious persecution and the arbitrary exercise of power. Consequently, though such coalitions were short-lived and abortive, they mostly represented a union of those men whose religious beliefs, at least in practice, were democratic and hopeful with those men whose political beliefs were equally democratic and hopeful. In many cases, these two sets of beliefs coexisted in the same person, with Walwyn as a conspicuous example of this fusion. At the same time, the Levellers served as a magnet to draw together such diverse men as the predominantly agnostic Wildman and the pious Chidley, and within the various popular fronts under the leadership of the Levellers it was not uncommon for a mystical millenarian like Saltmarsh to work with a skeptical opportunist like Sexby. In contrast, the Diggers never became strong enough really to qualify as a coalition or to exert much influence; the millenarian parties tended to be optimistic but not democratic; and the Cromwellian grouping of the center was neither predominantly hopeful in its theology nor particularly democratic in its politics: Milton and Cromwell, for instance, both retained a belief in a predetermined and small aristocracy of the elect, and both men placed liberty above democracy. Thus the Levellers, by organizing a party to do battle for a statutory and tolerant democracy, welded together, if only temporarily, certain Independents and sectaries who were optimists about salvation, and certain of their contemporaries who were, regardless of their religion, political democrats.

Second, the Levellers made their optimism clear, if not explicit, by articulating their assumption that pessimism and cynicism were insurmountable barriers to the growth of a democratic commonwealth. In philosophical terms, the Agreements of the People can be reduced to the assertion that most people are good and capable of becoming better. In this broader context, then, the Leveller conviction that power corrupts was not so much a belief in man's depravity as it was an affirmation of man's potentialities, provided he was given scope to develop them. In short, the Agreements of the People attempted to establish a permanent arrangement for practicing the optimism they preached.

The second major element that the Levellers supplied to the evolution of modern democracy was the push that they gave political theory in the direction of avowed secularism. Because the modern world has become increasingly pluralistic and complex, its democracies have developed along experimental and worldly lines — indeed, this method of growth seems necessary to any system of majority rule. But how was the impetus toward secularism in any way uniquely the contribution of the Leveller party?

In terms of the politics of the Interregnum, secularism's most aggressive manifestation was anticlericalism; and, since secularism has long been so protean in its expression as to be incapable of practical definition, it can best be examined in the light of this, its most obvious product. But anticlericalism itself was by no means a new phenomenon to the seventeenth century; at least since the time of Wyclif it had filtered into English politics. During the Civil War it flourished among such antipodal groups as Winstanley's Diggers and the skeptical Erastians led by Selden. In fact, except among the Presbyterians and conservative Independents, some form of anticlericalism broader and more sweeping than antiprelatism was one of the common denominators of all the non-Royalist factions. The problem therefore can be simplified: in what way was Leveller anticlericalism unique?

The anticlericalism of the sects tended to be at once democratic and religious. Most of the antinomian and millenarian groups believed that a professional clergy was one of the major obstacles to attaining God's truth. At the other end of the religious spectrum the anticlericalism of the skeptical Erastians was generally undemocratic and unreligious. In their view, the clergy, preferably a professional class, were to become the civil servants of an oligarchical government. At first sight the Leveller position seems to be essentially that of the sects. With them the Levellers advocated the separation of church and state, and an amateur, even a lay, clergy. Moreover, though Overton's jibes at religion and Wildman's indifference to things of the spirit may have displayed an attitude similar to that of Selden and Hobbes, the anticlericalism of the Leveller movement was by no means unreligious. Why?

The Leveller leaders were men of diverse religious backgrounds and attitudes. Lilburne never lost the basically Calvinistic conviction that he was an embattled member of the elect; and even after his conversion to Quakerism he could accuse a Baptist correspondent of being irretrievably damned.[8] Walwyn remained a lifelong antinomian. Overton spent most of his life as a nominal Baptist; and Wildman at least paid lip service to the religious sensibilities of his age. The political goal of these men involved them, too, in a series of coalitions designed to win mass support in an era of intense interdenominational competition. As a result, religious tolerance was essential to their mutual coöperation and to their political program — a program which, like that of most other contemporary left-of-center groups, insisted on freedom of conscience.

But the anticlericalism of the Levellers was not dominated by the idea of survival as a religious group in the face of hostile clerical forces, nor was it motivated by sectarian ambition. Instead, as part of the party's attempts to win mass support, Leveller anticlericalism was a plank in a political platform, part of the effort to win political rather than religious converts. But it was not unreligious. The Levellers preached the decentralization of religion, not its official subordination. The free exercise of religion, unimpeded by clerical or magisterial interference, was, in fact, one of the chief areas in which the individual in their brave new world could exercise his own genius inviolably and fully. Thus, for instance, the final Agreement of the People advocated as complete a democratization of ecclesiastical powers as it did of political powers. Hence Leveller anticlericalism — or, more broadly, Leveller secularism — stood somewhere between the mysticism or evangelism of the sects and the skepticism or autocracy of the Erastians.

However, it is impossible to understand this impetus toward secularism without an examination of the third component of the Levellers' contribution to the evolution of democracy: their emphasis on rationalism as a *sine qua non* of political progress — an emphasis made explicit in their stated creed that all men are educable. Because democracy must be basically hopeful and practicably secular, it must incorporate the conviction that human behavior is not only potentially intelligent, but that man will behave with increasing rationality as he is forced to exercise his reason. Thus freedom and responsibility, because they compel men to make decisions, are at once the characteristics of democracy and the route of its forward march. But since the history of rationalism is as old as the history of philosophy or of political theory, and since the seventeenth century — the age of Bacon and Descartes

— cannot be separated from the "Age of Enlightenment" which followed it, again the question arises: in what way was the Leveller contribution unique?

It was unique in two ways. First, the Leveller belief in the educability of all men, at least of all Englishmen, was inclusive. In Milton's war in heaven Abdiel won no new converts. In the program of the Fifth Monarchists an exclusive Sanhedrin of Saints was to prepare the nation for the coming of Christ.[9] Among the sects separation from the ungodly, not the conversion of the masses, was the rule rather than the exception. In contrast, the Leveller platforms and almost all their accompanying propaganda enunciated a credo of inclusiveness: government was the active right of all men, and all men were capable of exercising that right. Time after time the leaders of the party proclaimed that their agitation, by making men think, had laid the foundation for the establishment of democracy. Lilburne's recurrent appeals directly, and in a sense personally, to all who would listen, Walwyn's "meeting-house" antinomianism, and Overton's chronic defiance of authority were all aspects of this assertion of democratic rationalism. Moreover, the Leveller party emphasized administrative decentralization and a constitutional bill of rights as the national prerequisites to the continued growth of a thinking and effective citizenry. Thus Leveller rationalism, unlike that of most other contemporary groups, was distinguished by its inclusiveness.

It is true that such republicans as Vane and Marten paid allegiance to the same over-all political creed, as did, at least in theory, some of the Independents and left-wing sectaries. Indeed, the broad impetus of the Reformation was in the direction of individualism in church affairs, an impetus which, in turn, led to rationalism, even potentially to inclusiveness. In the case of the Levellers, however, the belief that all men were educable was central rather than peripheral. The difference between Rainsborough and Vane, for instance, was the difference between wholehearted democratic rationalism and the somewhat skeptical hope that the people could be prodded toward self-government.[10] The difference between Walwyn and George Fox was the difference between the full-fledged application of rationalism to politics and the devout wish that all men would some day see the light. As a result, the rationalism of the Levellers was not only inclusive, it dominated their political thinking. Leveller publicity was explicitly devoted to asserting that all men are educable, and, what is more important, intentionally to educating men to become free and responsible. Consequently both the inclusive range and the intensity of the Levellers' advocacy of applied rationalism served to distinguish it from the theories of those men who, though they believed that all men were capable of reason, shared with Swift the conviction that capacity and use were far apart. Ultimately, then, Leveller rationalism was interchangeable with Leveller optimism: each was the manifestation of the other; together they formed the philosophical justification for Leveller secularism.[11]

The fourth component of the Leveller contribution to the growth of democracy can be called pragmatism. Throughout history pragmatism in politics has manifested itself as expediency. The minor shifts in the programs of the Levellers, as well as their variations in tactics, were designed to win converts: as such, they were expedient, were indicative of the belief that the end can justify the means. But they can also be explained in terms of a larger pragmatism, of, that is, a philosophy which views truth as empirical.

Democracy, the practice of the rule of the majority, is necessarily empirical, and the proof of democracy's validity — its "truth" — tends to be practical rather than theoretical: it is good because it works. Yet in the long run all social theories, if they are more than bookish exercises, rightfully insist that they have to be put to the test of practice; and democracy is no exception. Hence the optimism on which it rests can be restated in pragmatic terms as the assurance that the rule of the majority will pass the test of practical application better than any other political theory.

During the Interregnum every political group strove to take this test, every group hopefully demanded power. Almost all of them cited their own experience of government to validate their claims to rule the nation. The monarchists had centuries of practice and precedent behind them. The Presbyterians had the examples of Geneva and Scotland to back up their arguments in the Westminster Assembly, just as the Independents had their own successful congregations. Even the Diggers had a few acres in Surrey to show that their brand of agrarian communism could meet the

test of practice. Consequently the Leveller desire to justify their
theories by putting them to the test of actual application was entirely typical of their own, and of any other, period of political controversy.

Yet the pragmatism of the Levellers was different from that of
most of their contemporaries in both its overtness and its explicit-
ness. Paradoxically, this party, born in the wrong century and
easily crushed by the political realities of the day, was the Interregnum group which most vociferously and most clearly insisted
on its own pragmatic sanction. The preambles to the Agreements
of the People stressed the fact that the constitutional reforms which
these documents advocated were not so much right as they were
feasible. Further, the majority of nonpersonal Leveller petitions
were essentially *ad hoc* and always allegedly practicable — in contrast to most of the hortatory or alarmist tracts and petitions which
refuted them. The typical Leveller appeal, though it might call on
the laws of nature and God, was directed at the institution of certain
specific changes which, once achieved, would become accepted and
permanent because they would work. Despite the fact that the
Levellers claimed for their reforms the blessings of tradition and
rejected the charge of revolution, they were recurrently willing to
acknowledge that their program was experimental.

This admission rested not so much on any external sanction as it
did on the very brand of democracy which the party advocated.
The extreme expression of the Royalist position, the doctrine of
the divine right of kings, in spite of its pragmatically anti-Papal
origins, was based on the external assumptions that it was justified
by tradition and sanctified by certain passages in the Bible. At the
opposite political extreme, the Diggers sought for validation largely
in the examples of the apostles and in their own reading of the
word of God; and the Millenarians found in Revelation the proof
that the rule of the Saints conformed to God's predictions. The
Levellers, too, cited history and Scripture, but such citations tended
to show not that their program of democracy was infallible, but that,
if given a chance, it could meet and pass the test of practice.

This inherent and avowed pragmatism can be clarified by comparing two significant documents, the final Agreement of the
People and the Scottish National Covenant, one of the charters most

central to militant Puritanism. The manifesto of Presbyterianism breathes out authoritarianism and infallibility. Here, in contrast, is the statement of the Levellers:

We tender this ensuing Agreement, not knowing any more effectuall means to put a finall period to all our feares and troubles. It is a way of settlement, though at first much startled at by some in high authority; yet according to the nature of truth, it hath made its own way into the understanding, and taken root in most mens hearts and affections, so that we have reall ground to hope . . . that our earnest desires and indeavours for the good of the people will not altogether be null and frustrate. The life of all things is in the right use and application, which is not our worke only, but every mans conscience must look to it selfe, and not dreame out more seasons and opportunities.[12]

It is not in the expedient humility of this and other similar statements that the pragmatism of the Levellers resides, but in their almost unique emphasis that their program made sense only if it was put to the empirical test of large-scale practice.

These four components of the Leveller contribution to the evolution of modern democracy are obviously interlinked, and it was partly their fusion by the Leveller party which constituted its contribution. But what is far more important, they were given a common denominator by the Levellers alone: the active and functional application of these ideas on a relatively massive scale to the implementation of political democracy. Had the Levellers not organized an apparatus for the actual promulgation of democracy, their ideological contribution would, at best, have been negligible and hypothetical. However, by the organization of a party, by the broad dissemination of their ideas, and by the persistent inculcation of a precise program, the Levellers specifically, if not in these exact terms, attempted to make optimism, secularism, rationalism, and pragmatism the basic elements of a democratic society and the working slogans of England's political development.

No other Interregnum party or political alignment either so combined these attitudes or so wedded them to actual democratic practice. The Royalists and Presbyterians were undemocratic. Those millenarians who advocated democracy lacked the political theory to support their views. The Diggers never achieved sufficient stature to put their ideas into effective operation. And even such Parliamentary Republicans as Vane and Marten, probably the Levellers' nearest intellectual kin, constituted only a small, aristocratic, and isolated group, untested and generally unheard outside the walls of Westminster. It is possible to view the Instrument of Government as a practicable charter based at least in part on the foregoing attitudes, and even to see it as an ideological forerunner of today's Parliamentary democracy. But basically it was a reaction against, not an affirmation of, democratic ideas; for Cromwell was almost certainly correct in thinking that the people of his day were not ready for democracy.

Assuming that Cromwell was right, what light can this analysis of the Leveller contribution to modern ideas cast on the nature of seventeenth-century Puritanism? Since the Interregnum by and large represented the achievement of militant Puritanism, it has become an accepted semantic convenience to refer to these years as the Puritan Revolution. But, if nothing else, the history of the Leveller party and the characteristics of its ideological contribution should indicate that Puritanism during the Civil War was not only an extremely complex phenomenon, but that it failed to develop any doctrine or trait which could hold together the diverse groups who precipitated the "Puritan Revolution." In fact, there seems to be no common denominator which can distinguish the members of the several Puritan coalitions from their various opponents. Thus Calvinism, though it constituted the chief original impetus to this revolution, created its own reaction in the form of sectarian antinomianism: Thomas Edwards and William Walwin were literally antipodal in their theology. Who was the Puritan? In politics, antiabsolutism ceased to separate the Puritan from his opposite number: Prynne and Sexby became monarchists, Hyde often urged that large concessions be made to the Levellers, and Buckingham paid lip service to republicanism. What, then, were Puritan politics? Nor did all the Puritans share a middle-class economic point of view: Selden and Vane generally spoke as aristocrats, both socially and economically, and on the far left the Anabaptists and Diggers voiced an incipient proletarianism. Finally, the groups composing Puritanism shared no common ground of philosophy: Milton's emphasis on freedom of will can be contrasted to the deterministic strain in Lilburne's religion; Overton's fledgling materialism had

nothing in common with the exalted mystcism of a man like Saltmarsh; and Wildman's skepticism was remote from the spiritual
intensity of Cromwell.

Consequently the history of the Puritan Revolution is largely the
history of a series of shifting coalitions. In this history the Leveller
party stands out for two reasons: first, the consistency of their belief
in political democracy helped to give them a clearer principle of
selection in choosing their allies than that used by other groups less
aware of the importance of political theory; second, this same consistent belief supplied greater pressure on them constantly to seek
an active and massive popular front to achieve their program. Hence
the conflicting thrusts of selectivity and popularity placed the
Leveller party in a position to illustrate more vividly than most
other Interregnum groups the fact that the Puritan Revolution was
a chain of changing political alignments, and of alignments that
tended to be neither selective nor popular.

The history of the Civil War also indicates that the nature of
any one of these changing alignments was determined not so much
by agreement on principle within a coalition as it was by the
nature of the opposition to that coalition. In the first years of the
war the opposition to the Puritan Revolution itself was led by a
combination of prelates and monarchists, while the Puritan forces
were largely dominated by the Presbyterians. As the momentum of
social change pushed the Presbyterians into the opposition, the
Independents took over. When, later, this group seemed to be
moving to the right, the Levellers joined forces with the Royalists —
the ones to reverse, the others to accelerate, this move, but united
by their common animosity to Cromwell and the Council of State.

To imply, then, that the word "Puritan" can include all the
diverse forces which were stimulated by and flourished during the
Puritan Revolution is to make the term meaningless by making it
too inclusive. At the same time, to equate Puritanism solely with
Presbyterianism is obviously to make it too exclusive a label. But
since Puritanism was essentially a product of the Reformation, the
diverse men who made and attempted to guide the Puritan Revolution at least shared an originally common source of motivation.
Thus the start of the Civil War in 1642 marked the coming to
power of a loose confederation, united by its opposition to prelatical

and kingly abuses, and still, in general terms, a product of the momentum generated by the Reformation. As such, it was largely a Puritan confederation. However, as the Royalist coalition crumbled and the Parliamentary coalition achieved power, so the adhesive force supplied by a strong antagonist grew progressively weaker. Where Laud, for instance, had served as a magnet to draw together the Puritan opposition to Charles and the prelates, so his removal helped to unleash the centrifugal forces inherent in any diverse coalition and in the coming to power of any political group. Historically, then, the Interregnum was the high point of Puritan strength, the crest in England of the wave of the Reformation. But these same years signified the end of Puritanism as a movement with sufficiently precise boundaries to make it capable of definition. The phrase "Puritan Revolution" is therefore valid as a description of the origins rather than of the achievements of the Interregnum.

In this sense, Napoleon's relation to the French Revolution or Stalin's relation to the Bolshevik Revolution parallel Cromwell's role in the Puritan Revolution. In each case what started as a movement with a certain ideological homogeneity began to break up as its opposition retreated; in each case a man on horseback took over in order to superimpose an ostensible and relatively rigid unity, and to curb a potentially endless series of disintegrative revolutions. Thus the final decade of the Interregnum is "Puritan" largely in the sense that Cromwell stamped it with his own Puritanism. Even so, in England as in France and Russia, each revolution lost most of its original characteristics as it came to power and ground to a halt.

The Leveller party had its existence in those few years between the defeat of the anti-Puritan coalition in the First Civil War and the solidification of Cromwell's rule immediately after the execution of Charles. Its story is therefore an excellent case history of the disintegration of Puritanism. The list of the allies and opponents of the Levellers is itself evidence that the Puritan Revolution, when it was most Puritan, was least revolutionary; that, when it seemed strongest, it was least capable of creating a program or a philosophy that could reunite its original adherents.

Consequently, though the springs of the Leveller movement are to be found largely in Reformation Puritanism, both its brief history and its contribution to the evolution of modern English democracy were essentially a product of the death throes of Puritanism — and, at the same time, the premature birth pangs of a new age. Indeed, the optimism, secularism, rationalism, and pragmatism which the Levellers attempted to fuse and to actualize by means of a constitutional democracy were less the ideological offspring of Luther and Calvin than they were the ideological ancestors of Jefferson and James Mill. In this respect, Cromwell was right: the Levellers were an anachronism.

But the Levellers were primarily a political party — one that obviously did not view itself as anachronistic. The men who led this party were as much the creatures of their age as were their followers and their opponents. No age spends much energy viewing itself as the end of an era or as the dawn of a new period; and certainly to call the manifestations of any age anachronistic is, at best, the privilege of historical hindsight. The day-to-day efforts of the Levellers were geared to their present, not to our recent past. The most significant of these day-to-day efforts involved the written word, and these words, in turn, were the product of the Levellers' immediate historical context. The Levellers explicitly and emphatically addressed themselves to a mid-seventeenth-century audience, not to posterity. However, if their message expressed political convictions more congenial to the nineteenth than to the seventeenth century, the question arises: did the Levellers make any significant contribution to, or foreshadow, modern prose style?

By and large the answer is no. On the simplest level, the fact that the party and its utterances so rapidly achieved oblivion meant that the Leveller influence on prose style was likely to be negligible. But the question remains: did the Levellers anticipate subsequent literary developments? Here, too, the answer is negative, though it is based on three ostensibly affirmative factors.

The first of these is that a group of men until then largely beyond the pale of literary history were doing the writing. Of the Leveller leaders, only Wildman had had a university education, and only Walwyn had read at all widely in the humane authors familiar to the educated man of the Renaissance. Not until late in life did Lilburne delve into such classical authors as Plutarch and Polybius, and Overton's smattering of Greek and Latin almost certainly came from translated compilations. But with most of their contemporaries, these men shared a profound familiarity with the Bible, and they enjoyed an only slightly closer acquaintance with the vocabulary of the law than did many of their fellow Englishmen. Hence they were far more typical of the literate common man than of the professional artist, the scholar, or the gentleman amateur. At the same time, with the exception of some of the sectarian pulpit orators, the Levellers as a group represented a new type of literary practitioner — unprofessional, relatively uneducated, and middle-class.

The second factor is that these men were specifically and intently addressing an audience which was also comparatively new to the written word; for the mass of people appealed to by Leveller petition and manifesto and by Lilburne's usually newsworthy outbursts was one that, by and large, had ignored the products of professional writers, just as these men and their wealthy amateur brethren had tended to ignore it. Except for the effusions of ballad-monger, journalist, and certain theological controversialists, this audience generally had little familiarity with the written word. Thus one of the major forces contributing to the disintegration of Puritanism during the 1640's was the flood of appeals pouring from the London presses which called on the people to take a variety of unprecedented actions. But because the ferment of the Civil War itself did much to create an audience to which all parties and all political writers addressed themselves in the competitive bidding for popular support, the Levellers were no exception in their interest in this new audience.

The third factor, then, is the nature of Levellers' interest in this new audience: since during the Interregnum many previously unliterary individuals had taken up the pen in the battle for political survival, and since it was common for such diverse authors as Edwards and Winstanley to appeal to the people, the Levellers were unique neither in their late arrival on the literary scene nor in the type of audience to which they appealed. But the nature of their interest in this audience does distinguish them from their contemporaries, for the Levellers alone consistently and enthusiastically preached political democracy. By so doing they identified themselves with their readers, not as a rhetorical device or as a calculated risk, but because their program made such identification fundamental and mandatory. Moreover, for this democratic program to have any chance of success, it had to gain mass backing. Consequently, though the advanced nature of Leveller ideology probably precluded mass support, and though on occasion the Leveller leaders were willing to see their brand of democracy superimposed on an apparently apathetic citizenry, still the major justification and *raison d'être* for Leveller propaganda lay in its ability to win converts. Such a criterion is of course applicable to most popular political writing, but in the case of the Levellers the very democracy which they urged largely determined the manner in which they tried to win converts.

The prime requisite of Leveller appeals was that they had to be understandable to the bulk of their readers. Unlike the appeals of most other contemporary groups, however, those of the Levellers usually demanded an active rather than a passive understanding. Royalist journals could shout alarm and plead for resistance to change or for indifference to left-wing blandishments; the Presbyterians could evoke reactionary terror; and even an official Commonwealthsman like Nedham could couch his polemics of the early 1650's in generally negative terms. On the other hand, the Levellers had to win adherents sufficiently active to support a positive program. Thus their appeals attempted to evoke the allegiance of large numbers of people who would be sufficiently aroused to work for their own democratization.

Because the Levellers were a highly organized and articulate group, they, more than any other coalition or aggregation of their contemporaries, directed a stream of publicity at the people in order both to win them to a program and to educate them to accept the responsibilities inherent in that program. The conspicuous reliance of the Levellers on the mass petition is itself evidence that their appeals were intended to be at once productive and educational. Signing a petition or reading a pamphlet in support of it meant, at least theoretically, that the person thus participating was not only being informed of certain grievances but that he was receiving a lesson in the techniques and burdens of political democracy.

Yet the entrance of these obscure men into the lists of controversy, hitherto the preserve of professionals, gentleman amateurs, and disputing divines, and their attempt to win and educate the mass of the people to democracy, had little qualitative effect on English prose, though it did add to its quantity. The reason for this negative conclusion lies in a combination of the foregoing factors. Since the Leveller leaders were intent on addressing an audience relatively new to the written word and even newer to the idea of active participation in the political decisions of the nation, they consciously or unconsciously adjusted their style to the expectations and capacities of that audience. This style, therefore, was on the whole traditional and conformist, not revolutionary or innovative; and like most of the commercial advertisements or political oratory of today, the appeals of the Levellers, despite their content, tended to follow the most worn rhetorical path.

This path was the stylistic tradition which was derived from the English Bible and fostered by the Reformation, and which found its fullest expression in the polemical Puritan sermon: not the brilliant performances of a Donne or an Andrewes, but the earthier preachments of that large number of men bracketed by Hugh Latimer and John Bunyan. Within this tradition the Bible, its ultimate source, was the predominant wellspring of images, *exempla*, allusions, and quotations. It was the book of the people, in many cases their only book. Every Interregnum controversialist interested in a wide audience utilized the Bible, and even Wildman's pages are interlarded with scriptural references. The Puritan sermon also represented a tradition that was oral rather than written. Perhaps as a result of this, the sentence had tended to become long, loose, and aggregative, structurally akin to what is now the paragraph. Interregnum prose offers few exceptions to this style. Finally, because this tradition was polemical and moralistic, it involved a minimum of sophisticated rhetorical devices. In this respect, too, a conventional lack of artistry marks the controversial political and religious prose of the 1640's. One rhetorical device, however, is common: the voluminous and undiscriminating citation of authorities. In most cases, every word in the Bible is treated as equally important, every historical statute as equally valid, every legal commentary as equally imposing. Hence the works of the Levellers, if viewed en masse, are stylistically indistinguishable from the contemporary outpourings of Royalist and Presbyterian, Independent and Fifth Monarchist, Quaker and Digger.

Even so, among the leaders of the Leveller party only Lilburne fully conformed to the tradition epitomized by the polemical Puritan sermon, and his contribution to the development of English prose style added nothing but volume. Wildman, too, bequeathed nothing to literary evolution, though his more discerning use of historical materials and his limited fund of classical lore did not divorce him so completely from the more humane tradition of Renaissance prose, and though his legal training gave his work a professional touch absent from that of "Legislative John." Overton's contribution would be more important were it not for the fact that many of his stylistic traits had already been displayed, fifty years earlier, in the zestful prose of the University Wits and of the original Martin Marprelate. Overton's skill as an ironist, his mastery in handling graphic and dramatic allegory, and his ability to make a scene come alive all serve to raise some of his works above the level of the ephemeral or the hackneyed. Yet such writers as Greene and Nashe had, two generations before, revealed similar literary skills; and certain of Overton's contemporary opponents — men like Bastwick or John Price — could, on occasion, enliven their prose with an irony, drama, and vividness not unlike his own. Consequently, despite his probable influence on Bunyan, Overton's literary achievements, in terms of their impact on modern prose, must also be considered negligible.

Walwyn's stylistic contribution is a little more difficult to evaluate, probably because, basically, his style is more eclectic. More than his fellows, he combined the polemical tradition of the Reformation with the humane tradition of the Renaissance, and the zeal of Lilburne with the ironic trenchancy of Overton. By and large, his style is restrained and clear, though it can jump from light irony to extremely personal intensity, or from hard-hitting denunciation to devout contemplation. Occasionally, in its disciplined clarity, Walwyn's prose suggests that of Sprat or Dryden, but on the whole it has little in common with the avowedly functional and "scientific" style of the Restoration. Rather, in oversimplified terms, it too harks back to an earlier tradition, in this case one that can be called Anglican. This tradition is possibly best epitomized in prose by the writing of that staunch and humane supporter of the established church, Richard Hooker. Like Walwyn, Hooker had a probing mind, a broad and tolerant sense of perspective, and an ability to be militant without being excessively vindictive. Though Walwyn lacked the careful artistry and the loftiness of style to which Hooker attained, some of his writing is worthy of being placed in the central current of late Renaissance prose, but a current that was then nearing its diffuse end.

Yet despite the over-all lack of importance to literary history and to modern prose of the individual Levellers, together in all probability they did make one stylistic contribution. In a few of their party petitions and in the Agreements of the People the Levellers achieved a directness and simplicity rare in their day. Such documents are not literature, and their stylistic ancestry is to be found in statutes and writs, not in works of art. None the less, those appeals of the Levellers which were composed for mass signature had to be terse and clear and easily comprehended; otherwise the process of securing signatures would have involved lengthy exegesis rather than urgent exhortation. As a result, certain of the party petitions and the Agreements of the People are among the few works of the Interregnum in tune with modern prose techniques; and notwithstanding certain legal and semantic formalities in which these documents had to indulge, stylistically they often achieved a functional precision of which the Royal Society would have approved. But these petitions and charters died almost aborning, and, at best, their direct impact on literary history was extremely slight.

It might be possible to claim that the Leveller movements's democratic agitation helped to produce a larger and more alert audience for the popular writers of the Restoration and eighteenth century; however — assuming that the Interregnum did raise the level of national literacy — this was the result of the cumulative ferment of the 1640's, not a specific contribution of the Leveller party. At the same time, the Levellers were both a cause and effect of that ferment. Yet in so far as they were ideologically though not literarily out of step with the dominant forces of the mid-seventeenth century, they were a political anachronism — hence their failure to achieve power, and hence the relative oblivion which has long shrouded them. None the less, the fact that the Leveller party, as a political movement, was born too soon suggests that the ideas and aspirations of that movement need not be anachronistic in the world of today. Indeed, the battle for an Agreement of the People is still being waged, though the arena is now larger and the price of failure higher.

Appendix: The Authorship of Mans Mortallitie

This problem can be boiled down to whether the "R.O." by whom *Mans Mortallitie* is signed was Richard Overton or the Robert Overton who subsequently became one of Cromwell's better-known colonels. The work went through three editions: the first early in 1644; the second in 1655, under the title of *Man Wholly Mortal*, in a slightly enlarged and revised form; and the third in 1675.[1] The first two editions give the place of printing as Amsterdam and the printer as John Canne. Thomason thought the "Amsterdam" fictitious, and cited London as the place of publication. Plomer concurs in this, and adds that the first two editions were probably printed at a secret press in Coleman Street, one utilized shortly thereafter by John Lilburne.[2] On the basis that Robert Overton had already used this Coleman Street Press, and because later, when he was governor of Hull, he appointed Canne as his chaplain, Plomer conjectures that Robert Overton was the author of *Mans Mortallitie*.[3] The second segment of evidence which identifies "R.O." with Robert Overton is based on the theory that Milton subscribed to the mortalist heresy, and that it was Robert, not Richard, Overton for whom Milton felt a warm friendship and whom he celebrated in his *Defenso Secunda*.[4]

Much of the above evidence, however, can apply with equal validity to Richard Overton. The press on which Plomer assumes *Mans Mortallitie* was printed was used from 1643 to 1645 by several of the more radical proponents of the Puritan cause. Also, Richard Overton might well have known Canne in Holland, where from about 1622 to 1640 Canne had been a Baptist minister.[5] It is possible, too, that the pamphlet was actually printed by Canne in Amsterdam, to which he returned around 1643, or by another of Richard's Dutch associates.

Except for one item, discussed in the next paragraph, the bulk of contemporary evidence is inconclusive. A pamphlet published at Oxford in 1645 in answer to *Mans Mortallitie*, entitled *The Prerogative of Man: or The Immortality of Human Soules*, gives no clue to the authorship of the tract in question; of "R.O." it merely says he will probably continue to "lie concealed, and his name unknowne." [6] In August 1644 the Stationers' Company petitioned for tighter enforcement of the printing ordinance, naming as special offenders against it the Milton who wrote *The Doctrine and Discipline of Divorce*, and the author, unknown, of *Mans Mortallitie*. A year later, three of the leading heresy-hunters of the time, William Prynne, Daniel Featley, and Ephraim Pagitt, coupled Milton, Roger Williams, and the unidentified "mortalist" as among those most worthy of suppression.[7] The most prominent of the witch-hunters, Thomas Edwards, specifically named Richard Overton among the "Anabaptists" who held the "mortalist heresy," though he also claimed that *Mans Mortallitie* was written by Clement Wrighter.[8]

But one item of contemporary evidence is quite conclusive in identifying "R.O." with Richard Overton. In May 1647 appeared an indirect attack on Lilburne, probably from a Royalist pen, entitled *The Recantation of John Lilburne. Opening all the Machinations of the Independent Partie.* Overton is its major target of abuse. In a marginal note on page 6 the anonymous author says of Martin Mar-Priest that "He writ the Booke of soules mortality, and maintaines the same." In the text, on page 7, the author again links Martin to the mortalist heresy, having already made it explicitly clear that Martin and Richard Overton are one and the same person.

Certain other evidence can be adduced in favor of Richard Overton's authorship. In his *The Araignment of Mr. Persecution*, 1645, Overton inserts the following into a speech by Sir John Presbyter against liberty of conscience:

Here the author of that Booke, intituled Mans Mortality, desires Mr. Edwards with those who are so invective against it in their Pulpits that they would cease their railing at it there, and come forth in Print against it; for the thing being so rare, so litle questioned, and the contrary so generally concluded as a principle of faith, any bumbast stuffe will passe there for authentick with the people without tryall, but if it be put forth to publike view, it must expect an encounter by one or tother, and therein the Author of that Booke observeth the policie of his Presbyterian Adversaries to maintaine their repute with the people, in being so hasty in the Pulpit, and so slow to the Presse.[9]

Such a parenthetical advertisement of himself and his views is not uncommon in Overton's works. Moreover, in his section of *The Picture of the Councel of State*, 1649, Overton tells how, when his house was "ransack'd," the soldiers took away, among certain other books and papers, his former

Meditations upon the works of the Creation, intituled Gods Word confirmed by his Works; wherein I endeavored the probation of a God, a Creation, a State of Innocencie, a Fall, a Resurrection, a Restorer, a Day of Judgment, &c. barely from the consideration of things visible and created.[10]

This statement does not necessarily conflict with the content of *Mans Mortallitie*, and it reinforces the supposition that he had a serious intellectual interest in theology.

Another, if negative, type of evidence in favor of Richard Overton can also be advanced. One of the objections to his authorship is that *Mans Mortallitie* displays a body of formal learning with which, presumably, a poor Baptist printer would not be acquainted. However, the little Latin in the tract consists largely of tags from Aristotle and an occasional Church Father. Then, too, its references to the fourth-century Bishop Nemesius, who attempted in part to reconcile classical thought with Christian theology, do not indicate that Overton read him in the original, for in 1636 the Puritan poet George Wither had translated Nemesius' major work, giving it the English title of *The Nature of Man*. Wither's translation probably served as the source of much of Overton's lore, and perhaps of some of his ideas.[11]

Finally, the style of *Mans Mortallitie*, though restrained when compared with Overton's political polemics, does show, on occasion, the flair for vivid analogy and incisive expression which characterizes his subsequent work. Further, the tract's close reasoning, its treatment of Biblical material, and its strongly materialistic bias are much more in keeping with the mind of Richard Overton than with that of the more mystical Robert Overton.

BIBLIOGRAPHY

I. SECONDARY SOURCES

A. *Works whose contribution has been largely bibliographical*

Bush, Douglas. *English Literature in the Earlier Seventeenth Century, 1600–1660.* Oxford: At the Clarendon Press, 1945.

Crane, R. S. and Kaye, F. B. "A Census of British Newspapers and Periodicals." *Studies in Philology*, XXIV (1927), 1–205.

Davies, Godfrey. *Bibliography of British History, Stuart Period, 1603–1714.* Oxford: At the Clarendon Press, 1928.

Fortescue, G. K., chief compiler. *Catalogue of the Pamphlets, Books, Newspapers, and Manuscripts relating to the Civil War, the Commonwealth, and Restoration, Collected by George Thomason, 1640–1661.* London: The British Museum, 1908.

Gabler, Antony J. "Check List of English Newspapers and Periodicals before 1801 in the Huntington Library." *Huntington Library Bulletin*, II (1931), 1–66.

Gerould, James T. *Sources of English History of the Seventeenth Century, 1603–1689.* Minneapolis: University of Minnesota Press, 1921.

Gillett, Charles R. *Catalogue of the McAlpin Collection of British History and Theology.* New York: Union Theological Seminary, 1927–1930.

Peacock, Edward. "Bibliography of John Lilburne." *Notes and Queries*, Seventh Series, V (1888), *passim*, January to June.

Wing, Donald, compiler. *Short-Title Catalogue.* New York: Columbia University Press, 1945 *et seq.*

Wolfe, Don M. *Milton in the Puritan Revolution.* New York: Thomas Nelson and Sons, 1941.

B. *Works whose contribution has been largely nonbibliographical*

Abbott, Wilbur C. *The Writings and Speeches of Oliver Cromwell.* Cambridge, Massachusetts: Harvard University Press, 1937–1947.

Allen, J. W. *English Political Thought, 1603–1660.* London: Methuen & Co. Ltd., 1938.

Ashley, M. P. *Financial and Commercial Policy under the Cromwellian Protectorate.* London: Oxford University Press, 1934.

—— *John Wildman, Plotter and Postmaster.* London: Jonathan Cape, 1947.

—— *Oliver Cromwell, the Conservative Dictator.* London: Jonathan Cape, 1937.

Baker, Herschel. *The Dignity of Man.* Cambridge, Massachusetts: Harvard University Press, 1947.
—— *The Wars of Truth.* Cambridge, Massachusetts: Harvard University Press, 1952.
Bamford, Francis, ed. *A Royalist's Notebook: The Commonplace Book of Sir John Oglander, Kt. of Nunwell.* London: Constable & Co., Ltd., 1936.
Barker, Arthur. *Milton and the Puritan Dilemma, 1641–1660.* Toronto: The University of Toronto Press, 1942.
Baxter, Richard. *Autobiography.* London: J. M. Dent & Sons, Ltd., 1931.
Beer, Max. *A History of British Socialism.* London: George Allen and Unwin Ltd., one-volume edition, 1940.
Beller, Elmer. "Milton and 'Mercurius Politicus'." *Huntington Library Quarterly,* V (1941–42), 479–487.
Bernstein, Eduard. *Cromwell & Communism, Socialism and Democracy in the Great English Revolution.* Transl. H. J. Stenning. London: George Allen & Unwin Ltd., 1930.
Beveridge, Sir William, with the collaboration of L. Liepmann, F. J. Nicholas, M. E. Rayner, and M. Wretts-Smith. *Prices and Wages in England from the Twelfth to the Nineteenth Century.* London: Longmans, Green and Co., 1939.
Beza, Theodore. *Life of Calvin.* Transl. Francis Sibson. Philadelphia: J. Whetham, 1836.
Braithewaite, William C. *The Beginnings of Quakerism.* London: Macmillan and Co., Limited, 1912.
Bredvold, Louis. *The Intellectual Millieu of John Dryden: Studies in Some Aspects of Seventeenth-Century Thought.* Ann Arbor: University of Michigan Publications in Language and Literature #12, 1934.
Brown, Louise Fargo. *The Political Activities of the Baptists and Fifth Monarchy Men in England During the Interregnum.* Washington: American Historical Association, 1912.
Bruce, John, ed., with David Masson. *The Quarrel Between the Earl of Manchester and Oliver Cromwell: An Episode of the English Civil War.* London: The Camden Society, 1875.
Brunton, D. and Pennington, D. H. *Members of the Long Parliament.* Cambridge, Massachusetts: Harvard University Press, 1954.
Buchan, John. *Oliver Cromwell.* Boston: Houghton Mifflin, 1934.
Burnet, Bishop Gilbert. *History of His Own Time.* London: William S. Orr & Co., 1850.
Burrage, Champlin. *The Early English Dissenters in the Light of Recent Research (1550–1641).* Cambridge: At the University Press, 1912.
—— "The Fifth Monarchy Insurrections." *The English Historical Review,* XXV (1910), 722–747.
Carruthers, S. W. *The Everyday Work of the Westminster Assembly.* Philadelphia: The Presbyterian Historical Society, 1943.
Clarendon, Sir Edward Hyde, earl of. *Calendar of Clarendon State Papers in the Bodleian Library.* Ed. O. Ogle, W. H. Bliss, H. O. Coxe, W. D.

Macray, F. J. Routledge, and C. H. Firth. Oxford: At the Clarendon Press, 1872–1932.

Clyde, William M. *The Struggle for the Freedom of the Press from Caxton to Cromwell.* London: Humphrey Milford, 1934.

Coates, Willson H. "Some Observations on 'The Grand Remonstrance'." *The Journal of Modern History,* IV (1932), 1–17.

Coke, Sir Edward. *The First Part of the Institutes of the Laws of England.* Ed. Francis Hargrove and Charles Butler. London: J. & W. T. Clarke, 1832.

Curtler, W. H. R. *The Enclosure and Redistribution of Our Land.* Oxford: At the Clarendon Press, 1920.

Darby, H. C., ed. *An Historical Geography of England Before A.D. 1800.* Cambridge: At the University Press, 1936.

Davies, Godfrey. "Arminian versus Puritan in England, ca. 1620–1640." *Huntington Library Bulletin,* V (1934), 158–179.

—— *The Early Stuarts, 1603–1660.* Oxford: At the Clarendon Press, revised edition, 1949.

de Beer, E. S. "George Masterson." *Notes and Queries,* CXCIII (1948), 57–59.

Dictionary of National Biography

Dietz, Frederick C. *An Economic History of England.* New York: Henry Holt and Company, 1942.

—— *English Public Finance, 1558–1641.* New York: The Century Co., 1932.

Evans, B. *The Early English Baptists.* London: J. Heaton & Son, 1862.

Feiling, Keith. *A History of the Tory Party, 1640–1714* Oxford: At the Clarendon Press, 1924.

Figgis, John Neville. *The Divine Right of Kings.* Cambridge: At the University Press, second edition, 1914.

Fink, Zera S. *The Classical Republicans: An Essay in the Recovery of a Pattern of Thought in Seventeenth Century England.* Evanston: Northwestern University, 1945.

Firth, Sir Charles Harding. *Cromwell's Army. A History of the English Soldier during the Civil Wars, the Commonwealth and the Protectorate.* London: Methuen & Co., 1902.

—— *The House of Lords during the Civil War.* London: Longmans, Green, and Co., 1910.

—— *The Last Years of the Protectorate, 1656–1658.* London: Longmans, Green, and Co., 1909.

—— *Oliver Cromwell and the Rule of the Puritans in England.* New York: The Knickerbocker Press, 1900.

—— ed. *The Clarke Papers.* London: The Camden Society, 1891–1901.

—— with Godfrey Davies. *The Regimental History of Cromwell's Army.* Oxford: At the Clarendon Press, 1940.

—— ed., with R. S. Rait. *Acts and Ordinances of the Interregnum, 1642–1660.* London: Published by His Majesty's Stationery Office, 1911.

Fisch, Harold. "The Puritans and the Reform of Prose-Style." *ELH,* XIX (1952), 229–248.

Forster, John. *Eminent British Statesmen*. London: Longman, Orme, Brown, Green & Longmans, 1838.

Foster, H. D. "The Political Theories of Calvinists before the Puritan Exodus to America." *The American Historical Review*, XXI (1915), 481–503.

Fox, George. *The Journal of George Fox*. Revised by Norman Penney. London: J. M. Dent & Sons Ltd., Everyman's Library, 1948.

French, J. Milton. *The Life Records of John Milton*. New Brunswick: Rutgers University Press, 1950.

—— "Milton, Nedham, and 'Mercurius Politicus'." *Studies in Philology*, XXXIII (1936), 236–252.

Gardiner, Samuel Rawson. *The Constitutional Documents of the Puritan Revolution, 1628–1660*. Oxford: At the Clarendon Press, 1889.

—— *Cromwell's Place in History*. London: Longmans, Green, and Co., 1910.

—— *The First Two Stuarts and the Puritan Revolution, 1603–1660*. New York: Charles Scribner's Sons, 1886.

—— *History of the Commonwealth and Protectorate, 1649–1656*. London: Longmans, Green, and Co., 1903.

—— *History of England from the Accession of James I to the Outbreak of Civil War*. London: Longmans, Green, and Co., 1904.

—— *History of the Great Civil War, 1642–1649*. London: Longmans, Green, and Co., 1893.

Gardner, Stanley. Letter on Interregnum pamphlet circulation. *The Times Literary Supplement*, March 7, 1952.

Gibb, M. A. *John Lilburne The Leveller, A Christian Democrat*. London: Lindsay Drummond Ltd., 1947.

—— *The Lord General: A Life of Thomas Fairfax*. London: Lindsay Drummond Ltd., 1938.

Gooch, G. P. *English Democratic Ideas in the Seventeenth Century*. Cambridge: At the University Press, second edition, 1927.

Gough, J. W. "The Agreements of the People." *History*, XV (1930–31), 334–341.

—— *The Social Contract, A Critical Story of Its Development*. Oxford: At the Clarendon Press, 1936.

Great Britain, *Reports of the Historical Manuscripts Commission*.

Haines, Charles Grove. *The American Doctrine of Judicial Supremacy*. New York: The Macmillan Company, 1914.

—— *The Revival of Natural Law Concepts*. Cambridge, Massachusetts: Harvard University Press, 1930.

Haller, William. "Before Areopagitica." *PMLA*, XLII (1927), 875–900.

—— *The Rise of Puritanism*. New York: Columbia University Press, 1938.

—— *Tracts on Liberty in the Puritan Revolution, 1638–1647*. New York: Columbia University Press, 1933–1934.

—— with Godfrey Davies. *The Leveller Tracts, 1647–1653*. New York: Columbia University Press, 1944.

———— with Malleville Haller. "The Puritan Art of Love." *Huntington Library Quarterly*, V (1941–42), 235–276

Harris, Victor. *All Coherence Gone*. Chicago: University of Chicago Press, 1949.

Haskins, George L. *The Growth of English Representative Government*. Philadelphia: University of Pennsylvania Press, 1948.

Henry, Nathaniel. "Milton and Hobbes: Mortalism and the Intermediate State." *Studies in Philology*, XLVIII (1951), 234–249.

———— "Milton and Overton." *The Times Literary Supplement*, Oct. 14, 1949.

Hill, Christopher. "The Agrarian Legislation of the Interregnum." *The English Historical Review*, LV (1940), 222–250.

———— "The English Civil War Interpreted by Marx and Engels." *Science and Society*, XII (1948), 130–156.

———— "Soviet Interpretations of the Interregnum." *The Economic History Review*, VIII (1937–38), 159–167.

———— as ed. *The English Revolution 1640*. London: Lawrence & Wishart Ltd., 1940.

———— as ed. with Edmund Dell. *The Good Old Cause, The English Revolution of 1640–1660: Its Causes, Course and Consequences*. London: Lawrence & Wishart, 1949.

Holorenshaw, Henry. *The Levellers and the English Revolution*. London: Victor Gollancz Ltd., 1939.

Horne, Andrew. *The Mirrour of Justices*. Transl. by William Hughes in 1646; ed. William C. Robinson. Washington: John Byrne & Co., 1903.

Huehns, Gertrude. *Antinomianism in English History, With special reference to the period 1640–1660*. London: The Cresset Press, 1951.

Ivimay, Joseph. *The Life of William Kiffin*. London: Printed for the Author, 1833.

James, Margaret. *Social Problems and Policy During the Puritan Revolution, 1640–1660*. London: George Routledge & Sons, Ltd., 1930.

———— "The Political Importance of the Tithes Controversy in the English Revolution, 1640–60." *History*, XXVI (1941), 1–18.

Johnson, A. F. "The Exiled English Church at Amsterdam and its Press." *The Library*, Fifth Series, V (1950–51), 219–242.

Jones, Richard Foster, and Others Writing in His Honor. *The Seventeenth Century: Studies in English Thought and Literature from Bacon to Pope*. Stanford: Stanford University Press, 1951.

———— *The Triumph of the English Language*. Stanford: Stanford University Press, 1953.

Jones, Rufus M. *Mysticism and Democracy in the English Commonwealth*. Cambridge, Massachusetts: Harvard University Press, 1932.

———— *Studies in Mystical Religion*. London: Macmillan and Co., Ltd., 1923.

Jordan, W. K. *The Development of Religious Toleration in England*. Cambridge, Massachusetts: Harvard University Press, 1932–1940.

———— *Men of Substance, A Study in the Thought of Two English Revo-*

lutionaries, Henry Parker and Henry Robinson. Chicago: The University of Chicago Press, 1942.

Judson, Margaret Atwood. *The Crisis of the Constitution, An essay in constitutional and political thought in England 1603–1645*. New Brunswick: Rutgers University Press, 1949.

Kirby, Ethyn Williams. *William Prynne, A Study in Puritanism*. Cambridge, Massachusetts: Harvard University Press, 1931.

Knappen, M. M. *Constitutional and Legal History of England*. New York: Harcourt, Brace and Company, 1942.

—— *Tudor Puritanism, A Chapter in the History of Idealism*. Chicago: The University of Chicago Press, 1939.

Krapp, George Philip. *The Rise of English Literary Prose*. New York: Oxford University Press, 1915.

Laird, John. *Hobbes*. London: Ernest Benn Limited, 1934.

Laski, Harold J., ed. *Vindiciae Contra Tyrannos: A Defence of Liberty Against Tyrants*. New York: Harcourt Brace & Co. n.d.

Leach, Robert J. *The Inward Journey of Isaac Penington*. Pendle Hill: Pendle Hill Historical Studies #6, 1943.

Lipson, E. *The Economic History of England*. London: A. & C. Black, Ltd., 1931.

London, Corporation of. *The Corporation of London: Its Origin, Constitution, Powers and Duties*. London: Oxford University Press, 1950.

Lyon, T. *The Theory of Religious Liberty in England, 1603–1639*. Cambridge: At the University Press, 1937.

MacIver, R. M., ed. *Great Expressions of Human Rights*. New York: The Institute for Social and Religious Studies, 1950.

Mathew, David. *The Social Structure in Caroline England*. Oxford: At the Clarendon Press, 1948.

McIlwain, C. H. *The High Court of Parliament and Its Supremacy*. New Haven: Yale University Press, 1910.

—— *The Political Works of James I*. Cambridge, Massachusetts: Harvard University Press, 1918.

McLachlen, H. John. Letter on Interregnum pamphlet circulation. *The Times Literary Supplement*, March 7, 1952.

Miller, Perry. *Orthodoxy in Massachusetts, A Genetic Study*. Cambridge, Massachusetts: Harvard University Press, 1933.

Milton, John. *Prose Works*. London: Henry G. Bohn, n.d.

Nayler, James. *A Collection of Sundry Books, Epistles and Papers Written by James Nayler*. London: J. Sowle, 1716.

Nef, John U. *Industry and Government in France and England, 1540–1640*. Philadelphia: The American Philosophical Society, 1940.

Neumann, Joshua. "Milton's Prose Vocabulary." *PMLA*, LX (1945), 102–120.

Nicholas, Sir Edward. *The Nicholas Papers*. Ed. George F. Warner. London: The Camden Society, 1886–1920.

Nicolson, Marjorie. "Milton and Hobbes." *Studies in Philology*, XXIII (1926), 405–433.

Onions, Charles T., ed. *Shakespeare's England: An Account of the Life and Manners of His Age*. Oxford: At the Clarendon Press, 1916.

Orme, William. *The Life and Times of the Rev. Richard Baxter: With a Critical Examination of His Writings*. Boston: Crocker & Brewster, 1831.

Orwell, George, and Reynolds, Reginald, eds. *British Pamphleteers*. London: Allan Wingate, 1948.

Patrick, J. Max. *Hugh Peters, A Study in Puritanism*. Buffalo: The University of Buffalo Studies, Vol. 17, No. 4, 1946.

Payne, E. A. "Milton and Overton." *The Times Literary Supplement*, Oct. 28, 1949.

Peacock, Edward. "Thomas Rainsborough." *Archaeologica*, XLVI (1880), 9–64.

Pease, Theodore Calvin. *The Leveller Movement: A Study in the History and Political Theory of the English Great Civil War*. Washington: American Historical Association, 1916.

Pepys, Samuel. *The Diary of Samuel Pepys*. Ed. Henry B. Wheatley. New York: Random House, n.d.

Petegorsky, David W. *Left-Wing Democracy in the English Civil War: A Study in the Social Philosophy of Gerrard Winstanley*. London: Victor Gollancz, 1940.

Plomer, Henry R. *A Dictionary of the Booksellers and Printers Who Were at Work in England, Scotland and Ireland from 1641 to 1667*. London: Printed for the Bibliographical Society, 1907.

———— "The Importation of Low Country and French Books into England, 1480 and 1502–3." *The Library*, Fourth Series, IX (1928–29), 164–168.

———— "Secret Printing During the Civil War." *The Library*, Second Series, V (1904), 374–403.

———— "Some Dealings of the Long Parliament with the Press." *The Library*, Fifth Series, V (1950–51), 90–97.

Pollock, Sir Frederick. *Essays in the Law*. London: Macmillan and Co., Limited, 1922.

Ramsey, Robert W. *Henry Ireton*. London: Longmans, Green, and Co., 1949.

Robbins, Caroline. "The Library of Liberty Assembled for Harvard College by Thomas Hollis of Lincoln's Inn." *William and Mary Quarterly*, V (1950), 5–23.

———— "The Strenuous Whig, Thomas Hollis of Lincoln's Inn." *Harvard Library Bulletin*, Third Series, VII (1951), 406–453.

Robertson, D. B. *The Religious Foundations of Leveller Democracy*. New York: King's Crown Press, 1951.

Robinson, Jane. "The Early Life of John Lilburne: A Study in Puritan Political Thought." Unpublished dissertation. University of California at Los Angeles, 1946.

Rollins, Hyder E. "Samuel Sheppard and His Praise of Poets." *Studies in Philology*, XXIV (1927), 509–555.

Rushworth, John. *Historical Collections*. London: D. Browne, 1721–22.

Sabine, George H. *A History of Political Theory*. New York: Henry Holt and Company, second edition, 1947.

—— ed. *The Works of Gerrard Winstanley*. Ithaca: Cornell University Press, 1941.

Schenk, Wilhelm. "A Seventeenth Century Radical." *Economic History Review*, XIV (1944), 74–83.

——*The Concern for Social Justice in the Puritan Revolution*. London: Longmans, Green, and Co., 1948.

Sensabaugh, George F. *The Tragic Muse of John Ford*. Stanford: Stanford University Press, 1944.

Shaw, William A. *A History of the English Church during the Civil Wars and under the Commonwealth*. London: Longmans, Green, and Co., 1900.

Shields, Alcuin. Letter on Interregnum pamphlet circulation. *The Times Literary Supplement*, Feb. 22, 1952.

Simpkinson, C. H. *Thomas Harrison, Regicide and Major-General*. London: J. M. Dent & Co., 1905.

Smith, H. F. Russell. *Harrington and His 'Oceana', A Study of a 17th Century Utopia and Its Influence in America*. Cambridge: At the University Press, 1914.

Smith, H. Maynard. *Pre-Reformation England*. London: Macmillan and Co., Ltd., 1938.

Somers Tracts. Ed. Walter Scott. London: T. Cadell and W. Davies, 1809–1815.

St. Germain, Christopher. *The Doctor and Student*. Ed. William Muchall. Cincinnati: Robert Clarke & Co., 1874.

State Trials: A Complete Collection of State-Trials and Proceedings for High Treason and other Crimes and Misdemeanours. London: J. Walthoe and T. Wotton, 1742.

Strauss, Leo. *The Political Philosophy of Hobbes, Its Basis and Its Genesis*. Transl. Elsa M. Sinclair. Oxford: At the Clarendon Press, 1936.

Surtees Society. *Depositions and Other Ecclesiastical Proceedings from the Courts of Durham*. XXI (1845).

—— *The Register of Richard Fox, Lord Bishop of Durham, 1494–1501*. CXLVII (1932).

Tanner, J. R. *Constitutional Documents of the Reign of James I, A.D. 1603–1625*. Cambridge: At the University Press, 1930.

—— *English Constitutional Conflicts of the Seventeenth Century, 1603–1689*. Cambridge: At the University Press, 1928.

—— *Tudor Constitutional Documents, A.D. 1485–1603, with an historical commentary*. Cambridge: At the University Press, 1922.

Tawney, R. H. *The Agrarian Problem in the Sixteenth Century*. London: Longmans, Green, and Co., 1912.

—— *Religion and the Rise of Capitalism, A Historical Study*. New York: Penguin Books, Inc., 1947.

Thompson, Faith. *The First Century of Magna Carta: Why It Persisted as a*

Document. Minneapolis: University of Minnesota Studies in the Social Sciences #16, 1925.

—— *Magna Carta, Its Role in the Making of the English Constitution, 1300–1629*. Minneapolis: The University of Minnesota Press, 1948.

Thompson, James Westfall, and Holm, Bernard J. *A History of Historical Writing*. New York: The Macmillan Company, 1942.

Thomson, Mark A. *A Constitutiontal History of England, 1642–1801*. London: Methuen & Co., Ltd., 1938.

Thurloe, John. *A Collection of the State Papers of John Thurloe*. Ed. Thomas Birch. London: F. Gyles, 1742.

Tindall, William York. *John Bunyan Mechanick Preacher*. New York: Columbia University Press, 1934.

Troeltsch, Ernst. *The Social Teaching of the Christian Churches*. Transl. Olive Wyon. New York: The Macmillan Company, 1931.

Tuveson, Ernest Lee. *Millennium and Utopia, A Study in the Background of the Idea of Progress*. Berkeley and Los Angeles: University of California Press, 1949.

Underwood, A. C. *A History of the British Baptists*. London: The Baptist Union Publication Dept., 1947.

Unwin, George. *The Gilds and Companies of London*. London: Methuen & Co., Ltd., 1908.

Usher, Abbott Payson. *The Industrial History of England*. Cambridge, Massachusetts, The Riverside Press, 1920.

Varley, Frederick John. *Mercurius Aulicus.* Oxford: Basil Blackwell, 1948.

Verney, Sir Ralph. *Notes of Proceedings in the Long Parliament*. Ed. John Bruce. London: The Camden Society, 1845.

Vincent, W. A. L. *The State and School Education 1640–1660 in England and Wales, A Survey Based on Printed Sources*. London: The Church Historical Society, 1950.

Watson, Foster. *The English Grammar Schools to 1660: Their Curriculum and Practice*. Cambridge: At the University Press, 1908.

Weber, Max. *The Protestant Ethic and the Spirit of Capitalism*. Transl. Talcott Parsons. New York: Charles Scribner's Sons, 1930.

White, Helen C. *English Devotional Literature (Prose), 1600–1640*. Madison: University of Wisconsin Studies in Language and Literature #29, 1931.

—— *Social Criticism in Popular Religious Literature of the Sixteenth Century*. New York: The Macmillan Company, 1944.

Whitehead, Alfred North. *Science and the Modern World*. New York: The New American Library, 1948.

Willey, Basil. *The Seventeenth Century Background: Studies in the Thought of the Age in Relation to Poetry and Religion*. London: Chatto & Windus, 1949.

Williams, J. B. (pseud. of J. G. Muddiman). *A History of English Journalism to the Foundation of the Gazette*. London: Longmans, Green, and Co., 1908.

Williams, Roger. *The Bloody Tenent of Persecution.* Ed. Samuel L. Cald-well. Providence: Publications of the Narragansett Club, Vol. III, 1867.

Williamson, George. "Milton and the Moralist Heresy." *Studies in Philology,* XXXII (1935), 553–579.

Wolfe, Don M. *Leveller Manifestoes of the Puritan Revolution.* New York: Thomas Nelson and Sons, 1944.

—— "Lilburne's Note on Milton." *Modern Language Notes.* LVI (1941), 360–363.

—— "Milton and Hobbes: A Contrast in Social Temper." *Studies in Philology,* XLI (1944), 410–426.

Wolfram, Harold W. "John Lilburne: Democracy's Pillar of Fire." *Syracuse Law Review,* III (1952), 213–258.

Wood, Anthony á. *Athenae Oxonienses.* London: Bennet, 1691–1692.

Woodhouse, A. S. P. *Puritanism and Liberty.* London: J. M. Dent and Sons Limited, second edition, 1950.

Zagorin, P. "The Authorship of 'Mans Mortallitie'." *The Library,* Fifth Series, V (1950–51), 179–183.

II. PRIMARY SOURCES

A. *Seventeenth-century newspapers* (The date given in parentheses indicates the year or years for which the newspaper has been particularly useful.)

Mercurius Britanicus: Communicating the affaires of Great Britaine: For the better Information of the People (1643).

Mercurius Aulicus, A Diurnall, Communicating the intelligence and affaires of the Court to the rest of the Kingdom (1643–44).

Mercurius Rusticus: Or, The Countries Complaint of the barbarous Outrages Committed by the Sectaries of this late flourishing Kingdome (1646).

Mercurius Anti-Pragmaticus (1647).

Mercurius Melancholicus: Or, Newes from Westminster and other Parts (1647–48).

Mercurius Pragmaticus (1647–49).

The Colchester Spie (1648).

Mercurius Aulicus: Againe Communicating Intelligence from all parts, touching all Affaires, Designes, Humours, and Conditions throughout the Kingdome (1648).

Mercurius Bellicus. Or, An Alarum to all Rebels (1648).

Mercurius Britanicus Alive Again (1648).

Englands Moderate Messenger (1649).

Heads of a Diarie (1649).

The Impartiall Intelligencer, Containing a Perfect Collection of the Weekly Passages in Parliament; the Proceedings of the Council of State, and the High Court of Justice (1649).

The Kingdomes Faithfull and Impartiall Scout (1649).

The Kingdomes Weekly Intelligencer, Sent Abroad to prevent mis-information (1649).

The Man in the Moon, Discovering a World of Knavery under the Sunne (1649).

Mercurius Aulicus (For King Charls II.) Communicating Intelligence from all parts, touching all Affairs, Designes, Humours, and Conditions throughout the kingdom (1649).

Mercurius Brittanicus, Communicating Intelligence from all parts of the Kingdome (1649).

Mercurius Elencticus (1649).

Mercurius Militaris, or the Peoples Scout (1649).

Mercurius Pragmaticus, (For King Charles II) (1649).

The Moderate: Impartially communicating Martial Affaires to the Kingdome of England (1649).

A Moderate Intelligence, Impartially Communicating Martial Affairs to the Kingdom of England (1649).

The Moderate Intelligencer: Impartially Communicating Martiall Affaires to the Kingdome of England (1649).

A Modest Narrative of Intelligence (1649).

The Perfect Weekly Account (1649).

Mercurius Politicus (1650, 1652, 1653, 1657, 1658).

B. *The writings of the Levellers, with other primary works directly related to them* (The Bibliography at the conclusion of Wolfe's *Milton in the Puritan Revolution*, which arranges by author most of the Leveller tracts, is useful as a supplement to the chronological listing which follows.)

Robert Browne, *A Treatise of Reformation without tarying for anie*, 1582.

Meredith Hamner, ed. and transl., *The Ancient Ecclesiasticall Histories of the first six hundred years after Christ*, 1584.

Leonard Busher, *Religious Peace*, 1614.

The Petition of Right, 1628.

George Wither, *The Nature of Man*, 1636.

John Bastwick, *Letany*, published in four parts in 1637.

The Scottish National Covenant, February 1638.

Lilburne, *A Christian Mans Triall*, March 1638.

Lilburne, *A Worke of the Beast*, April 1638.

Lilburne, *Come out of her my people*, September 1638.

Lilburne, *Coppy of a Letter written by . . . Lilburne*, November 1638 (reprinted in his *Innocency and Truth*, 1645).

Lilburne, *An Answer to Nine Arguments*, written December 1638, printed January 1645.

Lilburne, *The Poore Mans Cry*, December 1638.

Lilburne, *A Cry for Justice*, May 1639.

Lilburne, *To all the brave, courageous and valiant Apprentizes of . . . London*, May 1639 (reprinted in his *The Prisoners Plea for a Habeas Corpus*, April 1648).

Lilburne, *A copy of a letter . . . by John Lilburne*, October 1640.

Lilburne, *. . . to the Parliament assembled*, December 1640 (reprinted in his *Innocency and Truth*, 1645).

The Root and Branch Petition, December 1640.

The Act against Dissolving the Long Parliament, May 1641.

The Act for the Abolition of the Court of Star Chamber, July 1641.

Samuel Hartlib, *A Description of the famous Kingdome of Macaria*, October 1641.

Walwyn (?), *The Humble Petition of the Brownists*, November 1641.

Robert Greville, Lord Brooke, *A Discourse opening the Nature of that Episcopacie, which is exercised in England*, November 1641.

The Grand Remonstrance, December 1641.

Henry Archer, *The Personall Reign of Christ upon Earth*, January 1642.

Overton, *Articles of High Treason . . . against Cheapside Crosse*, January 1642.

Hay Any Work for Cooper, March 1642 (anon.).

Overton, *New Lambeth Fair newly Consecrated*, March 1642.

Henry Parker, *Observations upon some of his Majesties late Answers and Expresses*, July 1642.

John Hare, *St. Edwards Ghost; or, Anti-Normanisme*, written in October 1642, published in 1647.

John Goodwin, *Anti-Cavalierisme*, October 1642.

Walwyn (?), *Some Considerations tending to the undeceiving those, whose judgements are misinformed*, November 1642.

Daniel Felton, *The examination and confession of Captaine Lilbourne and Captaine Viviers*, December 1642.

"Martin Mar-Prelat," *The Character of a Puritan*, January 1643.

Dudley Digges, *The unlawfulnesse of Subjects taking up Arms*, January 1643.

Lilburne, *A Letter sent from Captaine Lilburne To divers of his Friends*, January 1643.

Parliament, *An Exact Collection of all Remonstrances, Declarations, Votes . . . and other Remarkable Passages betweene the Kings most Excellent Majesty, and his High Court of Parliament* (the "Book of Declarations"), March 1643.

William Prynne, *The Soveraigne Power of Parliaments and Kingdomes*, in four parts, the last of which appeared in August 1643.

Walwyn, *The Power of Love*, September 1643.

The Solemn League and Covenant, September 1643.

John Vicars, *Jehovah-Jireh: God in the Mount; or, A Continuation of Englands Parliamentary Chronicle*, published in sections between August 1642 and October 1643.

Thomas Goodwin, and others, *An Apologeticall Narration*, January 1644.

[Richard] Overton, *Mans Mortallitie*, first ed., January 1644.

Henry Robinson, *Liberty of Conscience*, March 1644.

Thomas Bakewell, *Confutation of Anabaptists*, June 1644.

Walwyn, *The Compassionate Samaritane*, July (?) 1644.

Thomas Edwards, *Antapologia*, July 1644.

Roger Williams, *The Bloudy Tenent*, July 1644.

William Prynne, *Independency Examined, Unmasked, Refuted*, September 1644.

John Goodwin, *The Grand Imprudence of Men running the hazard of fighting against God*, October 1644.

Henry Parker, *Jus Populi*, October 1644.

John Milton, *Areopagitica*, November 1644.

William Prynne, *Truth Triumphing over Falshood, Antiquity over Novelty*, January 1645.

Lilburne, *A Copie of a Letter . . . To Mr. William Prinne Esq.*, January 1645.

A Review of a certain Pamphlet Under the name of one John Lilburne, January 1645 (anon.).

Daniel Featley, *The Dippers Dipt*, February 1645.

Walwyn, *A Helpe to the right understanding of a Discourse concerning Independency*, February 1645.

The Self-denying Ordinance, April 1, 1645.

Overton, *The Araignement of Mr. Persecution*, April 1645.

Overton, *A Sacred Decretall*, May 1645.

Ephraim Pagitt, *Heresiography*, May 1645.

Henry Parker, *Jus Regum*, May 1645.

Lilburne, *The Reasons of . . . Lilbournes sending his Letter to Mr. Prin*, June 1645.

Overton, *Martins Eccho*, June 1645.

Overton, *The Nativity of Sir John Presbyter*, July 1645.

Lilburne, *A More full Relation of the great Battell fought betweene . . . Fairfax and Goring*, July 1645.

John Warre (?), *The Prerogative of Man; or, The Immortality of Human Soules*, July 1645.

William Prynne, *A Fresh Discovery of some prodigious new Wandring-Blasing-Stars & Firebrands*, July 1645.

Lilburne, *The Copy of a Letter . . . to a Friend*, July 1645.

John Bastwick, *A Just Defence of John Bastwick*, August 1645.

Englands Miserie, and Remedie, September 1645 (anon.).

Lilburne, *Englands Birth-Right Justified*, October 1645.

Walwyn, *Englands Lamentable Slaverie*, October 1645.

William Prynne, *The Lyar Confounded*, October 1645.

"E.A.," *Medico Mastx; or, A Pill for the Doctor*, October 1645.

Overton, *The Ordinance for Tythes Dismounted*, December 1645.

Lilburne, *Innocency and Truth Justified*, December 1645, published January 1646.

A Letter of the London Ministers . . . against Toleration, January 1646.

A Word in Season, January 1646 (anon.).

John Saltmarsh, *Smoke in the Temple*, January 1646.

Overton, *Divine Observations Upon the London-Ministers Letter against Toleration*, January 1646.

Walwyn, *Tolleration Justified and Persecution Condemnd*, January 1646.

Lilburne, *A true relation of the materiall passages of . . . Lilburnes sufferings*, February 1646.

Thomas Edwards, *Gangraena*, Part I, February 1646. (Part II appeared in May 1646 and Part III in December 1646.)

Walwyn, *A Whisper in the Eare of Mr. Thomas Edwards*, March 1646.

Walwyn, *A Word More to Mr. Thomas Edwards*, March 1646.

Overton (?), *The Last Warning to all the Inhabitants of London*, March 1646.

Walwyn, *A Word in Season*, May 1646.

To the Commons, } the Remonstrance and Petition of the Lord Mayor and
To the Lords, } Common Councell ("The City Petition"), May 1646.

Lilburne, *The Just Mans Justification*, June 1646. (A second edition appeared in August 1647.)

Lilburne, *The Free-Mans Freedome Vindicated*, June 1646.

Walwyn, *An Antidote against Mr. Edwards*, June 1646.

Lilburne, *To the . . . Parliament. The Humble Petition of L. C. John Lilburne, a Free man of England*, June 1646.

John Saltmarsh, *Reasons for Unitie, Peace and Love*, June 1646.

Walwyn, *A Pearle in a Dounghill*, June 1646.

Walwyn (?), *The Just Man in Bonds*, June 1646.

Lilburne, *A Copy of a Letter sent by . . . Lilburne to Mr. Wollaston*, June 1646.

The Propositions of the Houses sent to the King at Newcastle, July 1646.

Overton, *A Remonstrance of Many Thousand Citizens*, July 1646.

A Vindication of the City Remonstrance, July 1646 (anon.).

Overton, *An Alarum to the House of Lords*, July 1646.

Samuel Sheppeard, *The Famers Famd*, August 1646.

Walwyn, *A Prediction of Mr. Edwards his Conversion and Recantation*, August 1646.

Samuel Sheppeard, *The False Alarum*, August 1646.

Lilburne, *Liberty Vindicated against Slavery*, August 1646.

Overton, *A Defiance against All Arbitrary Usurpations*, written in August 1646, published in September 1646.

John White, *John Whites Defence of himself . . . against a lying pamphlet written by John Lilburne*, September 1646.

Elizabeth Lilburne, *To Parliament. The Petition of Elizabeth Lilburne*, September 1646.

Overton, *An Arrow Against All Tyrants and Tyrany*, written in September 1646, published in October 1646.

Walwyn (?), *A Demurre to the Bill for the preventing the growth and spreading of Heresie*, October 1646.

Lilburne, *Londons Liberty In Chains discovered*, October 1646.

Lilburne, *To the Honorable, the chosen, betrusted, and representative Body of all the Free-men of England . . . . The humble Petition of Lilburne*, October 1646.

Walwyn, *A Parable, Or Consultation of Physitians Upon Master Edwards*, October 1646.

Lilburne, *An Anatomy of the Lords Tyranny*, November 1646.

Henry Marten (?), *Vox Plebis*, November 1646.

Samuel Sheppeard, *Animadversions upon . . . Londons Liberty In Chains discovered . . . [and] An Anatomy of the Lords Cruelty*, November 1646.

Frederick Spanhemius, *Englands Warning by Germanies Woe*, November 1646.

Overton, *An Unhappy Game at Scotch and English*, November 1646.

Lilburne, *The Charters of London: or, The Second Part of Londons Liberty in Chaines Discovered*, December 1646.

Henry Robinson, *Some Few Considerations Propounded*, precise date unknown, 1646.

William Hughes, transl., *The Mirror of Justices*, precise date unknown, 1646.

Lilburne, *Regall Tyrannie discovered*, January 1647.

Lilburne, *The Oppressed Mans Oppressions declared*, January 1647.

Overton, *The Commoners Complaint*, February 1647.

Lilburne and Overton, *The out-cryes of oppressed Commons*, February 1647.

To the Commons. The Petition of the Inhabitants of Buckinghamshire and Hertfordshire, March 1647.

Walwyn, and others, *To the right honourable and supreme Authority of this Nation, the Commons in Parliament assembled, The humble Petition of many thousands . . .* , March 1647.

Mary Overton, *To the Parliament of England. The humble Petition of Mary Overton*, March 1647.

Overton, *A New Found Stratagem . . . put upon the inhabitants of Essex*, April 1647.

Walwyn, *A Still and Soft Voice from the Scriptures*, April (?), 1647.

Lilburne, *The Resolved Mans Resolution*, April 1647.

Advertisements for the Managing of the Counsels of the Army, May 1647.

The Recantation of John Lilburne, May 1647 (anon.).

Lilburne, *Rash Oaths Unwarrantable*, May 1647.

Henry Ireton, *A Solemn Engagement of the Army*, June 1647.

Marchamont Nedham, *The Case of the Kingdom stated*, June 1647.

Walwyn, *Gold Tried in the fire*, June 1647.

Henry Ireton, *A Representation of the Army*, June 1647.

A Copie of a Letter sent From the Agitators to All the honest Sea-men of England, June 1647.

"Amon Wilbee," *Plain Truth, without Feare or Flattery*, July 1647.

George Masterson, *The Devil in his Dumps*, July 1647.

Overton, *An Appeale from the Degenerate Representative Body . . . the Commons of England*, July 1647.

Lilburne, *A Copy of a Letter . . . to . . . Henry Marten*, July 1647.

Lilburne, *Jonahs Cry out of the Whales Belly*, July 1647.

Lilburne and Henry Marten, *Two Letters . . .* , July 1647.

Henry Ireton, *The Heads of the Proposals offered by the Army*, August 1647.

A Remonstrance from Sir Thomas Fairfax and the Armie . . . At . . . Kingston, August 1647.

Lilburne, *The Just Mans Justification* (second edition, enlarged, including a letter to the Agitators), August 1647.

Lilburne, *Two Letters . . . to Col. Henry Marten*, September 1647.

Lilburne, *The Juglers Discovered*, September 1647.

Lilburne, *Proposition . . . unto the Lords and Commons*, October 1647.

Wildman, *The Case of the Armie truly stated*, October 1647.

Propositions from the Adjutators of five Regiments of Horse, October 1647.

Lilburne, *The Grand Plea of . . . Lilburne*, October 1647.

John Saltmarsh, *Letter . . . to the Council of War*, October 1647.

Robert Everard, and others, *Two Letters from the Agents of the five Regiments of Horse*, October 1647.

Lilburne, *The Additional Plea of . . . Lilburne*, October 1647.

Wildman, *A Cal to All the Souldiers of the Armie*, October 1647.

. . . to the Generals Excellency . . . the Petition . . . from . . . Hertfordshire, November 1647.

The Levellers, *An Agreement of the People*, November 1647.

Two Letters from the Agitators, November 1647.

John Hare, *Plaine English To our wilful Bearers with Normanisme*, November 1647.

Lilburne, *For every Individuall Member of the House of Commons*, November 1647.

"Basilius Anonymus," *The Case of the King Stated*, November 1647.

Lilburne, *A new complaint of an old grievance*, November 1647.

To the Supream Authority . . . The humble Petition of many free-born people, November 1647.

A Bloody Independent Plot Discovered, November 1647 (anon.).

Lilburne, *A Plea for the honest . . . Soldiers*, November 1647.

Marchamont Nedham, *The Levellers Levell'd*, December 1647.

"Sirrahniho" (John Harris), *The Grand Designe*, December 1647.

Lilburne, *Englands Freedome, Souldiers Rights*, December 1647.

The Engagement between the King and the Scots, December 1647.

Wildman, *Putney Projects*, December 1647.

Henry Marten, *The Independency of England*, January 1648.

Lilburne, and others, *To the Supream Authority . . . . The Earnest Petition of many Free-born People of this Nation*, January 1648.

The mournfull Cryes of many thousand poor Tradesmen, January 1648 (anon.).

John Hare, *Englands Proper and onely way*, January 1648.

Lilburne, *A Defiance to Tyrants*, January 1648.

Wildman, *Truths Triumph*, February 1648.

John Cooke, *Unum Necessarium*, February 1648.

Henry Parker, *Of a Free Trade*, February 1648.

George Masterson, *The Triumph Stained*, February 1648.

Walter Frost, and others, *A Declaration of Some Proceedings*, February 1648.

Lilburne, *The peoples Prerogative and Priviledges*, February 1648.

William Prynne, *The Levellers Levelled to the very Ground*, February 1648.

"Jah. Norris," *A Lash for a Lyar*, February 1648.

Lilburne, *A Whip for the present House of Lords*, February 1648.

William Prynne, *A Plea for the Lords*, March 1648.

"J. Howldin" (Wildman), *The Lawes Subversion*, March 1648.

Lilburne (?), *A Plea, or Protest, Made by William Prynne*, March 1648.

John Vicars, *Coleman-street Conclave Visited*, March 1648.

Lilburne, *The Prisoners Plea for a Habeas Corpus*, April 1648.

Lilburne, *The oppressed mans importunate and mournfull cryes to be brought to the Barre of Justice*, April 1648.

"The Armies Petition," May 1648.

Lilburne, *The Prisoners mournfull cry against the Judges of the Kings Bench*, May 1648.

Lilburne, *The Lawes Funerall*, May 1648.

Gerrard Winstanley, *The Breaking of the Day of God*, May 1648.

Walwyn (?), *Englands weeping Spectacle*, June 1648.

Gerrard Winstanley, *The Saints Paradice*, July (?) 1648.

Sir John Maynard, *A Speech . . . in the . . . House of Commons*, delivered in July 1648, printed in August 1648.

To the Commons assembled in Parliament. The Petition of divers thousand wel-affected Citizens in the behalf of . . . Lilburne, August 1648.

Lilburne, *Letter to Cromwell* (reprinted in *Legall Fundamentall Liberties*), August 1648.

To Parliament. The Petition of divers Citizens of London, August 1648.

Walwyn, *The Bloody Project*, August 1648.

Lilburne, *To Every Individuall Member of the House of Commons, the humble Remonstrance of . . . Lilburne*, September 1648.

The Levellers, *To the Commons of England. The Petition of well affected Persons . . .* , September 1648.

Gerrard Winstanley, *Truth Lifting up its Head above Scandals*, October 1648.

Henry Ireton, *A Remonstrance of Lord Fairfax and of the Generall Councell of Officers, held at St. Albans* ("The Remonstrance of the Army"), November 1648.

The Declaration of . . . Fairfax, and his General Council of Officers, shew-

ing the grounds of the Armies advance towards . . . *London*, November 1648.

Gerrard Winstanley (?), *Light Shining in Buckinghamshire*, December 1648.

The Levellers, *Foundations of Freedom; or An Agreement of the People*, December 1648.

Walwyn (?), *No Papist nor Presbyterian*, December 1648.

John Jubbes, *Several Proposals for Peace & Freedom, by an Agreement of the People*, December 1648.

William Ashurst, *Reasons against Agreement with a late Printed Paper Intituled* . . . *the Agreement of the People*, December 1648.

Lilburne, and others, *A Plea for common-right and Freedom*, December 1648.

Elizabeth Poole, *A Vision wherein is manifested the disease and cure of the Kingdome*, December 1648.

St. Germain, "Doctor and Student" (*The Dialogue in English between a Doctor of Divinitie, and a Student in the Lawes of England*) — a new edition which, in part, superseded the earlier English editions of 1530, 1623, and 1638; precise date unknown, 1648.

Gerrard Winstanley, *The Mysterie of God, concerning the whole Creation, Mankinde*, precise date unknown, 1648.

Lilburne (?), *The Case and Vindication of John Poyntz*, probably written and published late in 1648.

John Goodwin, *Right and Might well met*, January 1649.

Overton (?), *To the* . . . *Supreme Authority* . . . . *The humble Petition of* . . . *Presenters* . . . *of the Large Petition of September 11* . , January 1649.

The Charge against the King, January 1649.

Lilburne, and others, *A Petition* . . . *Concerning* . . . *An Agreement of the People*, January 1649.

"A.P." (William Ashurst?), *An Appendix to the Agreement For the People*, January 1649.

Mrs. Mary Pope, *Behold, Here is a Word. Or an Answer to the late Remonstrance of the Army*, January 1649.

Gerrard Winstanley, *The New Law of Righteousness*, January 1649.

The Sentence of the High Court of Justice upon the King, January 1649.

William Cokayne, *The Foundation of Freedome Vindicated*, February 1649.

John Milton, *The Tenure of Kings and Magistrates*, February 1649.

The Act appointing a Council of State, February 1649.

Lilburne, and others, *Englands New Chains Discovered*, February 1649.

Robert Ward, and others, *To* . . . *Fairfax, and his Councel of Officers*, March 1649.

Overton, *To the Supreme Authority* . . . *the Petition of Richard Overton*, March 1649.

Lancashire Ministers, *The Paper called the Agreement of the People Taken into Consideration*, March 1649.

The Essex Watchmen's Watchword, March 1649.

Walwyn (?), *The Vanitie of the Present Churches*, March 1649.

The Act abolishing the office of King, March 1649.

George Lilburne, *To . . . the . . . House of Commons. The humble Remonstrance of George Lilburn, Esquire*, March 1649.

The Act abolishing the House of Lords, March 1649.

William Bray, *To the Supreme Authority . . . an Appeale . . . against the Lord Fairfax*, March 1649.

Overton, *The Hunting of the Foxes*, March 1649.

Lilburne, Overton, and Thomas Prince, *The second Part of Englands New-Chaines discovered*, March 1649.

More Light Shining in Buckingham-shire, March 1649 (anon.).

Thomas Shadforth, *Innocency modestly vindicated . . . against George Lilburne*, March (?), 1649.

Thomas Shadforth, *An Additional Answer to A Remonstrance written by Mr. George Lilburne*, April (?), 1649.

. . . Petition . . . from the Inhabitants of London, Westminster, the Borough of Southwark, Hamlets, and places adjacent, April 1649.

The Petition of several churches of God in London commonly, though falsly, called Anabaptists, April 1649.

William Bray, *To the Supreme Authority . . . A Second Appeale*, April 1649.

Peter Chamberlen, *The Poore Man's Advocate*, April 1649.

Lilburne, Overton, and Thomas Prince, *The Picture of the Councel of State*, April 1649. (A second edition appeared in October 1649).

Walwyn, *A Manifestation*, April 1649.

To the Supreme Authority . . . The Petition of divers persons of London in the behalf of . . . Lilburne . . . Walwyn . . . Prince . . . Overton, April 1649.

William Everard, *The Declaration and Standard of the Levellers*, April 1649.

Gerrard Winstanley, *The True Levellers Standard Advanced*, April 1649.

Elizabeth Lilburne (?), *To the Supream Authority . . . . The humble Petition of . . . Women . . . In behalf of . . . Lilburne . . . Prince . . . Overton . . . Bray . . . Sawyer*, April 1649.

"A Broadside from the Soldiers," April 1649.

Lilburne and Overton, *The Copie of a Letter to the General*, April 1649.

The Levellers, *An Agreement of the Free People of England*, May, 1649.

John Canne, *The Snare is Broken*, May 1649.

To the Supreme Authority . . . [in behalf of the four prisoners in the Tower], May 1649.

. . . The Humble Petition of . . . wel-affected Persons of . . . London, May 1649.

. . . Petition of Women, Affecters and Approvers of the Petition of Sept. 11. 1648, May 1649.

The Thankfull Acknowledgement . . . of . . . Apprentices, May 1649.

William Thompson, *Englands Standard Advanced*, May 1649.

John Price, and others, *Walwins Wiles*, May 1649.

A Declaration of the Wel-Affected in Buckinghamshire, May 1649.

The humble petition of divers young men and Apprentices of the City of London, May 1649.

The Levellers (Falsly so called) Vindicated, May 1649 (anon.).

The Resolved Apprentices, May 1649.

The Act declaring England to be a free Commonwealth, May 1649.

Henry Denne, *The Levellers Designe Discovered*, May 1649.

Humphrey Brooke, *The Charity of Church-Men*, May 1649.

Walwyn, *The Fountain of Slander Discovered*, May 1649.

Lilburne, *A Discourse Betwixt . . . Lilburne . . . and Mr. Hugh Peters*, written in May 1649, published in June 1649.

Gerrard Winstanley, *A Declaration from the Poor Oppressed People of England*, June 1649.

John Warre, *The Corruption and Deficiency of the Lawes of England*, June 1649.

John Canne, *The Discoverer*, June 1649.

Lilburne, *The Legall Fundamentall Liberties of the People of England*, June 1649. (A second edition appeared in July 1649.)

Gerrard Winstanley, *A Letter to the Lord Fairfax and his Councell of War*, June 1649.

Walwyn, *Walwyns Just Defence*, June (?), 1649.

Thomas Prince, *The Silken Independents Snare Broken*, June 1649.

Gerrard Winstanley, *A Declaration of the Bloudie and Unchristian Acting of William Star and John Taylor*, June 1649.

Edward Barber, *An Answer to the Essex Watchmens Watchword*, June 1649.

Humphrey Brooke, *The Crafts-mens Craft*, June 1649.

Overton, *Overtons Defyance of the Act of Pardon*, July 1649.

John Canne, *The Discoverer . . . the second part*, July 1649.

Overton, *The Baiting of the Great Bull of Bashan unfolded*, July 1649.

William Bray, *Innocency and the Blood of the slain Souldiers*, July 1649.

To all the Affectors and Approvers . . . of the Petition of . . . September 1648, July 1649.

Lilburne, *To . . . Mr. Cornelius Holland*, August 1649.

A New Bull-Bayting, August 1649 (anon.).

Lilburne, *An Impeachment of High Treason Against Oliver Cromwell and . . . Henry Ireton*, August 1649.

Lilburne, *A Preparative To An Hue and Cry After Sir Arthur Haslerig*, August 1649.

Lilburne, *An Outcry of the Young Men and Apprentices of London*, August 1649.

Gerrard Winstanley, *A Watch-word to the City of London and the Armie*, written in August 1649, published in September 1649.

Lilburne, *A Salva Libertate*, September 1649.

Lilburne, *The Remonstrance of many thousands of the Free-People of England*, September 1649.

John Milton, *Eikonoklastes*, October 1649.

Cuthbert Sydenham, *An Anatomy of . . . Lilburn's Spirits and Pamphlets*, October 1649.

Lilburne, *Strength out of Weaknesse*, October 1649.

Lilburne, *The Innocent Man's First Proffer*, October 1649.

Lilburne, *The Innocent Man's second-proffer*, October 1649.

To the Commons. The Humble Petition of the . . . Approvers of the Late Petition of the 11. of September, October 1649.

Henry Robinson, *A Short Discourse between Monarchical and Aristocratical Government*, October 1649.

Clement Walker, *The First Dayes Proceedings*, October 1649.

"L. R.", *A brief Discourse of the Present Power of Magistracy and Justice*, October 1649.

Truths Victory over Tyrants and Tyranny, October 1649 (anon.).

"Theodorus Verax" (Clement Walker), *The Triall of . . . Lilburne*, November 1649.

Albertus Warren, *The Royalist Reformed*, November 1649.

Clement Walker, *The Second Part of the Triall of . . . Lilburne*, December 1649.

Lilburne, *The Engagement Vindicated & Explained*, written in December 1649, published in January 1650.

Engagement to be taken by all men of the age of eighteen, January 1650.

Lilburne, *To the Supreme Authority. . . . The Humble Petition of . . . Lilburne*, March 1650.

Marchamont Nedham, *The Case of the Common-Wealth of England Stated*, May 1650.

Henry Parker, *A Letter of Due Censure . . . to . . . Lilburne*, June 1650.

To Parliament. The Petition of divers Inhabitants of London, promoters and approvers of the Petition of the 11. of Sept. 1648, August 1650.

Henry Robinson, *Certain Considerations in order to a more speedy, cheap, and equall distribution of Justice*, November 1650.

Lilburne, *To every individuall Member of Parliament, but more especially to George Thompson*, November 1650.

Wildman, and others, *London's Liberties*, December 1650. (A second edition appeared in 1683.)

John Milton, *A Defence of the English People*, December 1650.

Walwyn, *Juries Justified*, January (?) 1651.

A Declaration of the Armie concerning . . . Lilburne, February 1651.

Lilburne, *A Letter . . . to Mr. John Price of Colemanstreet*, March 1651.

Lilburne, *A Just Reproof to Haberdashers-Hall*, July 1651.

John Hedworth, *A Copy of a Letter Written . . . unto John Dodgson, Constable at Harraton*, September 1651.

John Hedworth, *The Oppressed Man's Out-Cry*, September 1651.

Lilburne, *The Case of the Tenants of the Manor of Epworth*, November 1651.

Lilburne, *To Every Individuall Member of the . . . Parliament . . . . The humble Addresse of . . . Lilburne*, November 1651.

George Primate, *To the Parliament. The Petition of Josiah Primate*, December 1651.

Lilburne, *A Declaration of . . . Lilburne To the Free-born People of England*, January 1652.

To the Parliament. The Petition of many well-affected people highly concerned in the sentence against . . . Lilburne, January 1652.

David Brown, *To the . . . Parliament. . . . . Petition for repairing certain wrongs done . . . by John Lilburne*, January 1652

Lilburne, *A Remonstrance of . . . Lilburn: Concerning the Lawes, Liberties, Privileges . . . of England*, January 1652.

Samuel Chidley, *The Dissembling Scot*, February 1652.

Gerrard Winstanley, *The Law of Freedom in a Platform*, February 1652.

Lilburne, *. . . his Apologeticall Narration*, April 1652.

Lilburne, *As You Were*, May 1652.

Walwyn, *A Memorandum in favor of free trade* (probably not published), precise date unknown, 1652.

Lilburne, *The Remonstrance and Declaration of . . . Lilburn . . . Sent in a Letter to the King of Scots* (probably written late in 1652).

Lilburne, *L. Colonel John Lilburne revived*, March 1653.

Wendy Oxford, *Vincit qui patitur*, April 1653.

The Declaration of the Lord General and the Council on the dissolution of the Long Parliament, April 1653.

John Moore, *The Crying Sin of England of not Caring for the Poor*, May 1653.

Lilburne, *The Banished Mans suit for Protection to . . . Cromwell*, June 1653.

Lilburne, *A Second Address . . . to . . . Cromwell and the . . . Councell of State*, June 1653.

Lilburne, *A Third Address directed to . . . Cromwell and the . . . Councell of State*, June 1653.

Lilburne, *A Defensive Declaration*, June 1653.

Samuel Chidley, *An Additional Remonstrance . . . . With a little friendly touch to . . . Lilburne*, June 1653.

A Jury-Man's Judgment Upon the Case of . . . Lilburn, June 1653 (anon.).

To the Parliament. . . . The humble Petition. . . . in behalf of . . . Lilburne, June 1653.

To the Parliament. . . . The humble Petition of divers afflicted Women, in behalf of . . . Lilburn, June 1653.

Lilburne, *The Prisoners Most mournful Cry*, July 1653.

Lilburne, *. . . Lilburnes plea in Law against an act of Parliament*, July 1653.

The fundamental Lawes and Liberties of England claimed, asserted, and agreed unto by several peacable persons . . . commonly called Levellers, July 1653.

Lilburne, *The Second Letter From . . . Lilburne . . . To . . . John Fowke*, July 1653.

Lilburne, *To the Supreme Authority For the Commonwealth of England. The Humble Petition of . . . Lilburne*, July 1653.

To Parliament . . . from Hertfordshire . . . in behalfe of . . . Lilburne, July 1653.

Several Informations and Examinations Taken concerning . . . Lilburn, his Apostasy to the Party of Charles Stuart, July 1653.

Lilburne, *Malice Detected,* July 1653.

To Parliament. The Petition of many grieved People . . . in behalf of . . . Lilburne, July 1653.

Lilburne, *The Exceptions of John Lilburne to a Bill of Indictment,* July 1653.

Lilburne, *A Conference with the Souldiers,* July 1653.

Lilburne, *Oyes, Oyes, Oyes,* July 1653.

A Caveat to those that shall resolve . . . to destroy J.L., July 1653 (anon.).

Unto . . . Parliament . . . The humble Representation of divers afflicted Women-Petitioners, July 1653.

Lilburne, *The Upright Mans Vindication,* August 1653.

To . . . Parliament. The humble Petition of . . . Youngmen and Apprentices, August 1653.

A Plea at large for John Lilburn, August 1653 (anon.).

A Voyce from the Heavenly Word of God . . . to every Member of Parliament in the behalf of . . . Lilburne, August 1653.

A Word to the Jury in the behalfe of John Lilburn, August 1653 (anon.).

Lilburne, *The humble and further demand of John Lilburn,* August 1653.

Lilburne, *More Light to Mr. John Lilburnes Jury,* August 1653.

Lilburne, *The Afflicted Mans Out-Cry,* August 1653.

Lilburne, *The Just Defence of John Lilburn Against Such as charge him with Turbulency of Spirit,* August 1653.

The Tryall of Mr. John Lilburn, published in three parts, August 1653.

A Letter to . . . Lilburn now Prisoner in the Tower, September 1653 (anon.).

"Anonimus," *An Hue and Cry after the Fundamental Lawes and Liberties of England,* September 1653.

John Canne, *. . . John Lilb. Tryed and Cast,* November 1653.

Albertus Warren, *A New Plea for the Old Law,* December 1653.

The Instrument of Government, December 1653.

Lilburne, *A Declaration to the Free-born People of England concerning the Government of the Commonwealth,* May 1654.

The Last Will & Testament of . . . Lilburn, May 1654 (anon.).

Wildman (?), *A Letter from an Officer of the Army in Ireland,* 1654 (?).

William Prynne, *The Quakers Unmasked,* February 1655. (A second edition appeared in June 1655.)

Overton, *Man Wholly Mortal,* precise date unknown, 1655.

Sir Henry Vane, *A Healing Question,* May 1656.

Lilburne, *The Resurrection of John Lilburne,* published in two editions, both in May 1656.

Marchamont Nedham, *The Excellencie of a Free-State,* June 1656.

James Harrington, *The Commonwealth of Oceana,* October 1656.

A Standard Set Up, May 1657 (anon.).

Elizabeth Lilburne, *The Petition of Elizabeth Lilburne . . . to the Protector*, November 1657.

Wildman (?), *The Leveller*, February 1659.

Lilburn's Ghost, June 1659 (anon.).

William Bray, *A Plea for the Peoples Good Old Cause*, October 1659.

William Bray, *A Plea For the Peoples Fundamentall Liberties*, October 1659.

John Milton, *The Readie & Easie Way to establish a Free Commonwealth*, March 1660.

William Walwyn (not the Leveller), *God Save the King*, May 1660.

Richard Blome, *The Fanatick History; or, An Exact Relation of the Old Anabaptists and New Quakers*, July 1660.

The Tales and Jests of Mr. Hugh Peters, December (?) 1660 (anon.).

Hugh Peters, *A Dying Fathers Last Legacy to an Only Child*, 1661.

Humphrey Brooke, *The Durable Legacy*, 1681.

NOTES

1. Throughout, "Interregnum" is used to designate the period from 1642 to 1660, when for most practical purposes England's government was kingless.

2. W. C. Abbott, *The Writings and Speeches of Oliver Cromwell* (1937–1947), IV, 877–899, summarizes Cromwell's fluctuating reputation. John Buchan, *Oliver Cromwell* (1934), makes his subject a somewhat Napoleonic figure; while the Cromwell who emerges from Abbott's comprehensive work and from the lectures of Samuel Rawson Gardiner (*Cromwell's Place in History* — 1910) bears many resemblances to Lincoln. M. P. Ashley, *Oliver Cromwell, the Conservative Dictator* (1937), suggests a semi-Hitlerian figure, as does Eduard Bernstein's *Cromwell and Communism* (transl. H. J. Stenning, 1930). C. H. Firth, *Oliver Cromwell and the Rule of the Puritans in England* (1900), projects a man temperamentally and politically akin to Franklin Roosevelt, a resemblance noted both favorably and unfavorably by certain commentators of the 1930's. Finally, Eisenhower's comparison of his "Crusade" to that of Cromwell became a minor issue in the presidential election of 1952.

3. The principal works on the Levellers are T. C. Pease, *The Leveller Movement, A Study in the History and Political Theory of the English Great Civil War* (1916); William Haller, *Tracts on Liberty in the Puritan Revolution, 1638–1647* (1934); William Haller and Godfrey Davies, *The Leveller Tracts, 1647–1653* (1944); Don M. Wolfe, *Milton and the Puritan Revolution* (1941), and *Leveller Manifestoes of the Puritan Revolution* (1944); W. Schenk, *The Concern for Social Justice in the Puritan Revolution* (1948); and A. S. P. Woodhouse, *Puritanism and Liberty* (revised edition, 1950). Indispensable to an understanding of the Levellers are the concluding volumes of Gardiner's *History of England from the Accession of James I to the Outbreak of the Civil War, 1603–1642* (1904), and the four volumes of his *History of the Great Civil War, 1642–49* (1893). Finally, no student of the Interregnum can accomplish much without the help of the Catalogue of the Thomason Collection, compiled under the supervision of G. K. Fortescue, *Catalogue of the Pamphlets, Books, Newspapers, and Manuscripts relating to the Civil War, the Commonwealth, and the Restoration, Collected by George Thomason, 1640–1661* (1908).

4. The political use of the word "Levellers" goes back at least to 1607, when a group of the common people of Northamptonshire who protested against enclosures by literally levelling fences and filling in ditches were so described (E. Lipson, *The Economic History of England* [1931], II, 403). In 1616 King James used the term to characterize certain antimonarchical dissidents (C. H. McIlwain, *The Political Works of James I* [1918], pp. xliv, 344). But "Levellers" used to describe a specific political movement first came into vogue late

in 1647, when Ireton during the debate at Putney so labelled his organized opponents on the left (Lilburne, *his Apologeticall Narration* [1652], p. 69). The fullest seventeenth-century discussion of the word occurs in Marchamont Nedham, *The Case of the Commonwealth of England Stated*, the second edition (May 1650), pp. 77–87.

5. See, for example, Beza's *Life of John Calvin*; Perry Miller, *Orthodoxy in Massachusetts* (1933); and F. D. Foster, "The Political Theories of Calvinists before the Puritan Exodus to America," *The American Historical Review*, XXI (1915), 481–503.

6. William Haller, *The Rise of Puritanism* (1938), p. 169.

7. The earliest English tract to express a distinctly separatist point of view was Robert Browne's *A Treatise of Reformation without tarying for anie*, 1582.

8. W. K. Jordan, *The Development of Religious Toleration in England* (1932–1940); W. A. Shaw, *A History of the English Church during the Civil Wars and under the Commonwealth* (1900); and the collections of constitutional documents listed in the Bibliography under J. R. Tanner, are all central to an understanding of Interregnum church history.

9. See, for example, R. H. Tawney, *Religion and the Rise of Capitalism* (Penguin Books, 1947), pp. 189–195.

10. See, for example, Haller, *Rise of Puritanism*, pp. 83–127; Max Weber, *The Protestant Ethic and the Spirit of Capitalism* (transl. Talcott Parsons, 1930), pp. 114ff; Tawney, *Rise of Capitalism, passim*; and Helen White, *English Devotional Literature (Prose) 1600–1640* (1931), *passim*.

11. Margaret James, *Social Problems and Policy During the Puritan Revolution, 1640–1660* (1930), p. 90; Tawney, *Rise of Capitalism*, p. 117.

12. See, for example, F. C. Dietz, *English Public Finance 1558–1641* (1932), pp. 3–7; Max Beer, *A History of British Socialism* (revised edition, 1940), pp. 44–47; Helen White, *Social Criticism in the Popular Religious Literature of the Sixteenth Century* (1944), *passim*; H. C. Darby, *An Historical Geography of England before A.D. 1800* (1936), pp. 394–443; and R. H. Tawney, *The Agrarian Problem in the Sixteenth Century* (1912), pp. 407ff.

13. Herschel Baker, *The Dignity of Man* (1947), pp. 69–83; C. G. Haines, *The Revival of Natural Law Concepts* (1930), pp. 3–15; and Sir Frederick Pollock, *Essays in the Law* (1922), pp. 31–61, represent a sampling of the large body of literature on the subject of natural law.

14. As recently as the summer of 1953 certain Catholic apologists cited UNESCO's violation of "natural law" to justify their opposition to this United Nations agency.

15. However, J. W. Gough, *The Social Contract* (1936), p. 78, probably overstates the case when he says that "by the early seventeenth century, contractarian principles had taken a firm hold of nearly all political thought."

16. See, for example, C. H. McIlwain, *The High Court of Parliament and Its Supremacy* (1910), pp. 41, 51; and Keith Feiling, *A History of the Tory Party, 1640–1714* (1924), pp. 32–35.

17. Faith Thompson, *Magna Carta, Its Role in the Making of the English Constitution 1300–1629* (1948), p. 19.

18. Faith Thompson, *The First Century of Magna Carta: Why It Persisted as a Document* (1925), p. 9; Thompson, *Magna Carta*, pp. 233, 249, 294ff, 325, 330f; and J. R. Tanner, *English Constitutional Conflicts of the Seventeenth Century, 1603–1689* (1928), pp. 34–67.

19. Cited in Gertrude Huehns, *Antinomianism in English History, With Special Reference to the period 1640–1660* (1951), p. 66.

20. John Nef, *Industry and Government in France and England, 1540–1640* (1940), pp. 98, 131f.

21. *Ibid.*, pp. 32ff, 115ff; and D. W. Petegorsky, *Left-Wing Democracy in the English Civil War* (1940), pp. 37–42.

22. See, for example, J. W. Allen, *English Political Thought, 1603–1660* (1938), p. 360.

23. McIlwain, *High Court of Parliament*, pp. 350, 385; and Margaret Judson, *The Crisis of the Constitution* (1949), *passim*.

24. S. R. Gardiner, *The Constitutional Documents of the Puritan Revolution, 1628–1660* (1889), p. xxiii; the Petition of Right is given on pp. 1–5. Thompson, *Magna Carta*, pp. 336ff, provides a relevant discussion of the debates on this petition.

CHAPTER II. JOHN LILBURNE: PURITAN APPRENTICE

1. The fullest biography of Lilburne is by M. A. Gibb, *John Lilburne the Leveller, A Christian Democrat* (1947). Jane Robinson, "The Early Years of John Lilburne: A Study in Puritan Political Thought" (UCLA dissertation, 1946) has also been helpful. Among the many brief biographies of Lilburne, the most valuable are the article by Firth in *Dictionary of National Biography*; Pease, *Leveller Movement*, pp. 87ff; Haller, *Rise of Puritanism*, pp. 273ff; Wolfe, *Milton*, pp. 139ff; and Schenk, *Social Justice*, pp. 20ff. Lilburne's own works are full of autobiographical references, including several conflicting figures ranging from 1614 to 1618 for the date of his birth.

2. In the register of the Lord Bishop of Durham, for instance, there is a reference to a local vicar, Jerard Lilborne, who in 1494 was granted Papal dispensation for illegitimacy (Surtees Society, *The Register of Richard Fox, Lord Bishop of Durham, 1494–1501*, CXLVII, 138f). The history of the Lilburnes can be gleaned from Surtees Society, *Depositions and Other Ecclesiastical Proceedings from the Courts of Durham*, XXI (1845), and from various published records of the County Palatinate of Durham. Much of it is summarized in Gibb, *Lilburne*, pp. 19–22.

3. The details of this much cited anecdote, which took place in 1636, are given in John Rushworth, *Historical Collections* (1721–1722), II, 788–790.

4. Lilburne, *Innocency and Truth* (1645), p. 8.

5. Lilburne's pride in his ancestry and in his learning can be most vividly seen in *A Worke of the Beast* (1638), p. 22; in *To all the . . . Apprentizes of . . . London* (1639), p. 3; and in the lengthy autobiographical passages in *Innocency and Truth*.

6. Lilburne, *Innocency and Truth*, p. 7; *Legall Fundamentall Liberties* (1649), p. 20.

7. Lilburne, *Legall Fundamentall Liberties*, pp. 20f. (Except for minor changes in punctuation for the sake of clarity, all quotations are, it is hoped, accurately transcribed.)

8. *Ibid.* p. 21.

9. *Ibid.* All of these books were readily available in English.

10. Haller and Davies, *Leveller Tracts*, p. 404.

11. The impact of these "histories" on Lilburne is evident in many of his early pamphlets. On his preliminary reading in law, see Haller, *Rise of Puritanism*, p. 274.

12. Quoted in Schenk, *Social Justice*, p. 25.

13. Lilburne, *Legall Fundamentall Liberties*, p. 21.

14. Haller, *Rise of Puritanism*, p. 274.

15. Lilburne, *Legall Fundamentall Liberties*, p. 21.

16. See Grossart's article on Bastwick in *Dictionary of National Biography*.

17. Bastwick, *A Just Defence of John Bastwick* (1645), pp. 11f; Lilburne, *A Christian Mans Triall* (1638), pp. 8, 9, 15. The *Letany* is reprinted in *Somers Tracts*, ed. Walter Scott (1809–1815), V, 407–437.

18. Bastwick, *A Just Defence*, pp. 11, 15.

19. *Ibid.*, pp. 12f.

20. Lilburne, *A Christian Mans Triall*, pp. 2ff; *To All the . . . Apprentizes of . . . London*, p. 1.

21. See Haller, *Rise of Puritanism*, p. 433; and A. F. Johnson, "The Exiled English Church at Amsterdam and its Press," *The Library*, Fifth Series, V (1951), 219–242. Subsequently, Lilburne at least twice refers to "my printers" in Holland.

22. Lilburne, *A Christian Mans Triall*, pp. 1, 4, 12.

23. See, for instance, McIlwain, *Political Works of James I*, pp. xv–xlii. Hampden's protest against an assessment of twenty shillings for ship-money in many ways parallels Lilburne's contemporaneous challenge to the bishops.

24. There is no extant copy of the first edition, which appeared in mid-March 1638. The second edition came out in December 1641.

25. Rushworth, *Historical Collections*, II, 463, relates that Lilburne's refusal to take the ex officio oath resulted in his thereafter being known as "Free-born John."

26. Lilburne, *A Christian Mans Triall*, p. 3.

27. *Ibid.*, p. 5.

28. *Ibid.*, p. 7.

29. *Ibid.*, p. 8.

30. For Lilburne's tacit admission of his guilt, see his *Copy of a Letter . . . to Ingram and Hopkins* (1640), p. 4.

31. *A Worke* appeared surreptitiously, probably in April or May 1638. A second edition appeared with *A Christian Mans Triall* in 1641. *A Worke* is reprinted in Haller, *Tracts on Liberty*, II, 3–34.

32. For corroboration of Lilburne's graphic details, see Rushworth, *Historical Collections*, II, 466.

33. Lilburne, *A Worke*, p. 8.

34. *Ibid.*, p. 21.

35. *Ibid.*, p. 26. The pamphlet actually ends with two pages of rough verse, allegedly written by Lilburne on the day after his punishment.

36. Like *A Worke of the Beast*, *Come out of her* very possibly was printed in Holland.

37. Part of the subtitle of *Come out of her* reads "A Just Apologie for the way of Totall Separation"; and the brief prefatory epistle is also markedly pro-separatist.

38. *Come out of her*, p. 25.

39. *Ibid.*, p. 4.

40. *Ibid.*, p. 24.

41. *Ibid.*, pp. 14f.

42. *A Coppy of a Letter . . . to one of his special friends when he was in his cruel close imprisonment* was first published by Lilburne in 1645 at the end of his *Innocency and Truth*.

43. Though this tract was not published until 1645, its full title includes the phrase "Written long since." Largely on the basis of internal evidence, December 1638 seems the most logical date for its composition. See also Haller, *Rise of Puritanism*, p. 437.

44. *An Answer*, p. 23.

45. For external corroboration of Lilburne's prison sufferings, see Rushworth, *Historical Collections*, II, 467f; and *Historical Manuscripts Commission, Fourth Report*, p. 33. Lilburne supplies his own most vivid details in *The Poore Mans Cry*, p. 10; *A True Relation*, p. 4; *A Cry for Justice*, pp. 23f; and *Copy of a Letter . . . to Ingram and Hopkins*, pp. 1f.

46. In his *To all the . . . Apprentizes of . . . London*, p. 3, Lilburne refers to his "multitudes of humble petitions" — among them one to the Queen of Bohemia, King Charles's sister.

47. Lilburne states that *A Cry* was printed in Amsterdam. Ten years later he reprinted it as part of *The Picture of the Council of State*.

48. *A Cry*, p. 23, also describes how he was "forced daily, in regard of barbarous cruelty, to cry out aloud at my iron grate, to the prisoners and strangers, to let them know the height of my misery wherein I live."

49. Dated by Lilburne May 10, 1639, this tract is reprinted in his *The Prisoners Plea for Habeas Corpus* of April 1648. In his *Innocency and Truth* he refers to the riotous effects caused by the distribution of this pamphlet.

50. *To all the . . . Apprentizes*, p. 2.

51. *Ibid.*, p. 3.

52. *A Coppy of a Letter written by John Lilburne . . . to James Ingram and Henry Hopkins, Wardens of the Fleet.*

53. *To the Honourable House of Commons . . . The humble Petition of John Lilburne Prisoner in The fleet* (November 1640, reprinted in *Innocency and Truth*, pp. 66f). Rushworth, *Historical Collections*, IV, 20, reports that

Lilburne was immediately given some liberty in order personally to further this petition.

54. John Vicars, *Jehovah-Jireh. God in the Mount. Or, Englands Parliamentary-Chronicle* (1644), p. 36; Rushworth, *Historical Collections*, II, 469.

55. Abbott, *Cromwell*, I, 120f.

56. Rushworth, *Historical Collections*, IV, 250.

57. Lilburne, *Innocency and Truth*, pp. 21f, 39, 46, 62, 75f.

58. Lilburne, *A Whip for the Present House of Lords* (1648), p. 18; *The Picture of the Councel of State* (1649), p. 10.

59. Lilburne, *Legall Fundamentall Liberties*, p. 22.

60. *Ibid.*

61. Lilburne, *Innocency and Truth*, pp. 39, 65; *Legall Fundamentall Liberties*, p. 70; Vicars, *Jehovah-Jireh*, p. 216.

62. This conjecture is based on Lilburne's affection for Brooke, on some echoes of Brooke's tract in Lilburne's later works, and on the indications that Lilburne was becoming more tolerant in his religious attitudes. (A minor aspect of his dispute with Colonel King concerned King's prosecution of certain of the townspeople and soldiers of Lincoln "for assembling together at a private meeting" — *Innocency and Truth*, pp. 41f.)

63. Parker's *Observations* obviously influenced Lilburne, though whether he read them in 1642 or 1645 cannot be ascertained.

64. *A Letter Sent from Captaine Lilburne to diverse of Friends . . . in London*, published in January 1643.

65. Vicars, *Jehovah-Jireh*, p. 234. For some of the more telling anecdotes of Lilburne's military imprisonment, see his *A Whip for the Present House of Lords*, pp. 4f; *Legall Fundamentall Liberties*, p. 70; Rushworth, *Historical Collections*, IV, 83; *Somers Tracts*, IV, 489; and Daniel Felton, *The Examination and Confession of Lilburne and Captain Viviers* (December 1642).

66. Lilburne, *Legall Fundamentall Liberties*, p. 23.

67. Lilburne's fullest accounts of his army career can be found in his *Innocency and Truth*, pp. 22–26; *The Just Mans Justification* (1646), pp. 2–11; *The Resolved Mans Resolution* (1647), pp. 32–40; and *Legall Fundamentall Liberties*, pp. 23f. See also Charles Firth and Godfrey Davies, *The Regimental History of Cromwell's Army* (1940), pp. xvff, 35; and David Masson, ed., *The Quarrel between the Earl of Manchester and Oliver Cromwell* (Camden Society, 1875).

68. Lilburne, *Innocency and Truth*, p. 46.

CHAPTER III. WALWYN AND OVERTON: THE EARLY FIGHT FOR RELIGIOUS LIBERTY

1. Walwyn's influence, as well as his life, are treated by Firth in *Dictionary of National Biography*; and by Pease, *Leveller Movement*, pp. 251ff; Woodhouse, *Puritanism and Liberty*, pp. [54]ff; Haller, *Tracts on Liberty*, I, 33–45, 56–63, 92–94, 107–110, 115–118, 121–127; Jordan, *Religious Toleration*, IV, 176–190; and Schenk, *Social Justice*, pp. 41–63.

2. Humphrey Brooke, *The Charity of Church-men* (1649), p. 10; Walwyn, *The Fountain of Slaunder Discovered* (1649), p. 1.

3. Brooke, *Charity*, p. 10.

4. *Ibid.*, p. 11; Walwyn, *Fountain of Slaunder*, pp. 2, 11; and his *Walwyn's Just Defence* (1649), p. 14.

5. Walwyn, *Just Defence*, p. 9. Walwyn also acknowledges, if derogatorily, his reading of Cicero (*ibid.*, p. 8).

6. *Ibid.*, p. 27.

7. *Ibid.*, p. 12.

8. Walwyn, *Fountain of Slaunder*, p. 22; Brooke, *Charity*, pp. 4f.

9. Brooke, *Charity*, p. 5.

10. Walwyn, *Just Defence*, p. 18.

11. Woodhouse, *Puritanism and Liberty*, pp. [57]–[60].

12. Brooke, *Charity*, p. 11, states explicitly that Walwyn never belonged to any "private Congregation." On the other hand, Walwyn's account of his break with certain of the Independents and Baptists in the late 1640's indicates that at one time he was a member of John Goodwin's church.

13. Walwyn, *Just Defence*, p. 8.

14. *Ibid.*

15. For the account of Walwyn's religious development, see in particular his *The Power of Love* (1643), pp. 20–24; *A Whisper in the Eare of Mr. Thomas Edwards* (1646), p. 3; *The Vanitie of the Present Churches* (1649), pp. 13, 33; and *Walwyn's Just Defence*, p. 3; also, the anti-Walwyn *Walwins Wiles* (1649), p. 5; and Schenk, *Social Justice*, pp. 43–49.

16. Walwyn, *A Whisper*, pp. 5f, 9f (corrected pagination).

17. *Ibid.*, p. 4.

18. For Walwyn's canon I am, in general, following that given in Haller, *Tracts on Liberty*, I, 121–127. The attribution of *The Humble Petition* to Walwyn is based on its ideas and style, and on a description by Brooke (*Charity*, p. 11) which in all likelihood refers to this tract. For support of this attribution, see Pease, *Leveller Movement*, pp. 256f; Haller, *Rise of Puritanism*, pp. 266, 396; and Wolfe, *Milton*, p. 481.

19. Walwyn, *Humble Petition*, p. 4.

20. *Ibid.*

21. *Ibid.*, p. 8. In arriving at this conclusion, one of the authorities Walwyn cites is Richard Hooker.

22. Schenk, *Social Justice*, p. 42.

23. See Haller, *Tracts on Liberty*, I, 123; and his *Rise of Puritanism*, p. 266.

24. Walwyn, *Some Considerations*, p. 2.

25. *Ibid.*, p. 9.

26. For the attribution of this tract to Walwyn, see Haller, *Tracts on Liberty*, I, 123.

27. Walwyn, *Power of Love*, "To Every Reader" — in Haller, *Tracts on Liberty*, II, 274f.

28. *Ibid.*, II, 277f.

29. Walwyn, *Power of Love*, p. 19.

30. *Ibid.*, p. 13.

31. *Ibid.*, p. 34.

32. *Ibid.*, p. 3.

33. *Ibid.*, p. 5.

34. *Ibid.*, p. 3.

35. For further bibliographical discussion of this tract, see Haller, *Tracts on Liberty*, I, 61–63, 123–125. Haller reprints the second edition, III, 61–104.

36. Walwyn wrote this tract partly in answer to two pamphlets which appeared in 1644, *An Apologeticall Narration* by five eminently respectable Independents, and Thomas Bakewell's *Confutation of Anabaptists*. The first of these, an extremely restrained plea for limited toleration, was, however, sufficiently impressive to stir up attacks on it from both the right and left, and Milton's *Areopagitica* was in part inspired by the conservative, non-Walwynian reaction to it.

37. Walwyn, *Compassionate Samaritane*, p. 37; see also, pp. 11f, 20f, 23, 26, 30, 33, 36, 42.

38. *Ibid.*, pp. 80–84.

39. At the height of the anti-Leveller agitation in 1649, for instance, an attack on Walwyn and the radicalism for which he stood had only this to say about Overton: "We know him but by his pen." (*Walwins Wiles*, p. 3.) The best biography of Overton is Firth's article in *Dictionary of National Biography*. There are brief accounts of his life in Jordan, *Religious Toleration*, IV, 190; Haller, *Tracts on Liberty*, I, 95; and Schenk, *Social Justice*, p. 36. Some data on his early life are also given in Champlin Burrage, *The Early English Dissenters in the Light of Recent Research (1550–1641)* (1912), I, 243ff.

40. B. Evans, *The Early English Baptists* (1862), I, 255f. See also Burrage, *Early English Dissenters*, II, 216–218.

41. See, for example, Jordan, *Religious Toleration*, III, 542; and A. C. Underwood, *A History of the British Baptists* (1947), pp. 82ff.

42. Overton, *A Defiance Against All Arbitrary Usurpations* (1646), p. 17.

43. Henry R. Plomer, "Secret Printing During the Civil War," *The Library*, Second Series, V (1904), 380–385; and *A Dictionary of the Booksellers and Printers Who Were at Work in England, Scotland and Ireland from 1641 to 1667* (1907), p. 142.

44. E.g., *Mans Mortallitie*, pp. 2, 36, 38, 43.

45. *Ibid.*, p. 10.

46. *Ibid.*, p. 33.

47. *Ibid.*, p. 35.

48. *Ibid.*

49. *Ibid.*, p. 36.

50. *Ibid.*

51. *Ibid.*, p. 43.

52. See, for instance, Ernest Lee Tuveson, *Millennium and Utopia, A Study in the Background of the Idea of Progress* (1949); and Victor Harris, *All Coherence Gone* (1949).

53. As early as 1534 Calvin wrote a tract entitled *Pscychopannychia*, which Beza describes as "an excellent little work" directed against the dangerous heresy of the "soul-sleepers." As late as 1648 certain Royalist newspapers still complained that the Mortalist Heresy was one of the more subversive ideas engendered by the Civil War, and that it was partly responsible for the revolutionary nature of that conflict. (See, for example, *Mercurius Bellicus*, No. 3, Feb. 8–14, 1648; and *Mercurius Melancholicus*, No. 30, March 20–27, 1648.)

CHAPTER IV. THE COMING TOGETHER OF THE LEVELLERS

1. The number of items in the Thomason Collection rises from 24 in 1640 to 721 in 1641, and to a height of 2134 in 1642. From then until 1648 the number remains between 1300 and 1500 a year. In 1648 the total rises to 2036, from which it drops to 1346 in 1649, and thereafter remains at or below 1000 a year. (*Thomason Catalogue*, p. xxi.)

2. For Prynne's Erastian connections, see Jordan, *Religious Toleration*, IV, 276ff; Haller, *Rise of Puritanism*, pp. 221ff; and Ethyn Williams Kirby, *William Prynne, A Study in Puritanism* (1931), pp. 77ff.

3. This letter, reprinted in Haller, *Tracts on Liberty*, III, 181–187, may well have been printed by Overton.

4. Lilburne, *Copie of a Letter*, p. 3.

5. Prynne, *The Lyar Confounded* (1645), p. 4. Lilburne was answered by an anonymous Presbyterian, who soundly berated him as a schismatic in a tract entitled *A Review of a Certain Pamphlet . . .* , which appeared in January 1645.

6. *A Helpe* is reprinted in Haller, *Tracts on Liberty*, III, 191–201. For its attribution to Walwyn, see I, 92, 121ff.

7. Walwyn's tangential plea for simplification of the laws both echoes a demand which English reformers had been making for at least three centuries and anticipates one of the recurrent planks in the platforms of the Levellers.

8. Walwyn, *A Helpe*, p. 8.

9. *Ibid.*, p. 7.

10. Though Prynne attributed this work to Henry Robinson, Overton acknowledged it as his own in *The Picture of the Councel of State*, pp. 36f. The identity of Martin was, however, fairly widely known by the summer of 1646. (See, for example, the testimony of Robert Eeles: *Historical Mss. Commission, Sixth Report, Appendix*, pp. 130bf.) *The Araignement* is reprinted in Haller, *Tracts on Liberty*, III, 205–256.

11. *Hay any Worke for Cooper* was reprinted in March 1642. In January 1643, *The Character of a Puritan, and his Gallimaufrey of the Antichristian Clergy*, "by Martin Mar-Prelat," appeared. These two works are the only items listed in Thomason, prior to *The Araignement*, written by "Martin"; but both the style and content of *The Character of a Puritan* strongly militate against Overton's authorship.

12. Overton, *The Araignement*, "To . . . the . . . Assembly of Divines" — in Haller, *Tracts on Liberty*, III, 207.

13. It is very possible that Bunyan drew on Overton for some of his trial scenes — as pointed out by Pease, *Leveller Movement*, p. 100; Haller, *Tracts on Liberty*, I, 97; and William York Tindall, *John Bunyan Mechanick Preacher* (1934), pp. 203, 281.

14. Overton, *The Araignement*, p. 11.

15. *Ibid.*, pp. 11f. Overton also points out that persecution prevents the conversion of the Jews, an act which some of his contemporaries felt must precede the Second Coming.

16. *Ibid.*, pp. 17f.

17. *Ibid.*, p. 24.

18. *Ibid.*, p. 44.

19. *Martins Eccho*, p. 3, explicitly compares the attempts to suppress its Martin with the vicissitudes of Barrow, Greenwood, and Penry.

20. Plomer, "Secret Printing," *Library*, pp. 383–385.

21. According to Prynne (*The Lyar Confounded*, 1645, p. 4), shortly after Lilburne's *Letter* had been turned over to the Committee for Examinations, Lilburne injured his eye; for this reason all charges against him were dropped.

22. Prynne, *A Fresh Discovery*, p. 17.

23. Lilburne, *Innocency and Truth*, pp. 4f.

24. Walwyn, *A Whisper in the Eare of Mr. Thomas Edwards* (1646), p. 4.

25. *Ibid.*, p. 6.

26. There is a lengthy and graphic account of this meeting in Bastwick's *Just Defence*, pp. 16f, though Bastwick here calls Walwyn "Worly." Walwyn, in his own *Just Defence*, says that "just before the New Model" he held "daily meetings and intimate discourse" with several of the "Independent" leaders, including Lilburne. This is, as far as I know, the only reference to any meeting between the two men prior to July 1645; and, in all probability, the sweeping reminiscences with which Walwyn begins his *Just Defence* are not wholly accurate in the details of their dates. This conjecture is confirmed by Lilburne's description of his meeting with "Worly" in his *The Copy of a Letter . . . to a friend*, dated July 25, 1645. (See also Haller, *Tracts on Liberty*, I, 100.)

27. *A more full Relation of the great Battell fought betweene Sir Tho. Fairfax and Goring.* (For a further account of this victory at Langport, see Gardiner, *Great Civil War*, II, 264–274.)

28. Lilburne, *Letter to a . . . Friend*, p. 8; and *The Just Mans Justification* (1646), p. 3 — where he accuses Colonel King of inciting Bastwick to make this false accusation.

29. Lilburne had been mistakenly arrested in May and June, in both cases apparently at Prynne's instigation (Lilburne, *Innocency and Truth*, pp. 9f; *Letter to a . . . Friend*, pp. 12f).

30. Lilburne, *Innocency and Truth*, pp. 13f.

31. Lilburne, *Letter to a . . . Friend*, p. 14.

32. *Ibid.*

33. Lilburne, *Innocency and Truth*, p. 16.

34. *Ibid.*; Prynne, *The Lyar Confounded*, pp. 71f.

35. Probably this list included Machiavelli, to whom Lilburne often refers in

his tracts of the later 1640's, though he shows no real familiarity with *The Prince* until *The Upright Mans Vindication* of 1653. It is very likely that Lilburne by this time knew the relatively famous *Vindiciae Contra Tyrannos*, which had appeared in English translation in 1622 and 1631. In 1646, in all probability, he read the new translation of Andrew Horne's fourteenth-century *The Mirror of Justices*, a work which deals in part with the violations by the Normans of a preëxisting contract between the Saxon rulers and the people of England. Finally, Lilburne was almost certainly familiar with the contemporary works of John Goodwin and Henry Parker.

36. It is dated by Thomason Aug. 30, 1645. It is here that Bastwick describes his first contacts with Lilburne in 1637.

37. Bastwick was directly answered in October by "A She Presbyterian," whose *Medico Mastix, Or A Pill for the Doctor* consists of a clumsy defense of the Independents and a rather scurrilous attack on her alleged coreligionists.

38. This petition is reprinted in Lilburne, *Innocency and Truth*, p. 29.

39. *Ibid.*, pp. 28f.

40. This tract was signed by an "Utter-Barrister." Thomason assigns it to Lilburne; and Wolfe (*Milton*, p. 480) conjectures that Overton might have written part of it. My own guess is that the "Utter-Barrister" was probably the young John Wildman, who had recently completed his formal study of the law.

41. *Englands Miserie and Remedie*, p. 5.

42. Though Lilburne in *Regall Tyrannie Discovered* (1647) implies that *Englands Birth-Right* is not his, its style, its content, and its surreptitious printing by William Larner all overwhelmingly support Thomason's attribution of it to Lilburne.

43. For the general attack on monopolies at this time, see James, *Social Problems*, pp. 131–158. This issue — and Lilburne's relationship to it — was further complicated by the fact that it was the larger monopolies which provided the government with its best source of loans.

44. Lilburne, *Englands Birth-Right*, p. 11.

45. *Ibid.*, pp. 31f — where Lilburne says that Cromwell is not only on the side of the Saints but their most effective leader.

46. *Ibid.*, pp. 32ff.

47. For the attribution to Walwyn, see Haller, *Tracts on Liberty*, I, 107, 125. *Englands Lamentable Slaverie* is reprinted in III, 311–318.

48. Walwyn, *Englands Lamentable Slaverie*, pp. 3f.

49. *Ibid.*, p. 4.

50. Lilburne, *Innocency and Truth*, pp. 30–34.

51. Prynne, *The Lyar Confounded*, p. 14.

52. Plomer, "Secret Printing," *Library*, pp. 382ff; Prynne, *The Lyar Confounded*, p. 6.

53. E.g., *Englands Birth-Right*.

54. For the major ordinances recently passed by Parliament which drew Overton's fire, see C. H. Firth and R. S. Rait, *Acts and Ordinances of the Interregnum, 1642–1660* (1911), I, 749–757, 789–797, 812f.

55. Overton, *Divine Observations*, p. 14.

56. *Ibid.*, p. 16. See also his attack on the Solemn League and Covenant on p. 5.

57. *Tolleration Justified* has been reprinted by the Sutro Branch, California State Library, Occasional Papers, English Series No. 6, Part III, 1940.

58. Haller, *Tracts on Liberty*, I, 8of. The three parts of *Gangraena* appeared in February, May, and December of 1646.

59. Thomason dates it March 13, 1646. It is reprinted in Haller, *Tracts on Liberty*, III, 321–336.

60. Walwyn, *A Whisper*, p. 5.

61. *Ibid.*, pp. 1of (corrected pagination).

62. According to Thomason, *A Word in Season* went through two successive editions, May 18 and May 26, 1646. Under date of May 18 Thomason states that it was written by a Mr. Sadler; however, Haller's attribution of it to Walwyn seems almost certain, not only on the basis of its style and content, but because Walwyn in his *Just Defence* strongly implies that *A Word in Season* was his.

63. Gardiner, *Great Civil War*, III, 107; Haller, *Tracts on Liberty*, I, 101.

64. For Lilburne's participation, see Thomason's comment on *A Word in Season* under date of May 26, 1646; for the contribution of Goodwin's parishioners, see Walwyn, *Just Defence*, p. 31.

65. Walwyn, *Just Defence*, p. 31.

66. Walwyn, *An Antidote*, p. 8.

67. *Ibid.*, p. 17.

68. It is reprinted in Haller, *Tracts on Liberty*, III, 339–348.

69. Walwyn, *A Prediction*, p. 7.

70. *Ibid.*, p. 18.

71. *Ibid.*, pp. 11f.

72. *Ibid.*, p. 16; see also pp. 9–13.

73. *Ibid.*, pp. 14f.

74. It is likely that Walwyn helped to write a tract which appeared on Oct. 7, 1646, *A Demurre to the Bill*. This pamphlet, in the form of a petition to the House of Commons, protests against a bill further to limit freedom of religion. There are also two or three tracts of mid-1646 in which Walwyn might have had a minor hand (Haller, *Tracts on Liberty*, I, 92, 122, 126).

CHAPTER V. THE GENESIS OF THE LEVELLER PARTY

1. Twice, however, he petitioned Parliament for his Star Chamber reparations, and he continued to press his charges against Colonel King.

2. Lilburne, *A true relation of the materiall passages of . . . Lilburnes sufferings* (February 1946) — reprinted in his *Apologeticall Narration*, 1652.

3. C. H. Firth, *The House of Lords during the Civil War* (1910), p. 156.

4. Lilburne, *Just Mans Justification* (1646), pp. 1f; *Legall Fundamentall Liberties*, pp. 24f.

5. Lilburne, *The Free-Mans Freedome Vindicated* (1646), p. 2.

6. A second edition appeared in August 1647.

7. Lilburne, *Just Mans Justification*, p. 20. Lilburne later dates the beginning of Cromwell's "apostasy" from his unwillingness at this time vigorously to prosecute Manchester.

8. Lilburne, *Free-Mans Freedome Vindicated*, p. 3; *An Anatomy of the Lords Tyranny* (1646), pp. 2ff.

9. This "Protestation" appears on pp. 6f of *The Free-Mans Freedome Vindicated*.

10. *To the . . . Parliament. The humble Petition of L. C. John Lilburne a Free Man of England* went through two editions, for on June 19, 1646, it appeared in slightly modified form.

11. *A Copy of a Letter Sent by . . . Lilburne to Mr. Wollaston Keeper of Newgate or his Deputy* (June 23, 1646).

12. Lilburne, *Londons Liberty in Chains discovered* (1646), p. 25; Walwyn, *The Just Man in Bonds* (1646), p. 3.

13. Lilburne, *Legall Fundamentall Liberties*, p. 26; Walwyn, *The Just Man in Bonds*, p. 4.

14. The probable dates for these two tracts are June 23 and June 29, 1646. *A Pearle* had a second edition in April 1647. For their ascription to Walwyn, see Haller, *Tracts on Liberty*, I, 122, 126.

15. Walwyn, *The Just Man in Bonds*, p. 2.

16. Walwyn, *A Pearle*, p. 4.

17. *Ibid.*

18. It is reprinted in Haller, *Tracts on Liberty*, III, 351–370. Though unsigned, *A Remonstrance* is undoubtedly by Overton.

19. In March 1646 he may have had a hand in *The Last Warning to all the Inhabitants of London* — a warning to the city to support the army, and a plea for toleration.

20. See Haller, *Tracts on Liberty*, I, 101.

21. Overton, *A Remonstrance*, pp. 3, 19f.

22. *Mercurius Aulicus*, No. 21 (May 26–June 2, 1643).

23. *Ibid.*, No. 4 (Jan. 21–28, 1644).

24. Thompson, *Magna Carta*, pp. 285–293.

25. See especially his *Jus Populi* (October 1644).

26. Woodhouse, *Puritanism and Liberty*, p. [56].

27. In *Plaine English To our wilful Bearers with Normanism* (1647) and in *Englands onely way to an Establishment in Honour, Freedome, Peace and Happinesse* (1648) Hare utilizes his interpretation of English history to support the king, the monarchy he envisages being essentially conservative and imperialistic.

28. Overton, *A Remonstrance*, p. 4.

29. *Ibid.*, p. 6.

30. *Ibid.*, p. 11.

31. *Ibid.*, p. 15.

32. *Ibid.*, p. 14.

33. Gibb, *Lilburne*, pp. 148f.

34. Lilburne, *Legall Fundamentall Liberties*, p. 26.

35. *Ibid.*

36. *Ibid.*; Overton, *An Alarum To the House of Lords* (1646), p. 5.

37. Overton's technique and ideas are in sharp contrast to a vilification of Lilburne which appeared two weeks later, *The False Alarm*, by Samuel Shepeard.

38. Overton, *A Defiance*, pp. 8–19, gives the story of his arrest and sentence.

39. *Ibid.*, p. 2.

40. For further discussion of the function of the petition at this time, see Jordan, *Religious Toleration*, IV, 355; Wolfe, *Leveller Manifestoes*, p. 72; William Clyde, *The Struggle for the Freedom of the Press from Caxton to Cromwell* (1934), p. 171; and Petegorsky, *Left-Wing Democracy*, p. 112.

41. *To the . . . supream Court of Parliament, the Humble Petition of Elizabeth Lilburne* (Sept. 23, 1646). It was probably written by Lilburne, who twice reprinted it — in *Londons Liberty* and in *Regall Tyrannie Discovered*.

42. *The humble Petition of . . . Lilburne, a legall Free-man of England* (October 1646). It is reprinted at the end of *Londons Liberty*.

43. For instance, Lilburne's antagonist, Colonel King, was originally appointed to his command in Lincolnshire largely because he was a resident of that district.

44. See James, *Social Policy*, pp. 193–240; Nef, *Industry and Government*, pp. 25ff; George Unwin, *The Gilds and Companies of London* (1908), pp. 339–350; and F. C. Dietz, *An Economic History of England* (1942), pp. 257–269.

45. Nef, *Industry and Government*, p. 26; Unwin, *Gilds of London*, p. 339.

46. Maurice Ashley, *John Wildman, Plotter and Postmaster* (1947), pp. 74f.

47. Lilburne, *Londons Liberty*, pp. 8, 21; *The resolved Mans Resolution* (1647), p. 12.

48. Lilburne, *Englands Birth-Right*, pp. 21ff, 38.

49. Overton, *A Remonstrance*, pp. 14f.

50. Lilburne, *Londons Liberty*, p. 41.

51. *Ibid.*, pp. 52f.

52. After a discursive introduction, this lengthy tract is mainly devoted to reprinting several of the Charters of London and to some correspondence and petitions in favor of free trade. In it Lilburne the editor is as undisciplined as Lilburne the polemicist.

53. Cited in Pease, *Leveller Movement*, p. 361. See also the three letters on this subject in *The Times Literary Supplement*, Feb. 22 and March 7, 1952, by Alcuin Shields, Stanley Gardner, and H. John McLachlen, which in general corroborate this figure.

54. Chidley, *The Dissembling Scot* (1652), pp. 8f.

55. In certain cases, such as *A Manifestation* (1649) and *An Agreement of the Free People of England* (1649), the press run might be as high as 20,000 (Lilburne, *Apologeticall Narration* [1652], p. 71); and some of the Leveller petitions circulated for mass signature may have been printed in quantities as large as 30,000 (Masterson, *The Triumph Stain'd* [1648], p. 14).

56. See C. H. Firth's article on Marten in *Dictionary of National Biography*.

57. Overton, *An Arrow*, p. 15.

58. Lilburne, *An Anatomy*, p. 21.

59. Though Wolfe, *Milton*, p. 481, attributes much of this tract to Overton, Marten seems the most likely author. (Haller and Davies, *Leveller Tracts*, p. 47, and Pease, *Leveller Movement*, p. 155, agree, despite the fact that *Vox Plebis* is mentioned neither by Firth in his article on Marten in *Dictionary of National Biography* nor by John Forster in his biography of Marten in *Eminent British Statesmen*.) The style of this tract is similar to that of Marten's *The Independency of England* (1648), and its knowledge of the conflict between Lord and commoner is appropriate to the man who was in charge of an official committee of Parliament to investigate that conflict. Finally, the republican sympathies which *Vox Plebis* displays indicate Marten's authorship, whereas its views on Magna Carta disqualify Walwyn, the other most likely candidate.

60. Gardiner, *Great Civil War*, III, 174–176.

61. It was entered by Thomason on Nov. 30, 1646. Overton acknowledges his authorship in *The Picture of the Councel of State*, p. 36. Though the title page of *An Unhappy Game* imitates that of the "Scotch Papers," it was surreptitiously printed in London, not Edinburgh. On the day of its publication the House of Commons ordered that it be suppressed, and two days later that it be publicly burnt (*Thomason Catalogue*, I, 477).

62. Overton, *An Unhappy Game*, p. 23.

63. Lilburne, *Regall Tyrannie*, p. 84.

64. Lilburne was concerned with answering certain heresy-hunting, anti-Lilburne tracts which had recently appeared, particularly *A Vindication of the City Remonstrance* of July 1646 and two tracts of August 1646, both by Samuel Shepeard, *The Famers Fam'd* and *The False Alarum*.

65. Lilburne, *Regall Tyrannie*, pp. 59–61.

66. *Ibid.*, p. 99. Lilburne cites as his major evidence three recent pro-monopoly statutes, Parliament's kind treatment of Manchester and Colonel King, and the improper management of affairs in Ireland.

67. It promptly had a second edition. On its composition, see Lilburne, *Legall Fundamentall Liberties*, p. 26.

68. Lilburne, *Oppressed Mans Oppressions*, p. 11.

69. *Ibid.*, pp. 26f.

70. The first of its two editions is reprinted in Haller, *Tracts on Liberty*, III, 375–395.

71. Overton, *The Commoners Complaint*, p. 3.

72. The Lords, in their endeavors to silence Overton, had early in 1647 arrested his wife and his brother.

73. This defection, the pamphlet points out, has just been dramatized by the House's refusal to receive a petition from Buckinghamshire and Hertfordshire in behalf of the two prisoners and allegedly signed by 10,000 sympathizers. (It is reprinted in *The out-cryes*, pp. 9ff; and on March 1, 1647, it was circulated in its own right in London.)

74. Lilburne and Overton, *The out-cryes*, pp. 14, 17.

CHAPTER VI. THE PARTY COMES OF AGE

1. E.g., No. 26 and No. 29 of June and July 1644.

2. Quoted in William Orme, *The Life and Times of the Rev. Richard Baxter* (1831), I, 47. The New Model Army was, of course, not a representative cross section of the people of England.

3. Quoted in Firth, *House of Lords*, p. 167.

4. Gardiner, *Great Civil War*, III, 225.

5. *Ibid.*, III, 212–230, 250–252.

6. For instance, it was probably Walwyn who was mainly responsible for a petition to the House of Commons from the inhabitants of Buckinghamshire and Hertfordshire, which Lilburne and Overton in *The out-cryes of oppressed Commons* claimed was signed by almost 10,000 names.

7. Haller, *Tracts on Liberty*, I, 115.

8. In 1649 Walwyn in his *Just Defence* (p. 4) and his *Fountain of Slaunder* (p. 7) implies that he was the author of this petition. This is corroborated by its nature and style.

9. For this narrative, see Walwyn, *Gold tried in the fire* (1647), pp. 1–3; Lilburne, *Rash Oaths Unwarrantable* (1647), pp. 29, 35ff; and Overton, *An Appeale from the Degenerative Representative Body* (1647), *passim*.

10. During this "lull" there was at least one Leveller petition in behalf of Nicholas Tue, the man still in jail for reading the certificate outside Westminster. On March 24, Mrs. Overton, still in Bridewell, added her petitionary bit by publicly detailing her own and her family's misfortunes and demanding personal and national remedial action. Several petitions and protests concerning the grievances of the army also appeared during this period.

11. *Gold tried in the fire* was obviously intended as a preface to the publication, in one pamphlet, of the original petition and its two subsequent modifications. Because *Gold* appeared alone, presumably these petitions were never reprinted in collected form. (See also Haller, *Tracts on Liberty*, I, 116, 122.)

12. George Masterson, *The Triumph Stain'd* (February 1648), details in alarmist language the extent of the Leveller organization at the close of 1647.

13. Walwyn, in his *Just Defence* (p. 4), complains that at this time "most of the uppermost Independents stood aloof and look'd on."

14. Ashley, *Wildman*, p. 9. The conjecture as to his possible friendship with Lilburne is based on their common interest in the reform of London's government.

15. In all probability the petition was first published on or shortly before March 15, 1647, and again in May. Thomason lists editions of Sept. 11 and Sept. 19, 1648 — the last of which is reprinted in Haller, *Tracts on Liberty*, III, 399–405. Lilburne promptly gave it wider circulation in his *Rash Oaths*, pp. 29–35.

16. *The humble Petition of many thousands, earnestly desiring the glory of God, the freedome of the Common-wealth, and the peace of all men* (1647), p. 4.

17. *Ibid.*, p. 5.

18. In the seventeenth century the attack on monopoly almost always had in view restraints on distribution, not on production.

19. The title page of *A Still and Soft Voice* states only that it was printed in 1647, and Thomason did not enter it. In his *Just Defence* (p. 4), Walwyn, after acknowledging his authorship, implies that it was published early in 1647. The political situation in April of that year, to which there are some indirect references in the text, indicates that the period shortly after Parliament's seizure of the March Petition is the most likely date for the composition of *A Still and Soft Voice*. (It is reprinted in Wolfe, *Milton*, pp. 363–374.)

20. In the summer of 1646, after Walwyn had probably assisted in drawing up and circulating a petition in behalf of toleration for Brownists and Anabaptists, some of the Independents, so Walwyn alleges, deliberately began to blacken his reputation by accusing him of atheism and lewd behavior, and later of communism. A few members of John Goodwin's congregation then constituted themselves a committee to examine into Walwyn's character. The majority of this committee concluded that he was a man of virtue; but, nevertheless, the accusations and innuendoes circulated against him at this time later formed the basis for *Walwins Wiles*, as well as much of the material which Walwyn now obliquely refuted in *A Still and Soft Voice*.

21. Walwyn, *A Still and Soft Voice*, p. 2.

22. *Ibid.*, pp. 7f.

23. *Ibid.*, p. 12.

24. Overton, *A New Found Stratagem*, pp. 6f.

25. *Ibid.*, p. 13.

26. Gardiner, *Great Civil War*, III, 242–249; Woodhouse, *Puritanism and Liberty*, p. [21].

27. This examination is given in *The Clarke Papers*, ed. C. H. Firth (1891), I, 403f.

28. This plan, *Advertisements for the Managing of the Counsels of the Army*, is given in Woodhouse, *Puritanism and Liberty*, pp. 398f. Petegorsky, *Left-Wing Democracy*, p. 98, suggests that it was printed on a press operated by the Agitators themselves.

29. Woodhouse, *Puritanism and Liberty*, pp. [23]f, 399–401. Two months earlier the officers of the New Model had drawn up a petition to Parliament asking for guarantees for the soldiers' material benefits but avoiding any larger issues.

30. Lilburne, "Letter to Cromwell," July 1, 1647, reprinted in his *Jonahs Cry out of the Whales Belly* (1647).

31. These two letters, dated respectively March 25 and April 10, 1647, are reprinted in *Jonahs Cry*.

32. Lilburne, in his *Rash Oaths*, p. 6, claims that it had a second edition.

33. One of the letters reprinted in *Jonahs Cry* accuses certain unnamed members of John Goodwin's congregation of plotting evil against Lilburne and of discouraging various petitions in his own and Overton's behalf. As far as I know, this letter (dated Feb. 13, 1647) is the earliest explicit evidence of the impending Leveller-Independent break.

34. *Clarke Papers*, I, 84–94, prints five letters to and from the Agitators, dated between May 18 and 20, 1647, which testify to such a plan; and Woodhouse, *Puritanism and Liberty*, pp. 400f, gives two similar conspiratorial letters of the end of May.

35. At about this time Walwyn was personally warning Cromwell to dissociate himself from certain of the Independent leaders (Walwyn, *Just Defence*, p. 6).

36. Lilburne, *Rash Oaths*, pp. 6f.

37. *Ibid.*, p. 18.

38. *Ibid.*, p. 47.

39. *Ibid.*, p. 50.

40. Walwyn, *Gold tried in the fire*, p. 4.

41. Gardiner, *Great Civil War*, III, 265–274. Marchamont Nedham, under the pseudonym of "Mercurius Pragmaticus," at the end of 1647 wrote a pro-Royalist closet drama, *The Levellers Levell'd*, in which their nefarious plot to murder the King is fortunately foiled.

42. Woodhouse, *Puritanism and Liberty*, pp. [23], 401–403. The *Engagement* was probably the work of Ireton.

43. Woodhouse, *Puritanism and Liberty*, p. [24]; Gardiner, *Great Civil War*, III, 280–296.

44. *A Representation* is reprinted in full in Haller and Davies, *Leveller Tracts*, pp. 52–63; and in part in Woodhouse, *Puritanism and Liberty*, pp. 403–409.

45. Ireton, *A Representation*, p. 4.

46. Gardiner, *Great Civil War*, III, 297–306.

47. Woodhouse, *Puritanism and Liberty*, pp. 409–412.

48. Gardiner, *Great Civil War*, III, 336–345.

49. It is reprinted in Gardiner, *Constitutional Documents*, pp. 232–241.

50. See, for example, the Leveller-inspired *A Copie of a Letter Sent from the Agitators . . . To All the Honest Sea-men of England*, dated June 21, 1647 (reprinted in Wolfe, *Leveller Manifestoes*, pp. 144–153).

51. It is reprinted in Wolfe, *Leveller Manifestoes*, pp. 156–195.

52. The "Amon Wilbee," by whom it was signed, was possibly a pseudonym for Marchamont Nedham, whose *The Case of the Kingdom truly Stated* of the preceding month had advocated a union of Royalists and Independents. *Plaine Truth* is well done enough to be by him, and since he was politically a chameleon, its views need not disqualify him.

53. Overton, *An Appeale*, in Wolfe, *Leveller Manifestoes*, pp. 167f.

54. In Wolfe, *Leveller Manifestoes*, p. 174.

55. *Ibid.*, p. 187.

56. None of these ideas were new, for the problems of public education, poor relief, and enclosures had inspired much seventeenth-century discussion. (See, for example, James, *Social Policy*, pp. 78–130, 243–250, 320–326). At least relatively new, however, was Overton's attempt to realize these reforms by specifically political means.

57. Two letters of the end of June and early July warned Cromwell against

apostasy. Toward the end of July, Lilburne wrote Marten that the rigors of continued imprisonment had brought him to his own breaking point. He then sent a letter to Fairfax threatening to appeal to the common people and soldiers if no relief was forthcoming; and at the end of the month Lilburne published a second letter to Marten, a pitiful account of the plight of his family — and with it Marten's rather chilly reply. Most of these letters appeared in *Jonahs Cry out of the Whales Belly* in July 1647, its seven items constituting an indirect history of the break between Leveller and Independent. Two of Lilburne's letters to Marten were published separately, while the letter to Fairfax appeared as the first item in *The Juglers Discovered* (September 1647).

58. Gardiner, *Great Civil War*, III, 348–352. Lilburne's latest charge was contained in a letter to Cromwell written on Aug. 13, 1647, and reprinted in mid-September in *Two Letters . . . to Col. Henry Marten*.

59. "A Letter to Fairfax," Aug. 21, 1647, reprinted in *The Juglers Discovered*, p. 9.

60. Lilburne, *The Additional Plea* (October 1647), pp. 22–24; Abbott, *Cromwell*, I, 540f; Gardiner, *Great Civil War*, III, 364.

61. Lilburne, "Advice to the Private Soldiers," in his *Juglers Discovered*.

62. Woodhouse, *Puritanism and Liberty*, p. [27]; Gardiner, *Great Civil War*, III, 364–369.

63. These three letters, and two earlier ones to Cromwell and Fairfax, were included in *Two Letters . . . to Col. Henry Marten*. In one of the letters to Marten, Lilburne warns the soldiers against allowing themselves to "come under a New England Independent tyranny."

64. The best testimony to Lilburne's activities among the soldiers comes from the antiradical press: see, for instance, the September and October issues of *Mercurius Pragmaticus*, especially No. 3 and No. 5; and the October issues of *Mercurius Anti-Pragmaticus*.

65. This proposition is reprinted in Lilburne's *The Peoples Prerogative and Priviledges* (February 1648).

66. *The Grand Plea* is addressed to Maynard, the man who had replaced Marten as chairman of the Parliamentary committee reviewing Lilburne's case.

67. At the end of *The Additional Plea* Lilburne threw himself on the mercy of Maynard's Committee. The result was that, early in November, Lilburne was granted permission to be absent from the Tower by day.

68. No. 2, Oct. 21–28, 1647.

69. No. 9, Oct. 23–30, 1647.

70. For a convenient breakdown of the various Agreements of the People, see J. W. Gough, "The Agreements of the People, 1647–49," *History*, new series XV (1930–31), 334–341. *The Case of the Armie* is reprinted in part in Woodhouse, *Puritanism and Liberty*, pp. 429–436; and in full in both Wolfe, *Leveller Manifestoes*, pp. 198–224, and Haller and Davies, *Leveller Tracts*, pp. 65–87.

71. Though probably the work of several hands, that of Wildman seems

dominant in *The Case* — a fact to which Ireton alluded in the course of the Putney Debate (*Clarke Papers*, I, 354).

72. Gardiner, *Great Civil War*, III, 378–380; Ashley, *Wildman*, p. 30.

73. These Engagements were principally *A Solemn Engagement of the Army*, June 5, 1647; *A Representation from* . . . *the Army*, June 14, 1647; and the Leveller-inspired *Remonstrance from Kingston*, Aug. 18, 1647.

CHAPTER VII. FROM PUTNEY TO WHITEHALL: THE ZENITH OF THE
LEVELLER PARTY

1. It was these "Propositions" to which Ireton referred on the first day of debate as the "Agreement"; as such, they technically represent the first "Agreement of the People"; and *An Agreement of the People*, circulated on Nov. 3, 1647, technically represents a second "Agreement." Since, however, the differences between these proposed constitutions are not important, the two are lumped together as the first "Agreement of the People" in the subsequent discussion of Leveller platforms.

2. This is made clear by Ireton's opening remarks, as well as by his later references to an already discussed "Agreement" (Woodhouse, *Puritanism and Liberty*, pp. 1, 34f; *Clarke Papers*, I, 227).

3. The full available transcript of the Putney Debate is given in Woodhouse, *Puritanism and Liberty*, pp. 1–124.

4. Woodhouse, *Puritanism and Liberty*, p. 7.

5. *Ibid.*, pp. 19f, 24, 31, 37.

6. *Two Letters from the Agents of the Five Regiments* (reprinted in part in Woodhouse, *Puritanism and Liberty*, pp. 437f).

7. *A Cal to All the Souldiers of the Armie*, dated Oct. 29, 1647 (reprinted in part in Woodhouse, *Puritanism and Liberty*, pp. 439–443). Its awareness of the details of the first day's debate, its style, and its many parallels to *The Case of the Armie* all indicate Wildman's authorship.

8. It is reprinted in full in Gardiner, *Great Civil War*, III, 392–394; in Woodhouse, *Puritanism and Liberty*, pp. 439–443, without the preamble; and in Wolfe, *Leveller Manifestoes*, pp. 226–234, along with two supporting letters from the Agitators.

9. Putney's proximity to London, the relative freedom then allowed to Lilburne and Overton, and the Independents' subsequent castigation of Walwyn's activities at this time all corroborate this inference.

10. In Gardiner, *Great Civil War*, III, 392.

11. The first clause of Article IV reads: "That matters of religion and the ways of God's worship are not at all entrusted to any human power, because therein we cannot remit or exceed a tittle of what our conscience dictate to be the mind of God without wilful sin: nevertheless the public way of instructing the nation (so it be not compulsive) is referred to their [future Parliaments'] discretion."

12. In the background of this discussion was the difference between *An*

Masterson's report reduced the figure from 30,000 to 3,000 — possibly a more likely number, since each petition was to be signed by many persons.

52. Another example both of collaboration between civilian and soldier and of Leveller frugality is this excerpt from *A Declaration*, p. 51: ". . . to one Lazarus Tindall, a private souldier . . . papers were delivered . . . to spread among the souldiers of that Regiment, and the same person who delivered them told him he should have one thousand of the Large Petitions also, to disperse in that Regiment, so soon as they were reprinted, which they were about to do in a smaller leter for the saving of charges."

53. *Ibid.*, p. 18.

54. This letter is reprinted in *A Declaration*, pp. 20–26.

55. *Ibid.*, p. 22.

56. See, for example, "Basilicus Anonymus," *The Case of the King Stated* (November 1647); Pease, *Leveller Movement*, pp. 254f.

57. Gardiner, *Great Civil War*, IV, 42–62, and his *Constitutional Documents*, pp. 248–268.

58. This is the petition referred to by Masterson and cited by the Levellers in the letter to Kent. It is reprinted in *A Declaration*, pp. 26–35; and in Wolfe, *Leveller Manifestoes*, pp. 263–272. It is not listed as a separate tract in the *Thomason Catalogue*.

59. Frost, *A Declaration*, p. 27.

60. On the concern occasioned at this very time by the national economic dislocations see, for instance, John Cooke, *Unum Necessarium* (Feb. 1, 1648); and Henry Parker, *Of a Free Trade* (Feb. 5, 1648).

61. See, for instance, *Mercurius Pragmaticus*, No. 19, Jan. 18–25, 1648.

62. It is reprinted in *A Declaration*, pp. 52–56; and in Wolfe, *Leveller Manifestoes*, pp. 275–278. Of all the Leveller writings, its language (which Frost says "looks more like the ebullition of wine than the cries of want") is closest to that of the Digger tracts of 1649.

63. Gibb, *Lilburne*, pp. 217–222; Ashley, *Wildman*, pp. 53f.

64. Frost, *A Declaration*, p. 13.

65. See also Abbott, *Cromwell*, I, 579.

66. Wildman, *Truths Triumph*, p. 9, says that Lilburne from the first denied the rumor that he had been offered a bribe by the Lords.

67. Also the House of Commons, as result of Lilburne's and Wildman's legalistic delaying tactics, was forced into a lengthy debate on the validity of Masterson's testimony. (Lilburne, *A Whip, passim; Mercurius Melancholicus*, No. 21, Jan. 15–22, 1648; Gibb, *Lilburne*, pp. 220ff; Ashley, *Wildman*, pp. 53f.)

68. In giving the Levellers credit for misleading a large number of people, Frost at the same time implies that they greatly exaggerate the number of their adherents (*A Declaration*, p. 6).

69. *Ibid.*, p. 40.

70. A week after *A Declaration*, Prynne, in one of his briefer tracts — *The Levellers Levell'd to the Very Ground* — amplifies this point.

71. After a discursive introduction, Lilburne reprints, among a great many other documents, the Petition of Right, four Chapters of Magna Carta, certain

statutes ranging from the time of Edward I to James I — with some of Coke's commentaries on them, four recent acts of Parliament, and several contemporary pamphlets and petitions, not to mention four of his own tracts.

72. Lilburne, *A Whip*, p. 3.

73. Frost's charge that Lilburne had been intellectually infected by the Royalists during his imprisonment at Oxford calls forth Lilburne's most bitter comments.

74. The author's signature, "J. Howldin," is almost certainly a pseudonym for John Wildman. Further, the clear and well-supported glorification of the law in which this pamphlet indulges strongly confirms Wildman's authorship.

75. There is a biography of Maynard by J. M. Rigg in *Dictionary of National Biography*.

76. *Thomason Catalogue*, I, 601.

77. That *The Prisoners Plea* is in the form of an epistle to Lenthall, the Speaker of the House, makes Lilburne's argument seem more cogent than if it had appeared in a pamphlet directed only to the general public.

78. Lilburne, *The oppressed mans importunate and mournfull cryes*, p. 4.

79. Gibb, *Lilburne*, p. 231.

80. Lilburne, *The Lawes Funerall*, p. 2, attributes his appearance before the judges to the efforts of those who had pushed his petitions for habeas corpus.

81. *Ibid.*, p. 20.

82. The over-all effectiveness of this tract suggests the hand of Walwyn, though its sentimentalism and stylistic exaggerations go beyond the manner of even his most religious writings.

83. This speech, given on July 27, 1648, was published on Aug. 11.

84. Gardiner, *Great Civil War*, IV, 175. (Wildman was released on the same day as Lilburne — Ashley, *Wildman*, p. 59.)

85. *The humble petition . . . in the behalfe of . . . John Lilburne.* It was reprinted at the end of Maynard's *Speech* of ten days later, where a note following the text states that the petition had "nigh ten thousand hands to it."

86. Gardiner, *Great Civil War*, IV, 175.

87. See, for instance, *Mercurius Pragmaticus*, No. 19, Aug. 1–8, 1648; and *The Colchester Spie*, No. 2, Aug. 10–17, 1648.

88. Lilburne was proud of this letter, reprinting it at least twice (*Legall Fundamentall Liberties*, p. 28; *Picture of the Councel of State*, p. 21), and later referring to it on numerous occasions with justified vanity.

89. *The Petition of divers Citizens of London . . . for the allaying and removall of . . . jealusies and discontents.*

90. It is almost certainly by Walwyn: both its style and ideas are his, and the "W. P. Gent." by whom it is signed could by no stretch of the imagination be identified with William Prynne. Further, Humphrey Brooke, in refuting the implication in *The Discoverer* that *The Bloody Project* was by Walwyn, did not deny this suggestion. (See, also, Haller and Davies, *Leveller Tracts*, p. 135. *The Bloody Project* is there reprinted, pp. 135–146.)

91. Walwyn, *The Bloody Project*, p. 4.

92. *Ibid.*

93. *Ibid.*, p. 6.

94. *Ibid.*, pp. 10f.

95. . . . *The Humble Petition*, often also referred to as the "Large Petition," is reprinted in Wolfe, *Leveller Manifestoes*, pp. 283–290; in Haller and Davies, *Leveller Tracts*, pp. 148–155; in part in Woodhouse, *Puritanism and Liberty*, pp. 338–342; and in *The Moderate* for mid-September 1648. A week later the Levellers reissued their other so-called "Large Petition," that of March 1647.

96. The only Leveller publication between *The Bloody Project* and the Whitehall Debate not directly connected with setting up and implementing this program was a petition from Lilburne, dated Sept. 4, 1648, asking for the reparations which he claimed were long his due, *the humble Remonstrance of . . . John Lilburne.*

97. *Old Parliamentary History*, XVII, 462, cited in Wolfe, *Leveller Manifestoes*, p. 282, notes 9 and 10. At this time, too, there were some signs of agitation in the New Model for the re-creation of the General Council of the Army.

98. On Sept. 13, 1648, the House of Commons was petitioned not to ignore *The Humble Petition.*

99. Gardiner, *Great Civil War*, IV, 232–275; Abbott, *Cromwell*, I, 684–704.

100. J. B. Williams, *A History of English Journalism to the Foundation of the Gazette* (1908), makes a good many anguished comments on *The Moderate* and on its editor, Gilbert Mabbott. Mabbott had been deputy to the clerk of the House of Commons, John Rushworth; and he also served as licenser of weekly news-books until, in May 1649, he was temporarily removed because of his ardent support of the Levellers.

101. In September 1648 Ireton had already begun to disagree with Fairfax concerning the best course to pursue in relation to the king, and on October 18 Ireton's own regiment petitioned for justice against Charles. At about this time Ireton began work on the "Remonstrance of the Army," which from the first included the demand that the king be brought to trial. (The "Remonstrance" is reprinted, in large part, in Woodhouse, *Puritanism and Liberty*, pp. 456–465.)

102. Gardiner, *Great Civil War*, IV, 233–238; Abbott, *Cromwell*, I, 685–688; and Woodhouse, *Puritanism and Liberty*, pp. [31]f.

103. Lilburne, *Legall Fundamentall Liberties*, p. 29. (This pamphlet, the major source for the narrative which follows, is reprinted almost in full in Haller and Davies, *Leveller Tracts*, pp. 400–449.)

104. Lilburne, *Legall Fundamentall Liberties*, p. 29.

105. *Ibid.*

106. *Ibid.*, p. 30. Walwyn later alludes to this incident in his own *Just Defence.*

107. Lilburne, *Legall Fundamentall Liberties*, p. 30.

108. *Ibid.*, p. 31; Gardiner, *Great Civil War*, IV, 239, 245.

109. These paragraphs, which come after a discussion of army arrears, appear in Woodhouse, *Puritanism and Liberty*, pp. 462–464. They are discussed in Gardiner, *Great Civil War*, IV, 239–242.

110. In Woodhouse, *Puritanism and Liberty*, pp. 463f.

111. Lilburne, *Legall Fundamentall Liberties*, p. 30.

112. To what extent Harrison's acceptance and Ireton's alleged acceptance committed their fellow officers became one of the focal points of debate between the Levellers and Independents in December 1648 and in the early months of 1649. The evidence does indicate, however, that Lilburne, while telling the truth, did exaggerate the scope and binding power of Ireton's yes — transmitted to Lilburne by Harrison from the bedside of Mr. and Mrs. Ireton.

113. Lilburne, *Legall Fundamentall Liberties*, pp. 32f. Four representatives of the Presbyterians were also invited to participate, but their refusal to do so was apparently taken for granted by all concerned.

114. *Mercurius Pragmaticus*, in mid-December 1648, was skeptical about the permanence of any such marriage, remarking that Cromwell and the Levellers "can as soon combine as fire and water; . . . consider that the Levellers aim . . . at pure democracy, or a Government by the many headed rabble, and the design of Oliver and his Grandees [is] for an Oligarchy in the hands of himself." On the other hand, the issues of *The Moderate* at this time were much more sanguine.

115. Gardiner, *Great Civil War*, IV, 263.

116. *The Declaration of . . . Fairfax and his General Councel showing the grounds for the Armies advance towards . . . London*. It is reprinted in Woodhouse, *Puritanism and Liberty*, pp. 456–467.

117. In addition to Marten and the four Levellers, this committee consisted of Colonels Tichburn and White, Daniel Taylor, and Richard Price — representing the London Independents; and Ireton, Sir William Constable and two other officers — representing the army (Lilburne, *Legall Fundamentall Liberties*, p. 33). The absence of three of the Parliamentary representatives can almost certainly be explained by their reluctance to participate in any group aiming at the dissolution of Parliament.

118. Petty, or Pettus — who, with Lilburne, Walwyn, and Wildman, was unanimously chosen "at a very large meeting" to represent the Levellers (Lilburne, *Legall Fundamentall Liberties*, p. 33) — had been active in Leveller circles since Putney, where he had been one of their civilian representatives. Ten years later he brought his ideas to Harrington's Rota (Pease, *Leveller Movement*, p. 352).

119. Lilburne, *Legall Fundamentall Liberties*, pp. 34f; Gardiner, *Great Civil War*, IV, 267f. Prior to this acceptance, Lilburne and Ireton engaged in vigorous debate.

120. Lilburne, *Legall Fundamentall Liberties*, p. 35.

121. Though Thomason dates *Foundations of Freedom* Dec. 10, 1648, and though Lilburne says it appeared on Dec. 16, two of its three slightly variant editions are dated Dec. 15 — a date confirmed by Gardiner (*Great Civil War*, IV, 276, note 3). It is reprinted in Wolfe, *Leveller Manifestoes*, pp. 294–303.

122. In Wolfe, *Leveller Manifestoes*, p. 295.

123. *Ibid.*, p. 297. Royalists were also excluded from voting for seven years, and for fourteen years were prohibited from sitting in Parliament.

124. Since it was not specified whether Parliaments were to be annual or biennial, there was a later disagreement between the Levellers and the Council of Officers on how long such a Council of State might have to function between Parliamentary sessions.

125. A third device to avoid the growth of "factions" was the added proviso that lawyers, while in Parliament, must give up their practice.

126. To this list the irrepressible Lilburne added, in a note at the end of *Foundations of Freedom*, four other categories of grievances which he thought needed correction. These reforms included ridding the nation of lawyers, setting up locally elected courts of justice and local public-accounting and assessment offices, and abolishing "all base Tenures."

127. The debates are given in Woodhouse, *Puritanism and Liberty*, pp. 125–178.

128. *Ibid.*, p. 126.

129. *Ibid.*, p. 160. Nye, though an Independent, was not a separatist.

130. *Ibid.*, p. 132.

131. *Ibid.*, pp. 144, 154.

132. Woodhouse's identification of this speaker as Overton seems conclusive (*ibid.*, p. 139, note 2).

133. *Ibid.*, p. 139.

134. *Ibid.*, p. 161.

135. Lilburne, *Legall Fundamentall Liberties*, p. 35. Also, Clarke, after Dec. 14, did not list the names of Lilburne and Overton as among those present.

136. *Clarke Papers*, II, 282. Clarke lists Walwyn and Wildman as present on Dec. 18, but not thereafter. Probably only the officers were given a vote at these meetings (*Clarke Papers*, II, 139) — an additional reason for the withdrawal of the Levellers, either of their own volition or at the request of the officers.

137. Its full title states that it was "offered" to the General Council of the Army. It is reprinted in Wolfe, *Leveller Manifestoes*, pp. 306–310.

138. Its views and its style suggest Walwyn; and the brief justification of "Idolatry" with which the tract ends makes it unlikely that it was written by a Catholic.

139. There are two additional proposals, each suggestive of Walwyn's advanced social thought. One urges that all who are in jail "for Conscience sake" be forthwith released. The other, as far as I know unique in the mid-seventeenth century and still today a spur to tumultuous debate, asks that the "excessive Fees of Physitians may be regulated and reduced, whereby the poore for a small and reasonable Fee may have the benefit of their skill."

140. Gardiner, *Great Civil War*, IV, 277.

141. The final form of the Agreement, as it was presented to the House of Commons on Jan. 20, 1649, is given in Gardiner, *Constitutional Documents,*

pp. 270–282. Woodhouse, *Puritanism and Liberty*, pp. 356–367, reprints the original Agreement along with the officers' revisions; while the actual proceedings involved in these modifications are given in *Clarke Papers*, II, 133–140, 147–150, 155–157, 170–186; and in Woodhouse, pp. 467–471. The version of the Agreement reprinted in Wolfe, *Leveller Manifestoes*, pp. 334–354, though it differs only slightly from the transcript in Gardiner's *Constitutional Documents*, includes a petition from the officers which accompanied the Agreement, as well as a recommendation from them to the people of England in mild support of this program.

142. Lilburne, *Legall Fundamentall Liberties*, p. 37.

143. Gardiner, *Great Civil War*, IV, 295f.

144. Ashurst, *Reasons against . . . the Agreement*, p. 11. Ashurst was answered in February 1649 by William Cokayne in *The Foundations of Freedome, Vindicated*, a pamphlet which emphasizes not the evils of the Leveller scheme but its improvements on existing plans and conditions. Ashurst was supported at the end of January 1649 by a Mr. "A.P.," whose *An Appendix to The Agreement For the People* also denounces Leveller disobedience, heresy, and schism.

145. It is reprinted in Wolfe, *Leveller Manifestoes*, pp. 313–321.

146. Gardiner, *Great Civil War*, IV, 281.

147. Schenk, *Social Justice*, pp. 172–177; Wolfe, *Leveller Manifestoes*, pp. 311f; and Gough's article in *History*, p. 377. It is interesting to note, however, that both Ashurst and Jubbes were worried about the future of Ireland, Ashurst's eighth "Particular" expressing a concern similar to that shown in Jubbes's eleventh and twenty-third proposals.

148. December 1648 and January 1649, despite Parliament's attempt to stem the flood, represent two of Thomason's busiest months of collecting.

149. Probably largely the work of Lilburne, *A Plea* was signed by the sixteen men who presented it to Fairfax.

150. Lilburne, *Legall Fundamentall Liberties*, pp. 35f.

151. It is reprinted in Wolfe, *Leveller Manifestoes*, pp. 326–330.

152. Thus the note at the end of the petition, signed by the Clerk of Parliament.

153. Clyde, *Freedom of the Press*, pp. 163f; Wolfe, *Leveller Manifestoes*, p. 323; and Williams, *History of English Journalism*, p. 109.

154. In Wolfe, *Leveller Manifestoes*, p. 328. Overton goes on to credit unlicensed printing with paving the way for Parliament's crucial declaration, early in January 1649, that "all just power . . . [is] in the people, & the Supreme Authority . . . [is] in this honourable House [of Commons]."

155. *Ibid.*, p. 327.

156. *Ibid.*, p. 328. The petition then comes to a quick end with four brief requests: that the supremacy of the House of Commons remain unencumbered by king or Lords, that tithes be abolished, that encroachments by the military be curtailed, and that full freedom of the press be guaranteed by law. The

sincerity of Overton's convictions is highlighted by the fact that Mabbott was still "chief licenser" of printed books and pamphlets.

157. Clyde, *Freedom of the Press*, pp. 165–167.
158. Lilburne, *Legall Fundamentall Liberties*, p. 36.

CHAPTER VIII. THE END OF THE LEVELLER PARTY

1. S. R. Gardiner, *History of the Commonwealth and Protectorate, 1649–1656* (1903), I, 1–6 (hereafter referred to as *C&P*); and his *Constitutional Documents*, pp. 291–293, 294–297.

2. Ashley, *Wildman*, pp. 69ff. See also the comments of Overton and Lilburne in the summer of 1649 (*Overtons Defyance of the Act of Pardon*, and Lilburne's *An Impeachment of High Treason Against . . . Cromwell*).

3. Lilburne, *Legall Fundamentall Liberties*, p. 42.

4. *Ibid.*, pp. 41–64. Lilburne also states that he turned down the chance of serving as one of the king's judges.

5. *Ibid.*, pp. 39, 42–44, 64–73. This trial — of Hamilton, Holland, and Capel — began on Feb. 10, 1649, and eventuated in their execution a month later (Gardiner, *C&P*, I, 10f).

6. Gardiner, *C&P*, I, 30f.

7. *Clarke Papers*, I, 191f.

8. Lilburne, *Legall Fundamentall Liberties*, p. 74.

9. It appeared in *The Moderate*, No. 34, Feb. 27–March 6, 1649. It is reprinted in Haller and Davies, *Leveller Tracts*, pp. 157–170.

10. In Haller and Davies, *Leveller Tracts*, p. 169 — Lilburne's pages being unnumbered.

11. *Ibid.*, pp. 157–160.

12. *Ibid.*, p. 166.

13. This petition is reprinted in Overton's *The Hunting of the Foxes*, in Wolfe, *Leveller Manifestoes*, pp. 372–375.

14. *To the Supream Authority . . . The Humble Petition of Richard Overton* (March 3, 1649) is given in *The Moderate*, No. 35, March 6–13, 1649.

15. It is reprinted in Haller and Davies, *Leveller Tracts*, pp. 252–275. Though the date of its imprimatur is Feb. 23, 1649, Thomason did not enter it until March 12. Haller, *Tracts on Liberty*, I, 122, suggests Walwyn as the author, as do Haller and Davies in their introductory note to this tract. Walwyn, in his *Just Defence*, praises this work, and its style and ideas are in keeping with his other writings. Moreover, a passage in *The Vanitie* (p. 26) strongly supports his authorship, for it shows Walwyn's intimate knowledge of the fact that certain of his former friends among the Independents had been, and were, engaged in assembling material for a concerted attack against him — that attack which early in May came to a head in *Walwins Wiles*.

16. Walwyn, *Vanitie*, p. 11.

17. In discussing the falseness of some of the extreme sects of his day, especially their departures from "the plaine expression of the Scripture,"

Walwyn at one point refers to Boehme as the "German madde man" (*Vanitie*, p. 16), though nowhere does he even hint that persecution might be the proper way to bring these wandering sects back to the true path of godliness.

18. *Ibid.*, pp. 19f.

19. *Ibid.*, p. 22.

20. *Ibid.*, pp. 45f. In all probability Walwyn did not know Fox, now just becoming conscious of his apostolic mission.

21. *Ibid.*, p. 21.

22. *Ibid.*, p. 43; also pp. 23f.

23. The fact that the Levellers were essentially crying in the wilderness is indicated by two pamphlets contemporaneous with Walwyn's tract. On March 6, 1649, Thomason entered a blast at the entire concept of an Agreement of the People signed by fifty-four Lancashire ministers; and two days later sixty-three Essex divines outdid their Lancashire brethren in *The Essex Watchmen's Watchword*.

24. Lilburne, in *The Picture of the Councel of State*, p. 2, declared in April that Walwyn "for some moneths . . . [had] never bin to any of our meetings." Walwyn's *Vanitie* was thus not a part of any planned Leveller propaganda campaign.

25. There is no biography of Bray in *Dictionary of National Biography*, but his military career is described in Firth and Davies, *Regimental History*, pp. 457–459, 608; and a summary of his life after 1647 is given in *Clarke Papers*, I, 411f. In the autumn of 1659, on the eve of the Restoration, he issued two pamphlets which continued to breathe forth Leveller ideas, *A Plea for the Peoples Fundamental Liberties and Parliaments*, and *A Plea for the Peoples Good Old Cause*.

26. *An Appeale in the Claim of Justice against . . . Fairfax* (March 19, 1649); *A Second Appeale in behalf of the Soveraignty of Justice . . . against Fairfax* (April 2, 1649).

27. It is reprinted in Wolfe, *Leveller Manifestoes*, pp. 358–383. Overton's authorship is confirmed by the circumstances under which it was written, by its style, and by its "Martinesque" title page.

28. Overton, *The Hunting of the Foxes*, in Wolfe, *Leveller Manifestoes*, p. 370.

29. *Ibid.*, p. 365.

30. *Ibid.*, p. 366.

31. *Ibid.*, p. 379, "The Examination and Answers of George Jellers."

32. Overton, in *The Hunting of the Foxes* (Wolfe, p. 368), tells the anecdote later repeated by Lilburne and several of the Royalist journals, that Colonel Hewson, a member of the Council of Officers, said in their meeting on Feb. 22, 1649: "We have had enough tryal of Civil Courts: we can hang 20 [Levellers] before they will hang one." Clarke's brief report of this meeting (*Clarke Papers*, II, 190–193) does not, however, mention this threat.

33. It is reprinted in Haller and Davies, *Leveller Tracts*, pp. 172–189; and in Wolfe, *Milton*, pp. 399–415. Two days after the appearance of this tract,

the Council of State asked Milton, now one of its secretaries, to "make some observations" on it. Milton never accomplished this task, for nowhere in his works is there any mention of the Levellers, much less an attack on *The Second Part of Englands New-Chaines.*

34. Lilburne, *Legall Fundamentall Liberties*, p. 74.

35. The title page provides these instructions.

36. The evidence for this is twofold: first, the prompt and militant measures taken against the leading London Levellers, including the fact that their early morning arrests were presumably timed to avoid popular demonstrations; second, the testimony of many different newspapers of March and April 1649 — in particular, *The Moderate*, No. 37 and No. 38; *The Kingdomes Faithfull and Impartiall Scout*, No. 8 and No. 10; and *The Moderate Intelligencer*, No. 208, which reported:

We begin . . . to be in amazement to see what is done in this Town [London], and in several parts of the Country, even upon the market days . . . Troopers coming with the late Printed papers and Petitions . . . affixing them upon posts, reading them at market places, making speeches to the people exhorting them to joyne with them, disswading them from paying excise before the faces of those that appeared to receive them, and . . . advising them not to give free quarter . . . . They tell the people they will live and die with them in their deliverance from such like slaveries and from this new Tyranny, naming the most eminent in the Army to the people as the causers of it; with these Troopers doe accompany many of the people of this Countrey, and some of the Militia; others underhand doe abet them. If those that governe doe not somewhat to stop these proceedings, and by way of ease, troubles will undoubtedly arise. . . .

37. The newspapers of the spring of 1649 are full of stories depicting the depression then gripping England. Peter Chamberlen's *The Poor Man's Advocate*, April 3, 1649, as well as the writings and activities of the Diggers in March and April, also testify to that economic unrest which immediately preceded the official establishment of the Commonwealth.

38. Gardiner, *C&P*, I, 34.

39. The first edition is reprinted in Haller and Davies, *Leveller Tracts*, pp. 191–246. Lilburne published a slightly altered second edition in October 1649.

40. That section of *The Fountain of Slaunder* relevant to Walwyn's arrest and examination is given in Haller and Davies, *Leveller Tracts*, pp. 246–251.

41. *The Picture*, p. 12.

42. *Ibid.*, p. 15; Abbott, *Cromwell*, II, 41f.

43. But one striking difference between the Lilburne of the late 1630's and of the late 1640's was the relationship to him of his early friend William Kiffin; for, on April 2, 1649, Kiffin presented to Parliament *The Humble Petition and Representation of Several Churches of God in London, commonly (though falsly) called Anabaptists,* a vitriolic indictment of the Levellers.

44. *The Picture*, p. 23.

45. *Ibid.*, p. 44.

46. Walwyn's *Fountain of Slaunder* is, however, a valuable supplement to his spiritual and intellectual biography.

47. Gardiner, *C&P*, I, 36.

48. This petition from "The Inhabitants of London . . . and places adjacent" is given in *The Moderate*, No. 38, March 27–April 3, 1649. Gardiner, *C&P*, I, 42, says that 80,000, not 10,000, signatures were claimed for it.

49. This petition was promoted by "divers thousands of London," and was printed in *The Moderate*, No. 41, April 17–24, 1649.

50. This petition was described in *The Moderate*, No. 40, a week before its presentation to Parliament.

51. The hostile comments in the press on this petition and on the *Petition of Women* of May 5, 1649, can be seen most graphically in *Mercurius Pragmaticus for King Charles II*, No. 3, May 1–8, 1649, and *Mercurius Militaris*, No. 1, May 22–29, 1649.

52. This was a broadside addressed to the New Model and "scatered about the Streets [of London]."

53. Gardiner, *C&P*, I, 42.

54. It is reprinted in Haller and Davies, *Leveller Tracts*, pp. 276–284; and in Wolfe, *Leveller Manifestoes*, pp. 388–396.

55 Its style is obviously Walwyn's, as the author of *Walwins Wiles* soon pointed out. Brooke subsequently added that *A Manifestation* was "principally" the work of Walwyn (*Charity of Church-men*, p. 12). See also Haller and Davies, *Leveller Tracts*, p. 276; and Wolfe, *Milton*, p. 384.

56. Walwyn, *A Manifestation*, p. 3.

57. *Ibid.*, p. 4.

58. *Ibid.*, p. 5.

59. *Ibid.*, p. 6.

60. *Ibid.*, p. 7.

61. Gardiner, *C&P*, I, 55–79; Abbott, *Cromwell*, II, 50ff.

62. Wolfe, *Leveller Manifestoes*, pp. 385f.

63. Though not entered by Thomason until May 10, 1649, *Walwins Wiles* was written shortly before the final Leveller *Agreement of the People* appeared. The authorship of John Price is strongly hinted at by Brooke (*Charity of Church-men*, p. 6), by Walwyn (*Just Defence*, p. 14), and by Price's own activities as a publicist for the Independents.

64. That the Independents had long been working on an indictment of Walwyn is attested to by their anti-Leveller activities since early 1647, by Walwyn's charge to this effect (*Just Defence*, p. 3), and by the manifestly painstaking nature of Price's "evidence" in *Walwins Wiles*.

65. Gardiner, *C&P*, I 44f.

66. *Ibid.*, I, 45f; Firth and Davies, *Regimental History*, pp. 219f.

67. The most graphic contemporary accounts of Lockyer's funeral are those in *The Moderate*, *The Kingdomes Weekly Intelligencer*, and *The Moderate Intelligencer*, the last of which gives the number of "green-ribboned mourners" as 4,000.

68. *An Agreement of the Free People of England* was signed by its four authors on May 1, 1649, and entered by Thomason on that same day. Besides appearing independently in at least two editions (one with and one without

Mabbott's imprimatur), it was also reprinted in Thompson's *England's Standard Advanced* (May 6, 1649), and in *The Levellers (Falsly so called) Vindicated* (May 14, 1649). Strangely enough, *The Moderate* did not reprint it; but it was given in full by *The Kingdomes Faithfull and Impartiall Scout* (No. 314, April 27–May 4, 1649), and by *Englands Moderate Messenger* (No. 2, April 30–May 7, 1649). Thomason also lists a later edition under date of July 23, 1649. *An Agreement* is reprinted in Haller and Davies, *Leveller Tracts*, pp. 318–328; and in Wolfe, *Leveller Manifestoes*, pp. 400–410.

69. Active Royalists are also disenfranchised for ten years.

70. The instructions to the people in the event of such a contingency are vague and somewhat contradictory, for they combine traditional arrangements with democratic innovations (Article VI).

71. However, only those qualified to vote for their representatives are eligible to choose their ministers and local officials.

72. *An Agreement of the Free People of England*, p. 7 (Article XXIX).

73. Gibb, *Lilburne*, pp. 260f; Gardiner, *C&P*, I, 49f.

74. These two petitions are mentioned in Gardiner, *C&P*, I, 48; and one of them is reprinted in *The Moderate*, No. 43, May 1–8, 1649.

75. This petition is reprinted in *The Moderate*, No. 43. It is also given, in large part, in Woodhouse, *Puritanism and Liberty*, pp. 367–369. For a straightforward account of its presentation by a contingent of Leveller women, see *The Kingdomes Weekly Intelligencer*, No. 310, May 1–8, 1649.

76. *The Thankfull Acknowledgement . . . of divers well-affected Apprentices . . . of Cripplegate*. On May 17 a group labeling themselves "The Resolved Apprentices" replied by upholding the Rump and castigating the Levellers.

77. *The humble Petition of divers young men and Apprentices of . . . London*, reprinted in *The Moderate*, No. 44, May 8–15, 1649. The revolutionary orientation of the petitioners and their appeal is given a lurid build-up in *Mercurius Brittanicus*, No. 3, May 8–15, 1649.

78. These two petitions are described respectively in *The Moderate Intelligencer*, No. 216, May 2–10, 1649, and in *The Kingdomes Faithfull and Impartiall Scout*, No. 15, May 4–11, 1649.

79. Firth and Davies, *Regimental History*, pp. 221–223; Gardiner, *C&P*, I, 48–54; Gibb, *Lilburne*, pp. 266–269.

80. Gardiner, *C&P*, I, 54. *A Moderate Narrative of Intelligence*, No. 13, early in June interpreted these events as a sort of obituary on the Leveller party.

81. For more on Denne (or Den), called "Judas" by the Levellers, see Firth and Davies, *Regimental History*, pp. 110–114; Huehns, *Antinomianism*, pp. 85f; and the biography by A. C. Bickley in *Dictionary of National Biography*.

82. *A Moderate Intelligence*, in the second of its two issues, reprinted a large portion of this interview. According to Lilburne, *A Discourse* had a second edition.

83. It is reprinted in Haller and Davies, *Leveller Tracts*, pp. 329–349.

Anthony á Wood has a brief biography of Brooke in *Athenae Oxoniensis* (1691), II, 803.

84. Though not entered by Thomason until May 30, 1649, the bulk of this pamphlet was probably written early in April. The account of Walwyn's arrest was in all likelihood excluded from *The Picture of the Councel of State* because he had had no hand in the publication of *The Second Part of Englands New-Chaines*.

85. Thomason did not enter *Walwyns Just Defence*, nor does the copy in the Newberry Library specify the date beyond saying that the pamphlet was published in 1649. Certain references in the tract, as well as some of Brooke's allusions to it, indicate that it was composed early in June. It is reprinted in Haller and Davies, *Leveller Tracts*, pp. 350–398.

86. Lilburne, *Legall Fundamentall Liberties*, p. 66.

87. *The Discoverer*, p. 4.

88. Frost and Canne assumed, or pretended to assume, that a tract by the Digger leader, Gerrard Winstanley — *The New Law of Righteousness* (January 1649) — expressed the religious principles of the Levellers. Since the Digger attempt to implement their theory of agrarian communism was very much in the news in April 1649, many of the attacks on the Levellers at that time strongly emphasized the alleged affinity between political democracy and economic egalitarianism.

89. It is reprinted almost in full in Haller and Davies, *Leveller Tracts*, pp. 400–449; and that section having to do specifically with the Second Agreemen of the People is given in Wolfe, *Leveller Manifestoes*, pp. 411–424, and in Woodhouse, *Puritanism and Liberty*, pp. 342–355. In July 1649 Lilburne published a slightly revised second edition.

90. Overton, *Defyance*, p. 5.

91. *Ibid.*, p. 6.

92. Within a month Thomason entered *A New Bull-Bayting*, a smutty Royalist attack on Cromwell which, by comparison, reveals Overton's skill in handling the weapon of political scurrility without resort to scatology or mere name-calling.

93. Gibb, *Lilburne*, pp. 272f. However, it is probable that Lilburne at this time wrote, to accompany Overton's *Baiting of the Great Bull*, a hortatory petition, *To All the Affectors and Approvers . . . of the Petition of . . . September 1648* (July 17, 1649).

94. Though it includes Lilburne's "Letter To . . . Mr. Cornelius Holland" and certain letters and speeches relevant to Masterson's charges, each item is so treated that it becomes a part of Lilburne's personal attack on the General.

95. Firth has a biography of "Hesilrige" in *Dictionary of National Biography*. The background for the dispute between him and Lilburne is given in Gibb, *Lilburne*, pp. 274f, 299f; Gardiner, *C&P*, I, 160–162; and Lilburne, *A Preparative*, pp. 7, 13.

96. Gardiner, *C&P*, I, 162f.

97. Lilburne's authorship is attested to by the militancy of the tract, by the

fact that he was responsible for its publication, and by his testimony about it at his trial.

98. Gardiner, *C&P*, I, 163f; Gibb, *Lilburne*, p. 276.

99. Because Lilburne refused to recognize the legality of this new warrant, he was not actually put behind bars until Sept. 27 (Gardiner, *C&P*, I, 164). *The Moderate*, no longer under the editorship of Mabbott, covered the events of the Oxford mutiny and Lilburne's recommittal in its final issues (No. 62, No. 63), though its coverage was neutral rather than markedly sympathetic to the Levellers. On the other hand, the Royalist press was now uniformly warm to Lilburne: e.g., *The Man in the Moon*, No. 23, Sept. 19–26, 1649; *Mercurius Pragmaticus (For King Charles II)*, No. 25, Oct. 9–16, 1649; and *Mercurius Elencticus*, No. 21 and No. 22, Sept. 10–24, 1649. In mid-September Lilburne told part of his story — namely, how he would refuse to obey any orders of the Council of State — in *A Salva Libertate*.

100. The article on Sydenham by W. P. Courtney in *Dictionary of National Biography* attributes this pamphlet to Sydenham, though its dedication is signed by "T.M."

101. In this interview Lilburne also gave a rather boyish description of some of his literary habits: his longer pamphlets, he said, took him three or four days to write; his shorter works considerably less time. He also acknowledged his excellent memory — to which *Strength out of Weaknesse* and *A Discourse Betwixt . . . Lilburne . . . and . . . Peters*, assuming that their lengthy transcripts are accurate, pay tribute.

102. Since the *First Proffer* had been addressed to an anti-Leveller Lord, and since the *second-proffer* was sent to Lilburne's brother, Colonel Robert Lilburne, for transmittal to certain of the Levellers' high-placed opponents, neither offer was intended to be officially presented by any person directly associated with the radicals.

103. This almost full list, consisting of forty-five separate numbered items, is invaluable as an aid in establishing a bibliography of Lilburne's works.

104. *To the Commons of England . . . The Humble Petition of the . . . Approvers of the Late Petition of the 11. of September* (Oct. 23, 1649). This lengthy and diverse list of all the Leveller grievances against the Rump and the Council of State was not even officially received by Parliament. From this same time date two other pro-Lilburne petitions and one public letter, all of them reprinted in Walker, *The Triall of . . . Lilburne*: a petition from Lilburne's wife and his brother Robert, Oct. 22, 1649; a petition from Robert Lilburne on the next day; and a letter from Lilburne to Lenthall written just before the trial began and very similar to Lilburne's *First Proffer*.

105. This trial is fully described in Gibb, *Lilburne*, pp. 278–294; and there are pertinent accounts of it in Gardiner, *C&P*, I, 164–170; Haller and Davies, *Leveller Tracts*, pp. 30f; and Pease, *Leveller Movement*, pp. 290–298. An uncorrected transcript of the trial appears in full in *A Complete Collection of State Trials* (1742–1756), II, 19–80. During the trial Theodorus Verax (Clement Walker) issued an account of the proceedings; and, on Nov. 28, 1649, with the help of Lilburne, he published an almost complete and revised

account, *The Traill of . . . Lilburne*. Three days later he supplemented this with the *Second Part of the Triall of . . . Lilburne*. On the second day of the trial itself appeared a pamphlet critical of Lilburne's courtroom behavior, *A Brief Discourse of the Present Power of Magistracy and Justice*. Within a few days this tract was jubilantly countered by the pro-Lilburne *Truths Victory over Tyrants and Tyranny*. The best newspaper accounts of the trial are those in *Mercurius Elencticus*, No. 26, and *Mercurius Pragmaticus (For King Charles II)*, No. 27 and No. 28.

106. Walker, *The Triall of . . . Lilburne*, p. 52.

107. For a broad contemporary perspective on the larger issues represented by this trial, see Henry Robinson's *A Short Discourse between Monarchical and Aristocratical Government*, which appeared on the day the trial began.

108. "L.R.," the author of *A Brief Discourse of the Present Power of Magistracy and Justice*, was sharply critical of Lilburne's histrionic turbulence; while the author of *Truths Victory* and Clement Walker took a contrary view, the former commenting at one point that the court's reading of selections from some of Lilburne's works "pleased the People as well as if they had acted before them one of Ben Johnsons [sic] Playes."

109. Lilburne was not being tried for the authorship of *The Second Part of Englands New-Chaines*, for which he had originally been arrested in March. Moreover, two new treason acts (of May and July 1649) were now cited against him (Walker, *The Triall of . . . Lilburne*, pp. 87–91).

110. Quoted in Gibb, *Lilburne*, p. 293.

111. Walker, *The Triall of . . . Lilburne*, p. 141.

112. *Ibid.*, p. 151.

113. *Ibid.*

114. Gibb, *Lilburne*, p. 294. The Royalist press, of course, made much of this antigovernment celebration.

115. Gardiner, *C&P*, I, 169.

116. *Ibid.*, I, 170–181, describes many of the ways in which the Commonwealth government was then strengthening its position. Probably the pamphlet which is most pertinent to the growing prestige of this government, notwithstanding Lilburne's moment of victory, is *The Royalist Reform'd* (November 1649) by Albertus Warren, "Gentleman." Addressing himself in dignified terms to lawyers, ministers, and Royalists, Warren avers that now the Puritan Revolution has indeed become respectable.

CHAPTER IX. AFTERMATH: NOVEMBER 1649 TO MAY 1660

1. Gardiner, *Constitutional Documents*, p. 298. Gardiner's *Commonwealth and Protectorate* and C. H. Firth's *The Last Years of the Protectorate* (1909) tell the story of the years from 1649 to 1658, while the official government newspaper of this period, *Mercurius Politicus*, provides a valuable contemporary supplement.

2. Except for the pamphlets noted below, Walwyn too slips from the news of the day. Firth's biography in *Dictionary of National Biography* ends in

1651, and, as far as I know, there is no mention of his name in the journals of the Commonwealth and Protectorate. The adulatory sermon by a William Walwyn, *God Save the King* (May 1660), was composed by a Royalist minister, not by William Walwyn the Leveller.

3. Schenk, *Social Justice*, pp. 43, 60.

4. This memorandum, probably never published, is described in James, *Social Policy*, pp. 155–157.

5. Schenk, *Social Justice*, p. 63. Humphrey Brooke's *The Durable Legacy* of 1681 indicates that Walwyn's son-in-law then enjoyed a similar high status.

6. No. 31, Nov. 21–28, 1649.

7. *Mercurius Politicus*, No. 162, July 14–21, 1653.

8. Overton's name crops up between 1654 and 1657 in *A Collection of the State Papers of John Thurloe* (1742); and in the *Calendar of Clarendon State Papers Preserved in the Bodleian Library* (1876) there are two letters to Charles II in which Overton, Sexby, and one of Wildman's agents are said to have offered to serve the King (III, 55–57). In the *Nicholas Papers* (1886 *et seq.*) Overton's name recurs with relative frequency between July 1655 and December 1656. The extent of his dislike for Cromwell's rule can be seen in his willingness to deal with a collection of unsavory characters, as well as with agents of the repressive government of Spain. Finally, *Mercurius Politicus*, No. 418, May 27–June 3, 1658, mentions a Royalist conspiracy in which a "Captain Overton" took part — in all probability the indefatigable Richard Overton.

9. Presumably Overton had no connection with the third edition of 1674–1675.

10. Firth, "Overton," *Dictionary of National Biography*.

11. Ashley, *Wildman*, p. 70. There is also a biography of Wildman by Firth in *Dictionary of National Biography*; and his career, during the Commonwealth and Protectorate, can be followed, like Overton's, in the papers of Thurloe, Clarendon, and Nicholas.

12. Ashley, *Wildman*, pp. 71ff; *Thurloe Papers*, IV, 179, 215, 333, 340.

13. Ashley, *Wildman*, pp. 73–75.

14. Wildman entitled the published reprint of his speech *Londons Liberties*, the important sections of which are reprinted in Woodhouse, *Puritanism and Liberty*, pp. 369–378. In 1683, when the problem of London's government was again a matter of heated public discussion, Wildman published a second edition of *Londons Liberties*.

15. In Woodhouse, *Puritanism and Liberty*, p. 372.

16. *Ibid.*, p. 378.

17. Ashley, *Wildman*, pp. 88ff; *Thurloe Papers*, IV, 743; V, 45, 694; VI, 829ff; VII, 80.

18. Ashley, *Wildman*, p. 133, conjectures that Wildman knew Harrington by 1654; and he suggests that, if Wildman wrote *A Letter from an Officer of the Army in Ireland*, he probably helped to criticize *Oceana* while it was still in the process of composition.

19. Pepys in his *Diary* on three occasions refers in very unflattering terms

to Wildman's relationship with Villiers (Dec. 7–8 and 12–13, 1667, and Nov. 4–5, 1668).

20. In 1688–89 Wildman wrote and published five short and generally approving tracts on the subject of the "Glorious Revolution."

21. Gardiner, *C&P*, I, 177; Gibb, *Lilburne*, p. 296.

22. Lilburne, *The Engagement Vindicated and Explained* (January 1651).

23. Gardiner, *C&P*, I, 177f.

24. No. 1, June 6–13, 1650.

25. This reconciliation between Lilburne and Cromwell is described in Gardiner, *C&P*, II, 79; and Lilburne refers to it in a letter he wrote to Cromwell in the summer of 1650. In March 1650 he petitioned the Rump for the £1,583 he claimed was the reparation owed him, avowing that he now wanted to stick to a quiet, remunerative, and nonpolitical way of life.

26. For the Leveller-Royalist negotiations, see Gardiner, *C&P*, I, 195f, 249. The petition, "from some that are called Levellers," is described in *Mercurius Politicus*, No. 12, Aug. 22–29, 1650.

27. Gibb, *Lilburne*, pp. 296f; and Lilburne's *humble Addresse* to Parliament of Nov. 6, 1651, protesting against an increase in the excise tax on soap.

28. As early as Dec. 1, 1650, in the letter to Lenthall appended to *The Second Part of the Triall of . . . Lilburne*, Lilburne had complained that Attorney General Prideaux was blocking his efforts to learn more law.

29. In November 1651, Lilburne published *The Case of the Tenants of the Manor of Epworth*, which describes his first year of involvement in the case. (Though signed by the four "trustees" of these tenants, this legalistic document seems largely the work of Lilburne.) The case is discussed in Ashley, *Wildman*, pp. 77–88, and in Gibb, *Lilburne*, p. 298. An interesting contemporary light is thrown on the enclosure problem by a pamphlet which appeared in May 1653, John Moore's *The Crying Sin of England of not Caring for the Poor*.

30. By the summer of 1654 it had still not been finally settled.

31. The case is described in Gibb, *Lilburne*, pp. 299–301, and in Gardiner, *C&P*, II, 80. Lilburne summarizes it one-sidedly in the forty pages of *A Just Reproof to Haberdashers-Hall* (1651), and, far more briefly, in his *Apologeticall Narration* (1652). His first mention of the case occurs in his *Letter . . . to . . . John Price* (April 1651). See also his *Copy of a Letter . . . unto . . . the Constable at Harraton* (September 1651); *The Oppressed Mans Out-Cry* (September 1651) (very possibly the work of Lilburne); and his anti-Haselrig petition to Parliament of Nov. 26, 1651. The other side is most effectively presented in John Canne's *John Lilb. Tryed and Cast* (1653).

32. Gardiner, *C&P*, II, 79f; Lilburne, *Apologeticall Narration*, p. 19.

33. Gardiner, *C&P*, II, 80; Gibb, *Lilburne*, p. 300; Lilburne, *Apologeticall Narration*, pp. 62–68; and *Mercurius Politicus*, No. 85, Jan. 15–22, 1652.

34. Pease, *Leveller Movement*, pp. 346f, points out that the act proclaiming Lilburne's banishment was not properly engrossed, that it was passed early in the morning when, presumably, few members were present, that no formal charge was made, and that Lilburne was not allowed to speak in his own

defense. Moreover, Lilburne's wife was then asked to surrender any papers she had concerning the case of the Harraton colliery. Thus it is not surprising that, in February 1658, Parliament acknowledged the irregularity of its own action and reversed its sentence against Lilburne. Lilburne, *Apologeticall Narration*, pp. 20f, lays most of the blame on Cromwell's ambition; but the Royalist insurrections of mid-1651, the continued war in Ireland, and Lilburne's apparent approach toward renewed political activity are all factors to be considered.

35. *The Petition of many well-affected people highly concerned in the sentence against . . . Lilburne* (Jan. 20, 1652).

36. *A Declaration* consists of two sections: Lilburne's speech to Parliament on hearing his sentence, and his subsequent "Remonstrance to the Freemen of England." On January 22 a David Brown joined in the hue and cry with an anti-Lilburne petition to the Rump, to which Samuel Chidley replied a week later in *The Dissembling Scot*. Then, on Jan. 28, 1652, just before leaving England, Lilburne issued a second "Remonstrance" — . . . *concerning the Lawes, Liberties, and Inheritances of the Freeborn People of England*.

37. No. 90, Feb. 19–26, 1652. Lilburne, however, had already petitioned one of the local magistrates against any attempts by agents of the Commonwealth to have his pamphlets suppressed in Holland.

38. Part of it (pp. 69ff) also seems a deliberate attempt on Lilburne's part to divorce his ideas from those which Winstanley had recently put forward in *The Law of Freedom in a Platform*.

39. Lilburne repeatedly refers to his persecution of the 1630's and includes several quotations from his works of that period. He also reprints *A true relation of the material passages of . . . Lilburnes sufferings* of February 1646, along with four documents relevant to his most recent persecution.

40. See also Don M. Wolfe, "Lilburne's Note on Milton," *Modern Language Notes*, LVI (1941), 360–363.

41. Sometime in 1652 Lilburne published a letter to Charles, *The Remonstrance and Declaration . . . concerning the Crown and Government of the Commonwealth of England*, which outlined his conditions for helping the King. (See Nicholas' report to Hatton of April 1652, *Nicholas Papers*, I, 291.)

42. Gibb, *Lilburne*, pp. 304–309, gives the intriguing highlights of this year.

43. *Nicholas Papers*, I, 291.

44. *Ibid.*, I, 301; II, 13; *Calendar of Clarendon State Papers*, II, 146.

45. *Nicholas Papers*, I, 321; *Calendar of Clarendon State Papers*, II, 121.

46. Lilburne, *A Defensive Declaration* (1653), p. 7; *Apologeticall Narration*, pp. 44ff. Some of these agents, Lilburne alleges, were commissioned not only to defame but to murder him.

47. Gibb, *Lilburne*, p. 306.

48. Lilburne, *A Defensive Declaration*, p. 4.

49. Lilburne, *Lilburne Revived*, first letter, p. 9, second letter, p. 5; *A Defensive Declaration*, p. 14. Oxford repeated his charges in *Vincit qui patitur* (April 1653).

50. It is in this tract that Lilburne states he has been reading Polybius and Plutarch.

51. Gibb, *Lilburne*, pp. 306–309; Lilburne, *A Defensive Declaration, passim*; and the government-sponsored *Several Informations and Examinations* (July 1653).

52. Lilburne, *A Defensive Declaration*, p. 4.

53. This letter is the first item in *A Defensive Declaration*.

54. Gibb, *Lilburne*, pp. 310f; *Several Informations and Examinations*, p. 10; *Mercurius Politicus*, No. 157, June 9–16, 1653; and Lilburne, *The Upright Mans Vindication* (1653), pp. 5f.

55. Gardiner, *C&P*, II, 293f.

56. This letter is given in *The Upright Mans Vindication*, pp. 3–19.

57. *Mercurius Politicus*, No. 158, June 16–23, 1653.

58. According to *Mercurius Politicus* (No. 157), Mrs. Lilburne and William Kiffin personally delivered this tract to Cromwell.

59. The first "Address" was the one Lilburne had written from Calais.

60. Gardiner, *C&P*, II, 295.

61. *The humble Petition . . . in behalf of . . . Lilburne.*

62. *The humble Petition . . . in behalf of M: John Lilburne.*

63. *The Fundamental Lawes and Liberties . . . claimed, asserted, and agreed unto by several peacable persons . . . called Levellers* (July 9, 1653); a petition from Hertfordshire "in behalfe of . . . Lilburne" — referred to in *Mercurius Politicus*, No. 161, July 7–14, 1653, and described in Gardiner, *C&P*, II, 295.

64. It seems likely that Lilburne helped to write this pamphlet — many of the ideas, personal references, and legal citations suggest his hand; but the title page, the circumstances of composition, and in spots the style all indicate a collaborator.

65. The first letter to the Lord Mayor had been *The Prisoner's Most mournful Cry.*

66. *To the Supream Authority . . . The Humble Petition of . . . Lilburne.*

67. The trial is given in *State Trials*, VII, 354–370. It is described in Gibb, *Lilburne*, pp. 315–323; Gardiner, *C&P*, II, 295–300; and Pease, *Leveller Movement*, pp. 336–346. Among contemporary accounts, the most important are the three parts of *The Tryall of . . . Lilburne*, almost certainly by him, which came out during the later days of August 1653; Canne, *John Lilb. Tryed and Cast*, November 1653; *Mercurius Politicus*, No. 161 through No. 167, July 7–Aug. 25, 1653; and, for the first three days of the trial, Lilburne, *A Plea at large for . . . Lilburne*, Aug. 6, 1653.

68. *The Tryall of . . . Lilburne*, Part I, pp. 1f. It should be noted that, had Lilburne pleaded guilty, the jury needed only to find that he was the John Lilburne intended by the act of banishment for him to be automatically executed as a felon. Gardiner, Gibb, and Pease all state that this was the first time in the history of English law that a prisoner asked, and was granted the right, to see his indictment.

69. On July 14 certain of Lilburne's supporters, among them Overton,

petitioned Parliament to intervene in the case, *The Petition of many grieved People*. When Parliament ignored the petitioners, they seconded Lilburne's request that he see a copy of the indictment. Lilburne published his exceptions to this indictment on the same day he presented them (July 16, 1653), *The Exceptions of John Lilburne*.

70. *The Tryall of . . . Lilburne*, Part I, pp. 3ff.

71. Gardiner, *C&P*, II, 296.

72. *A Caveat*, pp. 4f.

73. *The Humble Representation of divers afflicted Women-Petitioners on the behalf of . . . Lilburne* (July 29, 1653).

74. *The Humble Petition of . . . Youngmen and Apprentices. Mercurius Politicus*, No. 164, July 28–Aug. 4, 1653, describes how Parliament voted this petition scandalous and ordered the arrest of the six young men who presented it.

75. It is reprinted in Haller and Davies, *Leveller Tracts*, pp. 450–464.

76. Lilburne was here paraphrasing a remark Henry Marten had previously made about him (Rushworth, *Historical Collections*, II, 468).

77. Lilburne, *Just Defence*, p. 5.

78. *The Tryall of . . . Lilburne*, Part I, pp. 6–8; Part II, pp. 2–6.

79. For the greater tension outside the court, see *Thurloe Papers*, I, 430; *Calendar of Clarendon State Papers*, II, 241.

80. *A Word to the Jury in the behalfe of John Lilburne*.

81. Gardiner, *C&P*, II, 297; *The Tryall of . . . Lilburne*, Part III, pp. 2f.

82. *The Tryall of . . . Lilburne*, Part III, p. 4.

83. That Lilburne had long planned this angle of his defense is shown not only by *Lilburnes Plea in Law* of June 1653, but by his dropping of the "Lt. Colonel" from before his name in his pamphlets of July and August 1653.

84. *The Tryall of . . . Lilburne*, Part III, pp. 4–6; Canne, *John Lilb. Tryed and Cast*, pp. 127–141; Gardiner, *C&P*, II, 297–299; Pease, *Leveller Movement*, pp. 340–342; and Gibb, *Lilburne*, pp. 319f — all of which deal with Lilburne's appeal to the jury.

85. *The Tryall of . . . Lilburne*, Part III, p. 6.

86. *Calendar of Clarendon State Papers*, II, 245f; *Mercurius Politicus*, No. 167, Aug. 18–25, 1653.

87. Quoted in Gibb, *Lilburne*, p. 320. G. P. Gooch, *English Democratic Ideas in the Seventeenth Century* (1927), p. 215, adds that five years later the accounts of this trial were still listed by London booksellers as among their "most vendible books."

88. Gardiner, *C&P*, II, 300.

89. Canne, *John Lilb. Tryed and Cast*, pp. 157–164, describes their interrogation.

90. *A Letter to . . . Lilburne now Prisoner in the Tower* — inappropriately signed by a "Christian friend."

91. Gardiner, *C&P*, II, 300.

92. It is dated Sept. 26, 1653. Its style and its indirect approach strongly militate against Lilburne's authorship.

93. Canne's authorship is confirmed by the marked similarity between this tract and the two parts of *The Discoverer.*

94. Gardiner, *C&P*, III, 2.

95. Ashley, *Wildman*, p. 83, points out that the writ of the common law did not extend to the Channel Islands.

96. Gibb, *Lilburne*, pp. 326–329; *Thurloe Papers*, III, 512, 629.

97. Four days later, on May 27, 1654, the anti-Lilburne and pro-Commonwealth *Last Will and Testament of . . . Lilburne* cleverly mocked the prisoner.

98. Gibb, *Lilburne*, pp. 329f.

99. This "Letter to his Wife," dated Oct. 4, 1655, is reprinted in *The Resurrection of John Lilburne*, the first edition of which was entered by Thomason on May 16, 1656, the second — "with additions" — on May 21. On Oct. 5, 1655, Lilburne wrote to a friend detailing the spiritual excitement and solace of his conversion and recommending some of the Quaker books which Lilburne had found most inspiring ("to William Harding," also reprinted in *The Resurrection*). A third letter in *The Resurrection* ("to Elizabeth Hunniwood"), dated March 16, 1656, suggests that Lilburne may have had a hand in writing two Quaker tracts, but other than the two foregoing letters I can find no substitute for, or sign of, any such tracts.

100. "To Robert Barrington," March 25, 1656, reprinted in *The Resurrection*, pp. 18–22.

101. Gibb, *Lilburne*, pp. 344f.

102. "The Petition of Elizabeth, widow of John Lilburne . . . to the Protector," Nov. 4, 1657, cited in Gibb, *Lilburne*, p. 345.

103. No. 399, Aug. 27–Sept. 3, 1657. Rushworth, *Historical Collections*, II, 468, adds that 4,000 persons followed Lilburne's corpse to the grave.

104. This anonymous tract was entered by Thomason on June 22, 1659. It may seem strange that *Lilburns Ghost* was probably the only published invocation to Lilburne's spirit during the turmoil of the end of the Interregnum, but his death two years earlier had been greeted largely by silence in pamphlet and newspaper.

CHAPTER X. THE CONTRIBUTION OF THE LEVELLER PARTY

1. *Thomason Catalogue*, p. xxi. The figures for the two eight-year periods are, respectively, 12,581 and 6,177.

2. It is reprinted in Gardiner, *Constitutional Documents*, pp. 314–325.

3. Louise Fargo Brown, *The Political Activities of the Baptists and Fifth Monarchy Men in England During the Interregnum* (1912) contains the fullest description of this movement.

4. *Ibid.*, p. 134.

5. As Bernstein, *Cromwell and Communism*, p. 171, points out, in England only the Chartists can be considered the direct political heirs of the Levellers.

6. This anonymous tract was published in London sometime late in 1660 — a few months after Richard Blome issued his *Fanatick History*, a distorted

collection of anecdotes which reviews the "blasphemies" of the Good Old Cause with mockery and horror.

7. His *The unlawfulness of Subjects taking up Arms* (1643) is permeated with this view.

8. Lilburne, *The Resurrection of John Lilburne*, second edition, pp. 18, 22.

9. A full expression of Fifth-Monarchy thought can be found in the party manifesto issued in May 1657, *A Standard Set Up.*

10. See, for instance, Vane, *A Healing Question* (1656); here, despite his compliments to the people on their potential wisdom (e.g., pp. 19f), Vane still did not lose that air of aristocratic skepticism toward the political capacities of the masses which characterized his republicanism. In a somewhat similar manner, Nedham's *The Excellencie of a Free-State* of the same year testified on behalf of the government that Cromwell's mission was to rule for, not by and with, the people.

11. Logically, if not historically, the secularism inherent in Leveller democracy could have contributed to the growth of deism: God would never have to be called on to intervene directly in the affairs of a functioning and self-regulating democratic society.

12. *An Agreement of the Free People of England*, pp. 1f.

APPENDIX. THE AUTHORSHIP OF "MANS MORTALLITIE"

1. *Short-Title Catalogue*, under Robert Overton; Schenk, *Social Justice*, p. 168; and P. Zagorin, "The Authorship of 'Mans Mortallitie,'" *The Library*, Fifth Series, V (1951), 179–183. This last article, which I discovered after this Appendix was written, repeats some of the information which follows, and arrives at the same conclusion.

2. Plomer, "Secret Printing," *Library*, pp. 377–380.

3. *Ibid.*, p. 381. For further details concerning Robert Overton's use of this press, see the Examination of Nicholas Tew, under date of February 10, 1645, in *Historical Manuscripts Commission, Sixth Report, Appendix*, p. 46a.

4. This is the main point made by Nathaniel Henry, "Milton and Overton," *The Times' Literary Supplement*, Oct. 14, 1949, p. 665. E. A. Payne, in a letter published two weeks later in the same journal, partially refutes Henry's contention.

5. E. A. A. Axon, "Canne," in *Dictionary of National Biography.*

6. Warre (?), *The Prerogative of Man*, p. 45.

7. Prynne, *Twelve Considerable Serious Questions*; Featley, *The Dippers Dipt*; and Pagitt, *Heresiography*. (I am indebted to Wolfe, *Milton*, p. 58, for these references.)

8. Edwards, *Gangraena*, I, 81f; II, 17f.

9. Overton, *The Araignment*, p. 20.

10. *The Picture of the Councel of State*, p. 28.

11. I am indebted to a conversation with Professor Haller for this suggestion. I have not seen Wither's translation of Nemesius, but I have glanced through a Greek-Latin edition of *The Nature of Man* and there are certain

obvious parallels between it and *Mans Mortallitie*. (Schenk, *Social Justice*, p. 168, suggests that Overton drew his Aristotelian conception of the soul from this work by Nemesius.) A second source from which Overton might have drawn some of his more learned-sounding scriptural discussion was Meredith Hamner's translation of the Church Fathers, which ran through five editions between 1584 and 1650. This work, *The Ancient Ecclesiasticall Histories of the first six hundred years after Christ . . . Written in the Greek Tongue by . . . Eusebius, Socrates, and Evagrius,* has a "Chronographie" and an index, both of which made its use as a reference especially feasible. A third possible source for Overton was the widespread rationalistic theology of Socinius, with which he undoubtedly had many indirect contacts.

INDEX